New Jersey Cemeteries and Tombstones

« *New Jersey* »

CEMETERIES

and

TOMBSTONES

History in the Landscape

Richard F. Veit ~ *Mark Nonestied*

RIVERGATE BOOKS

AN IMPRINT OF
RUTGERS UNIVERSITY PRESS
NEW BRUNSWICK, NEW JERSEY, AND LONDON

LIBRARY OF CONGRESS CATALOGING-IN-PUBLICATION DATA

Veit, Richard Francis, 1968-
    New Jersey cemeteries and tombstones : history in the landscape / Richard F. Veit and
Mark Nonestied.
      p. cm.
    Includes bibliographical references and index.
      ISBN 978–0-8135–4235–5 (hardcover : alk. paper)—ISBN 978–0-8135–4236–2 (pbk. : alk.
paper)
      1. Cemeteries—New Jersey. 2. Historic sites—New Jersey. 3. Sepulchral monuments—New
Jersey. 4. Landscape architecture—New Jersey. 5. Cemeteries—New Jersey—History. 6.
Sepulchral monuments—New Jersey—History. 7. Burial—New Jersey—History. 8.
Landscape—New Jersey—History. 9. New Jersey—History, Local. I. Nonestied, Mark. II.
Title.
      F135.V45 2008
      363.7'509479—dc22
      2007015497

A British Cataloging-in-Publication record for this book is available from the British Library.

Visit our Web site: http://rutgerspress.rutgers.edu

❨ CONTENTS ❩

❮ ILLUSTRATIONS ❯

❰ ACKNOWLEDGMENTS ❱

Although there are two authors listed on the cover of this book, we could not have completed it without the help of numerous co-conspirators. First and foremost, we would like to thank our families and friends. They not only tolerated but supported our fascination with old cemeteries. Only they remember how many trips to the mall, the shore, or to visit relatives, were interrupted by a slight detour to see what was in the old cemetery up on that hill.

Our colleagues in gravestone studies generously shared their knowledge, pointed out our missteps and misinterpretations, and directed us towards some excellent sites that might otherwise have been overlooked. Undoubtedly there are burial grounds and gravemarkers we have missed. This is not for lack of trying.

We especially appreciate the invaluable encouragement and support shown by Laurel Gabel, the dean of gravestone studies, when we first began framing the outline for this book. Similarly, R. Alan Mounier, South Jersey archaeologist, provided encouragement and suggested ways that we might improve the text. He was joined by Budd Wilson, David Mudge, Bill Liebeknecht, Paul Schopp, and Renee Brecht, who pointed us toward some particularly interesting South Jersey cemeteries. A special thanks to Linda Waller, who generously shared information about Lawnside's historic African American cemeteries.

Art historian John Zielenski is the recognized authority on Newark's colonial carvers. He has the skills of a detective. His work has transformed our understanding of the previously poorly documented carvers located in and around Newark. Moreover, his conversations with us regarding colonial gravestone carving and carvers have proven invaluable. As he continues his research we will undoubtedly learn more of the men who carved New Jersey's first markers.

Paul McLeod, one of the first individuals to systematically study New Jersey gravemarkers, shared his unpublished senior thesis on Monmouth County's colonial gravemarkers (1979), and his encyclopedic knowledge of gravestone carving techniques. Special thanks to Matt Tomaso for helping us connect with Paul. Adam Heinrich, a graduate student at Rutgers University, has picked up where Paul left off, examining some of the family connections evident in Monmouth County's early gravemarkers. His help is also appreciated.

Bob Kelly, deacon at Christ Church in Shrewsbury, and Trevor Kirkpatrick, Christ Church Cemetery Historian, have hosted innumerable cemetery tours for Monmouth University students, and shared their extensive knowledge of one of Monmouth County and eastern New Jersey's finest historic cemeteries. Joseph Hammond, whose knowledge of Monmouth County history is unrivaled, generously shared some rare copies of early gravestone invoices. Megan Springate at the Monmouth County Historical Association also proved particularly helpful.

Steven Baeli shared his research on Ocean County cemeteries and helped us find some particularly well-hidden Monmouth County markers. Dawn Turner provided useful information on Burlington City's historic burial grounds, while Thomas Hope of Will Hope & Son Memorials gave us a guided tour of one of New Jersey's oldest active monument shops and showed us how craftsmen turn blocks of granite into pieces of art.

David Gradwohl advised us regarding etiquette for Jewish cemeteries and provided assistance with translations, both linguistic and cultural. Susan Tunick kept up a steady stream of facts about terra cotta gravemarkers. Alicia Batco shared useful information on early Sussex County cemeteries. Gary Collinson was instrumental in unraveling some Pennsylvania connections. Kathy Fisher helped with Montville area cemeteries. We would also like to offer a special thanks to the numerous students at Monmouth University, both graduate and undergraduate, especially JoAnn Aiton, Chris Cosgrove, Michael Gall, Jillian Henehan, Kimberly Keene, Koorleen Minton, Tom Minton, Wednesday Shaheen, and Kathy Shapiro, who brought photos and articles about their favorite old New Jersey cemeteries to class.

Many other individuals graciously shared their knowledge of historic burial grounds and gravemarkers over the course of our study. We wish to thank John Bolt, Gordon Bond, Gary Chapman, Robert Craig, Dudley Gardner, Connie Grieff, Stephanie Hoagland, Paul Huey, Paul Hutchison, Bob Kelly, Joseph Klett, Anthony Mauro, Linda McTeague, Theodora Noordzy, Fred W. Sisser III, Carl Stein, Dorothy Stratford, James Turk, Dawn Turner, and Charles Webster.

The number of cemetery superintendents, monument workers, and office staff that have generously shared their knowledge over the past decade has been countless. We would like to especially thank Frank DeGeeter Jr., who provided photographs and information on George Washington Memorial Park. Alan Kroboth and Frank Garzon offered pertinent material on early crematoriums. Kearney Kuhlthau at Elmwood Cemetery has been a longtime supporter of research endeavors into New Brunswick–area cemeteries. Scott Willman at Mount Pleasant Cemetery has added to our understanding of this important New Jersey landmark. Ronald Nelson of the

Clinton Monumental Company shared his knowledge of the modern memorial business. The office staff of Greenwood Cemetery and Cemetery Management Services provided wonderful information on Greenwood Cemetery and its early community mausoleum.

Staff at the Camden Library, Jersey City Public Library, Union Public Library, Elizabeth Public Library, New Jersey State Archives, New Jersey Special Collections, and Winterthur Library gave valuable assistance. The late Charles Cummings of the Newark Public Library was never without an interesting tidbit on Newark cemeteries.

We also wish to thank Marc Mappen, Anna Aschkenes, Chris DeRosa, Brian Greenberg, Fred McKitrick, William Mitchell, and Katie Parkin for their support. The folks at Rutgers University Press, particularly Marlie Wasserman, Marilyn Campbell, and Barbara Glassman, were a pleasure to work with.

The encouragement of our family and friends was invaluable. Terri, Douglas, Rebecca, and Maryann Veit were always helpful. George, Rosemary, and Todd Nonestied provided tremendous support.

We are very grateful to Terri and Karen, whose many weekends were spent navigating New Jersey's roads in search of burial grounds. Karen is also especially thanked for her support in reading and commenting on the manuscript.

New Jersey Cemeteries and Tombstones

« 1 »

Why Study
Historic Burial Grounds?

For many individuals, graveyards and cemeteries are scary, spooky places. They are to be avoided for as long as humanly possible. Our view is different. We see cemeteries as oases of history set in a constantly changing cultural landscape. A resident of colonial New Jersey returning to Elizabethtown, Burlington, or Trenton after an absence of two centuries would find little familiar, except, perhaps, the gravemarkers in the local burial ground. This book is a cultural history of New Jersey's historic burial places from High Point to Cape May and from the banks of the Delaware River to the wave-washed shore. We begin our tour in the seventeenth century and end the day before yesterday. Our goal is not simply to provide a guide to some of the more intriguing and unusual burial grounds in the state, though many are listed and described, but more importantly to illustrate how gravemarkers reflect the state's varied history and diverse cultures. New Jersey's cemeteries and burial grounds are important repositories of historical information and public art. The gravemarkers they contain are of great value to historians, archaeologists, anthropologists, sociologists, art historians, and, of course, genealogists. The designs carved on gravemarkers, the materials they were made from, the languages inscribed upon them, and the stories they tell provide us with glimpses of the past. From lonely forgotten burial plots in rural communities to the green islands of the state's urban cemeteries, burial grounds are focal points of local history.

According to the New Jersey State Cemetery Board, there are several hundred active nonsectarian cemeteries in the state. There are probably two or three times as many that are inactive, and many that are abandoned and forgotten. These burial grounds are as varied as the people who rest in them. They range from tiny burial places, such as the Michael Field gravesite, located along a country road in Monmouth County, to vast necropolises, cities of the dead, associated with Newark, East Orange, Camden, and Trenton.

New Jersey's burial grounds are a vast and varied resource and it should come as no surprise that tackling such a topic for publication has been many years in the making. In researching this book we developed a methodology that coupled what we had previously found with what had yet to be studied. We started with a physical examination of New Jersey cemeteries from every corner of the state. Although we certainly have not covered every one, our field research did include over nine hundred New Jersey burial grounds. Often we would pass through the same cemetery on various occasions, seeing the same site from different viewpoints, which helped to round out our study. In addition, photographs and notes from trips to cemeteries in other states, and even other countries, have helped us to frame New Jersey's burial grounds against a larger backdrop. This process took over a decade, as we recorded carvers' signatures, photographed markers, and made detailed observations. With this compilation the story of New Jersey cemeteries began to unfold in voluminous notes and thousands of images.

Archival research helped to bring the story to life. From state archives to personal collections we sought out every source we could find on New Jersey cemeteries. In our quest for information we sent out a mailing to over one hundred New Jersey monument companies asking for information about their businesses. Those known to be historic received personal phone calls: polite and yet sometimes perhaps pestering, we asked them to check every nook and cranny for any information. Online auctions and antique shops have added to our personal collections of New Jersey cemetery and gravestone ephemera. On countless occasions, the name of New Jersey's most prolific eighteenth-century gravestone carver, Ebenezer Price, has been typed in as an eBay search; it is perhaps wishful thinking that his ledgers or carving tools may turn up someday. But with the help of modern technology our collections of photographs, postcards, and monument catalogs have grown, adding to what we could not find in the archives and ultimately enhancing our understanding of New Jersey cemeteries.

With a framework in place for understanding New Jersey tombstone and cemetery history, we turned to local historical societies and several county organizations to help us conduct a series of lectures. These talks were meant to educate the public about our findings and encourage them to share with us their knowledge and stories about New Jersey cemeteries. We learned much and yet there is still much to know.

What has developed is this volume. It is, however, not a guidebook to finding individual cemeteries, though many are mentioned (see appendix A for a listing of culturally and historically significant cemeteries). Rather, it is a guide to understanding the state's historic burial places and the gravemarkers they contain. We begin by briefly reviewing what might be termed the prehistory of gravemarking, the markers used by New Jersey's Native American people, the Lenape and their ancestors. Then we examine the initial European settlers of the state. A handful of seventeenth-century grave-markers survive in some of New Jersey's oldest settlements: Elizabeth, Newark, Perth Amboy, Piscataway, and Woodbridge. The images that deco-rate these gravemarkers—skulls, hourglasses, and crossed bones—speak to the brevity of life in colonial New Jersey and the religious sentiments of these early settlers. Next, we move on to the eighteenth century and study the rich, but distinctive, gravestone carving traditions of colonial New Jersey. Settlers in Quaker-dominated southwestern New Jersey employed white marble gravemarkers, simple and often undecorated, to commemorate their loved ones. In eastern New Jersey, the descendants of dour Puritans, Scot-tish proprietors, and Dutch yeoman farmers transformed rich brown sand-stone into stunning but somber works of art that have stood the test of time. Northwestern New Jersey, once a sparsely settled frontier, contains locally produced German- and English-language markers and some of the finest cal-ligraphy to be found in colonial burial grounds anywhere. Further east, the Dutch stronghold of Bergen County contains a smattering of stones carved in Dutch, emphasizing the persistence of this distinctive cultural group well into the nineteenth century. The shore, once a haven for smugglers and pri-vateers, is dotted with gravemarkers from Rhode Island, Massachusetts, and New York, highlighting the important trade routes of colonial America.

Early-nineteenth-century cemeteries represent a transitional period. The death's heads and cherubs so popular on gravestones carved before the Rev-olution are replaced by monograms, urns, and weeping willow trees. Note-worthy artisans, like Rahway's John Frazee, sometimes called America's first sculptor, and Henry Sillcocks in New Brunswick experimented with new styles of carving. They were among a unique group of transitional carvers who produced the final flourish of the brownstone tradition before new national styles of commemoration, employing marble carved in neoclassical forms, whitewashed away the local folk traditions.

As gravemarker styles were changing, so too were the designs of the cemeteries. Small rural family plots and church-associated burial grounds in urban communities began to be replaced by purposefully designed ceme-teries governed by a board of lot holders. These cemeteries were an answer to society's concerns over the proper treatment of the dead. This era of bur-ial reform would lead to a larger movement and new ideology of cemetery design—the rural or garden cemetery movement. A combination of con-cerns—overcrowding in urban cemeteries, a profit motive, questions of health and hygiene, and increasingly sentimental views of death—led burial reformers to advocate relocating cemeteries to new sites outside of crowded urban areas. Many of the state's major cities have cemeteries dating from this period. Their parklike appearance is no accident. Designed as picturesque landscapes, they provided a refuge from the dreary tenements found in so many cities. Particularly noteworthy cemeteries include Mount Pleasant in

Newark, Riverview in Trenton, Evergreen in Camden, Willow Grove in New Brunswick, and Evergreen in Hillside. They survive in varying states of preservation and provide a glimpse of Victorian mourning customs.

The Victorians erected gravemarkers that, much like the houses they lived in, reflected an individual's success and place in the world. They transformed graveyards full of squat sandstone and marble tablets into cemeteries, monument-filled Valhallas, with granite and marble obelisks, pillars, statuary, and sculpture in all shapes and sizes and reflecting the full panoply of funereal iconography. Mechanized carving using pneumatic drills, a well-developed rail transportation network to move raw stone, and the increasing use of granite allowed for larger and more ornate markers than was previously possible.

By the end of the nineteenth century it was becoming clear that the products of the rural cemetery movement shared some of the same problems as earlier burial grounds. Their pleasing vistas and open spaces were full of marble obelisks, columns, and tablets commemorating families and individuals. An alternative was the lawn park cemetery, which focused more on landscaping and relied less on monuments. The goal was a more natural landscape, without the rows of stock memorials to mar the view (Sloane 1991, 122). Continued concerns about the healthiness of enormous cemeteries and the growth of the public-health movement led to the creation of crematoriums and columbaria to store ashes. New Jersey's first crematorium was constructed in 1907, and several outstanding twentieth-century columbaria still survive, including one at Rosedale & Rosehill Cemetery in Linden and another at the Garden State Crematory in Bergen County.

In comparison to the ornate resting places of the Victorians, most twentieth-century cemeteries seem restrained. The markers, except for the occasional mausoleum, are often smaller and less elaborate. Indeed in the postwar period, the rise of the memorial park corresponds with the widespread use of flat bronze tablets, which were inexpensive to produce, long-lasting, and facilitated mowing but also left little room for inscriptions, individuality, or art of any kind. Like the man in the gray flannel suit and the cookie-cutter suburbs of the postwar period, mid-twentieth-century cemeteries have a sameness that, at first glance, makes them seem unworthy of study. Nevertheless, they too reflect the ethos of a particular period, when the ostentation of the Victorians seemed garish, and rational, functional designs prevailed. Moreover, modern cemeteries should not be dismissed out of hand. New Jersey's memorial parks aren't simply the byproduct of some cold economic calculus, which looked to replace cluttered cemeteries with easy-to-mow lawns. Rather, they were an attempt to bring beauty back into the cemetery, with sweeping vistas, carefully selected plantings, and works of high art. A particularly good example of this type of cemetery is George Washington Memorial Park in Paramus.

Nineteenth- and twentieth-century ethnic cemeteries are often repositories of unusual and artistic memorials, in contrast to the uniform white and gray markers of the larger society. Jewish cemeteries in urban and rural areas are full of richly ornamented gravemarkers, often displaying menorahs, the Lion of Judah, and Torah scrolls. Burial places associated with immigrants from Southern and Eastern Europe contain stones decorated with enameled portraits of patriarchs and matriarchs only recently arrived from Italy, Greece, and the Jewish Pale of Settlement. Immigrant blacksmiths from Southern Germany and Austria transformed bar iron into elaborate crucifixes to commemorate their deceased countrymen, and talented masons from Italy and Greece used inexpensive concrete to make crosses, obelisks, statues, and sometimes even mausoleums.

Middlesex and Mercer Counties also have dozens of colorful ceramic gravemarkers made from fired clay and tile. They are reminders of the brickworks, terra cotta factories, and potteries that once were so common in the central part of the state. Today the clay mines have been filled in with shopping malls and the potteries paved over, but the gravemarkers tell us of the talented artisans, Danish, English, Italian, and German, who turned dull clay into high art among the sand hills of central Jersey.

At the beginning of the twenty-first century, art is making a reappearance in New Jersey's burial grounds. Laurel Grove Cemetery and Memorial Park in Totowa contain outstanding artistic markers for Turkish immigrants and other Islamic groups, as well as Eastern European immigrants. Rosedale & Rosehill Cemetery in Linden, which may be the largest cemetery in the state, provides a glimpse of modern New Jersey's ethnic diversity, with Asian, African American, Italian, Polish, Muslim, Hispanic, and Gypsy sections. Some of the individual markers are amazing, such as the life-size granite Mercedes-Benz for Ray Tse and colorful Gypsy markers. Evergreen Cemetery in Hillside also contains an exceptional collection of Gypsy markers.

New Jersey's burial grounds are in flux at the beginning of the twenty-first century. Newspapers regularly carry articles on the restoration of particular burial grounds by historical societies, Boy Scouts hoping to attain the rank of Eagle Scout, and concerned local citizens. Cemetery tours are quite popular, especially around Halloween, sometimes drawing hundreds of visitors. Modern congregations of Korean and Latin American immigrants take pride in maintaining the historic burial grounds associated with older church edifices. Balancing these happy tales are articles about endangered and disappearing cemeteries. Colonial burial grounds are being plowed under for development, and archaeologists are digging up older urban cemeteries so that land more precious than gold can be recycled to serve the living rather than accommodate the dead. Abandoned urban cemeteries are a particular sore spot. Rather than providing much-needed green space, they sometimes serve as temporary homes for the homeless and as places of business for drug dealers and prostitutes. In modern America, a society that values youth and vitality, and attempts to compartmentalize death and dying, cemeteries remain places where the dead and the living interact in ways planned and unplanned.

Burial places are also changing; witness the rise of massive mausoleums, the burial ground equivalent of the big-box stores that have replaced Main Street's storefront businesses. Cremation, once considered a dirty word by cemetery professionals, has turned out to be less ominous than once feared. Families unsure of how to house the ashes of their late loved one often opt to bury them in cemeteries, complete with gravemarkers. In other cases, columbaria with hundreds of niches are erected to house cremains and a few mementos of the dead. Nonetheless, lack of space is a constant concern for cemeteries, because once burials stop, the regular cash flow for maintenance, mowing, tree care, and security trickles to a halt.

Modern cemeteries and gravemarkers are every bit as reflective of American society today as their colonial and Victorian precursors. Not surprisingly, large corporations are acquiring funeral homes and cemeteries. These transformations involve economies of a scale that cemetery managers of the past never would have dreamed of. Globalization is also affecting cemeteries. Today the granite employed for a gravestone or mausoleum is as likely to come from India or South America as it is to hail from Barre, Vermont, or Elberton, Georgia. Designs carved on markers are no longer drawn by hand with copper stencils and cut with cold chisels as was the case in the eighteenth century, nor are they sketched on drafting paper and cut with the pneumatic drills favored by early-twentieth-century artisans. Instead, they are laid out on a computer and printed on rubberized templates that can be affixed to markers and sandblasted.

Computers are also working to keep the dead alive in a way that Egyptian pharaohs would have envied. In Rahway's Hazelwood Cemetery, the gravemarker of Bruce Berman has the deceased's hands and face etched into the stone and bears the address of his former website. For a period after his death, interested visitors were able to view the deceased's artwork. Similarly, in Franklin Memorial Park, by pressing the appropriate buttons at a kiosk, visitors can view pictures and prerecorded messages about the deceased. One can only imagine what the next development in commemoration might be.

Tombstone Hounds: Previous Studies

Gravemarkers have long fascinated historians and antiquarians. In 1814 Timothy Alden compiled a volume titled *A Collection of American Epitaphs and Inscriptions with Occasional Notes*. Alden sought out the unusual and the famous and included several New Jersey epitaphs, including one for Mrs. Katharine Eck-

1.1 A view of Trinity Episcopal "Old Swedes" Church and Burial Ground in Swedesboro from Barber and Howe's *Historical Collections of the State of New Jersey* (1868). John Barber and Henry Howe wrote histories of many northeastern states in the mid-nineteenth century. They often provided vignettes of burial grounds as noteworthy historic sites.

ley, whose 1772 gravemarker survives today in East Hanover. The marker shows Mrs. Eckley at repose in a small coffin with lid ajar. According to Alden, the unfortunate Mrs. Eckley was riding in a carriage accompanied by her pedestrian husband. The horse bolted and Mrs. Eckley, who had been peeling an apple with a pen knife, fell out of the carriage and onto the blade. As Alden notes, "Mrs. Eckley, by her sudden removal, exhibited a most striking exemplification of the precarious tenure of human life" (Alden 1814, 193–194). John Barber and Henry Howe, traveling historians who wrote an intriguing history and guide to New Jersey in 1844, included numerous epitaphs and some illustrations of gravemarkers in their book, *Historical Collections of the State of New Jersey* (fig. 1.1).

Recording inscriptions and epitaphs was a popular pastime for nineteenth-century historians. One of the earliest surviving examples of this activity is a volume titled "Inscriptions from Monumental Stones in Newark Cemeteries," recorded by John S. Condit in 1847. As Newark's colonial cemeteries have all been removed or lost, this volume is especially valuable, as are the illustrations it contains (fig. 1.2). Later still, books of genealogical data from some of the state's most famous burial grounds, such as that of the First Presbyterian Church in Elizabeth (Wheeler and Halsey 1892), were printed. Moreover, illustrations of early gravemarkers are common in late-nineteenth- and early-twentieth-century histories (see Wickes 1892). Of course, genealogists have long had a keen interest in cemeteries, and during the 1920s and later a cadre of genealogists from the New Jersey Genealogical Society, who titled themselves "tombstone hounds," recorded hundreds

1.2 John Condit recorded some of the markers in Newark's Old First Presbyterian Burial Ground before its removal. This 1847 drawing is an example of his work (Condit 1847). (From the collections of The New Jersey Historical Society, Newark.)

of cemeteries and their inscriptions (fig. 1.3). They even wrote a bit of verse about their work, which bears repeating:

> *A Slave of the Wire Brush*
>
> Whenever I don my thorn-proof pants
> And my poison ivy–proof socks,
> And rub my legs with tick-proof oil
> And get out my First Aid box,
> They know I'm off with the Tombstone Hounds
> And not any amount of talk
> Will dissuade this slave of the wire brush
> And the crowbar, trowel and chalk.
>
> And whether the skies are overcast,
> Or the mercury ninety-four;
> Or whether a storm is on the way,
> Or the winds of winter roar—
> So what? I'm off with the Tombstone Hounds
> And weather or not, it can't mar
> The fun of a slave of the wire brush
> And the trowel, chalk and crowbar.
>
> You'll not find me in the baseball parks,
> Or wasting time on the links;
> Night clubs and hot-spots leave me cold,

The ponies to me are jinx;
But when I'm off with the Tombstone Hounds
You can hear the joyous howl
For miles of this slave of the wire brush
And the chalk, crowbar and trowel.

So sound the call to the Tombstone Hounds!
Come on, you huskies—Mush!
Here is the crowbar, trowel and chalk,
Where is that wire brush? (Rankin n.d., 70)

While the members of the Genealogical Society of New Jersey continue to
energetically record graveyard inscriptions and publish detailed cemetery
locators (Raser 1994, 2000, 2004), they no longer recount their work in dog-
gerel verse. Moreover, wire brushes have been discarded as much too damaging, replaced by mirrors, flashlights, and rubbing paper.

More recently, art historians and anthropologists have begun studying
gravemarkers for what they can tell us about the artisans of early America
and cultural trends in commemoration. In 1964 Mary K. Stofflet, a student
at Skidmore College in Saratoga Springs, New York, wrote a noteworthy
paper titled "A Study of the Characteristics of the Gravestones Located in
Monmouth County, New Jersey 1664–1800." Then in 1972 Emily Wasserman
published *Gravestone Designs, Rubbings, and Photographs from Early New York and New*

1.3 Genealogists have long maintained an active interest in the state's burial grounds. This 1939
photograph shows a group of "tombstone hounds" from the New Jersey Genealogical Society,
about to begin a gravestone recording foray at the Spruce Run Heights Evangelical Church.
(Reproduced with permission of the Genealogical Society of New Jersey.)

Jersey. This was the first widely distributed study of New Jersey's early grave-markers. It was followed in 1979, by Paul McLeod, who wrote a detailed study of Monmouth County's eighteenth- and early-nineteenth-century gravemarkers for an undergraduate honors thesis at the College of William and Mary.

The pace of research picked up in the 1980s. Historian Richard Welch, building on Wasserman's work, identified many of the state's colonial carvers (1983, 1987). Elizabeth Crowell, then a doctoral student at the University of Pennsylvania, wrote her doctoral dissertation on Cape May's colonial grave-markers (1983) and Richard Veit wrote his M.A. thesis on Middlesex County's eighteenth-century markers (1991). Crowell's work focused on determining why Cape May's markers were so plain and simple. She concluded that they reflect the Quaker influence in southern New Jersey and Philadelphia, which avoided rich iconography. Veit examined the shifting styles of Middlesex County gravemarkers from skulls to cherubs to mono-grams. More recently, Adam Heinrich has looked at the family connections that shaped gravemarker choice in colonial Monmouth County (Heinrich 2003), and John Zielenski has documented the colonial carvers of Newark and their distinctive work (Zielenski 2004). His meticulous research should serve as a model for future researchers.

New Jersey's ethnic cemeteries have also seen some study. Folklorist Thomas Graves (1993) documented the spectacular artwork associated with St. Andrew's Ukrainian Cemetery in South Bound Brook, which includes life-size bronze Cossacks and granite markers shaped like suspension bridges. The terra cotta memorials of Middlesex County, produced and used by Danes, Englishmen, Italians, and Germans, have also been documented (Veit 1995; Veit and Nonestied 2003). Other scholars have studied Jewish cemeter-ies in northern (Gould 2005) and southern New Jersey (Kraus-Friedberg 2003).

New Jersey has also played host to a variety of cemetery programs. The Association for Gravestone Studies held its annual conference in New Jer-sey in 1985 and again in 1998. County cultural and heritage commissions, local historical societies, and churches regularly sponsor cemetery work-shops, lectures, and tours. Particularly noteworthy are cemetery tours and preservation programs sponsored by Middlesex County Cultural and Her-itage Commission as well as the Bergen County Division of Cultural and Historic Affairs. For close to fifteen years the East Brunswick Museum has been sponsoring evening candlelit tours of Chestnut Hill Cemetery in East Brunswick. The popular event, held in October, brings over fifteen hundred people out to learn about the rich history of the cemetery and region. Other historical societies have also sponsored tours, including the Mer-chants and Drovers Tavern Museum, which runs regular events at the Rah-way Cemetery.

Keeping the Record

The study of historic gravemarkers is, for many people, more than simply a hobby. For genealogists, art historians, archaeologists, and others it can become an obsession. Models of how to record burial grounds are provided by publications of the American Association for State and Local History (Newman 1971; Jones 1971; Strangstad 1988) and the Association for Gravestone Studies (www.gravestonestudies.org). There are also computerized databases available for use in recording historic burial grounds. These define what pieces of information are useful to record.

While wire brushes were once used to clean lichen from the faces of old stones for recording, modern cemeterians prefer more mild methods, soft bristle brushes, and deionized water. Some researchers like to make grave rubbings as a record of interesting or artistic gravemarkers. Rubbings allow details unseen in photographs to be visible. However, unless it is done with great care, rubbing can deface a marker, contribute to spalling and weathering, and may damage the surface in the act of trying to record it. Photography provides a low-impact alternative. However, photographing gravemarkers can be a challenge. Often researchers have to visit and revisit a cemetery, waiting for the sun to be in just the right spot so that a marker will be well lit. With mirrors and photographer's reflectors these repeated trips can be avoided. So long as the sun is shining and the grass or shrubs are trimmed, a good photograph should be possible. Digital cameras also provide an advantage in that a photographer can see just how poor a photograph is before leaving the cemetery.

While thousands of new gravemarkers are erected every year, others disappear, victims of vandalism, weathering, and development. A good photograph of a gravemarker and written record can be an invaluable piece of evidence for future researchers. By studying the markers that our predecessors erected we can better understand their lives and culture, the art they created, their sorrows and successes. Gravemarkers provide us with a personalized glimpse of the past meant to instruct and inform future generations.

The Importance of Cemetery Studies

Cemeteries provide a physical record of a community's former inhabitants. By viewing the stones that mark their final resting places we can learn about their beliefs, their lives, their accomplishments, their relationships, and the tragedies that laid them low. For genealogists, cemeteries are an important source of raw data, which allow family relationships to be traced, pedigrees to be perfected, and ancestors to be rediscovered. The memorials contained in cemeteries and graveyards provide a unique artistic record reflecting the styles of the time, and in some cases the sensibilities of the individuals resting there. New Jersey's historic burial places are an unsurpassed source of information about our state's history and people.

Whether dating from the seventeenth century or the twenty-first century, cemeteries provide a long-lasting record of a community's history and inhabitants. There is the equivalent of Edgar Lee Masters' *Spoon River Anthology* (1924) in every local cemetery. By careful study and analysis we can make these mute stones speak. The goal of this book is to help tell their tales.

« 2 »

Early American Burial Grounds and Gravemarkers

There is no better place to come face to face with the ideas and beliefs of New Jersey's first settlers than a burial ground. The names scratched onto split fieldstones, or chiseled into brown sandstone and white sugar marble, remind us of early settlers—English, Dutch, Swedish, Scottish, African, and German—who made new homes in a new land. Colonial New Jersey was home to four distinct gravemarking traditions, each reflecting the beliefs of a different cultural group. This chapter provides a brief history of New Jersey's burial grounds from the seventeenth century to the present. It examines the types of burial grounds employed by New Jerseyans from prehistory to the current day. Also discussed are the major types of gravemarkers, how gravestones were carved, the inscriptions and epitaphs they bear, and what they cost. It concludes with a brief discussion of how gravemarkers can be effectively recorded.

Native American Burial Grounds

Long before there were any professional carvers in New Jersey, Native Americans were commemorating their dead. The first gravemarkers in New Jersey were undoubtedly placed over the final resting places of Native Americans, the people known today as Lenape or Delaware and their precursors. Although Native Americans had lived in New Jersey for millennia before the first European colonists arrived on these shores, we know less than we would like to about their memorial traditions. Some of the earliest graves located in the state are cremations. These date back thousands of years and were found by archaeologist Drew Stanzeski at the West Creek site in southern Ocean County (Stanzeski 1996, 44). In fact, the West Creek site is the earliest known cemetery in the state (Mounier 2003, 168). Later burials included cremations; in-flesh burials, sometimes in the fetal position; and even ossuaries, where the bones of many individuals were commingled in a single grave.

Some Native Americans were buried with rich accompaniments—stone tools, smoking pipes, and exotic minerals brought from a distance (Kraft 2001, 174–179; Mounier 2003, 161–192). Others were returned to the earth as naked as they were born. No Native American gravemarkers predating the arrival of the Dutch and English have been unequivocally identified. Although many nineteenth-century authors noted the presence of low earthen mounds or tumuli, which once marked the graves of ancient Native Americans, it appears that these were in fact natural eminences, which suited Native Americans as burial places. As reported in Alanson Skinner's pioneering survey of Native American sites in New Jersey:

> Artificial burial mounds do not exist in New Jersey. They are frequently reported, but investigation has invariably shown that the Indians have made use of a natural elevation for their interments. No earthworks or mounds of aboriginal manufacture are known in the State, popular tradition to the contrary notwithstanding. . . . The typical Indian cemetery in New Jersey is practically impossible to locate except by accident, as there are rarely if ever any surface indications to point out the spot. (Skinner 1913, 12–13)

Oral traditions passed down from generation to generation, as well as the writings of Dutch traders and Moravian missionaries who lived with the Delaware and Munsee, provide a glimpse of their burial traditions during the seventeenth and eighteenth centuries. Adrian Van Der Donck, a seventeenth-century resident of New Amsterdam, noted that when a Native died

> they place a pot, kettle, platter, spoon, with some provisions and money, near the body in the grave. . . . They then place as much wood around the body as will keep the earth from it. Above the grave they place a large pile of wood, stone or earth, and around above the same they place palisades resembling a small dwelling. All their burial places are secluded and preserved with religious veneration and care, and they consider it wicked and infamous to disturb or injure their burial places. (1968, 87)

Although current-day archaeologists typically take great pains to avoid disturbing the graves of Native Americans, the researchers of a century ago were less restrained than their modern counterparts and regularly unearthed burials for the anatomical information and artifacts they might yield. During the late nineteenth and early twentieth centuries an extensive burial ground located near the Delaware Water Gap was repeatedly probed by archaeologists and dozens of skeletons were unearthed (Heye and Pepper 1915; Ritchie 1949; Kraft 1993; Lenik 1996). Eventually, archaeologist George Heye proved to be such a nuisance that he was arrested on charges of desecrating graves (Kraft 1993, 75)! Later, in the 1930s, in West Long Branch, Mrs. Wallace

Markert, tilling her garden, chanced upon a cluster of Native American burials, which were later formally excavated by an archaeologist from the Museum of the American Indian in New York (Veit and Bello 2002). George Heye, Mrs. Markert, and other early excavators who unearthed Native American burials from the historic period regularly recorded finds of shell and glass beads, copper and iron bracelets, copper or brass projectile points, kettles, spoons, and ornaments. These excavations corroborate Van Der Donck's observations.

David Ziesberger, a Moravian missionary living with the Delaware Indians in Ohio during the late eighteenth century, after many of them had removed from New Jersey, recorded the use of wooden gravemarkers by Native Americans. He wrote, "At the head of the corpse a tall post is erected, pointing out who is buried. If the deceased was a chief this post is neatly carved but not otherwise decorated. If it was a Captain the post is painted red and his head and glorious deeds are portrayed upon it. The burial post of a physician is hung with a small tortoise shell" (Hubert and Schwarze 1999, 89). While no such gravemarkers survive today, these descriptions remind us of how Native American burial grounds in colonial New Jersey may have looked.

Despite the loss of these first gravemarkers to the elements, it is still possible to visit the graves of several prominent Native American leaders in colonial burial grounds. In the Friends Burial Ground in Burlington City, visitors can find the final resting place of Ockanickon, a Native leader who died in 1681. It is marked by a boulder and a bronze plaque presented in 1910 by the YMCA and YWCA campers of Camp Ockanickon. Similarly, the Delaware Indian Chief Tuccamirgan, who died in 1750, is buried in the Case Family Cemetery in Flemington. Tucked into a cozy residential neighborhood, Tuccamirgan's burial place is marked by a marble shaft that dwarfs the fieldstone and plain marble gravemarkers of the Case family, which keep it company in the cemetery. Tuccamirgan is reputed to have helped the Case family, the first settlers of the area, survive a particularly harsh winter (Deats 1925; Sarapin 1994, 98). His reward was burial in the family plot and presumably a gravemarker. The current commemorative marker was erected in 1925 when the rundown cemetery was restored. Although neither of these markers is more than a century old, they commemorate the presence of New Jersey's first people in the state's burial grounds.

It is worth noting that Oratam, the chief or sachem of the Native Americans who lived in the Hackensack River Valley, is reputed to have been buried in Wyckoff, New Jersey. Extensive research by archaeologist Edward Lenik has revealed this legend to be in error (1987). Oratam, today most famous as the namesake of a busy road, the Oraton Parkway, in Essex County, rests in an unmarked grave.

2.1 This unusual marker in the burial ground of the First Reformed Dutch Church of Hackensack, or Church on the Green, is dated 1713. It may mark the grave of a Native American. In addition to the initials A.B., the marker is inscribed with what appear to be a canoe, an arrow, and a tobacco pipe.

One possible Native American gravemarker deserves notice. It is located in Hackensack's First Reformed Dutch Churchyard. An almost triangular sandstone slab is reputed to mark the "grave of a female Indian slave" (Sarapin 1994, 73). Carved on it are the initials A.B., the date 1713, and what appears to be a two-headed arrow, as well as a tobacco pipe and canoe (fig. 2.1). When questioned, the church sexton noted that there were Native Americans buried in the graveyard, near the grave of General Poor. Enoch Poor, a hero of the American Revolution, is buried near the southwestern corner of the burial ground. However, the sexton was unable to state if this curious stone was for a Native American. Equally puzzling is the fact that the church building incorporates numerous carefully carved sandstone blocks from the original 1696 church, many dated and marked with initials of founding church members, but there are no seventeenth- or early-eighteenth-century gravemarkers, with the exception of the anonymous A.B., in the burial ground. One wonders why the skillful carvers who produced these building stones did not try their hand at making gravemarkers.

In Burlington County's Tabernacle Cemetery a simple granite tablet marks the burial place of "Indian Ann" (d. 1894). Like the markers for Tuccamirgan and Ockanickon, this also is a commemorative stone. Ann, who is described on the gravemarker as "The Last of the Delawares," was not actually the last of her tribe, but one of the last local descendants of the Native Americans who resided at the Brotherton Indian Reservation in today's Indian Mills (Flemming 2005, 111–118).

More recently, in 1998, when James "Lone Bear" Reevey, a Sand Hill Indian who had served as a prominent spokesman for local Native Americans, died, he was buried in Hillside Cemetery in South Plainfield. This burial incorporated some aspects of traditional Lenape practices. Lone Bear's grave was marked by both a small pillow-shaped granite memorial inscribed "Lone Bear" and a wooden memorial similar to those once used by the Lenape. These are two fitting memorials for a man who lived in two worlds.

Early American Burial Places

Burial grounds in colonial New Jersey fall into several basic categories: family or domestic burial grounds, public burial grounds, potter's fields, and burial grounds associated with churches and meetinghouses (Sloane 1991, 4–5). Later, in the nineteenth and twentieth centuries, garden and rural cemeteries, the lawn park cemetery, institutional cemeteries, memorial parks, and columbaria developed. They are discussed in chapters 5 and 6.

Today family burial grounds are truly endangered historic resources. However, these were once the most common form of burial place in the state. They were often located on hills, or in locations where the soils were not particularly good for agricultural purposes. In the words of W. Woodford Clayton, writing in the 1880s about then rural Piscataway, "At an early day plots of ground were set apart in one corner of a farm called the family burial-ground, and in this township there were many such, but in later years the stones have been removed and the ground leveled with the rest of the field" (Clayton 1882, 600). Although exact numbers are impossible to come by, many, if not most, larger farms probably had associated burial grounds. Today, as former farms are snapped up for development, family plots are in danger of disappearing.

The practice of burial on the family's farm presumably began in the seventeenth century, when there were precious few organized churches and formal burial places in the state. Often these family burial grounds contained only a handful of stones. Good examples are the French Family Burial Ground in Burlington County and the Swayze Family Burial Ground in Hope Township. As time went by, if the family remained in the same area, the number of interments could reach into the dozens or beyond. Monmouth County has several good examples of these larger, abandoned family burial grounds: the Luyster family's plot on Williams Way in Holmdel, the Polhemus Family Burial Ground, tucked away off Laird Road, and the Schenck-Covenhoven Burial Ground in Holmdel are good examples (Raser 2002). Often modern visitors assume that the unkempt appearance of these abandoned family burial grounds is the result of recent neglect. If left untended, a burial ground will begin to return to forest in a few short years. The Schenck-Covenhoven Burial Ground, which is today largely overgrown, was described as being in horrible shape as early as 1910 (Stofflet 1964, 7). Sadly, neglect is not something new.

As families move away and once-farmed fields are planted with condominiums and McMansions instead of potatoes and corn, family plots are
abandoned. These historic cemeteries are at high risk. Sometimes the gravestones were laid down years ago to increase the amount of acreage that could
be farmed (Mounier 2003, 191). Today, with farming on the wane and family
plots lost in thickets and brambles, it is quite easy for an unscrupulous individual to pull out or knock down the remaining headstones and redevelop
the property regardless of the site's history. Occasionally when this happens
a few interesting headstones will be salvaged and end up in the collections of
a local historical society—the Gloucester County Historical Society has a
significant collection of such orphan stones and there are smaller collections
at the East Brunswick Museum and the Monmouth County Historical Association. But more often than not the headstones that remain are buried some-
place inconspicuous and forgotten. Happily, the New Jersey Genealogical
Association has made great strides toward recording the locations of the
state's cemeteries (Raser 1994, 2000, 2002). They began this important but
time-consuming task in the 1920s when a group of genealogical sleuths, who
called themselves tombstone hounds, began recording historic burial
grounds and their inscriptions. This genealogical fieldwork continues today,
though the results are as likely to be published on the Internet as in some
local historical or genealogical publication.

In colonial New England, graveyards were often located near the center
of town, typically adjacent to the meetinghouse (Stilgoe 1982, 266). In New
Jersey this tradition also held true. However, in some cases the burial ground
far predates the meetinghouse. The Piscatawaytown Burial Ground has several gravemarkers that date from the late seventeenth century, but sits next to
St. James Episcopal Church, which was chartered in 1704. An early Baptist
meetinghouse also stood at the site.

Of course churches also established burial grounds for their congregants.
Numerous early examples survive. Some fine ones include the Woodbridge
First Presbyterian cemetery, Yellow Frame Presbyterian Church burial ground
on the Sussex/Warren County border, and Old St. Mary's Church burial
ground in Burlington City, New Jersey.

In Virginia it appears that having a family burial ground was a mark of
status. Philip Vickers Fithian, a native of Cumberland County, New Jersey,
who spent some time as a tutor in the family of Robert Carter, the owner of
Nomini Hall Plantation in Virginia, provides an interesting tidbit on colonial burial grounds. Writing a diary entry in January 1773, he noted:

> At the Church today I heard an impious Expression from a
> young Scotch-Man, Tutor in Mr. Washington's Family; he
> meant it for a Satire upon the neglect of the people in suffer-
> ing their Grave Yard to lie common—He saw some Cattle &
> Hogs feeding & rooting in the yard, "Why, says he, if I was

buried here it would give me pause to look up and see Swine feeding over me!"—But I understand only the lower sort of People are buried at the Church, for the Gentlemen have private burying-Yards.   (Fithian 1990, 223)

There are also seemingly random gravemarkers that can be found on the side of the road. Some are all that remain of a forgotten family plot, but there are also solitary markers that have interesting stories to tell. The grave of Michael Fields, a Revolutionary War soldier who died from injuries suffered during the Monmouth campaign and was buried where he fell along Heyer's Mill Road in Colts Neck, is a good example. Today his simple marble headstone is surrounded by an ornate Victorian cast-iron fence, a roadside oddity but also a very small and historically interesting burial ground (Di Ionno 2000, 130). Sometimes an outlaw was purposefully buried near a crossroads. Joe Mulliner was an infamous Tory who terrorized inhabitants of the Pine Barrens during the Revolution. Ultimately, his luck ran out and he was captured and hanged. He was buried on the Pleasant Mills–Weekstown Road, a few miles east of Pleasant Mills, near his old haunts, presumably as a discouragement to others considering a life of crime.

It is also worth noting that early American burial grounds were often racially segregated. The state's earliest African American burial ground may have been located in Tinton Falls, close to the site of Lewis Morris's seventeenth-century ironworks. Morris had over sixty enslaved African Americans living and working at this plantation in the early nineteenth century. A 1787 deed noted the presence of "an ould grant of a Negro berying [sic] ground" (Raser 2002, 273).

During the nineteenth century, as old urban burial grounds filled up and became unsanitary and unsightly, new burial places developed. The transition to these new, privately owned commercial burial places is described in detail in chapter 4. The nineteenth century also saw the rise of a variety of social institutions, prisons, hospitals, and asylums, all of which sometimes have associated burial grounds. Later still, in the twentieth century memorial parks introduced a new aesthetic into places of burial. The rise of memorial parks is discussed in chapter 10. By the early twentieth century, as space came to be at a premium in older nineteenth-century cemeteries, managers looked for new ways to make more room. The family mausoleums of the nineteenth century gave way to community mausoleums, constructed on cemetery grounds. Large ones could hold thousands, maximizing a space that may have held only several hundred with traditional in-ground burials. Cremation became the pinnacle of space saving as cemeteries constructed columbaria, structures that contained niches for cremated remains. The evolution from family mausoleums to large, space-saving community mausoleums and columbaria is discussed in chapter 9.

Early Gravemarkers

The first formal gravemarkers in the state were probably wooden headboards and simply lettered fieldstones. According to historian Richard Welch,

> at the time of the first large-scale English migrations to the New World (1620–1660), there was no widespread method of identifying graves in England by means of stone markers. During this period, English graves, with the exception of those of the nobility and gentry, were identified by wooden markers constructed like a section of fence with two posts anchored in the ground and a plank fitted between them.
>
> (Welch 1983, 2; see also Mytum 2004, 26)

These markers were also called grave boards and grave rails. The horizontal plank would be painted with the pertinent information about the deceased and sometimes carved and ornamented as well (Welch 1983, 2; Mytum 2004, 26). Unlike headstones, which almost always run perpendicular to the burial, a grave board would have been placed over and aligned parallel to the burial. In Cape May County, the probate records of John Hand, who died in 1736, list among the expenses charged to the estate "Item By Moneys pd for the Coffin and Grave Posts" (Crowell 1983, 94).

In 1886, when John Stillwell surveyed the Shrewsbury Friends Burial Ground, he recorded 133 markers, 4 of which were "wooden head pieces" (Raser 2002, 268). As late as the 1930s, 2 wooden markers, which dated from the 1790s, survived in this burial ground (Raser 2002, 268). Although no colonial grave boards survive today in New Jersey, it is clear that wooden markers were among those employed by the region's first settlers. Archaeologists excavating in burial grounds may yet recover the shadowy stains that mark their former locations.

Wooden markers from much later periods do remain, and indeed are still being crafted today. They were produced in a variety of forms; some are simple arched planks resembling wooden gravemarkers, others are cruciform, while still others have what has been called a head and shoulders form, and look like the silhouettes of miniature people. Wooden gravemarkers were once quite common; a description of a nineteenth-century Irish Catholic cemetery in Newark noted hundreds of wooden crosses. None survive today. At Weymouth, in the Pine Barrens, a small, timeworn wooden marker still stands. It appears to have been made from cedar or some other decay-resistant wood and may once have been painted. It is a good example of a head and shoulders marker.

Probably the most common form of wooden gravemarker is the wooden cross. They are particularly common in Eastern European burial grounds. A recent trip to St. Vladimir's Church in Cassville, New Jersey, revealed a half dozen new wooden markers standing next to the caretaker's shed. Similarly,

St. Andrew's Ukrainian Orthodox Cemetery in South Bound Brook contains dozens of birch branch crosses. The Atlantic City Cemetery even holds a particularly elaborate multilayered stained and polyurethane-coated plywood cross. Inexpensive, easy to work, and simple to erect, wooden gravemarkers remain an alternative to professionally carved gravestones.

Although wooden gravemarkers were once quite common, stone has long been the preferred material for permanent markers. New Jersey is a small state with a highly varied geology. The Highlands in the northwestern corner of the state consist of rugged mountains containing some of the oldest rocks in North America (Stansfield 1998, 15). Rich beds of sandstone, which have been worked since the late seventeenth century, are also present in New Jersey (McKee 1973, 13). Known to geologists as the Stockton and Brunswick formations, these stones have been extensively quarried for building material (Widmer 1964, 66). They are quite common in the Piedmont region of the state. However, the southernmost three-fifths of the state is coastal plain, a generally flat region of clays, sands, marls, and gravels (Widmer 1964, 95). This area contains little stone suitable for the creation of permanent memorials. Individuals living there who wanted permanent gravemarkers had to import the stone from Pennsylvania, northern New Jersey, or elsewhere.

Fieldstone markers, both inscribed and plain, are found in many of New Jersey's older cemeteries. Sometimes the stones were carefully squared up, such as the numerous fieldstone markers at Old Tennent Church in Manalapan. In other cases, they were left in their natural forms, and initials were carefully pecked out on their faces with a hammer and chisel, or perhaps simply scratched with a handy nail. The water-worn cobble that marks the grave of Hendrik Van Liew in the Three Mile Run Cemetery of New Brunswick, bearing his monogram HVL, is a good example of this type of marker. Presumably these simple memorials were produced by the friends and family members of the deceased rather than by professional stonemasons and carvers.

Occasionally an ambitious farmer-turned-gravestone-carver went so far as to cut a fieldstone into the tri-lobed arch popular among eighteenth-century carvers. Examples of these markers can be found in the Deerfield Presbyterian Cemetery in Cumberland County and in Rosemont, Hunterdon County, as well as numerous other burial grounds in between. Fieldstone gravemarkers are also particularly common in Hunterdon County, with good examples to be found in the Rockefeller Family Burial Ground at Larison's Corner. Although fieldstone markers were used into the nineteenth century, formal gravemarkers were being produced in New Jersey by the beginning of the eighteenth century, if not before. It can be assumed that the rough fieldstones found in rural New Jersey were the expedient memorials of individuals without access to professional stonecutters, due to geographic isolation or financial circumstances. Their prevalence into the late eighteenth and early nineteenth centuries, particularly in northwestern New Jersey, is likely a byproduct of this area's relative remoteness and distance from professional carving centers.

Types of Gravemarkers

HEADSTONES

Colonial gravemarkers came in many different varieties. These include headstones and footstones, tombstones, graveslabs, table stones, and box tombs. Headstones and footstones were the most common. These markers consist of a pair of shaped stones, often topped with a three-lobe arch, used to mark the head and feet of the deceased, creating, by inference, a permanent grassy bed of repose for the individual buried there. The headstone is typically larger than the footstone and often bears a much more elaborate inscription and decoration. In Middlesex County, eighteenth-century headstones range from 10 to 70 inches tall and from 11 to 29 inches wide. Footstones are considerably smaller.

Early markers tend to be quite thick, often with rough-hewn backs, showing the bedding planes of the sandstone formations from which they were cut. Later markers are thinner and more regular and may show chisel marks or saw marks on the reverse faces, where careful carvers cleaned up their work. Occasionally the designs on the backs of the stones are elaborate and highly patterned, though it is not clear whether this reflects the zeal of energetic young apprentices practicing with chisels or a more conscious attempt at ornamentation. Most seventeenth- and early-eighteenth-century headstones have a gently arched top or a larger central arch flanked by two smaller arches. In the late eighteenth and early nineteenth centuries, a design that consisted of both inward- and outward-curving shapes became common (Little 1998, 12). The shapes of the headstones, and by association the footstones, closely resemble the form of doorways from the same time periods, a symbolism that is likely intentional, as gravemarkers, like doorways, marked portals from one state of being to another: outdoors versus indoors and living versus dead (St. George 1988). The uppermost portion of the stone, which is often the most highly decorated part of the marker, is called the tympanum.

Although the ancient Greeks and Romans used gravemarkers that resemble headstones, headstones were first extensively used in Great Britain at the end of the Middle Ages, and became common in the seventeenth century (Mytum 2004, 27; see also Little 1998, 12). The earliest surviving headstones in the Northeast date from the mid-seventeenth century. In Massachusetts, the oldest marker is for a couple, Bernard and Joan Capen, who died in 1638 and 1653, respectively (Chase and Gabel 1997, 5). Virginia's earliest surviving tombstone is dated 1627. It is located in Jamestown, and marks the grave of Sir George Yeardley. New York City's oldest surviving marker is dated 1681 and marks the final resting place of Richard Churcher, who died at age five. It is found in Trinity Churchyard in lower Manhattan.

Mary Jones's headstone in the Piscatawaytown Burial Ground, Edison, is New Jersey's oldest intact legible headstone. It dates from 1693. However, there is an older fieldstone memorial in Woodbridge's First Presbyterian Burial Ground, dated 1690. But both of these are surpassed in age by the gravemarker of Thomas Lawrance, which is dated 1687, and is affixed to the rear wall of Elizabeth's First Presbyterian Church. Both the Jones and Lawrance markers are carved from dense dark brown sandstone.

FOOTSTONES

Footstones are smaller and may bear just the initials of the deceased, or sometimes his or her initials and date of death. Occasionally, one is found with a small cherub or other design in the tympanum. At the Old Prospect Cemetery in Jamaica, Queens, there are a number of footstones that are handily inscribed with the deceased's name, then the words "Foot Stone" followed by the date (John Zielenski 2005, personal communication). While headstones survive in some numbers, footstones are less common. Zealous groundskeepers seem to have removed many footstones during the late nineteenth and twentieth centuries to expedite mowing, and careful observers can sometimes find piles of displaced footstones on the peripheries of colonial cemeteries. For reasons that are not clear, many of the surviving New England slate headstones in New Jersey retain their footstones, though often in displaced locations.

LEDGERS AND TOMBSTONES

Horizontal slabs, which are also called tombstones or ledgers, also appeared in New Jersey in the late seventeenth century. Ledgers are typically quite large, and were often erected by members of the elite (Mytum 2004, 29). They provided more space for inscriptions than the typical headstone. Measurements of Middlesex County ledgers indicate that most were approximately six feet long and roughly three feet wide. In Europe many churches have ledgers covering interments underneath their floors (Lees 2000, 53). Given that space was limited inside churches, some individuals erected similar markers outdoors. Grave ledgers were also very common in colonial Tidewater Virginia (Crowell and Mackie 1990, 118). Ledgers have a rich folklore. In colonial New England they were sometimes called wolf stones or wolf

2.2 A fragment of David Lyell's armorial tombstone, formerly at Topanemus Burial Ground, now at St. Peter's Episcopal Church, Freehold.
(Reproduced courtesy of the Monmouth County Historical Association.)

slabs on the supposition that they would prevent wolves from uprooting the corpses of the deceased. Other authors argue that their great weight would have prevented souls from returning to haunt the living, or that they would have prevented bodysnatching and grave robbing (Chase and Gabel 1997, 5; Lees 2000, 54). While there is evidence that graves were robbed in the seventeenth century, particularly Native American graves, for the rich grave goods they contained, there is little evidence that these markers served as postmortem insurance policies.

Ministers and other important individuals often received ledger-type markers. The Presbyterian minister Azariah Horton in Madison's Bottle Hill Cemetery is marked by one, as is the Reverend John Tennent in Old Scots Burial Ground, Monmouth County. Ledgers are particularly common in Morristown's Presbyterian Burial Ground and at Old St. Mary's Cemetery in Burlington. Some particularly noteworthy markers of this type include the ledger of Revolutionary War hero General Enoch Poor in Hackensack, and French émigré Louise Douillard Van Schalkwyck de Boisaubin (1805) in Morristown.

A handful of New Jersey ledger stones contain armorial crests. Some are even inscribed in Latin. These markers are associated with the intelligentsia of colonial New Jersey. One of the finest marked the resting place of East Jersey proprietor David Lyell, who emigrated to New York City from England in 1699, and established his residence in Perth Amboy. Lyell was a merchant, goldsmith, and member of the Governor's Council. He died in 1725 at the age of fifty-five. His marker has been called "one of the finest examples of early eighteenth century American stone carving extant today" (Williams 1949, 67). It is decorated with the Lyell coat of arms and a Latin inscription (fig. 2.2). Today the broken marker rests at St. Peter's Episcopal Church in Freehold, New Jersey. However, it was moved there for safekeeping from Topanemus Burial Ground in Marlboro. Another fine armorial ledger marks the grave of merchant Peter Bay (died 1743), who is buried in Old St. Mary's Cemetery, Burlington City.

Occasionally ledgers had cast metal plates, sometimes brass or lead, inset into their faces to mark the graves of particularly illustrious individuals. A very curious story relates to a large sandstone ledger located just outside the door of Christ Episcopal Church in Shrewsbury. A marble plaque inset notes that it marks the grave of William Leeds, an early benefactor of the church. However, Leeds, who died in 1735, was buried on his farm in Lincroft, which on his death he willed to Christ Church. When that property was sold off in 1906 his remains were removed to Shrewsbury and a place of honor by the church he favored. However, the sandstone marker was not originally his. It may have belonged to Lewis Morris Ashfield, a prominent local citizen (Raser 2002, 215). It was this marker that originally bore a lead plaque, an embellishment that was removed and melted down into musket balls during the Revolutionary War.

Piscatawaytown Burial Ground in Edison contains several early ledgers, including one marking the grave of two unfortunate boys, Charles and Richard Hoopar, who consumed poisonous mushrooms (fig. 2.3). While the earliest ledgers are quite simple, later examples may have carefully carved

2.3 The ledger of Charles and Richard Hoopar (d. 1693) at the Piscatawaytown Burial Ground in Edison. The unfortunate Hoopar brothers were poisoned by eating mushrooms.

edges, and are sometimes embellished with cherubs, roses, fleurs-de-lis, or other decorative elements on their corners. Sandstone and marble were both employed for ledgers, though the marble examples are often illegible today due to the damaging effects of acid rain.

Within some of New Jersey's earlier churches there are ledgers set in the floor. In Great Britain ledgers that were placed outside of churches are sometimes termed external ledgers, while those placed within churches are called internal ledgers (Mytum 2004, 28). Christ Episcopal Church in Shrewsbury has two ledgers within the sanctuary. Similarly, ledgers have been reported from Old St. Mary's Episcopal Church in Burlington, St. John's Episcopal Church in Elizabeth, and St. John's Episcopal Church in Salem. However, it is not always clear which came first, the church or the ledgers (personal communications, Paul Schopp, Connie Grieff, Linda McTeague, and James Turk, 2005). In one particularly unusual case, a ledger for the Reverend Bateman forms the top of the communion table in the Locktown Stone Church in Delaware Township (personal communication, John Bolt, 2005). In some cases growing congregations necessitated the expansion of churches that resulted in old burial grounds being built over. This occurred at both the First Presbyterian Church in Trenton and St. Michael's Church in the same city. This resulted in some very well preserved marble gravemarkers within the crawl space under the church.

TABLE AND BOX TOMBS

Ledgers generally sit directly on the ground or on low supports. Close relatives of the ledger include the table tomb and the box tomb. The table tomb requires somewhat more skill to erect than a ledger. It consists of a horizontal stone slab resting on four or six turned legs. They form a sort of commemorative table, hence the name. They were never particularly common in New Jersey, and many of those that were erected have fallen prey to vandalism and neglect—a settling base or shattered leg spells disaster for a table tomb.

Box tombs, also called chest tombs, are the most elaborate memorials in the ledger family. Cranbury's Presbyterian Cemetery contains a fine example; Morristown's First Presbyterian Church Cemetery contains several, as does St. Peter's Episcopal Churchyard in Perth Amboy. Like ledgers, box tombs were often topped by marble slabs, though sandstone could also be employed. The pieces were cut to fit together, forming a strong box, which supported a flat horizontal slab above. The slab was typically inscribed with the pertinent information about the deceased. Each side of the box might be two or three inches thick. Sometimes copper fasteners were used to brace the corners. The expense entailed in erecting a box tomb was substantial, and only a handful of individuals opted for this form of commemoration. Box

2.4 An unusual box tomb in St. Peter's Episcopal Churchyard, Perth Amboy. The inscription, which is highly eroded, indicates that it marked the burial place of a woman named Catherine, whose last name is illegible. She died in the mid-eighteenth century. The marker strongly resembles English box tombs from this period and may have been imported from overseas.

or chest tombs provided several advantages over simple headstones or ledgers. They provided a large area for inscriptions and ornamentation—five surfaces. They were also highly visible.

One of the most curious box tombs in New Jersey is in St. Peter's Episcopal Churchyard in Perth Amboy. It was carved from what appears to be limestone, and has an almost baroque appearance, with curvaceous pillars supporting a badly weathered top. It marks the grave of a woman named Catherine, whose last name is illegible. She died in 1747. It strongly resembles some of the lyre-ended chest tombs found in Great Britain (Lees 2000, 64) and may have been imported. It is more similar to imported English box tombs found in Virginia's Tidewater region (see Crowell and Mackie 1990, 103–138) than it is to the other locally produced gravemarkers in the cemetery (fig. 2.4).

Cardinal Directions

Archaeologists have spent considerable time attempting to determine the direction that early gravemarkers most commonly faced. In the Christian tradition the deceased expected a literal Second Coming of the Lord, and individuals were often buried with their feet to the east and heads to the west so that they could sit upright in their graves at the last trumpet's sound. However, this is only the most general of patterns, and burials also were placed to follow the lay of the land, oriented toward existing road networks, toward houses of worship, and sometimes faced west instead of east. During the nineteenth century in garden cemeteries and later in twentieth-century memorial parks, orientation ceased to be important. However, in modern Muslim cemeteries graves are, whenever possible, oriented toward Mecca.

The organization of gravemarkers in a cemetery may be irregular or may follow a plan. In colonial cemeteries, where stones have not been reset, clear family clusters may be present. At Hope in Warren County, the burials of eighteenth-century Moravians did not follow family groups; instead individuals were buried in the order in which they passed on. Archaeologists John Lawrence, Robert Lore, and Paul Schopp, excavators of a mid-eighteenth-century Lutheran burial ground in Somerset County, found that infants were segregated from adults, a common practice in Roman Catholic cemeteries, and that adults were buried in rows and columns. However, this rather regular pattern broke down over time, presumably due to the dissolution of the congregation, and, as the community broke down, family clusters become evident (Lawrence, Lore, and Schopp 2001, 15–17).

From Quarry to Grave

The majority of the gravemarkers discussed in this book were carved from stone. Others, discussed in chapter 8, were made from ceramic, concrete, glass, wood, and even plastic. The earliest surviving formal gravemarkers in New Jersey are found in the northeastern portion of the state. They were carved from a dense chocolate-brown sandstone and date from the late seventeenth century. Fewer than a dozen of these gravemarkers remain. Many are associated with prominent individuals. Interestingly, these markers are not the rough-hewn memorials we might expect in an area that was still a frontier. They are well carved. Over the course of the eighteenth and nineteenth centuries, the sandstone carving tradition of northeastern New Jersey would develop into an art form. In other parts of the state, marble and other stones were preferred; nevertheless, the techniques employed in colonial America remained largely unchanged until the mid-nineteenth century and the advent of steam power and pneumatic drills.

New Jersey has substantial deposits of sandstone, also called freestone or brownstone, that is suitable for carving. Much of it dates from the Triassic period, some 251–200 million years ago. New Jersey sandstone was widely employed for building purposes and provided the raw material for

New York City's famous brownstones (Widmer 1964, 65). This sandstone was quarried in Newark and Belleville and along the Delaware. Deposits are also found scattered through the Watchung Mountains, and in the area north of Paterson and Newark (Widmer 1964, 66). Near Feltville in the Watchung Reservation, an abandoned nineteenth-century quarry, complete with some half-finished foundation blocks, can still be seen. This quarry may have been worked by Jonathan Hand Osborn, who carved in nearby Scotch Plains.

Sandstone's color varies depending on its constituent elements, and ranges from grayish to buff to dark brown. It also varies in density, with some stone being more easily lettered than others.

Quarrying in New Jersey had probably begun by the late seventeenth century, as evidenced by the earliest dated gravemarkers. Quarries were worked progressively from the top down in terraces (McKee 1973, 16). Sandstone is a sedimentary rock and laborers using chisels and wedges were able to split blanks of stone free from the surrounding bedrock. It seems likely that the stone blanks were shaped into the rough forms of headstones at the quarry. These blanks were sold to carvers, who in turn lettered and decorated them. According to Harriet Forbes, carvers would keep a variety of markers on hand so that customers could select a marker that fit their taste (Forbes 1927, 11). Although we have no illustrations of eighteenth-century stonecutters' shops, Victorian monument dealers are often depicted with a stock of gravemarkers in all shapes and sizes. The sandstone quarries in Newark and Belleville were particularly well known, and were first worked in the late seventeenth or early eighteenth centuries (Cook 1868). Some of the earliest carvers, all of whom are anonymous to us today, were probably quarry owners; partnerships between carvers and quarrymen were not uncommon (Zielenski 2004, 3:10, 1).

Uzal Ward, a Newark stonecarver, published the following advertisement in 1771:

> Uzal Ward–Newark, Quarry stone. Whereas many persons in New York, who have occasion for Newark quarry stone have met with difficulty and disappointment in being supplied not knowing where or to whom to properly apply. The public may have therefore this notice that I the subscriber . . . will indeavor speedily and punctually to supply all demands for such stone. . . . Uzal Ward.
>
> (*New York Gazette* 1771)

William Grant, a Boston stonecutter who relocated to New York in the 1740s, advertised his partnership with Samuel Hunterdon, "Quarrier of Newark" (*New York Weekly Post-Boy* 1745).

Seventeenth- and early-eighteenth-century northern New Jersey gravemarkers are made from very dark brown sandstone, composed of well-indurated or cemented quartz sand. They are nearly unaffected by the weather. Later gravemarkers were carved from lighter-colored sandstone, which was somewhat less durable, and contained substantial quantities of muscovite (McLeod 1979, 19). Sadly, sandstone can be badly affected by the freeze-thaw cycle, and water can permeate stones, leading to a slow-motion explosion, as the frozen water pushes the layers of stone apart.

Marble, always a popular material for gravemarkers in southern New Jersey, became the norm in all parts of the state after about 1800. In New England, marble gravemarkers were uncommon until the end of the eighteenth century (Forbes 1927, 12). When first introduced they cost roughly a third more than comparable slate memorials (Sloane 1991, 22). The introduction of marble seems to correlate with other whitening trends in late-eighteenth-century and early-nineteenth-century America, where white table ceramics and houses painted white were also becoming common. Marble remained popular until mid-century, when granite began its rise to dominance. However, marble is still used. Among other things, it is employed by the federal government for military memorials. Most early marble markers are illegible today. Marble and limestone are easily eroded by acid rain.

Slate was also employed as the raw stuff of gravemarkers. It retains its appearance better than sandstone or marble and appears unaffected by acid rain. Some slate gravemarkers found in Middlesex and Monmouth Counties look little different today than when they were first carved.

Local fieldstones, particularly the ironstone found in the southern portion of the state, and on occasion non-local stones that may have been previously employed as ship's ballast, also found their way into burial grounds as expedient markers.

Granite, a hard igneous rock, became the preferred material for gravemarkers in the mid-nineteenth century. True granites are composed of quartz and orthoclase and are often dark in color. It is also a dense stone. Marble is a metamorphic rock formed from limestone or dolomite. It is relatively soft and easy to cut by hand; however, it also weathers easily. Granite is much harder. While granite was occasionally used for colonial gravemarkers in New England, its weight and hardness limited its popularity. With the introduction of steam-powered machinery, saws, polishers, and pneumatic hammers, it became more practical to carve markers from granite. Moreover, due to the nation's growing railroad network, it was possible to ship the markers and even the raw material by rail. This, combined with the increased investment needed to purchase the machinery required to shape granite, resulted in the growth of certain larger firms (Little 1998, 231). With increasing popularity, due in part to granite's excellent resistance to weathering, the material had come to dominate the market by the fourth quarter of the nineteenth century.

Carving Gravestones

After the stone was cut free from the bedrock in a quarry, the roughly shaped stone blanks were transported to the carver's shop, where they were finished. This involved smoothing the sides of the stone and carving a design using a mallet and chisels. In some cases the stones' backs were left rough as they came from the quarry. However, in general, later sandstone gravemarkers were more carefully finished than early markers. With marble and soft stones it was even possible to saw the blanks to the desired size. Transporting these large stones, many of which easily top one hundred pounds, must have taxed the muscles of many a carver. In New England, where records are somewhat more complete, there is good evidence that stones were moved in winter on sleds drawn by oxen (McKee 1973, 19). Waterborne transportation is another possibility. Uzal Ward, a carver in Newark, was co-owner of a sloop, which may have carried his gravemarkers to distant customers (Levitt 1973, 306). His stones are quite common in northern New Jersey and New York, but are also found scattered across Long Island, and even in the Caribbean (Zielenski 2004, 33).

The diary of James Parker, a Perth Amboy merchant, notes the cost of transporting two gravemarkers, presumably a headstone and footstone, from Rhode Island to Ezekial Bloomfield of Woodbridge for six shillings in freight (McGinnis 1960, 79). Since Moses Bloomfield is the only Bloomfield marked with a gravestone from that period, it seems likely the account refers to his marker.

Carvers also made mistakes. They range from minor misspellings and spacing errors to major gaffes. Stone is not a particularly forgiving material, as shown by the marker of the twice-married Martha Moore of Woodbridge. Sadly, the carver inscribed the names of her husbands, Michael Moore and Samuel Jaques, in the wrong order and had to, quite literally, rub out the wrong husband, at least in name, to correct his mistake!

All early gravemarkers were carved by hand and as such they show considerable variability. Some markers are clearly the work of master craftsmen, while others, cruder and error laden, are perhaps the work of apprentices or novices. The carvers worked in shops and, like other artisans of the time, trained apprentices. Ebenezer Price, one of the most active carvers of the eighteenth century, had several known apprentices, and there were other carvers, possible apprentices, who also worked in his style. In two cases, gravemarkers are known that were signed by two artisans; one combined the signatures of Stewart, presumably Abner, and Aaron Ross; while the other, for William Muirhead (d. 1776), in the Pennington Presbyterian Churchyard, was signed by Ebenezer Price and his apprentice Abner Stewart.

Straight edges, compasses, and copper stencils were used to lay out the stone before carving (Frazee 1835, 7). The degree of ornamentation, depth of carving, and competency of the sculpting varied considerably. Some carvers, such as Uzal Ward (1725/26–1793), focused most of their attention on the upper portion or the tympanum of the gravemarker and on careful lettering, leaving the body of the marker largely unornamented. Others, such as Ebenezer Price (1728–1788), could, when cost was no object, lavish floral ornamentation in baroque profusion all over the face of a marker.

IDENTIFYING GRAVESTONE CARVERS

Each carver had his own distinct style, which is reflected in their lettering or epigraphy and in their carving. New Jersey's earliest gravemarkers were all produced by craftsmen who chose to remain anonymous. However, with careful study it is possible to determine, with some degree of surety, who carved a particular marker. This sort of meticulous detective work involves photographing, in some cases taking rubbings of and recording a group of similar markers, and then searching for regularities in how the carvers produced certain designs, particularly the secondary decorations on the sidebars, and the lettering (Williams 2000, 163). With careful study it is possible to identify a body of work and hence to identify a carver (Luti 2002, xix).

As carvers typically learned their trade as apprentices under the watchful eyes of masters, it is often challenging to separate out the work of a master and his apprentices. The works of Ebenezer Price and his probable apprentice Jonathan Acken (fl. 1760–1800) are quite similar. This was no accident as a customer making a purchase at Price's shop presumably wanted a marker that appeared to be the master's work. Of course, imitation is also the sincerest form of flattery and carvers imitated the work of their more successful brethren, particularly as this was a world without robust copyright laws. John Zielenski, a master at carver identification, has found at least five mid- to late-eighteenth-century carvers who produced cherubs with pear-shaped heads like those carved by Uzal Ward, the originator of the style (Zielenski 2004). However, by the nineteenth century, the identification of carvers based on lettering starts to break down. Increasingly, carvers seem to have taken their characters from popular typefaces, eliminating much of the variation that is so helpful in telling one from the other.

The earliest signed gravemarkers in New Jersey date from the mid-eighteenth century. Carvers typically marked their work in inconspicuous locations, such as the base of the marker near the grass line. On rare occasions carvers might also sign their name across the back of the stone, as John Solomon Teetzel did on Catharina Flack's gravemarker in the Long Valley Union Cemetery (Veit 2000, 146), or on the thin sides of the marker, a technique occasionally employed by John Zuricher (Welch 1987, 29).

It is curious that after half a century of carving, New Jersey's artisans began to sign their markers. A growing economy meant that more individuals than ever before were able to afford permanent memorials. This, in turn, meant more business for carvers, who increasingly signed their works, probably in the hopes of acquiring more patrons.

Very little is known about the process of selecting a gravemarker, though much has been written about the cultural trends that may have influenced marker selection. Did gravestone carvers maintain a stock of blank stones, as was later the norm in the nineteenth century? How much say did a customer have about the decoration on the gravemarker?

William Hornor (1932, 238), writing about colonial funerals in Monmouth, noted that "for the first 30 years no stones were used to mark graves. After that date those desiring to so mark their graves ordered thru the local store-keeper, who, in turn, ordered them from New York. This accounts in part for the frequent errors in dates and spelling found on our early headstones." Most gravestones were erected well after the death of the individual whose grave they mark (Benes 1977, 5). A range of two to four years after death seems to have been the norm. For instance in the Piscatawaytown Burial Ground, the gravemarker of Ephraim F. Randolph notes Ephraim's death in 1793, but was signed by the carver "Cut by Jonathan Hand Osborn 1796." Similarly, a receipt signed by gravestone carver J. Sillcock, dated 1813, survives for the marker of Abraham Powelson, who died in 1809 and is buried in the Bedminster Cemetery.

It seems likely that in many cases a letter was sent to a carver outlining the inscription for the marker and then the carved stone was cut and shipped. For instance, the Three Mile Run Burial Ground in Middlesex County contains the gravemarker of Treyntje Sleght, who died in 1763. The marker is carved on slate and is probably a product of Gabriel Allen of Providence, Rhode Island. The inscription is in Dutch. While Mrs. Sleght, the wife of a Dutch Reformed minister, Johannes Leydt, could undoubtedly speak Dutch, it seems less likely that Gabriel Allen could. Presumably her bereaved husband, or perhaps a merchant acting as an intermediary, sent a letter north containing the desired inscription for his departed wife's memorial. Morristown's First Presbyterian Church Burial Ground contains a sandstone marker for Sarah, the wife of Jonathan Crane, dated 1787. It is decorated with a cherub and appears to be the work of the Osborn family. It is inscribed in large letters, "Purchased by Ichabod Crane."

Professionally carved gravemarkers could represent a substantial investment. Most individuals in colonial New Jersey did not receive gravemarkers. Fieldstones and headboards had to suffice. Information about the costs of early gravemarkers comes from several sources. The account books of the Stevens family, carvers in Newport, Rhode Island, survive. They indicate that in the early eighteenth century a headstone and footstone together cost between two and three pounds, while tombstones cost between ten and twenty pounds (Benson 1980). In New England, researchers have been able to discover the names of many otherwise anonymous artisans using probate records. These records, drawn up after the death of an individual, sometimes list expenses to be paid from the decedent's estate, and on occasion note the cost of a gravestone and who was to be paid for it. In New Jersey, tombstone costs from probate records are buried in reels of microfilm at the New Jersey State Archives. The process of examining the records to find the occasional payment is tedious. The search, however, can be rewarding; to date, an examination of several New Jersey counties has yielded evidence of nearly ninety payments for gravestones dating from 1778 to 1876.

A receipt for a pair of Luyster family gravemarkers survives in a private collection and documents a rather austere sandstone marker for Anne Luyster with ninety-five letters, which cost 1 pound, 12 shillings, and 10.5 pence. It was crafted by a New York City carver, and the bill was dated eight years after Anne's death. A handful of gravemarkers in the Orange Presbyterian Churchyard, Rosedale Cemetery in Orange, and Madison's Bottle Hill Burial Ground have faintly carved prices cut at the grass line. They date from 1814 to 1823 and range in cost from $4.25 to $14, depending on the marker's size. It seems all of the markers were cut by the same carver, but he chose not to sign his work. They are also rather austere, with no decoration whatsoever. Presumably, more elaborate gravemarkers would have cost proportionally more.

Elijah Hughs (1744–1797), a resident of Cape May County who served in the New Jersey legislature, kept a detailed diary of his daily activities in 1774 and 1775. At the end of his diary is a short accounting noting the costs associated with a funeral of Lydia Crowell. Ezekial Eldredge was paid seven shillings sixpence for digging the grave. The shroud also cost seven shillings and sixpence. Catherine Swain received two pounds seventeen shillings for funeral charges, and Daniel Hunt of Philadelphia provided one marble tomb. An itemized breakdown of the tombstone's cost was also provided.

1 marble tomb	£9–7–6
4 Banisters for Do @ 37	£6–7–10
To lettering of Do.	
222 letters @ 3 cents	2–9–6
To caseing the tomb	0–15–0
To caseing the Banisters	0–11–3
	£20–13–3

Which is in Dollars and Cents
55 Doll'rs 10 cents   (Dickinson 1965, 99)

As is seen in this ledger, a large marble table tomb represented a sizeable investment, well beyond the reach of most individuals. Conversely, a simple wooden gravemarker could be expediently produced by a carpenter, or even a family member, and serve, albeit temporarily, the same purpose. John Weever's *Ancient Funeral Monuments* (1631) states, "By the tomb everyone might be discerned what rank he was living: for monuments answerable to men's worth, status and places, have always been allowed, and stately sepulchers for base fellows have always lien open to bitter jests" (Ludwig 1966, 55). Not until the late eighteenth century did gravemarkers become inexpensive enough that people of lesser means could afford them.

Reading the Stones

Gravestones often combine art and text, providing two different glimpses of the past. The designs carved on gravemarkers are known collectively as iconography. The study of these graven images is an important area of research for anthropologists, archaeologists, and art historians. Moreover, hobbyists intrigued by these designs often collect photographs of historic gravemarkers or make grave rubbings. On early American gravemarkers ornament is often confined to the top of the marker, which is typically arched, and is called the tympanum. Occasionally the face of the marker is also decorated, framing the inscription in the center. The designs themselves varied through time and from region to region across the state and are a major focus of this volume.

The shapes of markers also carried meaning. Colonial markers, even when undecorated, were often shaped like doorways, reflecting the grave's position as a doorway between two worlds, the living and the dead. It is no surprise that headstones and footstones resemble beds as well, for they served as final beds of repose.

Nineteenth-century markers followed earlier Greek, Roman, and Egyptian originals. Urns, broken columns, and obelisks abound, as do mausoleums shaped like miniature Greek temples. Roman Catholic immigrants in the twentieth century ornamented their markers with statues of Mary and Jesus, while Jews preferred the Star of David and menorahs. Today markers are more likely to bear secular images, a laser-etched wedding picture, a colorized carving of a tractor trailer, or even the logo of the New York Yankees, showing a true fan's undying allegiance to his team. The effect is quite different from the didactic markers of early America, where skulls and hourglasses served to remind visitors of their inevitable fate.

Inscriptions on gravemarkers provide the grist for genealogists' mills. They typically provide the name of the deceased and the date of death, though sometimes they are so minimalist that only initials are provided. They may also provide the date of birth, marital status of the deceased, information about military service, parentage, children, or occupation, and other pertinent information. Causes of death may also be noted. For instance, the marker of William Christie in the Cranbury Presbyterian Burial Ground noted that the unfortunate Mr. Christie was "cut off in the flower of his youth by falling from the stage-coach near Cranberrey" [*sic*]. For individuals interested in family history, gravemarkers like Margaret Elisabeth Winde-muthin's in Stillwater are treasures. Its German inscription is provided below with an English translation.

M.E.W.	M.E.W.
ALHIER	HERE
RUHET	RESTS
MARG: ELIS.	MARG: ELIS.
WINDEMUTHIN	WINDEMUTHIN
GEBOHRNE BERNHART	BIRTH NAME BERNHART
IST GEBORN ANO	BORN ON
1721 D:5 AUG ZU	THE 5TH OF AUGUST IN THE YEAR 1721
KERZENHEIM IN DER IN	IN KERZENHEIM IN THE
GRAFSCHAFT BOLAN	EARLDOM OF BOLANDEN
DEN IN EUROPA.	IN EUROPE.
IN AMERICA KOMEN	CAME TO AMERICA
MIT VATER U. MUTTER	WITH HER MOTHER AND FATHER
U. 2 SCHWESTER.	AND TWO SISTERS.
ANO 1731. STARB	IN 1731. DIED
D. 15 FEBRUARY ANO	THE 15TH OF FEBRUARY IN THE YEAR
1800. IHR ALTER	1800. HER AGE
WAR 78 JAHR 6	WAS 78 YEARS 6
MONATH U. 10 TAG	MONTHS AND 10 DAYS

Epitaphs differ from inscriptions in that they typically are composed of rhymed verse relating to the deceased individual. One of the most popular colonial epitaphs reads:

> Stranger stop and cast an eye
> As you are now, so once was I
> As I am now so you shall be
> Prepare for death and follow me

Epitaphs for noteworthy women, military heroes, and religious figures were often quite lengthy and could sometimes include prose. As carvers charged by the letter a lengthy epitaph could be quite an investment in commemoration.

German-language markers from the eighteenth century often are inscribed with funeral sermons or *Leichen* text (Graves 1988, 60–95). These recount the scriptures read at the funeral.

In a general sense epitaphs became less morbid with time and by the late eighteenth century emphasized resurrection and rebirth instead of death and mortality. By the nineteenth century they had been replaced by simple sentimental inscriptions, such as "gone home" or "at rest."

Not all stones found in graveyards mark actual graves. Some are cenotaphs, commemorating individuals who died far away, in wars, in mine or

2.5 Monument to shipwreck victims lost off the Jersey shore. It was erected by the state of New Jersey in 1904 in the Old Manahawkin Cemetery, Manahawkin.

other industrial disasters, during travels, as missionaries or sailors. Before the American Civil War, embalming was rare and bodies were rapidly disposed of. A particularly fine example is the marker of John Vredenburgh in Somerville's Old Cemetery. Vredenburgh died on July 19, 1844, at Batavia on the island of Java. He had gone to Batavia for reasons of health after graduating from the University of the City of New York (http://familytree maker.genealogy.com). Sadly, he failed to escape whatever was ailing him.

There are also, of course, gravemarkers for unknown individuals. Willow Grove Cemetery in New Brunswick contains the grave of an unknown World War I soldier, who died from influenza but was unclaimed by his family for so long that his name was lost. He rests in an honored grave in the cemetery, purchased by members of a local VFW. Similarly, unknown Revolutionary War soldiers rest in a mass grave behind Mendham's Hilltop Presbyterian Church. At the Old Manahawkin Cemetery in Manahawkin, Ocean County, there is a monument marked "The Unknown from the Sea." This monument, erected in 1904, commemorates shipwreck victims (fig. 2.5). Other mass graves commemorate victims of industrial disasters, such as the casualties from the explosion on October 4, 1918, when the T. A. Gillespie Shell Loading Plant in Morgan, New Jersey, exploded. The unfortunate victims share a single marker in South Amboy.

« 3 »

New Jersey's
Colonial Gravemarkers

The Subscriber begs leave to inform the public,
That he has taken a shop in New-Brunswick,
Burnet-Street, near the sign of the Leopard, where he proposes
carrying on the STONE CUTTING business,
Where all orders for grave, hearth, building stone &c. &c. will be
attended to with punctuality, and the work executed with neatness.

~ Aaron Ross, New Brunswick, May 13, 1797 ~

Colonial New Jersey was home to four major schools of gravestone carving, each reflecting the cultural traditions of a particular region of the state. Northeastern New Jersey from Bergen and Essex Counties south to Monmouth County and west into Morris and Somerset Counties contains hundreds of reddish brown sandstone gravemarkers. The earliest of these markers date from the late seventeenth century. They are an extension of New England's seventeenth- and eighteenth-century gravestone carving traditions. The symbolism they employ—death's heads, hourglasses, crossbones, and later cherubs or soul effigies and monograms—reflects the Puritan origins of so many of northern New Jersey's first settlers. Congregationalists, Presbyterians, Anglicans, and Baptists all employed similar gravemarkers. They tell us something of the attitudes of these people toward death and also highlight the incredible artisanship of local stone carvers, such as Ebenezer Price and Uzal Ward.

Concentrated in Bergen County but also thinly scattered through Somerset, Middlesex, and Monmouth Counties are the gravestones of early Dutch settlers. Though they were often carved from sandstone, they are distinctive in the use of the Dutch language, preference for minimal decoration, and persistent use of carved fieldstone.

In northwestern New Jersey, particularly western Morris, Warren, and Sussex Counties, the colonial gravestones are quite different. Only a few professionally carved gravemarkers were lugged from Newark or Elizabeth over the steep hills of Warren and Sussex Counties; isolated by geography, and in some cases by language and culture, German immigrants looked inward to their own folk traditions and produced unique works of folk art, which still survive in some numbers.

Heading south, modern Route 33 seems to reflect a historic dividing line between the markets served by northern New Jersey, New York, and New England carvers and Philadelphia carvers. To the south of this line, Philadelphia-carved marble was the primary gravemarking material. Most of these Philadelphia-made gravemarkers are devoid of ornamentation, reflecting the Quaker distaste for the ostentatious. However, some of the oldest burial grounds in southern New Jersey hold cherubs and mortality images carved on marble, soapstone, and sandstone. Philadelphia was a cultural center in early America, and its talented artisans dominated the South Jersey market well into the nineteenth century, when local carvers started to establish their own shops in Salem, Absecon, Pleasantville, and Cape May Courthouse.

These four traditions, the New England–influenced settlers of Essex, Union, Middlesex, and Morris Counties; the German-language carvers of northwestern New Jersey; the Dutch stonecarvers of far northeastern New Jersey; and the Philadelphia-dominated southern tier of the state, reflect the distinct groups who settled New Jersey in the colonial period and provide us with a window into their cultures, aesthetics, and histories.

East Jersey Gravemarkers

Out of New Jersey's colonial gravemarkers, few have seen as much concerted attention as those found in the northeastern corner of the state (Wasserman 1972; McLeod 1979; Welch 1987; Veit 1991; Zielenski 2004). Early attempts by the Dutch to establish settlements on the western shore of the Hudson River were largely unsuccessful. It was not until the 1660s that permanent communities took root in Bergen County. Shortly thereafter, in 1664, the English conquered New Netherland and what would become New Jersey was opened up to English settlement.

Eastern New Jersey's early settlers showed considerable religious diversity. Newark was settled by Congregationalists, most of whom changed their form of church organization to Presbyterianism during the eighteenth century. Puritans from New England settled Woodbridge. Baptists settled in Middletown, Piscataway, and the surrounding region. Presbyterians settled in Elizabeth, while Quakers were present in Rahway, Shrewsbury, Woodbridge, and Plainfield. The Scotch proprietors, including Quakers, Anglicans, and Presbyterians, attempted to establish a great trading center at Perth Amboy. Later, at the end of the seventeenth century and beginning of the eighteenth century, Dutch settlers, the sons and daughters of immigrants already established in the Dutch strongholds of Albany, New York, and on Long Island, moved south and west to the fertile Raritan Valley, and into Monmouth County.

With the exception of the Quakers, who rarely used formal gravemarkers, since they believed that all people were equal in the eyes of God, all of these groups participated in a commemorative tradition that employed the reddish brown sandstone found near Newark and at scattered quarries in the Watchung Mountains.

Broadly speaking, the gravemarkers of northeastern New Jersey underwent a three-stage evolution over the course of the eighteenth century from mortality images—skulls, crossbones, hourglasses, and other signs of life's brevity—to cherubs, and then on to monograms and urns and willows. This pattern is by no means unique to the state. In the 1960s archaeologists James Deetz and Edwin Dethlefsen, who argued that historic gravemarkers could be important tools for studying and tracing cultural change through iconography, noted the same patterns in New England (Deetz and Dethlefsen 1966, 1967; Dethlefsen and Deetz 1966). There they found an evolution from mortality images to cherubs, and finally to urns and willow trees. Their three-part evolutionary model attempted to explain the changes in New England gravestone iconography, particularly in the Massachusetts Bay area, in relation to known social movements. They believed the shift from death's heads to less ominous cherubs corresponded with the Great Awakening, a religious revitalization movement that emphasized the possibility of salvation through faith. The movement may also be seen as a reaction against the growing influence of Enlightenment ideas. Deetz and Dethlefsen further hypothesized that a second iconographic shift, from cherubim to urns and willow trees, which occurred in the late eighteenth century, corresponded with the advent of new Protestant denominations, such as Unitarianism and Methodism (Deetz 1977).

New Jersey was settled, in part, by Puritans moving south from New England and was a major center of the religious movement known as the Great Awakening. In fact, Jonathan Edwards, one of the most famous New Light or Great Awakening ministers, was briefly president of the College of New Jersey, now Princeton University. However, the stylistic shifts noted by Deetz and Dethlefsen, while also found in northeastern New Jersey, do not correlate perfectly with the spread of the new religious ideology. Rather, the markers found today in historic burial grounds reflect the changing religious philosophies of the time as well as ties with New England, carvers' abilities, consumers' preferences, and various other factors.

Some of the earliest surviving gravemarkers in New Jersey date from the late seventeenth century and are found in Perth Amboy. As might be expected, several bear mortality images. In the 1680s, a group of Scottish investors purchased large tracts of land in New Jersey, in the hopes of establishing a Scottish colony (Landsman 1985). Many of these new immigrants had been victims of terrible religious persecution in Scotland (Wildes 1943, 57). In New Jersey they found a refuge. Two particularly interesting early gravemarkers are known to survive from Perth Amboy's Old Burying Ground. They mark the final resting places of Thomas Gordon and his wife, Hellen. The Gordons came to Perth Amboy in 1684 from Aberdeen, Scotland, with four children and seven servants (Clayton 1882, 497). Hellen had two more children after her arrival in New Jersey, but she and several of her children soon succumbed to illness. Her gravemarker, dated 1687, notes that Hellen and four of her children once rested beneath it. At the base of the stone is a rather crudely carved skull and crossbones as well as an hourglass. The marker, though almost certainly carved in New Jersey, is remarkably similar in both form and decoration to tombstones used in Scotland during this period (Willshire and Hunter 1979).

Mortality images, such as those found on Hellen Gordon's marker, would become standard designs for stonecutters in northeastern New Jersey. They emphasized the brevity of life. Also carved on the marker is a sawtooth row of triangles, perhaps to indicate the pall, a richly ornamented cloth that would have been placed over the coffin of a deceased individual of great merit. Nearby is Hellen's husband, Thomas Gordon, 1722. Thomas is also marked by a large sandstone ledger inscribed in Latin.

The anonymous craftsman who produced Hellen Gordon's stone had an elite clientele. He is likely responsible for two ledgers now affixed to the rear wall of the First Presbyterian Church in Elizabeth. Although today upright, these large sandstone slabs were presumably once placed flush with the ground over the graves of Samuel Lawrance, who died at age fifteen in August 1687, and his brother Thomas Lawrance, who died at age nineteen in October 1687 (Wheeler and Halsey 1892, 273, 277) (fig. 3.1). According to John Weever's *Ancient Funeral Monuments*, markers such as these were associated with "the meaner sort of gentrie" (Crowell and Mackie 1990, 118). Both ledgers show the same stylized crossbones as seen on Hellen Gordon's marker. The Lawrance brothers were the sons of Elizabeth Lawrance by her first marriage. The widow of a wealthy Long Island planter, she later married Philip Carteret, New Jersey's first governor (Thayer 1964, 51).

Thomas Warne, one of the twenty-four original proprietors of East Jersey, also received a marker that was probably carved by this same craftsman. Warne, who died in 1722 with the "dead paulsey," was buried in Monmouth County's ancient Topanemus Burial Ground. However, his marker, now broken, may be found at St. Peter's Episcopal Church in Freehold, where it was

3.1 The Lawrance Brothers, who died in 1687, are commemorated by these ledgers set into the rear wall of Elizabeth's First Presbyterian Church. These are two of the handful of surviving seventeenth-century markers in the state.

removed to protect it from vandalism. The stone informs the reader that Warne was born in Devonshire in Great Britain and lived some time in Ireland before coming to East Jersey (Martin 1979, 21) (fig. 3.2).

Other seventeenth-century markers are found in the Piscatawaytown Burial Ground by St. James Episcopal Church in Edison, Woodbridge's First Presbyterian Burial Ground, and in Mount Pleasant Cemetery in Newark. Of these burial grounds, Piscatawaytown contains the largest collection of markers, five, that date from the seventeenth century. However, it is worth noting that these markers are not clearly associated with St. James Church, but rather with an earlier burial ground that preceded the establishment of the Episcopal church. The ledger of Charles and Richard Hoopar is, perhaps, the most interesting surviving seventeenth-century marker in the state. It commemorates the untimely deaths of two boys who made the mistake of eating "poyseond" mushrooms. Another early slab marks the graves of Captain John Langstaff and his wife, Martha (1697) (Hunt 1880, 8). Nearby, a substantial sandstone headstone commemorates Mary Jones, who died in 1693. Other large blocks of the same dark pock-marked sandstone may be the remains of other seventeenth-century gravemarkers. The cemetery of Woodbridge's Old White Presbyterian Church contains a single seventeenth-century gravemarker. It is crudely carved with the letters EFB and dated 1690. It was not the work of the same craftsman who carved the ledgers in Elizabeth and Piscataway. In the late nineteenth century, Newark's oldest downtown burial grounds were removed. However, two seventeenth-century gravemarkers survive at Mount Pleasant Cemetery in Newark. They mark the final resting places of Ellena and Thomas Johnson, who died in November 1694.

Sadly, many of New Jersey's historic communities have lost their earliest burial grounds. The situation in Newark is representative of what happened

3.2 Fragments of a ledger stone for Thomas Warne (d. 1722), an East Jersey proprietor, survive in the basement beneath St. Peter's Episcopal Church in Freehold. (Reproduced courtesy of St. Peter's Episcopal Church, Freehold.)

across the state. Newark's first burial grounds were located in the heart of the community. By the mid-nineteenth century the property had become too valuable to be preserved and was developed. Only a handful of markers survive in a small garden behind Newark's First Presbyterian Church. Given the large number of carvers who plied their trade in Newark, their loss is keenly felt by students of gravestone studies.

By the 1730s, markers inscribed with mortality images, cherubs, and simple rosettes were being regularly produced in East Jersey. The mortality images present in East Jersey's colonial cemeteries represent the southern extension of New England's colonial gravestone carving tradition, and reflect the origins of many of the settlers in this region. To our modern eyes, these designs—toothy skulls, fleshless bones, and empty hourglasses—seem quite morbid. However, they reflect both the religious sensibilities of the times and larger cultural trends.

Harriette Forbes was the first scholar to notice and write about this pattern of change (1927). Later, archaeologists James Deetz and Edwin Dethlefsen elaborated, attributing the change from mortality images to cherubs to urns and willows to changing religious sensibilities.

The earliest mortality images in New Jersey are generally carved in shallow relief. The decoration is primarily in the arch or tympanum at the top of the stone. Sometimes a crown or possibly a tulip or even a cloud is shown floating above the skull of the deceased. This design may show the soul of the deceased crowned in heaven, or possibly the soul's triumph over death, particularly with winged skulls (Wasserman 1972, 25).

Most of the carvers of early mortality images have not yet been successfully identified. However, their images remain some of the most striking artwork produced in colonial America. Elizabethtown's Presbyterian Church has a rich collection of unattributed mortality images. Two active but anonymous carvers have been identified by earlier researchers. They are styled the Old Elizabethtown Soul Carvers I and II.

The Old Elizabethtown Carver I produced some of the most striking memorials in the state. He carved headstones for Hannah Ogden (1726) and

3.3 The marker for Leonard Harriman (d. 1726) in the cemetery of Woodbridge's First Presbyterian Church is a good example of the work of an anonymous colonial craftsman known as the Old Elizabethtown Carver I. His work is distinguished by the well-executed skulls. Note the peacocks, symbolizing eternity, and the flames surrounding the image.

Sarah Woodruff (1727), both in Elizabeth's First Presbyterian Churchyard. He was active in the 1720s and 1730s, and outside of Elizabethtown is represented by markers in Woodbridge and Monmouth County (fig. 3.3). He also carved the gravemarker of David Lyell (1725), a colonial merchant, lawyer, and silversmith (Williams 1949, 63–65). It is an armorial ledger, complete with coat of arms, engraved in English and Latin, with an ornamental border and finely carved skull and crossbones. The marker was originally located at the Topanemus Burial Ground but was later moved to St. Peter's Episcopal Church in Freehold (see fig. 2.2).

The Old Elizabethtown Carver II cut curious masklike mortality images with rectangular mouths and arrow-shaped nasal orifices (Welch 1987, 7; Trask 1985, 2). He too was active in the 1720s and 1730s in Elizabeth (fig. 3.4). However, his work also shows up farther afield. There is a fine ledger for the minister John Tennent, at Old Scots Burial Ground in Marlboro Township, that is clearly his work. Given that so many of Elizabeth's earliest gravemarkers are for members of the Ogden family, and that John Ogden, the progenitor of the family, was a well-known stonemason, one wonders if one or two of his seven sons tried their hands at stonecarving.

Another anonymous artisan active during this period who is well represented in the burial grounds of colonial Middlesex County, particularly Pis-

3.4 The marker of Jonathan Ogden (d. 1732) in Elizabeth's First Presbyterian Churchyard shows the handiwork of the Old Elizabethtown Carver II. The image combines elements of the mortality symbols common among the Puritans and their descendants with the cherubs that became popular in the mid-nineteenth century.

cataway town, Metuchen, and Woodbridge, is known as the Rosette Carver, after his preferred decorative motif. His work has also been found in Monmouth County at the Old Tennent Churchyard in Manalapan, and Topanemus, an early Episcopal burial ground in Marlboro. While the Rosette Carver's contemporaries spent their time putting skulls on stones, this carver chose to use his dividers to scribe circles and rosettes on thick, buff-colored sandstone fieldstone tablets. His markers date from 1714 through the 1730s. Given the narrow geographic distribution of these works, it is quite possible that they are the work of a local artisan.

A far cry from this homespun artisan's work are the well-executed mortality images and cherubs that began to appear in northern New Jersey's burial grounds by the third decade of the eighteenth century. Many of these markers are the work of an anonymous craftsman known today as the Common Jersey Carver (fig. 3.5). His work is well represented in Elizabeth and Woodbridge but is also found in Rahway, Morristown, and farther afield. He carved elegant wigged cherubs, with wings that reach outwards and swirl upward at their tips. He also produced well-proportioned mortality images with rows of neat teeth (Zielenski 2004, AA-GG2). His last known work is dated 1763.

Although we don't yet know the name of the Common Jersey Carver, it seems likely that his shop was in either Newark or Elizabeth, the cultural hubs of northern New Jersey. By the 1740s, the work of two other talented carvers starts to appear in this area, as well as several less well documented workers. The two noteworthy artisans were Uzal Ward of Newark and Ebenezer Price of Elizabethtown.

Both Price and Ward had imitators, and/or partners and apprentices. Blessed with exceptional talent, they served more than simply local markets. Price gravemarkers, typically ornamented with cherubs, but also tulips, and scallop shell or fan designs, are found scattered across the central portion of

3.5 The Common Jersey Carver produced both mortality images, seen here, and cherubs. This marker is located in the cemetery of Woodbridge's First Presbyterian Church.

the state as well as on Manhattan, Staten Island, Long Island, and as far away as the Carolinas, Georgia, and the Caribbean (Welch 1983; Combs 1986; Paonessa 1990; Little 1998). Ward had a similar reach.

Thanks to the meticulous research of John Zielenski, the life and career of Uzal Ward are now better documented than those of any other colonial New Jersey carver. Ward, born in 1725 or 1726, was a native of Newark (Zielenski 2004, 2). He was married at the age of twenty to Sarah Johnson, also of Newark, and together they had at least four children. His house was located close to Trinity Episcopal Church, which still stands by Military Park. Ward produced hundreds of gravemarkers, mostly ornamented with puffy-cheeked cherubs, often surmounted by crowns of righteousness. He also carved mortality images, winged skulls, and on occasion monograms and floral designs (Zielenski 2004, 31) (fig. 3.6). He struck his letters with a bold, sure hand. Only rarely did he sign his work. Perhaps his handiwork needed no advertisement. His workshop seems to have operated at a fever pitch during the 1760s (Zielenski 2004, 8–9). Then, in 1765, tragedy struck: Ward's wife and daughter died. Ward found the silver lining in this cloud by marrying the recently widowed owner of two "valuable stone quarries," Hannah Meadlis. With his own source of raw material, his own boat to ship the stone, and a crew of busy workmen, Ward ran quite an operation. However, fewer of his markers survive from the 1770s than previously. For Ward and his family the American Revolution proved disastrous. Like many successful businessmen, he sided with the British, and ultimately served with Loyalist troops in New York. His properties in Newark were vandalized and confiscated. His second wife, a refugee, died. After the war, Ward's trail becomes

3.6 Newark stonecutter Uzal Ward produced very distinctive cherubs, an image which has been linked to the Great Awakening. Note the cherub's puffy cheeks, perhaps representing the exhalation of the soul through the cherub's mouth. This marker for Rachel Denman is located in Madison's Hillside or Bottle Hill Cemetery.

harder to follow. He may have moved to Nova Scotia with other displaced Loyalists (an individual named as Uzal Ward, perhaps a son, is present in records of that province), but he seems later to have returned to Newark, where he carved a few more gravemarkers (Zielenski 2004, 2). He died in Newark in 1793.

Perhaps the most distinguishing characteristic of Ward's work is the pear-shaped head that he commonly employed for his cherubs. This design was also used by other carvers active in northern New Jersey and was most popular with artisans based in and around Newark. One of the most prolific of the pear-head carvers was William Grant. However, there were at least three other anonymous stonecutters who also worked in this style. Thanks to meticulous epigraphic research by John Zielenski it is now possible to distinguish their work (Zielenski 2004). One of these carvers, whom Zielenski terms the "Rounded Pear Carver," cut an unusual tree-of-life marker for Jabesh Marsh (fig. 3.7).

The better-known William Grant was a very busy carver, who was active from 1740 to 1791 (Zielenski 2004, 66). Woodbridge's First Presbyterian Burial Ground contains a large number of his markers. Grant came from Boston to New York and was advertising his abilities by 1740. In a 1745 advertisement he proclaimed that he was working in partnership with an English carver named Samuel Hunterdon and that "he carves and cuts all Manner of Stones in the neatest and most curious Fashions ever done in America" (Gottesman 1938, 231). Despite these claims of neat and curious fashions, it appears that Grant and Hunterdon were carving cherubs and mortality

3.7 An anonymous carver produced this fine marker for Jabesh Marsh, which shows a tree of life cut down. It is located in the Rahway Cemetery.

images resembling the work of Uzal Ward and the Common Jersey Carver. Perhaps this is what the market desired.

Although Ward and Grant were able and talented carvers, they faced stiff competition from Ebenezer Price and his apprentices, working only a few miles to the south in Elizabeth. Price was born in 1728 and operated a shop at a place he called the "white house." He carved realistic high-relief cherubs, with secondary decoration that sometimes approached the baroque. It is not clear where Price acquired his training. Unlike most of his predecessors, he occasionally signed his work. He was actively carving from the 1750s until his death in 1788.

Price carved two forms of cherubs. Some were stylized and very lightly incised, while other were much more naturalistic and were carved in high relief (fig. 3.8). He often carved a crown or spirit image above his cherubs. Other popular primary motifs by Price included a shell or fan design, not unlike that seen in Georgian architecture and furniture from the period (Welch 1987, 17). This design was preferred for children and may represent the voyage of the soul through life. In the Elizabeth Presbyterian Burial Ground the fan design appears on fifteen gravemarkers dating from the 1750s through the 1790s. All of the individuals commemorated were children. They range in age from two days to five years old.

Tulips were another common image employed by New Jersey stone-carvers (fig. 3.9). Research on New York City cemeteries showed a correlation between this design and individuals with Dutch surnames (Baugher and Winter 1983, 46–54). This correlation does not hold true in New Jersey. In Elizabeth, tulip-decorated markers were used for Abigail and Mary Crane, Abigail Cory, Elizabeth Ross, and Charlotte Scudder, among others. They were popular from the 1750s through the first decade of the nineteenth century. Fourteen gravemarkers are ornamented with tulips carved with varying

3.8 A fine cherub carved by Ebenezer Price graces this marker for Martha Winans in Madison's Bottle Hill or Presbyterian Burial Ground.

degrees of elaboration. With only a handful of exceptions, tulip-decorated markers were erected for unmarried women and girls.

Men who had served in the military sometimes had swords as secondary decorations. Masonic symbols are rare but do occur. The borders on Price's stones are festooned with myriad secondary designs, ivy and clover, diamonds, hearts, and pilasters. Other carvers were even more innovative. An

3.9 Although tulips are often associated with the Dutch, they were a widely popular gravemarker motif in eastern New Jersey. This example from the Price shop is for Catharine Thane and is located in Elizabeth's First Presbyterian Churchyard.
(Reproduced from Wheeler and Halsey 1892.)

3.10 This unusual marker in the Schenck-Covenhoven Family Burial Ground combines a rising or setting sun and a cherub. It marks the grave of Ruleff Covenhoven (d. 1786). (Photo by John Zielenski.)

unknown carver produced the Ruleff Covenhoven marker in Holmdel, which combines a cherub with a rising sun (fig. 3.10).

Although most of the markers that the Price workshop produced were simple trilobate or triple-arch stones, they also pioneered the use of a new stone shape that had seven small lobes protruding from the central arch (Welch 1987, 17). Other markers also had unusual shapes. Several in Elizabeth had very complicated outlines, to accommodate the profusion of ivy, pansies, and tulips that Price carved on their faces. The John Davis Jr. (d. 1760) marker in Westfield is also particularly interesting. It has an hourglass shape, which hearkens back to a design element common on early-eighteenth-century markers.

Price and his apprentices signed their markers much more often than Ward or Grant. This may relate to growing competition among carvers as the number of artisans in central New Jersey rose, or pride in craftsmanship, or both.

During his career, Ebenezer Price trained several apprentices and had many imitators. They included Jonathan Acken (fl. 1760–1800), David Jeffries (fl. 1760–1800), and Abner Stewart. Thanks to a 1788 newspaper advertisement we get a fleeting glimpse of apprentice stonecutter Abner Stewart. In that year Ebenezer Price advertised:

Three Pounds Reward

Run away from the subscriber about 4 weeks ago, an apprentice boy, named Abner Stewart, strong and able, near 20 years, 5 feet 8 inches high, brown hair, bluish eyes, cloathed in a half worn suit of blue coating, plated buttons, and good wool hat; went away on account of a riot, &c. committed in this town in which he was supposed to have been an aggressor; it all being settled by his father who is desirous that he should return to his master and serve out his time, being his duty and interest to do so.

—All persons are hereby forewarned entertaining, employing or carrying him off, but should he return immediately, all shall be well, if not, whoever will take up said apprentice and bring him home or secure him in any gaol, so that his said master may have him again shall have the above reward, and all reasonable charges paid by

Ebenezer Price,
Stonecutter.
Elizabethtown, June 3, 1788   (*New Jersey Journal*)

The advertisement appears to have worked, as the following year, after Price's death, Stewart advertised that he was now in charge of his master's old shop. He continued to carve cherubs, monograms, and floral designs in Elizabethtown as late as 1798 (Wasserman 1972, 16). Later, he relocated to Marksboro in northwestern New Jersey, where he continued to produce markers into the early nineteenth century.

By the 1770s there were half a dozen carvers in Elizabethtown and surrounding communities, including Scotch Plains, Westfield, and New Providence, who worked in Price's style. They included the brothers Jonathan Hand and Henry Osborn, Abner Tucker, J. Tucker, and David Stewart.

Among the most productive were the Osborn brothers, Jonathan Hand (1760–1846) and Henry (1770–1839). They were two of the sons of Jonathan H. Osborn, a resident of the Westfield Ward of Elizabeth Township (Cook 1971), and part of a large family; their parents had six other children. The place of their training is unknown. However, it is possible that the elder Jonathan H. Osborn was also a carver, as his inventory lists a "lot of mason's tools" worth twelve shillings. Jonathan Hand Osborn served in the American Revolution as a drummer boy and later received a pension (Cook 1971, 86). He had an older brother Jonathan Baldwin Osborn, and perhaps because of this, he sometimes called himself Hand Osborn; several stones signed "Hand Osborn" are found in New Providence's Presbyterian Burial Ground. He may also have signed stones simply "H. Osborn," a source of confusion as his brother Henry also carved gravemarkers. Jonathan Hand Osborn was listed on the ratable list for Westfield Ward, Elizabeth Township, in 1782, 1783, 1789, and 1790, and in 1820 in Westfield Township, Scotch Plains District (Cook 1971). He was a member of the Scotch Plains Baptist Church. He and his wife, Martha Shotwell (1766–1846), had seven children. He died in March of 1846.

Both of the Osborn brothers carved cherubs, though theirs are somewhat less refined than the work of Price and his apprentices (fig. 3.11). They also carved floral motifs, monograms, and other designs (fig. 3.12). In the early nineteenth century, as many carvers were switching to the neoclassic

3.11 Jonathan Hand Osborn of Scotch Plains was one of many carvers who made stones in a style similar to that of Ebenezer Price. This cherub for John Lindsley is a good example of his work. It is located in the Morristown Presbyterian Burial Ground.

3.12 A rather unusual eagle graces this marker for Charity Thompson in the Piscatawaytown Burial Ground by St. James Episcopal Church in Edison. It may have been carved by one of the Osborns.

designs of weeping willows and urns, Jonathan Osborn instead was a prolific carver of a regional design with tulips, script monograms, and border patterns of vines and repeating diamonds patterns. The designs, carved on sandstone, were imitated by others, including Elizabethtown carver Noah Norris, and seem to slow the spread of the willows and urns in this region. But, like many carvers, he made the switch to marble and dropped the distinct regional style he had created in sandstone.

While Jonathan Hand Osborn's shop was in Scotch Plains, his brother signed his markers "Woodbridge." Both were active by the 1770s and carved into the nineteenth century, when the increasing use of marble, which they also worked, makes it nearly impossible to track their work.

Some of the most intriguing eighteenth-century carvers are, today, completely anonymous. In the Orange Presbyterian Churchyard there are a number of markers by a carver active in the late 1770s who produced striking three-dimensional cherubs, who wear their hair carefully combed forward in a Roman style. Farther west in Morristown, Chester, Whippany, and elsewhere, there is a series of cherub-ornamented markers dating from the 1770s, with tightly coiled wigs like those carved by Price, but which are often topped by orbs. Art historian John Zielenski has termed this craftsman the Orb Carver.

While eastern New Jersey's earliest carvers are anonymous and known only by their carving styles, many of the later artisans signed their work, allowing us to trace their careers, follow the distribution of their products, and learn a bit more about their motivations.

The Osborns and other artisans who began their careers carving rather doleful cherubs on sandstone, in many cases, ended their days carving monograms and urns and willow trees on marble. Thanks to John Frazee, one of the last of eastern New Jersey's sandstone carvers, we have a better understanding of this transition. While Frazee started his stonecutting career as a mason's assistant, working on a bridge in Rahway, he ended it as one of North America's great sculptors. In 1835 he sat down and began to write his autobiography. His reminiscences provide a glimpse into the stonecutter's world during the early nineteenth century. Describing the beginning of his career, he wrote:

> There was not, nor had there ever been any stonecutter in Rahway. The headstones in our burying ground were purchased in Woodbridge, Elizabethtown, and Newark. I had, from time to time, examined the work of other workers in marble, and noticed particularly their respective styles and manner of execution. But none possessed anything like genius, or the powers of invention, as applied to fine art. The ornaments, with which they enriched the borders of their tomb-tables and headstones, had neither germ nor root in nature. . . . I did not think such

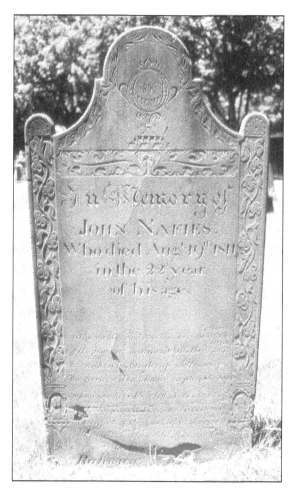

3.13 John Frazee, the carver of this fine sandstone marker for John Nafies in Rahway, parlayed his skill as a gravestone carver into a career as one of America's first sculptors. Note the light and refined lettering and the pair of profile silhouettes at the base of the pilasters.

kinds of enrichment were altogether appropriate upon monuments for the dead; nor was I in any way inclined to imitate their style or taste. I was resolved to strike out a new path, both in ornament and lettering.   (Frazee 1835, 7)

Frazee and a group of his contemporaries succeeded in their goal of striking out a new path, but contrary to his autobiography it was not that far from the path his contemporaries and predecessors had been following (fig. 3.13).

The mortality images produced in eighteenth-century Elizabethtown and Newark stem from the medieval *memento mori* (remember thou diest) tradition of depicting the body as corruptible and life as fleeting (Tarlow 1999, 188). The cherubs, which replaced them, represent a new cultural horizon, only loosely correlated with the Great Awakening, but also tied to changes in carving styles in England, and a shifting interpretation of death. They typically avoid graphic depictions of the decay of the body. Finally, the use of urns and willow trees, or locally designed monograms, represents a third cultural horizon. This one was linked to the new neoclassical style that was so popular both in England and in the young United States, and drew its inspiration from archaeological excavations in Italy and Greece and a renewed interest in the classical world. Although in some parts of New England death's heads, cherubs, and urns and willows do correlate with changing religious sensibilities, they also reflect broader cultural traditions that influenced Puritans and non-Puritans alike.

The gravestones of east central New Jersey show a pattern very similar to that first noted by Deetz and Dethlefsen in New England. There are, however, some significant differences. Urns and willows are infrequent; instead undecorated gravemarkers (Baugher and Winter 1983, 36:50) and monograms are more common. Locally designed monograms were popularized by Ebenezer Price's apprentices, as well as the Osborn brothers and Jonathan Frazee. Their presence probably has little to do with changing religious sensibilities, but much to do with the increasing democratization of permanent gravemarkers and the rise of a consumer culture, in which individuals besides elites could afford to purchase gravemarkers.

The development of the monogram style in East Jersey is curious. After years of aping New England's fashions, why did the region's carvers decide to go their own way? The change seems to have little to do with the shifting religious sentiments of the time. In fact, John Frazee, describing his own work, wrote:

> I knew nothing strictly speaking of emblematic ornaments, and I had not means whatever afforded me for obtaining a knowledge of such things. I began my career among the tombstones, utterly ignorant of every rule of art, and all those symbols, images, and attributes that had their origin in the classical ages, and that lived and breathed in the beautiful sculptures upon the tombs and sarcophagi of Egypt and Greece.
>
> (Frazee 1835, 7)

At least from this statement it does not appear that religion played much of a role in determining Frazee's choice of design. However, he was no atheist. In fact, he was an active member of the Presbyterian Church in Rahway, where he served as choir leader (Frazee 1835, 2).

While most carvers in the sandstone belt produced script monograms and other localized styles, a few introduced the urn and willow. Urns first appear by the late eighteenth century in the New England states, where their style was popularized through mourning jewelry and printed material, including early pattern books, such as Asher Benjamin's *The American Builder's Companion*. Benjamin's book published plates and descriptions for the building trade but has one plate with six designs for urns that "ought to be principally confined to monuments, wall pieces, churches, mausoleums, mourning pieces, etc." (Benjamin 1827, 72).

Although the book was written by Benjamin, the designs are signed by Daniel Raynerd. Raynerd was a stucco worker who traveled to England in the 1790s to learn his trade and it is there that he may have picked up the inspiration for the designs (Quinan 1975, 1). Raynerd had partnered with Benjamin to publish the designs in the early nineteenth century but shortly afterward left the partnership to pursue different endeavors. Although Benjamin's book was updated and published into the late 1820s, the Raynerd plates date to the first printings in the early nineteenth century. The book helped to introduce the urn and neoclassical style into the New England states, from where it would spread rapidly.

In New Jersey urns appear in the late eighteenth century. An early example is the Elizabeth Kinney ledger in the Morristown Presbyterian Cemetery. The large sandstone slab is from 1789 and has a round urn with handles carved into the top surface. By the early nineteenth century urns appear with some regularity in the sandstone-rich regions of the state. They were produced by both skillful carvers, who executed finely crafted urns, and amateurs, who produced less refined examples.

Prior to 1810, some urns sprout willow branches from just under the lid. This design seems to have been utilized more in the New England states, where one can find many examples in cemeteries, but had limited use in New Jersey. Among the early New Jersey examples is a worn marble gravestone dated 1798 and located in a family burial ground on the property of Rutgers Preparatory School in Somerset. A deeply modeled urn was carved with two well-defined willow branches emerging from under the lid. They then droop down and sweep toward the shoulders of the gravestone. The carver of this stone is unknown and its style is unlike any other examples found in the region, making its background unique and worthy of further research.

Other transitional and regional variations of urns and willows exist in central and northern New Jersey. By the 1810s script monograms, a unique regional design, became common. At the same time designers partnered the urn with a willow tree, creating a stunning mourning scene at the top front face of the gravestone. Springfield and Connecticut Farms carver J. C. Mooney was among the earliest to introduce the design to central New Jersey. Although others had adopted the style prior to him, Mooney was prolific in its use and his willow and urn depictions were skillfully carved. In this sandstone-rich region he carved a number of examples. Of note is the memorial he carved for the Wade children in the Springfield Presbyterian Churchyard. A single marker commemorates the three children of Oliver and Phebe Wade, who died in 1808, 1809, and 1818. Mooney carved a stone with three tops, each with a weeping willow and urn.

Noah Norris, an Elizabeth carver of the same time period, carved a number of examples on the correct classically inspired material, marble. During the 1810s and 20s he carved modeled urns with willows that appear to be

3.14 As the number of carvers increased in the early nineteenth century, they resorted to advertising to help sell their wares. While most carvers signed their stones discreetly near the base, Jonathan Hand Osborn placed his calling card in a much more obvious place, the top or tympanum of the marker. This headstone in the Scotch Plains Burial Ground marks the grave of William Darby.

inspired by church wall plaques of the same vintage. Mooney and Norris, along with their contemporaries, began by carving spindly willow trees bending over simple or pedestaled urns, all of the branches hanging to one side. Later willow trees became straight and fuller with branches flowing from both ends. This style is more typical of the mid-nineteenth century and will be discussed in chapter 5.

Signed gravemarkers first appear in New Jersey in the mid-eighteenth century. Although they peaked in popularity in the 1780s, they continued to be used into the modern era. Many carvers chose to sign their works just above the grass line, which has led to the loss of some information as stones sink into the ground. Other artisans, perhaps more aware of the growing market for memorials, placed their imprimaturs in more prominent locations. Jonathan Hand Osborn was not above giving himself equal billing with the deceased in the tympanum of the stone (see fig. 3.14).

Gravestone carvers in northwestern New Jersey, such as the bilingual carver John Solomon Teetzel, also signed many of their works. Teetzel carved roughly one hundred gravemarkers that survive, dated from the 1770s through 1800, and signed forty-four of them (Veit 2000, 146–147). Although he commonly signed with a capital letter *T* or his last name, *Teetzel*, at the base of the marker, he would also at times sign *J. S. Teetzel*, and in some cases put his whole name on the back of the markers. Carvers such as Teetzel, the Osborns, and even earlier Ebenezer Price and Uzal Ward sometimes also put their place of business on the markers.

The use of signed markers appears to correlate with an increasingly active market for gravestones at the end of the eighteenth century. In a general sense, it appears that carvers signed more elaborate stones, perhaps to highlight their handiwork, and also stones shipped some distance away from their home bases (Stone 1987). It is also clear that some families preferred the work of certain carvers (Heinrich 2003, 12).

Sadly, New Jersey probate records and wills only rarely contain information on the costs of gravemarkers. However, a handful of early-nineteenth-century gravestones by an unidentified carver or carvers have been found in Morris and Essex Counties. These markers have faintly inscribed prices carved near their bases, complete with dollar signs. Modest, minimally decorated memorials, they ranged from four dollars and twenty-five cents to fourteen dollars in cost. These prices were likely meant to be hidden beneath the soil, but erosion and restoration projects have revealed them.

The monogrammed sandstones and lightly inscribed floral designs of the 1820s would soon disappear, whitewashed away by a sea of marble memorials as Philadelphia-style gravemarkers became the first truly national style. However, two other influences on northeastern New Jersey's colonial carving styles bear noting: New England's finely carved slate gravemarkers and New York City's sandstone carvers.

New England Gravemarkers in New Jersey

New England is the heartland of American gravestone studies. Its historic gravemarkers have seen scholarly attention for longer than those of any other region of the country (Forbes 1927; Caulfield 1991; Benson 1980; Ludwig 1966; Benes 1977). New England gravemarkers were imported in small numbers into eastern New Jersey from the second decade of the eighteenth century through the 1790s. The earliest example that we were able to locate is dated 1722/23—the double date reflects the fact that the Julian calendar, which started the new year in March instead of on January 1, remained in use in colonial America. It marks the grave of Joyce Hance, who is buried in the Rumson Burial Ground. The latest example is for Isaac Winslow, a native of Berkley, Massachusetts, buried in the Old Presbyterian Cemetery in Middletown, New Jersey. Mr. Winslow died in 1790 and his grave is marked by a large gray slate marker carved by his uncle Ebenezer Winslow in Berkley, Massachusetts (Vincent Luti 2005, personal communication).

3.15 The John Saltar gravemarker is one of the finest examples imported from New England into New Jersey. It is located in the Old Yellow Church Burial Ground in Upper Freehold.

The New England markers found in New Jersey are predominantly bluish gray and flinty black slates carved by the Stevens Shop of Rhode Island, the Allens of Providence, Rhode Island, and the Lamsons of Charlestown, Massachusetts. Other carvers' products are present but in much smaller numbers. For instance, several beautifully carved but now highly eroded marble headstones imported from Connecticut stand in the burial ground of the Orange Presbyterian Church. They marked the graves of Abigail Condit (1784), Caleb Condit (1797), and John Smith Condit (1800).

Imported slate gravemarkers can be found in Hunterdon, Mercer, Middlesex, Monmouth, Somerset, and Union Counties. They are particularly common in Shrewsbury, New Brunswick, and the Piscatawaytown section of Edison, with smaller numbers in Rumson, Middletown, Perth Amboy, Lamington, Chester, Elizabeth, Matawan, Trenton, and Readington. Many are stunning examples of the gravestone carver's art. Flinty black slate headstones carved by John Stevens I are found in the Rumson Burial Ground, as well as in the burial ground of Christ Episcopal Church in Shrewsbury. Perhaps the finest example of Rhode Island stonecarving in New Jersey is the John Saltar (1723) stone in the Old Yellow Church Burial Ground in Upper Freehold (fig. 3.15).

The Stevens family of Newport, Rhode Island, carved the vast majority of New England gravemarkers imported into New Jersey. Their shop, which opened in 1705 on Thames Street, remains open today under the ownership of Nick Benson, and the clink of mallet and chisel on cold stone still sounds. During the colonial period, hundreds of Stevens markers were erected in Rhode Island and Massachusetts burial grounds, while smaller numbers found their way south to New York, New Jersey, and even the Carolinas and Georgia. Gravemarkers by John Stevens I (1646/47–1736) (fig.

3.16 The Joyce Hance marker in the Rumson Burial Ground was carved in Newport, Rhode Island, by John Stevens I. Despite its great age it is in excellent shape.

3.16), John Stevens II (1705–1778), his brother William (1710–c. 1790), and possibly his brother Philip (1706–1736) (Luti 2002) are all found in New Jersey. Particularly intriguing is the possibility that a small group of previously unattributed gravestones in New Jersey are the work of Philip Stevens, a shadowy member of this artistic family. These markers date primarily from the 1720s and 1730s and include both mortality images—with pointed teeth—and beautifully carved cherubs. Philip Stevens, who spent much of his time at sea, was murdered in 1736 about the time that this talented carver stopped producing stones (Luti 2002, 143). Could Philip Stevens have been murdered in New Jersey? Was he working with a partner? For now, the answers and the circumstances of his untimely death remain unknown. What is clear is that the Stevens family provided both gravemarkers and inspiration to New Jersey carvers from the 1720s through the 1760s.

Family ties played an important role in the decision to purchase a New England gravemarker. Rumson and Shrewsbury were settled by immigrants from Rhode Island, many of whom purchased land from Christopher Almy. Almy, a Newport merchant, apparently maintained the link with Rhode Island during his life, actively shipping goods to coastal New Jersey (Ellis 1885, 370). Even after his death, Newport gravemarkers continued to be shipped south. Another connection was through Isaac Stelle, the son of Gabriel and Elizabeth Stelle of Shrewsbury and later Perth Amboy. As a young man Isaac relocated to Newport, where he became a prominent merchant. The Stelle family, Isaac's parents, siblings, and other relatives, purchased seven of thirty-two slate gravemarkers carved by the Stevens family in New Jersey. Gabriel Stelle's wife Elizabeth and son Edward both rest under

Newport slates in Shrewsbury. After Isaac's death in 1763, the number of Rhode Island gravestones imported into New Jersey sharply declined.

The work of other New England carvers can also be found in New Jersey's colonial burial grounds. Gabriel Allen of Providence, Rhode Island, carved the Dutch-language markers of Treyntje Sleght (1763) and her daughters, Anna Leydt (1760) and Elizabeth Leydt (1760) in the Three Mile Run Cemetery in New Brunswick. It is likely that the Reverend Johannes Leydt, a founder of Rutgers University, sent a letter north with the inscriptions he wished carved on the gravestones, which the Allens carved in Dutch and sent south. George Allen Jr., also of Providence, carved a fine cherub-decorated marker for David Cowell, minister of Trenton's First Presbyterian Church (Vincent Luti 2006, personal communication).

Massachusetts stonecarvers are less well represented in New Jersey. The headstone of Moses Bloomfield (1724) was carved probably in the Lamson shop in Charlestown, Massachusetts, and freighted south by Captain Sayre on October 28, 1725 (McGinnis 1960, 79). Another product of the Lamson shop is a very expressive slate cherub for David Lewis (1760) of Elizabethtown, formerly of Stratford, Connecticut. The stone notes that Mr. Lewis was a schoolmaster who died with the smallpox.

In additional to the easily identifiable slate gravemarkers from New England, a small number of sandstone markers carved in the New England style can be found in New Jersey. These include distinctive cherubs from the Stevens shop for Tabitha Trowbridge in East Hanover and Nathanael Bonnel (1736) in Elizabeth, and a mortality image for Jerusha Chichester (1742) carved in the Lamson style in Jersey City's Old Bergen Burial Ground. Family ties, traditions, and trade networks that made it easier to ship a stone hundreds of miles by water rather than dozens by land brought New England gravemarkers to New Jersey. However, given a growing population, talented local carvers, and a readily accessible supply of high-quality brownstone, New England imports had largely disappeared before the Revolution.

New York City Carvers

Given the number of New England–carved stones in northeastern New Jersey, one might expect there to be even more New York City–carved markers in the burial grounds of colonial New Jersey. Such is not the case. The primary reason is that New York City, while underlain by Manhattan Schist, lacks the slate, sandstone, marble, and soapstone that colonial carvers preferred to work. In fact, New York City's carvers were largely dependent upon the quarrymen of Newark for their favorite raw material—sandstone, though they also imported marble from New England, Pennsylvania, and even overseas.

Perhaps the most recognizable of the New York City carvers whose work
is represented in New Jersey is John Zuricher. Zuricher was active from the
1740s through the 1770s (Welch 1983, 44). He was bilingual and carved stones
in English and Dutch, according to his customers' dictates. His markers are
decorated with cherubs, some rather square in the face, others somewhat
pear-shaped, and others still with pendantlike chins. On occasion his cherubs
were surmounted by crowns. At the end of the inscription he often carved a
small trumpet-shaped device, as though announcing further what he had
written. In New York State many of his markers, particularly later ones, were
signed. Very few in New Jersey were signed. A rare exception is in the Mof-
fatt Road Lutheran Cemetery in Mahwah, Bergen County (Sarapin 1994, 78).

John Zuricher and his wife, Elizabeth Ensler, lived in New York City.
Theirs was a fruitful relationship, and resulted in ten children (Welch 1983,
47). Zuricher, like so many of his contemporaries, was a stonemason. In
addition to carving gravestones, he is reputed to have "cut cornices and
arches for City Hall in Manhattan and milestones for the Albany Post Road"
(Mellett 1991, 46). During the Revolution Zuricher fled New York City for
Haverstraw in Rockland County. There he continued to carve stones, but not
in the numbers he previously had produced. His will, written there, described
him as a stonecutter (Welch 1983, 47). Zuricher died in May 1784. Sadly, his
own gravemarker, if one was made, has not been found.

His stones are numerous in New York City, the Hudson Valley, particularly Rockland County, and on Long Island. They have also been found in
South Carolina and northeastern Pennsylvania (Mellett 1991, 43).
Researchers have yet to produce a detailed study of Zuricher's work. Given
the long time he was active, and the large number of stones he produced, it
seems quite likely that he worked with apprentices. This may account for
some of the variation seen in what appear to be his markers. One stone in
Rockland County, New York, shows the initials "NH" below Zuricher's signature, perhaps indicating the work of an apprentice (Mellett 1991, 45).

Scattered examples of Zuricher's carving are found in eastern New Jersey. Known specimens are found in Cranbury, Edison, Hackensack, Mahwah,
Metuchen, Middletown, Montgomery, New Brunswick, and Woodbridge. A
handful of sandstone markers in the Trinity Methodist Church Burial
Ground in Marmora and the Second Cape May Baptist Churchyard in
Palermo, Cape May County, may also be his work. One of the finest surviving examples of Zuricher's carving in New Jersey is the Sarah Van Harlingen
marker in the Harlingen Reformed Churchyard (fig. 3.17). Its inscription is
entirely in Dutch.

Another New York City carver whose work is well represented in New
Jersey's colonial cemeteries is Thomas Brown. Brown, who came to New York
from London, England, was advertising his handiwork in New York City
newspapers by the 1760s (Welch 1987, 36). His repertoire included simple

3.17 Sarah Van Harlingen was buried in the Harlingen Reformed Churchyard. Her marker was carved by John Zuricher of New York, whose work was popular with Dutch settlers in New Jersey and New York. It is one of a handful of Dutch-language gravemarkers in the Raritan Valley.
(Photo by Wednesday Shaheen.)

crossbones, as well as very attractive, naturalistic cherubs and Masonic images. His work is present in New Brunswick and West Long Branch. New York City carvers, including William Valentine and Thomas Gold, may be responsible for many of the undecorated sandstone tablets found in Monmouth County.

Dutch Burial Grounds of Northeastern New Jersey

The products of New York City carvers are particularly well represented in northeastern New Jersey, especially Bergen, Hudson, and Passaic Counties. This area was a stronghold of the Jersey Dutch from the seventeenth century well into the 1800s. They built distinctive houses and churches, and carved their own gravemarkers from fieldstone, with simple Dutch inscriptions, or, when the spirit moved them, purchased a marker from John Zuricher or another New York City carver. An extraordinary collection of Dutch-language markers survives in the Old Paramus Reformed Church Burial Ground in Ridgewood. Also of great importance is the Hackensack First Reformed Dutch Churchyard. It contains two examples of John Zuricher's work, as well as stones by other unknown carvers. The church, twice rebuilt, is particularly interesting as the current structure incorporates several finely cut sandstone blocks from the original 1696 structure. Many of these blocks are cut with interesting monograms and other designs. Interestingly, very few Dutch-language markers are to be found in

Monmouth or Somerset Counties, despite the large number of Dutch families that settled there. One of the rare exceptions is Teunis Post's (1764) headstone in the North Branch Cemetery in Branchburg. It has a particularly interesting inscription.

Hier Liegt myn Oude Vriend	Here lies my old friend
Die gods raad heeft gedien	Who has served God's council
Hier Leg Zyn Arme Overschot	Here lie his poor remains
Zyn Zielgeniet nu Zynen godt	His soul now enjoys his God
Wel Rust myn Broder	Rest well my brother
Gy had aw Loop en Werk voleynd	You have completed your course and work

By the 1820s, even in Bergen County, the Dutch language was no longer being used for gravemarkers. It did, however, continue to be spoken occasionally as late as 1900 (Leiby 1964, 118).

The Dutch-settled areas of northern New Jersey also contain large numbers of simple rectangular and irregular fieldstones with crudely lettered inscriptions. The reason these rustic markers were preferred over more formal gravemarkers remains unknown. However, in a recent study Brandon Richards has argued that the simple fieldstone markers may have been inspired by wooden markers, and relate to a long tradition of folk memorials in Europe dating back to the Viking rune stones (Richards 2007). Finally, in the early nineteenth century, the simple fieldstone markers, long preferred by Dutch settlers, were replaced by professionally carved marble markers no different from those of their English neighbors.

Germanic Gravemarkers in Northwestern New Jersey

Northwestern New Jersey is isolated by rugged mountain ranges from the rest of the state. Because of this a distinctive local carving tradition developed there. The eighteenth-century cemeteries of northwestern New Jersey's Highlands are quite different from those in the rest of the state. The earliest surviving legible markers date from the mid-eighteenth century. There were few professionally carved gravestones in western Morris County, Warren, or Sussex Counties before the Revolution. The sandstone carvers of Newark and Elizabeth rarely penetrated this market. A handful of gravestones carved by Uzal Ward and Ebenezer Price were lugged over the mountains to mark the graves of settlers who had family members in Newark or Elizabeth. Philadelphia's marble workers also sent markers north to the upper Delaware Valley, but their numbers are quite few. The strongest influence was Germanic and came from Pennsylvania. Early markers were generally carved on fieldstone and show a minimum of decoration. In Greenwich, Warren County, there are some thick, lichen-covered stones that resemble the tri-lobed gravemarkers of eastern New Jersey, but are completely unornamented and carved from local stone.

Pennsylvania Dutch or Pennsylvania German gravemarkers from the colonial period share a unique iconography, which differentiates them from English-language carvers. Six-pointed stars are common, as are tulips and hearts (Barba 1954, 10, 21). The earliest dated German-language gravemarkers in Pennsylvania are from the mid-eighteenth century (Messimer 2000, 89). Earlier markers may have been wood (Graves 1988, 61). Pennsylvania German gravestones reached their highpoint in the period from 1770 to 1790, when sandstone, schist, and slate markers were carved in what might be termed a folk style. Skulls and other mortality images rarely appear, and cherubs are relatively uncommon. More numerous are stars, suns, moons, tulips, and hearts (Farber and Farber 1988; Lichten 1946, 128). Rather than reiterating the Puritan theme of death and life's brevity, these markers reflect different folk traditions. Some German markers are decorated with skulls and crossed bones, or hourglasses, but others emphasize salvation, God's love, and the kingdom of heaven, through cherubs, hearts, the crown of the kingdom of heaven, or the tree of life. Some markers were even painted, a practice once common in the region of Germany known as the Palatinate (Messimer 2000, 75).

Early Germanic gravemarkers are found in Long Valley at the German Valley Union Churchyard and at St. James Lutheran Church in Phillipsburg. In Long Valley there are simple markers carved of local fieldstone whose inscriptions are almost telegraphic in their brevity. Everything is abbreviated—names, biographical information—only the date of death is spelled out. Other early markers survive in the St. James Lutheran Cemetery in Warren County, including the wonderfully ornamented gravemarker of Peter Henitz (1777) (fig. 3.18). Peter's stone has his biographical information on one face and a wonderful relief image of tulips in a vase on the reverse. The marker is probably the work of a Northampton County, Pennsylvania, carver.

The small town of Hope in Warren County is also home to an important collection of German-language markers. Small, flat marble tablets, set flush with the ground, they mark the graves of Moravian immigrants who founded a community here in 1769. The Moravians were German-speaking immigrants from an area that today spans the Czech Republic, Germany, and surrounding nations. The Moravian Church, which was founded by John Hus in the mid-1400s, is the oldest extant Protestant denomination. The community at Hope was an offshoot of the larger Moravian communities at Bethlehem and Nazareth in Pennsylvania. Every Moravian community had a God's Acre, which was typically located on a hilltop and enclosed by a border of cedar trees (Little 1998, 86). The example in Hope lacks the border of cedar trees, but is on a hillside, and has typical Moravian gravemarkers,

3.18 Philip Henitz is buried in the St. James "Straw Church" Lutheran Cemetery in Greenwich Township, Warren County. He has a distinctive German-language marker carved by a German craftsman known as the Northampton County Carver.

carved from marble with the names and death dates of the deceased. The stones also note the birthplace of the deceased and are numbered.

In the 1780s two talented carvers began to regularly provide gravestones for the settlers of northwestern New Jersey. One is an individual who signed his stones simply "D." The other carver active in the region was John Solomon Teetzel. Both men were bilingual and lettered stones in German and English, and both men carved very similar stones. Teetzel lived and worked in Hardwick (also spelled Hartwick) in what was then Sussex, but today is Warren County. The area was first settled in the 1730s and 1740s by Germans and Quakers. These two craftsmen, the D Carver and Teetzel, almost certainly knew each other, though we have no idea if they were competitors, master and apprentice, or merely acquaintances. There are seven signed examples of the D Carver's work in the Stillwater Cemetery. The earliest dates from 1748 and marks the graves of two sisters, members of the Windem or Windemuth (also spelled Wintermuth and Windenmuthen) family (fig. 3.19). This family grouping is one of the most interesting and elaborate set of eighteenth-century markers in the state. The memorial for the sisters is signed on the reverse IWM 1785 D. Nearby is the gravestone of John Peter Bernhard, who, according to his gravemarker, was born in Kersenheim in the Earldom of Bolanden in Europe and came to America with his wife and children in 1731. It too is inscribed on the reverse IWM 1785 D. Even more extraordinary are the markers of John George Windemuth (died 1782) and his wife Marg:Elis (presumably Margaret Elisabeth) Windemuth, who

3.19 This gravestone marks the burial site in the Stillwater Cemetery of two sisters.

died in 1800. Both markers are roughly anthropomorphic and are signed. The husband's marker is signed on the reverse in German, "Dieser Stein ist Gemacht Ano 1785 D," which translates, "This stone was made in 1785 AD." Its lengthy inscription notes that Herr Windemuth was born in 1711 in Pungstad in Europe, came to America in 1736, married M. Elis. Bernhardt in 1739, had eight children, was married forty-three years, and died at the age of seventy-one, leaving three sons and three daughters still living. Making this extraordinary piece of folk art even more interesting is the fact that it was originally ornamented with a very crude cherub. A cherub was also carved on the accompanying footstone. However, the eyes, nose, and mouth of the cherub have been scraped away. Then, the initials of the deceased were repeatedly carved over the excised image. Perhaps the family found the image on the gravemarker offensive. A marker for John Schuster completes the group. It is dated 1785 and is decorated with a small soul or ghost carved at the base of the stone. It seems likely that the markers cut with the initials IWM, date 1785, and initial D on the reverse were a group of stones commissioned by a surviving relative in 1785.

The inscriptions on these early markers employ two conventions also seen on Pennsylvania's German-language markers: the spousal biography and the immigration biography. According to folklorist Thomas Graves, "The 'spousal' or 'family' biography names the husband or wife and usually one or more of the following items: the wife's maiden name, the year the couple was married, the number of children" (Graves 1988, 67). Herr Windemuth's stone has all of these. Graves further notes, "The features of an immigrant biography include the immigrant's place of birth and sometimes the year of immigration" (Graves 1988, 67). The markers of the Schusters, Windemuths, and Bernhardts provide a glimpse into the lives of immigrants coming from the myriad duchies and principalities that a century later would become Germany to the New World.

While the D Carver produced a small body of extraordinary folk art, John Solomon Teetzel (1762–1836) produced well-carved but more mainstream German- and English-language markers in New Jersey, from 1780 to 1800. At least ninety-nine stones that he carved survive. In 1780 Teetzel came to America from Cobourg, Upper Saxony, Germany. At the time, he was eighteen years old. He settled in New Jersey and married Rachel Van Till on November 5, 1786 (Gary Chapman 2000, personal communication). He was apparently not a landowner, but he was literate, and perhaps because of this he was soon witnessing the wills and recording the household inventories of his neighbors. Sadly, he left no records of his carving business. His work has been found in fourteen cemeteries in four counties: Morris, Somerset, Sussex, and Warren, with exceptional collections of stones at Stillwater in Sussex County, Yellow Frame in Frelinghuysen Township, Warren County, and Long Valley, Morris County. Most of his surviving ninety-nine markers were inscribed in English. Only thirteen were carved in German. His earliest stones from the 1770s were clearly backdated. He signed forty-four of his gravemarkers, about 45 percent of those that survive. On Catharina Flack's gravemarker in the Long Valley Union Cemetery he carved "TEETZEL" in large capital letters across the back of the stone, while the Debra Dowe marker in the Swayze Family Burial Ground in Hope Township is signed "Teetzel in Hardwick."

Teetzel was a master at lettering stones (fig. 3.20). His English-language markers are strongly carved and often surmounted with swirling curlicue initials of the deceased. His German-language stones show fraktur-style lettering. Most of his stones are unornamented. He occasionally carved simple flowers, ivy, and four-pointed stars, but no cherubs or mortality images. In comparison with his fine lettering, his artwork is primitive. Teetzel also preferred to carve what appears to be a tight-grained buff- to gray-colored sandstone.

Teetzel's inscriptions varied. All of his German-language markers have either an epitaph or Bible verse in addition to the typical genealogical information. About half of his English-language markers have Bible verses or epitaphs, with the latter being much more common. Several of the German-language markers designate these verses as *Leichen Text* or funeral sermons. The presence of texts read at the funeral on gravemarkers is commonly seen in Pennsylvania German cemeteries.

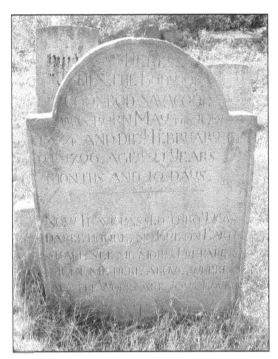

3.20 The Conrod Savacool marker in the Stillwater Cemetery is a good example of the handiwork of John Solomon Teetzel, a German immigrant who carved in Marksboro, Warren County, during the 1780s and 1790s.

On occasion, Teetzel employed epitaphs such as those seen on other gravemarkers in northeastern New Jersey. Patrick Brown's marker in the Lamington Presbyterian Cemetery, an important burial ground with interesting stones by New Jersey, New York, New England, and Philadelphia carvers, reads:

> My Glass is Run
> My Time is Spend [*sic*]
> No Mortal Souls
> Can Death Prevent

German epitaphs differ from those on English-language markers. For instance, Matthias Flach's (1793) gravemarker in the Union Church Cemetery in Long Valley has both an epitaph and a Bible verse in German. Translated, they read:

> Here in this
> Grave Rests
> Mathias Flach
>
> . . .
> Under This Stone
> Over My Bones
> From All Troubles and Problems
> Until the New
> Day.

The Bible verse is Job 14:11:

> Man That is
> Born of Woman
> Is of Few Days
> And Is Full Of
> Trouble

In 1800, as the new century began, John Solomon Teetzel stopped carving gravemarkers in the hill country of northern New Jersey. He next surfaces in Grimsby Township, Halton County, Ontario, Canada. There his earliest surviving markers are dated 1790 and 1800. The first may be backdated. In Grimsby he farmed and served on the town council as a tax assessor and warden and was the secretary of a local Masonic Lodge (Gary Chapman 2000, personal communication; Paul Hutchison June 2003, personal communication). He continued to carve gravemarkers, in the same style that he had employed in New Jersey. His family Bible notes, "As well as farming John Solomon was engaged in his trade of chiseling and cutting stone" (Gary Chapman 2000, personal communication). He died in 1836 at the age of seventy-five.

With Teetzel's departure for a new frontier, German-language markers disappear from northern New Jersey. Happily, Teetzel's old haunts were not without a carver for long. Abner Stewart, Ebenezer Price's talented apprentice and ultimately his successor at his Elizabethtown shop, was also carving in Hardwick Township. Oddly enough, Stewart's gravemarkers, which had previously been near clones of Ebenezer Price's work, now became close copies of Teetzel's. They are masterfully carved. Most are decorated with monograms, and occasionally ornamented with sidebars. Good examples of Stewart's work during what might be thought of as the second phase of his career are found in Long Valley and also at the Yellow Frame Presbyterian Church. He apparently carved in the crossroads town of Marksboro (Veit 2000, 156).

Philadelphia-Style Gravemarkers

Gravemarkers in southern New Jersey differ significantly from those found in the northern half of the state. Most were the products of Philadelphia carvers, and minimally decorated marble gravemarkers are most common. Today acid rain and lichen have conspired to render many of these stones illegible. Often they are an unsightly gray color. Nevertheless, a brand new polished white marble gravestone is beautiful to behold.

Philadelphia artisans were producing marble gravemarkers by the first decade of the eighteenth century, if not before (Keels 2003, 10). The stone employed in these markers, sometimes called sugar marble, is very grainy, and was quarried from the limestone belt of Montgomery and Chester Counties in Pennsylvania (Crowell 1981, 23). A geological description of the stone from the 1960s classified it as "a fine grained marble composed of white crystalline calcite and sparkling flakes of white mica" (Stose 1965, 111). Gray slaty banding is present on some of the markers.

Unlike the gravemarkers of northern New Jersey, Philadelphia-carved stones are rarely decorated. The reasons for this likely relate to Quaker religious beliefs. The Quakers, who dominated Philadelphia's cultural life for much of the colonial period, eschewed highly ornamented gravemarkers. In the words of Pearson Thistlethwaite, gravemarkers were a "stone of stumbling" for Quakers (Fischer 1989, 521), with meetings in London recommending that all gravemarkers be removed in the 1760s. Quaker burial grounds, which are common in southern New Jersey and present in smaller number along the shore, typically contain only small and unornamented markers. These minimalist memorials can be tied to two aspects of Quaker belief. First, the Quakers felt that all people were equal in the eyes of God, therefore there was no need for an elaborate gravemarker; furthermore the Quaker ethos emphasized simplicity. In some instances Quaker burial grounds are bereft of gravemarkers entirely. The expansive Quaker burial grounds of Salem, Burlington, and Mount Holly are good examples of the Quaker ethos as reflected in the landscape. Some of New Jersey's most famous Quakers, such as John Fenwick of Salem, today rest in unmarked graves.

As gravemarkers became more widely available during the eighteenth century, they became a source of controversy among Friends. Woodbridge, Rahway, and the Plainfields had significant Quaker settlements in the eighteenth century. Most of their burial grounds have been lost. However, Joseph Dally, in his *Woodbridge and Vicinity: The Story of a New Jersey Township* (1873), noted that at the monthly meeting held in Woodbridge on the seventeenth of February 1751, "Some friends having been concerned in setting up grave Stones in our Burying ground, John Vail and Joseph Shotwell are desired to treat with them and to desire them to have them removed." Friends Vail and Shotwell faced a tough task. Four months later they reported that some stones had been taken down and laid flat on graves while others had not been removed (Dally 1873, 209). Ultimately, with much cajoling these markers were also taken down.

Shrewsbury, twenty miles to the south, apparently saw an even more violent reaction to the placement of gravemarkers in a Friends' burial ground. Local historian John Stillwell, writing in 1903, stated, "The stones in this yard are noticeable for their small size and absence of ornament. It was considered among this sect, perhaps more so formerly than now, a mark of pride and too great ostentation to erect tablets over their dead" (Raser 2002, 268). Furthermore, Stillwell noted that when some Quakers strayed from this unwritten rule and began to erect gravemarkers, a Friend named Parker "applied sledge-hammers to the most prominent stones, and only ceased when the debris of many was thrown into the highway as a warning to others" (Stillwell 1903, 1:375; Raser 2002, 268). Despite these energetic iconoclastic efforts, a handful of undecorated slate gravemarkers carved in the Quaker style survive in Shrewsbury. Curiously enough, a single sandstone carved with an East Jersey mortality image survives in the burial ground. Perhaps it was this sort of thing that so upset Friend Parker!

The Quaker influence was not limited to members of the Society of Friends. Archaeologist Elizabeth Crowell's research (1981, 1983) has shown that undecorated marble gravemarkers were the norm in colonial Philadelphia and in its associated hinterlands, including southern New Jersey. Philadelphia carvers could produce stunning skulls and crossed bones, as well as cherubs, when they so desired. There are fine examples in Old St. Mary's Cemetery in Burlington as well as in Somerset, Hunterdon, and Salem Counties, but more often than not, they carved unornamented headstones. They also produced fine box tombs, table tombs, and ledgers. They could carve inscriptions in Latin or German as their clients desired. There are several eighteenth-century German-language markers at the Emanuel Lutheran Church in Friesburg, Salem County.

Elizabeth Crowell's research on Philadelphia and Cape May County, New Jersey, gravemarkers shows that while these markers were generally unornamented, Philadelphia-carved headstone forms reflect an evolution paralleling that seen in the more highly ornamented sandstone markers in the northern portion of the state and indeed in New England. When tracked through time it appears that the earliest headstones show either a heart-shaped top or a central elevated arc, flanked by two wings (Crowell 1981, 21). These styles were popular into the 1770s. While the heart presumably represents life (Ludwig 1966, 160), the cherub-shaped stones, though generally undecorated, seem ready to receive a cherub. They are followed by transitional markers, and finally, at the end of the eighteenth century, by urn-shaped or neoclassical markers. Crowell also notes that the epitaphs on these markers closely parallel those noted on New England cherub stones, which are typically inscribed "Here lies the body of . . . ," implying that only the body is interred, the soul having departed heavenward; while the urn-shaped stones are more commonly inscribed "In Memory of . . ." or "Sacred to the Memory of . . ." (Crowell 1981, 26), projecting a more secular world view.

Although the majority of Philadelphia gravemarkers were carved from a soft white marble, Philadelphia artisans did, on occasion, employ other materials, and when they did the results were stunning. Some of the earliest gravemarkers in southern New Jersey are found in Burlington's Old St. Mary's Cemetery. Several markers appear to be the work of an anonymous artisan or artisans active in the first and second decades of the eighteenth

3.21 Some of the earliest gravemarkers in the Delaware Valley were produced by an anonymous craftsman who worked soft gray soapstone. This marker for Mary Steward (d. 1706) at Old St. Mary's Cemetery in Burlington City is his work.
(Photo by Dawn Turner.)

century. For the purposes of this discussion, we will call him the Column Carver (fig. 3.21). He carved large, thick, greenish gray soapstone blanks, probably quarried in southeastern Pennsylvania. His lettering was even, though his spelling often left something to be desired. His trademark motif was a pair of columns flanking the central block of the stone. The columns are carved in bas relief and show Doric and Ionic capitals. A similar gravemarker displaying paired columns and a cherub is found in Christ Church, Philadelphia, and there are ledgers by the same carver set into the floor of the church. The Column Carver appears to have ceased his labors by the 1720s.

Later, in the mid-eighteenth century, another carver, or carvers, probably operating out of Philadelphia, crafted several masterpieces from soapstone. These markers are quite rare. Two of the finest are the Hannah Kelly gravemarker in the Daretown Presbyterian Churchyard and the Jonathan Davis marker in the Shiloh Baptist Cemetery (fig. 3.22). Again, these soapstone markers with imagery more familiar in the northeastern portion of the state are the exception rather than the rule.

The End of an Era

At the end of the eighteenth century, New Jersey's distinctive regional gravemarking traditions began to fade. The colorful blue and gray slates and

3.22 This lifelike cherub was produced by an anonymous Philadelphia craftsman. It marks the grave of Jonathan Davis and is located in Cumberland County.

soapstones, red and brown sandstone tablets, and buff fieldstones began to be replaced by marble neoclassical designs. The urn and willow motif, popular in New England during the late eighteenth century, began to appear in New Jersey burial grounds in the 1790s (fig. 3.23). A new generation of carvers in central New Jersey, including John Frazee, Noah Norris, John Sill-

3.23 A new design that first appeared at the tail end of the eighteenth century and became popular in the nineteenth century was the urn and willow tree.

3.24 Undecorated, Philadelphia-style gravemarkers became very popular in the nineteenth century. This one commemorates an exceptional individual, Abraham Van Gilder, who lived to be 116 years old. He was buried in the Stelton Baptist Churchyard, Edison.

cocks, and A. Wallace, carved simple, spindly willow trees draped over commemorative urns on sandstone and also marble. Unornamented gravemarkers also became common as the elaborate imagery, cherubs, tulips, and the like of the mid-eighteenth century faded.

Ultimately, it was this plain-style marble marker, carved in neoclassical forms, that would become the first truly national style at the beginning of the nineteenth century (fig. 3.24). Marble had been available to local carvers for some time, but it was in the nineteenth century that it became the norm. The reasons for this shift are unclear, but it stretched up and down the eastern seaboard. Essentially, the Philadelphia style had become the standard. Perhaps this relates to Philadelphia's brief tenure as the nation's capital (1790–1800) and its much longer stint as the nation's cultural center. At the same time white neoclassic gravemarkers, inspired by archaeological discoveries in Greece and Rome, allowed the burgeoning middle class to purchase refined memorials for family members. During the nineteenth century burial grounds would be transformed into cemeteries, gravestones became monuments, and America's commemorative habits were transformed.

« 4 »

From Graveyards and Burying Grounds to Cemeteries

The nineteenth century was a period of great burial reform. From the European continent to the United States, cemetery reformers were looking for ways to better handle the dead. The old church graveyards, filled to capacity, had become unsanitary, uncivilized, and unacceptable. A great upheaval was taking place in the way new cemeteries were to be designed and managed. In this chapter you will read about the first hints of burial reform in New Jersey, which took place in the 1830s and early 1840s with the formation of the Jersey City and Harsimus Cemetery, the Trenton Cemetery Company, and the Mercer Cemetery in Trenton. These were New Jersey's answer to reform, moving burials from the chaotic, crowded urban church graveyards to the fringes of the cities and establishing cemeteries that were systematically laid out and better managed.

The chapter continues into the mid-nineteenth century, when New Jersey was caught in the grasp of the rural cemetery movement, with its emphasis on bucolic sites designed with garden qualities. The movement would impact cemetery design for much of the nineteenth century, with many New Jersey cities and towns having their own example by century's end. The Orange Cemetery Company in South Orange, Riverview Cemetery in Trenton, Evergreen Cemetery Company in Camden, and Mount Pleasant Cemetery Company of Newark were among the earliest of these reformed cemeteries and incorporated impressive structures, large monuments, and landscaped grounds into their designs. They would transform the overcrowded, unsanitary graveyard and burial ground into an attractively landscaped garden cemetery.

In the decades following the Civil War another style of cemetery became popular—the lawn park cemetery. This concept arose as cemetery and landscape architects explored better ways to design burial grounds that would meet new standards in taste and maintenance. In addition, the role of cemetery superintendent would be defined and different management styles introduced. What developed was a professionally operated cemetery.

The chapter concludes with a look at the various structures that were built in cemeteries. Entrances gates, offices, superintendent homes, chapels, and receiving vaults were all important support buildings to the large garden and lawn park cemeteries. Their architectural styles mimicked broader patterns of taste and enticed people to purchase lots within the cemetery.

Early-Nineteenth-Century Burial Reform in New Jersey

In order to provide a fit and proper burial place
~ *Act to incorporate the Jersey City*
and Harsimus Cemetery, 1831 ~

In 1835 Mr. E. Hersy Derby of Salem, Massachusetts, made a shocking discovery in the town's ancient graveyard. He made his visit after reading an announcement published by John Winn Jr., the secretary of the Board of Health. The notice directed owners of plots in the public burial ground to see that they were appropriately marked, as the Board of Health planned a sale of those that were unused or unclaimed. Mr. Derby arrived at the graveyard to check on the tomb of the Browne family, relatives of his wife, only to find that the graves had been violated, the coffins broken up, and the silver coffin plates stolen. Several family members whom Mr. Derby had "deposited . . . so recently that their grave clothes hardly had time to decay" lay "exposed to the dogs of the fields and the winds of heaven, with only a slight covering of the earth" (*Jersey City Gazette*, Sept. 16, 1835).

Mr. Derby, whose deceased relatives were wealthy and respectable citizens of Salem, voiced his dismay in an editorial in the *Salem Gazette*. With eloquent sarcasm he wrote about the irrationality of the town authorities by asking how this action would benefit the graveyard. After all, who in the future would want to be buried here knowing that their "descendants may in like manner have their feelings outraged."

He ends his editorial with a series of emotionally charged questions: "I ask of the public, as a fellow-citizen, if this outrage is to be permitted? I ask, as a lately bereaved father, if the sanctity of the tomb is no longer inviolate? I ask, as a husband and father, if the mother of my wife and the grandmother of my children is to be thus cast out to common earth? I ask, if those already deeply afflicted, and whose crushed affections are turning to that *church yard* as the last resting place of what was loveliest and dearest to them on earth . . . are to have their breaking hearts lacerated anew by learning that the remains of those whose memory they have been taught to venerate from childhood, have been thus rudely turned from the tomb" (quoted in the *Jersey City Gazette*, Sept. 16, 1835).

The editorial was picked up by a newspaper in Boston, where this "violation on the grave" had caused such a sensation that a group of respected Bostonians went to Salem to investigate the matter. The editors of the *Boston Transcript* added that "this is not the first instance, by many, of similar outrages, that we have noticed." They wanted the legislature, then in session, to pass new statutes for the preservation of burial grounds; if burial grounds had to be moved it must be specified how, when, and by whom (*Jersey City Gazette*, Sept. 16, 1835).

The publication of "Violation on the Grave" in the *Jersey City Gazette* on September 16, 1835, brought to New Jersey, in print, a description of the appalling nationwide conditions of early-nineteenth-century burial grounds. But the citizens living in the urban areas of New Jersey were already familiar with these problems and, as if to answer Mr. Derby's questions, were also looking to reform the way society handled the dead.

The seeds of New Jersey burial reform were first planted in 1829, when the body of an unidentified man washed up along the banks of Harsimus Cove in Jersey City. The body was pulled from the shoreline and dragged onto the grass. Soon afterward several local citizens gathered and, feeling compassion for the individual, they took it upon themselves to find him a burial plot. In addition, they wanted to mark the plot with a stone in case his relatives or friends came in search of the body (*Hudson Dispatch*, July 28, 1955).

To help pay the cost of the burial and stone, these kind-hearted citizens took up a collection for this unfortunate soul. As burial in early-nineteenth-century urban areas like Jersey City generally meant interment within a churchyard, they approached the nearby Bergen Church on the corner of Vroom Street and Tuers Avenue, to execute their good deed (*Hudson Dispatch*, July 28, 1955; Sarapin 1994, 55; *Hudson County Magazine*, Fall 1991). They were shocked, however, when the sexton told them it would cost $12 to dig the grave. Compared to other New Jersey cemeteries the cost was indeed high. In East Windsor, for instance, the estate of Asher Applegate paid just $3 on June 22, 1835, for the digging of his grave (Middlesex County unrecorded estate papers). In nearby Essex County the cost for digging a grave was between $1.50 and $7 in the years 1828 to 1830 (Essex County unrecorded estate papers, reel 2–43). For the concerned citizens of Jersey City, fulfillment of their noble intentions must have seemed out of reach.

More than likely, thoughts of matters other than cost were also going through the minds of these generous individuals. In the early nineteenth century they would also have been well aware of the deteriorating condition of church graveyards. The phenomenon was not just a New Jersey problem, but an issue that was sweeping the young republic and engaging burial reformers in England and the European continent, whose ancient churchyards had long since been filled to capacity. Many of the problems arose as urban populations exploded, placing a strain on the limited space within the church burial grounds. Considering that many of New Jersey's graveyards had their roots in the seventeenth and eighteenth centuries, it should be no surprise that by the early nineteenth century they were filled with a dizzying arrangement of headstones and footstones. Any earlier plans for expansion were quickly thwarted as the cities grew around the graveyards, boxing them in.

In an increasingly health-conscious society, overcrowded burial grounds equaled unsanitary burial grounds and often took the blame for outbreaks of disease. Cholera and yellow fever had a devastating impact on early-nineteenth-century communities and the deaths attributed to these outbreaks further strained the limited space in the graveyards (Sloane 1991, 37; Curl 2002, 135). In the urban areas of other states, forward-thinking citizens attempted to solve the problem of overcrowding by designing new burial grounds, as quasi-businesses managed by a board of trustees. An official act of state legislation was needed to form such cemetery companies.

The earliest of these endeavors in the United States was the New Haven Burying Ground, commonly known today as the Grove Street Cemetery in New Haven, Connecticut. It was incorporated by the state of Connecticut in 1797, when local citizens, led by U.S. Senator James Hillhouse, sought to remedy the problem of overcrowding in the ancient town burial ground located in the heart of New Haven (Sloane 1991, 30).

In Jersey City the matter of the burial of the unidentified drowned man was taken up at a public meeting at Hugh McCutcheon's Farmers Hotel at 42 York Street (*Hudson Dispatch*, July 28, 1955). "Destitute of a suitable and convenient place for the interment of their dead," the group decided to form a cemetery company "in order to provide a fit and proper burial place" (Justice 1831, 87–89). Citizens David C. Colden, Robert Gilchrist, Jonathan Jenkins, John K. Goodman, John Haight, John Gilbert, and Joseph Dodd became the first trustees of the Jersey City and Harsimus Cemetery on February 9, 1831.

JERSEY CITY AND HARSIMUS CEMETERY

The Jersey City and Harsimus Cemetery ushered in a new era of burial reform in New Jersey with the legal formation of a cemetery as a company—a cemetery company. The cemetery was not tied to a church but governed by a board of trustees who were elected by the lot holders to manage the cemetery according to its incorporation papers and bylaws. The concept of lot holders as decision makers was a unique feature of the new cemetery. Historically, society had long been concerned with the less than permanent nature of graveyards. Graves were often moved by church authorities with little say from the descendants (Sloane 1991, 31).

The citizens of Jersey City did not need to go far to find moved graves and misplaced tombstones. The *Jersey City Gazette* published accounts of violated graves and lost tombstones during the summer of 1835. On July 11 the paper carried an article about an "ancient relic" that was unearthed in Boston during the excavation of a cellar. The object was the tombstone of one-year-old Samuel Browne, who died September 9, 1690. The paper would further reinforce the notion of impermanence just two months later on September 16, when Mr. Derby's editorial "Violation on the Grave" was published. As a contrast to the way society handled the dead previously and in order to allay the fears of those purchasing plots, the cemetery companies gave lot holders the power to vote on a managing board that would make decisions in the best interest of the cemetery, thereby helping to ease the concerns about moved graves (Sloane 1991, 32).

In order to lend legitimacy to early cemetery companies, prominent citizens often made up the governing board of trustees (Sloane 1991, 69). Sitting on the board of the Jersey City and Harsimus Cemetery was David C. Colden. Born in Flushing, New York, in 1769, Colden was descended from a family of New York politicians. He was well-educated, having studied in Jamaica, New York, and London, England. After studying law he was admitted in 1791 to the New York Bar Association. He became a New York City district attorney in 1798 and later served in the state Senate and Assembly. In 1818 Colden was elected mayor of New York City. By the 1820s he had moved to Jersey City and became an important figure in the development of the Morris Canal, along with Robert Gilchrist, another trustee of the cemetery, who acted as cashier for the Morris Canal and Banking Company (*Jersey City Gazette*, May 8, 1835). Colden's prominence was typical of those involved in this new movement. He had the political clout, knowledge, and legal background to legitimize this new ideology and strengthened hopes of making it prosper.

In keeping with the ideology of many nineteenth-century cemetery reformers the new cemeteries were laid out in a systematic way. Author James Curl has examined the work of John Claudius Loudon, England's premier cemetery architect and critic, whose burial reform ideology had far-reaching consequences. According to Curl, Loudon felt that the "untidiness" of the church graveyard was due to the fact that they were not "laid out to a systematic plan" (Curl 2002, 258). The new cemeteries were situated away from the chaos of congested urban areas. The grounds were planned on a grid system with larger family lots being the norm rather than the single plots found within church graveyards.

In Jersey City, a similar systematic philosophy was implemented. In 1831 the Jersey City and Harsimus Cemetery consisted of three acres and was documented as having had a substantial stone wall, with the grounds laid out with plots and vaults (Justice 1831, 87). Today, although somewhat difficult to decipher, traces of its original design concept survive. The cemetery is accessed from Newark Boulevard by a gated entrance. From the gate, a single road dips down to traverse the lower portion of the cemetery. From this section the visitor has a view of the entire burial ground. The main paths are laid out with slate flagging. This must have been an exorbitant and draining cost and certainly a risky undertaking for a new burial ground since the investment placed it in debt, offering a design concept that had little practical use. Perhaps because of the practicality issues and with the view that financial resources would be better spent on other embellishments, flagging was not extensively utilized in other New Jersey cemeteries of this period, making this one unique.

The cemetery was built on the eastern declivity of Bergen's Hill. Near the base of the hill the ground gradually levels off, only to drop sharply at the eastern portion of the grounds. The cemetery must have been difficult and expensive to construct as design elements necessarily included walls and stone stairs to reach the upper portion, where a series of family vaults had been constructed.

In the period between 1831 and 1855 there were a number of interments in the Jersey City and Harsimus Cemetery. During that time both simple gravestones and monuments were erected. The earliest is a sandstone grave-marker for Andrew Gammel, "who departed this life June 22, 1830." A smattering of early monuments exist, including a mid-nineteenth-century square marble tablet marker with a draped urn. In addition two early obelisks can be found, including one for John C. Dows, who, while traveling on the clipper ship *Sea Serpent*, fell overboard and drowned in the 1850s.

Other stones give insight into the early patrons of the cemetery, a number of whom are of English descent. Mary Rood Drayton was born in 1790 in West Lambrook, Somersetshire, England. She died in North Bergen in 1847. Her husband, also from Somersetshire, would follow nine years later. The marker to commemorate their lives as well as their two children is a Gothic Revival brownstone monument from the mid-nineteenth century. The main tablet is set into a base and decorated with raised crockets along its edge, as well as a recessed surface outlined with Gothic tracery. A later granite monument for the Roberts family memorializes Joseph Roberts, a native of Liverpool, England.

With competition from the larger New York Bay Cemetery, which opened in 1850, the Jersey City and Harsimus Cemetery became a localized burial ground, interring members of a community whose demographics had changed. By 1880 Germans made up a larger percentage of the burials than previously. The thick, deeply carved brownstone tablet marker for Sophia Hanstein features a raised tablature for the epitaph and a deeply modeled winged hourglass on the tympanum. The marker is sunken, obscuring the date, but is typical of the German-produced brownstone memorials found in Jersey City and westward to Newark in the third and fourth quarters of the nineteenth century. Nearby an earlier German marker for Katharina Gunther is dated 1857. The brownstone tablet marker is carved in German with a heavily modeled urn on the tympanum. An 1883 monument commemorates Charles Finke in durable granite. The family chose to remember him not only by carving his name and date of death but proudly added "A native of Bremen."

By 1890 markers with epitaphs in Russian dotted the cemetery landscape. The burials continued into the 1910s with markers like the diminutive Turko family memorial from 1914 with a small iron Russian cross placed behind the stone. By the 1910s and 1920s Italian burials could also be found, giving the cemetery a multicultural mix with monuments in a number of different languages and styles. During this time additional property was purchased along the front of Newark Boulevard, expanding the grounds to its present five acres (*Jersey Journal*, May 23, 1912, 9; *Jersey Journal*, July 18, 1916, 5). The cemetery went into decline after World War II and was in a state of disrepair until a group of concerned plot owners gathered to resurrect the burial ground. They have since made substantial improvements and by 2005 the cemetery was filling to capacity with members of the city's Latin American community, a reflection of the ever-changing demographics of Jersey City.

TRENTON CEMETERY AND THE MERCER CEMETERY

During the 1830s and into the early 1840s other cemetery companies formed around the state. In New Jersey's capital, Trenton, early church graveyards had also grown, leaving little room to expand. A cholera epidemic had swept through the city around 1835 and must have strained the space even more. A large number of victims had to be taken from Trenton to a burial lot west of Sandtown, which was owned by Nottingham Township (West 1876, 15).

Just three years later, on February 24, 1838, the city's first enterprise of this type, the Trenton Cemetery Company, was incorporated (Adams 1838, 138). The cemetery was located on the western side of Princeton Avenue, north of Gordon Street (Podmore 1964, 118). Among the trustees was wealthy Trentonian Elisha Gordon, who helped develop the cemetery as well as the later Mercer Cemetery. The Trenton Cemetery was divided into four sections with a total of 572 burial plots. Some were sold, but the soil, having too much clay, proved difficult to dig. The cemetery was eventually abandoned, bringing an end to Trenton's first cemetery company (Trenton Historical Society 1929, 521).

With problems at the Trenton Cemetery and a continuing need for burial reform, the Mercer Cemetery Company at Trenton was incorporated within five years. The cemetery was situated on farmland fronting South Clinton Avenue and Barlow Street, on the fringes of urban Trenton. Following the reformist ideology, this new burial ground contained family-sized plots and vaults laid out on a grid system. Although the cemetery was incorporated in 1843, the first interment actually took place the year before (Walsh n.d., 4).

Visiting the cemetery today, one notes that the earliest stones are marble gravestones similar to those found in the churchyards of downtown Trenton. Some are void of iconography while others exhibit motifs common in the first decades of the nineteenth century. About half a dozen have weeping willow motifs, including the Deborah Temple marker from 1848, depicting a weeping willow draped over a monument. Most gravestones appear to be the work of Trenton marble carvers, with at least one weeping willow for Ann Prandt, who died in 1847, signed by tombstone carver Luther Ward, who had recently arrived in Trenton from New Brunswick (*Kirkbride's New Jersey Business Directory*, 1850). The other style popular during this time has the words "In Memory of" carved at the marker's top face in decorative script. Several markers display this motif, with some notable examples including the matching Eliza Howell and William R. Howell marble markers.

The Mercer Cemetery at Trenton contains a snapshot of Trenton's mid-nineteenth-century demographics and wealth; on display are a variety of high-style monuments as well as simple gravestones. In addition to the traditional markers, a new phenomenon took place at the Mercer Cemetery. Unlike church burial grounds with limited space, the Mercer Cemetery sold plots as family groupings with room to erect large, central family monuments. By the 1850s, the small gravestones in the cemetery were quickly overshadowed, and a number of impressive monuments began to dominate the landscape, turning the cemetery into a marble sculpture garden.

One of the earliest monuments is that of William Bradford, who died in the late 1840s. The Classical Revival monument has a marble cap that exhibits Greek motifs. Like many other markers found in southern New Jersey cemeteries, the complex and skillfully carved monuments were often produced in nearby Philadelphia. The memorial for Henry J. Weisman, who died at the Naval Academy in 1854, is in the form of a draped shaft supported by a square base, known as a die. Henry's name, inscribed on the shaft, is surrounded by a wreath and anchor. The base bears the name of the Philadelphia monument company Day & Wright. One of the unique Philadelphia monuments in Mercer Cemetery is that of Trenton iron industrialist William Borrow, who died in 1854 (fig. 4.1). The monument depicts Borrow's invention for rolling iron and was carved by J. Baird of Philadelphia, who has numerous other signed stones in the cemeteries of southern New Jersey.

By the late nineteenth century, with little room for expansion and with competition from nearby Riverview Cemetery, Mercer Cemetery saw its burials beginning to decrease. It was noted in 1964 that an occasional burial still took place (Podmore 1964, 118), but by the early 1990s the cemetery had

4.1 Trenton industrialist William Borrow developed a machine for rolling iron and arranged for its likeness to be carved onto his family monument when he died in 1854. The monument is located in the Mercer Cemetery in Trenton.

fallen into disrepair and the Friends of Mercer Cemetery formed. In 1992 the group was awarded a Green Acres grant and restoration work commenced: the site was cleaned up, paths were uncovered, new granite benches put in place, and interpretive plaques installed (Walsh n.d., 4).

The Jersey City and Harsimus Cemetery, the Trenton Cemetery Company, and the Mercer Cemetery at Trenton are among a handful of cemeteries that were formed in New Jersey during a time of burial reform. They represent the wishes of a society in search of a better way to combat overcrowded church burial grounds and to reform the way its dead were handled. This new breed of cemeteries bridges a gap between the eighteenth-century church graveyard and a new movement of cemetery design that would sweep the nation and flourish in New Jersey—the large, landscaped garden cemeteries of the rural cemetery movement.

The Rural Cemetery Movement: New Jersey's Garden Cemeteries

These tokens of respect to the memory and ashes of the venerated dead are in accordance with the best feelings of our nature, and it is to be hoped that this laudable example will be more generally followed in other places.
~ Description of the Orange Cemetery,
Barber and Howe, 1844 ~

By 1844 several cemetery companies had formed in New Jersey. Some, like the Mount Holly Cemetery Company, incorporated in 1841, followed the design concepts of their predecessors in Jersey City and Trenton. Others, like

4.2 The Orange Cemetery in South Orange was an early rural cemetery. Barber and Howe printed an illustration of the burial ground in 1844. After falling into neglect by the 1950s, the monuments were removed and the site was turned into a park (Barber and Howe 1844).

the Orange Cemetery Company, incorporated in the autumn of 1840, were laid out on rolling terrain with a gated entrance, landscaped grounds, walks, and a "variety of trees, shrubbery, and evergreens" (Barber and Howe 1844, 187). The new design impressed John Barber and Henry Howe, who published an image and description of the cemetery in *Historical Collections of the State of New Jersey* in 1844 (fig. 4.2).

The Orange Cemetery had many subscribers, among them the Reverend Asa Hillyer, a graduate of Yale and pastor of the Presbyterian Church in Orange. He died on August 28, 1840, and his was among the earliest burials in the cemetery (Barber and Howe 1844, 188). The interment of a prominent person such as Hillyer helped ensure the future success of the cemetery, and by 1926 the ten-acre site had an estimated 430 marked graves when the Orange Township Board of Health passed an ordinance prohibiting burials within the township limits. By the 1950s the cemetery was in decline and was turned into a park. All the memorials were removed and today the site is marked only with a tall, central granite monument inscribed with the names of those interred there (Edith Clack, personal communication).

Despite the eventual demise of the Orange Cemetery Company, nineteenth-century historians Barber and Howe were so impressed with the cemetery's landscape that they wished this "laudable example [would] be more generally followed in other places." Within four years their wish came true with the formation of one of New Jersey's most laudable examples— the Mount Pleasant Cemetery Company of Newark. This cemetery has the distinction of being New Jersey's first landscaped garden cemetery, a product of the rural cemetery movement that was sweeping across the nation by the mid-nineteenth century.

The rural cemetery movement was based on a revolutionary ideology in cemetery design. The roots of the movement can be traced back to Europe in the late eighteenth century as burial reform was under way in the Old World. In 1804 the Parisian cemetery Père-Lachaise was laid out after earlier graveyards in the city became too crowded. The severity of the crowding reached a crisis point when a portion of a wall holding back the thousand-year-old Cimetière des Innocents collapsed, sending hundreds of rotting corpses into the basement of an adjoining building (Sloane 1991, 28; Curl 2002, 154). It was against this backdrop of post-Revolutionary France that a new and more civilized way of handling the dead was born. Père-Lachaise was embellished with fine monuments and cemetery structures. Its rolling terrain and landscaped grounds were so favorably received by nineteenth-century society that it became the model for numerous other cemeteries across Europe and America.

The first rural garden cemetery in the United States was Mount Auburn in Cambridge, Massachusetts, which opened in 1831. It was followed quickly by Laurel Hill in Philadelphia, incorporated in 1836, and Brooklyn's Green-Wood Cemetery, incorporated in 1838 (Sloane 1991, 56, 93). Mount Pleasant in Newark was incorporated in 1844, and by 1851 about a dozen gardenlike cemeteries had opened in New Jersey.

"PASSAIC'S GREENWOOD REPOSE"— MOUNT PLEASANT CEMETERY, NEWARK

New Jersey's first landscaped garden cemetery, a product of the rural cemetery movement, was Mount Pleasant in Newark (fig. 4.3). Approximately nineteen acres of land for the cemetery was first acquired in 1843. Over the next several decades additional land would bring the total number of acres to thirty-six. The location for this new cemetery could have not had a more perfect setting. It was situated on undulating ground with its eastern border along the picturesque Passaic River. The western border was located along a road to Belleville, which one writer in 1843 regarded as "one of our most agreeable drives" (*Newark Daily Advertiser*, Dec. 16, 1843).

Horace Baldwin was the cemetery's initial promoter, pitching the idea of a rural cemetery to a group of civic-minded residents on December 7, 1843 (Senkevitch 1986, sec. 8). Baldwin was only twenty-eight years old and would become instrumental in developing and designing the cemetery. Just nine days after the initial meeting, the *Newark Daily Advertiser* published an article on the proposed cemetery. Clearly, the article stated, Newark was in need of a better place to deposit the dead.

The reporter took great pains to justify the importance of this proposed cemetery, describing what had been the common method of burial up to that time and explaining its inadequacies: "In this city of Newark, the inconven-

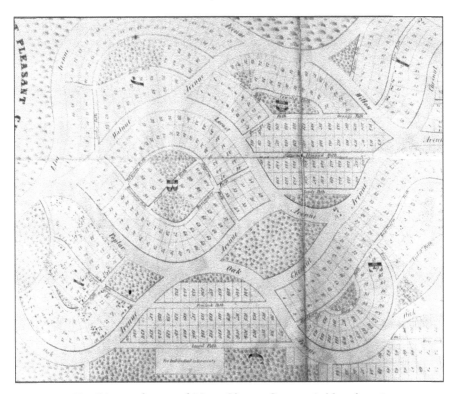

4.3 Detail image of a map of Mount Pleasant Cemetery in Newark, c. 1844.
This early map may have belonged to Horace Baldwin, one of the founders of the
burial ground. Common design elements of the rural cemetery movement, such as
the serpentine roads and secondary paths, are evident on the map.
(From the collections of The New Jersey Historical Society, Newark.)

iences of the present modes of burial are severely felt." The article further
proclaimed how a new cemetery to be established on the outskirts of the city
would solve their problems: "The proposed establishment seems to furnish
every facility for gratifying the desire which must rank among the purest and
strongest of the human heart" (*Newark Daily Advertiser*, Dec. 16, 1843). The
worries of these early promoters were quickly put to rest, for Mount Pleasant Cemetery would not be a hard sell to Newark's residents, who were more
than ready for a better place of interment for their dead.

By the 1840s Newark's population was swelling and many of the
ancient churchyards that had served the city for well over a century and a
half had been filled to capacity. Among them was the ancient graveyard of
the First Presbyterian Church, which by the mid-nineteenth century was a
disorderly eyesore, the old headstones having been placed in a great pile
(fig. 4.4) (*Harper's New Monthly Magazine*, October 1876, 670). Many of the
other urban graveyards in Newark were equally crowded and in an appalling
condition.

4.4 In 1876 *Harper's New Monthly Magazine* published this image of the First Presbyterian
Burial Ground in Newark. The cemetery dated from the late seventeenth century
and had been closed for almost seventy-five years when this illustration was completed.
The site was in a ruinous condition with most of the markers having been placed
in a large pile. The condition of Newark's church graveyards in the early nineteenth
century helped pave the way for the founding of Mount Pleasant Cemetery.
(Reproduced with permission from the Newark Public Library.)

The new cemetery that was being proposed would relieve the strain on
the older burial grounds and move the dead from the center of congested
urban Newark to its more pleasing and rural outskirts. The article published
in the *Newark Daily Advertiser* makes numerous references to better, more successful models followed in other parts of the world, including Père-Lachaise
in Paris. With other examples in nearby Boston, Brooklyn, and Philadelphia,
Newark's residents seemed ready for a rural cemetery of their own.

The person who oversaw many aspects of Mount Pleasant was Horace
Baldwin, who with his father, Isaac, operated a jewelry store in Newark. In
addition to the logistics involved with organizing a cemetery, he oversaw the
design concepts as well. Cemetery board minutes show that Baldwin was
involved in a number of design projects, including the grounds and gatehouse (Senkevitch 1986, sec. 8, 4). No records exist as to where Baldwin's
inspiration came from but he certainly had a clear understanding of the rural
cemetery and its design. He may have been inspired by a nearby model,
Brooklyn's Green-Wood Cemetery, but this is speculation based partly on

the fact that the first name proposed for Mount Pleasant was "Passaic's Greenwood Repose" (Senkevitch 1986, sec. 8).

As with many early garden cemeteries, a board of trustees was established to govern the enterprise. Many of those on the board were prominent civic-minded citizens. William Rankin, the first president of the board, was a well-known lawyer with many political connections. Rankin was also involved with the Presbyterian Church and was a representative of the Newark Presbytery to the General Assembly (Senkevitch 1986, sec. 8, 2). Rankin's experience with the Presbyterian Church would have made him an ideal person to understand the need for a new cemetery.

Algernon S. Hubbell was the secretary of the organization and also a well-known lawyer and politician, who served as a member of the New Jersey legislature during the 1847/48 session (Senkevitch 1986, sec. 8, 3). Hubbell's law office at 330 Broad Street was the location for the initial board meetings and from which residents could purchase plots (*Newark Daily Advertiser*, Dec. 16, 1843).

Along with Rankin, John P. Jackson was responsible for applying to the New Jersey state legislature for an official act of incorporation. Jackson, like Rankin and Hubbell, was a distinguished lawyer and politician. In addition, Jackson served as the editor of the *Newark Daily Advertiser*, which may explain the lengthy article about the cemetery that appeared just nine days after Baldwin met with the group.

Mount Pleasant would follow the design concepts of the other newly established rural cemeteries in the northeast; however, the architects involved with Mount Auburn, Green-Wood, and Laurel Hill would not have a hand in Mount Pleasant. The minutes of the board of trustees for Mount Pleasant show that Horace Baldwin was the head of the design committee and that Peter Soms had been hired to be the engineer (Senkevitch 1986, sec. 7, 1). It is possible that by 1844 the concept of the rural cemetery was fully entrenched in the psyche of this group of citizens. It appears that the design would come from within the talent of Newark, aided only by the knowledge of what existed at other rural cemeteries.

The cemetery was laid out in three-hundred-foot-square plots along a serpentine road system, with the primary roads named after trees and the secondary paths named after plants. The main entrance was accessed from Bellville Avenue where the ground gently rolled toward the Passaic River. Near the eastern border, along the river, the landscape dropped sharply, providing an area for terraces and vaults that could be built into the side of the hill.

On June 18, 1844, Mount Pleasant Cemetery was officially consecrated by the Reverend James Scott, D.D., of the Dutch Church (Senkevitch 1986, sec. 7, 8). Having a religious service was key to the acceptance of this new cemetery, especially in a society were church-associated graveyards had been the norm. Scott's presence helped to solidify the religious connection of this new mode of burial. In his address he stated that "the burial-place should therefore always be selected in consistency with this natural sympathy; in places lonely, but not deserted, where the beauty of nature is heightened by the care of man, and where the labor of life does not come in too close contrast to the stillness of the dead" (*Sentinel of Freedom*, June 25, 1844).

Reverend Scott's comments reflected much of the ideology of the new rural cemetery movement. Like its contemporaries, Mount Pleasant was situated away from the industrial life of the city and the ills associated with it; yet the location was not so rural as to be wild and untamed. At Mount Pleasant nature was subdued by the hand of man, engineering a perfect balance between the two forces and creating a place of great beauty and respite. People flocked to see the new cemetery, to meander through its grounds and for a moment to escape from urban life. The rural cemetery had come to New Jersey and became the "resting place for the living as well as the dead" (Sloane 1991, 64).

To commemorate the incorporation of the cemetery, in 1854, at a cost of about $1,500, the cemetery association erected a monument to the founders (Senkevitch 1986, sec. 7, 7). This action was not common; only a handful of other examples can be found, including one in the Washington Monumental Cemetery in South River and another in Willow Grove Cemetery in New Brunswick. At Mount Pleasant an impressive three-sided brownstone monument in Gothic Revival style with pointed arches, crockets, and pinnacles was erected near the front entrance. The monument commemorates Horace Baldwin, William Rankin, Isaac Baldwin, and Algernon S. Hubbell, and lists the date of the cemetery company's formation and the date the grounds were consecrated by Reverend Scott. Although the cemetery records do not identify who was hired to create it, the monument is signed on the base by "Struthers." Struthers and Son was a well-known Philadelphia monument company founded by marble carver John Struthers, whose son took over after his father's death in 1851.

Mount Pleasant Cemetery gained acceptance and great admiration from the citizens of Newark. Families purchased plots in increasing numbers, with some disinterring the remains of relatives in the crowded churchyards and moving them to Mount Pleasant. Today one can find older gravestones in the cemetery dating from the seventeenth and eighteenth centuries.

In 1866 a proposed rail line along the cemetery's eastern border following the Passaic River caused much outcry among those who had loved ones buried there. An editorial entitled "Our Cemetery" and published in the *Newark Daily Advertiser* stated that the cemetery would be "brought within a very few feet of the din and clatter of a Railroad with its bells and whistles and clangor, almost enough to awaken the dead, totally destroying the quiet and solemnity of this holy place" (January 30, 1866). Protracted court battles kept the railroad out until the early part of the twentieth century,

4.5 Large family plots became the standard lot size in nineteenth-century rural cemeteries. The larger lots permitted the erection of family monuments.
The photograph shows an ornate monument from the mid-nineteenth century in Mount Pleasant Cemetery, Newark.

assuring that the peace and quiet remained at least throughout the nineteenth century.

Mount Pleasant Cemetery was well patronized by the citizens of Newark, as evidenced by the number of high-style monuments and markers that grace its grounds. Visitors in the mid-nineteenth century must have been awed by the sea of polished, gleaming white, classically inspired memorials. The cemetery landscape was filled with a wonderful array of skillfully carved monuments and markers. Gravestones with weeping willows, allegorical figures, angels, and urns pushed the limits of two-dimensional carving. The marble gravestone for Mary Ann Adams from 1846 exemplifies such skill, its top front surface carved with a rose, an urn, and a funeral pall. The marker also includes a carving of a miniature gravestone that reads, "Our First Born."

It was the three-dimensional monuments that separate Mount Pleasant from anything the citizens of Newark had seen before (fig. 4.5). Artistically produced monuments of pedestaled columns, concave dies, draped urns, obelisks, and statuary transformed the cemetery into an outdoor sculpture garden. The monuments were further embellished with heavy garland and architectural elements, making them stunning and elaborate memorials. The list of high-style monuments that can be found in the cemetery is endless, including those bearing renowned Newark family names, such as Janes, Waters, Goble, Ward, and Robertson.

Newark's marble carvers are well represented in Mount Pleasant Cemetery, where signed markers and monuments by Czar Duncomb, the Wilcox family, George Brown, and the shop of Passmore and Meeker can be examined. The latter team executed some stunning examples, including the marble monument for the Morrison family, which dates from 1861 and is carved in a Baroque Revival style with concave die and floral moldings. The towering shaft is topped with a cross that has a pair of books leaning against it. In addition to local talent, the work of out-of-state carvers can be found in Mount Pleasant (Senkevitch 1986, sec. 7, 16). The Baldwin plot located in the southeastern section of the cemetery contains three marble canopy graves, one broken column, and two draped urns on dies by the Philadelphia monument firm of Struthers.

It is also possible that well-known sculptors from New York had their hands in the monuments at Mount Pleasant. A number of stones bear resemblance to markers produced by sculptors Robert Launitz and John Frazee. Frazee initially produced gravestones in central New Jersey; after working in Rahway and New Brunswick he later moved to New York City and formed a partnership with Launitz. A monument in Mount Pleasant Cemetery simply inscribed "Our Mother" features the soul of a robed female figure taking flight toward heaven, a motif employed by Launitz (Dimmick 1992, 170). The marker is topped with an urn and garland and is similar to an 1866 example published in *Collection of Monuments and Headstones, Designed by R. E. Launitz, New York* (see Dimmick 1992, 169, 172).

Competing for recognition among the marble monuments are a number of carved brownstone memorials. On the diminutive side but no less decorated is the monument for George Ross. The thick brownstone tablet marker has a heavily draped funeral pall and two deeply modeled books entitled *Time*, vol. I, and *Eternity*, vol. II. Other brownstone monuments bear signatures from Newark carvers J. Stevens and the shop of Wheaton and Brown.

By the 1870s Mount Pleasant Cemetery had become the fashionable cemetery for Newark. A visitor to the grounds in 1871 remarked, "No piece of ground was ever better adapted to a required purpose than that occupied by Mount Pleasant Cemetery" (Senkevitch 1986, sec. 8, 6). Throughout the nineteenth century impressive marble monuments were followed by large vaults and then granite monuments and mausoleums. In the early decades of the twentieth century Mount Pleasant continued to be an important burial ground for Newark's citizens, with a number of large monuments and mausoleums erected during this period. But by midcentury Mount Pleasant's heyday was coming to an end. Much of the cemetery had been filled and new, larger cemeteries had opened and were gaining popularity.

Since its formation in 1844 the city of Newark has grown and engulfed this once rural location. But visitors can still escape from the modern world by entering through the impressive gates of Mount Pleasant and wandering through its grounds. Although some of its marble markers have suffered the indignity of erosion, Mount Pleasant Cemetery is still awe-inspiring and continues to be New Jersey's finest example of the rural cemetery movement.

RIVERVIEW CEMETERY, TRENTON

Following the formation of Mount Pleasant, rural cemeteries began to appear in other urban areas of New Jersey as well. With the Mercer Cemetery in Trenton filling up, Riverview Cemetery was incorporated in 1858. The earliest section was a Quaker burial ground that was reputed to date from the late seventeenth century (Trenton Historical Society 1929, 519). Although this section of the cemetery still exists—its simple markers a contrast to the surrounding monuments—the earliest dated stones do not predate the mid-nineteenth century. There are, however, eighteenth-century markers in other sections of Riverview, which were most likely removed from older churchyards in Trenton.

Riverview Cemetery followed the design ideology of many rural cemeteries. Its roads were laid out in a serpentine manner, though not as curvilinear as its predecessors.' The cemetery's western boundary overlooked the Delaware River. It was in this scenic location that Trenton's wealthy elite opted to purchase family plots and adorn them with elaborate monuments. Trenton's middle class occupied the middle section of the cemetery, with some of the secondary paths there laid out with brick paving. The landscape at the opposite end of the cemetery, its southeastern boundary, dipped down and then leveled out. This section was reserved for families with fewer financial resources, many of whom were newly arrived immigrants. It was in this location that the cemetery association decided to construct a receiving vault in 1859. The vault was built into the side of a hill with the facade constructed of brownstone. Two other family vaults were constructed nearby, utilizing the steep decline in the landscape. Dating from the third quarter of the nineteenth century, the vaults are a contrast to the later aboveground mausoleums for the Lee and Bowman families near the cemetery's entrance.

The monuments and markers in Riverview Cemetery range from pattern book quality to truly one-of-a-kind examples. High-style monuments with draped urns, angels, and statuary were erected in marble and later in granite. Among the more notable are those for the Stokes family and the granite monument for the Buchanan family. The latter features a life-size angel carved from a large granite slab that serves as its backdrop. The angel points upward, as a kneeling woman, head bowed down, clings to the angel's robe.

4.6 The Truman S. Betts marker in Riverview Cemetery in Trenton dates from 1872. It makes a striking allusion to Edgar Allan Poe's "The Raven." The marble tablet marker is set on a base and was carved to mimic a door with the word *Lenore* across its surface. A marble raven, now missing, was perched above the door.

The monument was carved by T. Delahunty of Philadelphia, who also had a hand in many of the other granite monuments in Riverview.

The marker for Trenton cable industrialist John Roebling, whose firm supplied the cables for the Brooklyn Bridge, is an early granite example made by Batterson Canfield and Company of Hartford, Connecticut, after Roebling's death in 1869. Meant to mimic a sarcophagus, the monument features a bronze plaque of Roebling's bust. Smaller individual footstones are placed directly in front of the family monument.

Perhaps Riverview's most notable burial and monument is the massive granite memorial for George Brinton McClellan, commander of the Army of the Potomac during the Civil War and governor of New Jersey from 1878 to 1881. McClellan died in 1885 and his marker was erected "as a tribute of respect and admiration by personal friends." The monument features a stepped base with a die and capstone. A towering column rises from the monument and terminates with an eagle perched on a sphere. The memorial's height and scale is impressive and it can be viewed from many locations within the cemetery, clearly conveying the "respect and admiration" felt by his friends.

Close to McClellan's monument is one of the state's most unique stones. The tablet marker for Truman S. Betts, M.D., who died in 1872, makes a striking allusion to Edgar Allan Poe's "The Raven" (fig. 4.6). The marble tablet marker is set on a base and was carved to mimic a door with the word *Lenore* across its surface. A marble raven, now missing, was perched above the door.

Trenton's carvers also contributed heavily to Riverview's landscape, where monuments from leading firms such as J. Payran and J. H. Conroy can be found. Conroy carved several impressive monuments, including one for the Speeler family that is topped with a draped urn and rests on a blue-stone marble base cut to look like stone blocks. Conroy also carved a marble tablet marker set on a base for twenty-three-year-old Caroline Sandt. Dated 1866, it is carved with two pilasters that frame a heaven-bound angel.

The markers at Riverview Cemetery illustrate a wide cross-section of Trenton society, from those who toiled in local industry to those who owned the factories. Today the cemetery still affords a wonderful view of the Delaware River and continues to be an active place of interment.

EVERGREEN CEMETERY, CAMDEN

By the mid-nineteenth century almost every large urban area of New Jersey had a rural cemetery. In Camden, the first rural cemetery was Evergreen. Incorporated in 1848, the cemetery quickly became the fashionable place for interment. The eighty-five-acre cemetery was laid out along Ephraim Avenue on the outskirts of the city. Its architects dispensed with the serpentine road system common to other rural cemeteries and opted for a more linear design.

As in many rural cemeteries, Camden's wealthy were buried near the front entrance on what was the highest ground. Numerous high-style marble monuments with statuary, draped urns, floral wreaths, and garlands were erected by notable citizens, including the Sawyers, Richter, and Carpenter families. Many of the mid-nineteenth-century marble monuments were carved by well-known Philadelphia firms and are signed on the base. In addition to the large monuments, at least one vault with a marble facade was built in the cemetery for the Hansell family.

The Evergreen Cemetery board authorized the construction of a Gothic Revival superintendent's home and office at the entrance along Ephraim Avenue. The cemetery's masterpiece, however, would be a stunning chapel with Moorish influences. A turn-of-the-century photograph shows the box-like structure built on raised ground at the crossing of two cemetery roads (fig. 4.7). Lining the roads leading up to the chapel are numerous family lots surrounded by marble enclosures and cast iron fencing.

Unfortunately, Evergreen Cemetery went into decline and eventually went bankrupt. With no one to maintain the site it quickly became over-grown and vandalized. Its impressive chapel has long since been demolished and recently its abandoned superintendent's home was also taken down.

4.7 Evergreen Cemetery was Camden's grand nineteenth-century garden cemetery.
This photograph, taken around 1900, shows a Moorish-influenced chapel
that was located near the front entrance.
(Reproduced with permission from the Camden County Historical Society.)

Today the cemetery is uncared for and it is difficult to access the important
monuments that can only be seen poking through the overgrown brush.

WILLOW GROVE CEMETERY, NEW BRUNSWICK, AND CHESTNUT HILL CEMETERY, EAST BRUNSWICK

By 1870 approximately seventy cemetery companies had been incorporated in
New Jersey, most designing their grounds in the garden cemetery style.
Some, like Willow Grove Cemetery in New Brunswick, had been founded
almost twenty years earlier and were experiencing great popularity. Willow
Grove became the leading burial ground for mid-nineteenth-century New
Brunswick, with many of the city's elite resting under elaborate monuments.
In addition to the movers and shakers of the time, Willow Grove, like many
garden cemeteries, encompassed members of all social classes and ethnic
backgrounds, including several Japanese students who died while attending
Rutgers University in the 1870s (Sarapin 1994, 17).

   In contrast to the rural cemeteries in urban areas, in the rural, agricultural community of East Brunswick Township, the Chestnut Hill Cemetery
Association was incorporated in February 1863 by leading citizens who lived
in the Old Bridge section of town. The cemetery was laid out on Chestnut
Hill, offering a breathtaking panoramic view of the small communities it
served. Some large-scale monuments were erected, but most markers were
modest in size, reflecting the meager financial means of the working-class
community. Although relatively small, Chestnut Hill Cemetery, like larger

4.8 This scene at Chestnut Hill Cemetery in East Brunswick shows a
Memorial Day celebration in the early 1930s. The boy in the foreground is standing
in a lot reserved for veterans; he is reciting the Gettysburg Address.
(Reproduced with permission from the East Brunswick Museum.)

garden cemeteries, was a gathering place for the living as well as the dead.
Historically, on Memorial Day the community came together at the veterans'
plot to hear a local student recite the Gettysburg Address (Nonestied 1999,
29). Photographs from the period show large crowds amassed in the cemetery for this mingling of life and death (fig. 4.8).

Chestnut Hill was just one of many rural cemeteries that epitomized
the movement as a "change in custom and culture" moved the rural cemetery of the urban areas to the rural areas as well (Sloane 1991, 66). The
movement was now spreading broadly; after the Civil War small towns
across New Jersey were creating their own rural cemeteries to embrace.
Today many nineteenth-century rural cemeteries still survive and function
as an integral part of their communities, serving as the resting place of their
ancestors as well as the newly departed.

The Lawn Park Cemetery

*The landscaping of "Harleigh" has received the most thoughtful attention,
whether through woods or beside placid water.*

~ Harleigh Memorial, 1928 ~

The garden-style cemeteries of the rural cemetery movement were the precursors to parks in the country and would spawn a generation of landscape
architects. In its formative stage the rural cemetery movement became the

answer to society's concerns over the treatment of the dead. Just after the Civil War, however, garden cemeteries were filling with burials, displaying a haphazard collection of monuments and encroached upon by the very urban areas from which they sought to escape. Cemetery and landscape architects looked for better ways to design cemeteries in order to meet new needs in terms of both taste and maintenance. The result was the lawn park cemetery.

The lawn park design was developed at Spring Grove Cemetery in Cincinnati, Ohio, when landscape architect Adolph Strauch was placed in charge of expanding the cemetery (Sloane 1991, 100). The new design would give the cemetery a more pastoral aspect, reflecting the design of parks, which were gaining popularity in the mid-nineteenth century and beginning to replace the garden cemetery as a popular place of respite for the living.

Strauch's new plan would create open spaces by dispersing trees and plantings and limiting the size and styles of the markers (Sloane 1991, 97). The narrow serpentine paths found in garden cemeteries would be replaced by wider, slightly curved roadways. Strauch's landscape design also incorporated a series of lakes, which, combined with the open lawn features, provided an unobstructed pastoral view.

To complement the landscape designs, restrictions were placed on the monuments. It was apparent by the mid-nineteenth century that the cluttered garden cemeteries were losing the rural garden atmosphere to which they had initially aspired. Monuments were not only confusing the landscape but the artistic feeling was being lost due to the increasing use of generic pattern book–style memorials (Sloane 1991, 104). Promoters of the lawn park cemetery looked for ways to tastefully join monuments with the landscape features.

Strauch's plan went much deeper than the landscape designs. In order to run an efficient and orderly cemetery, he needed to take maintenance responsibilities away from the lot holders. With garden cemeteries, it was the lot holders who were responsible for plantings and maintenance; therefore, what developed was a chaotic style with both well-maintained and ill-cared-for cemetery plots. In order to achieve a "landscape of unity and beauty," restrictions had to be placed on the owners of cemetery lots (Sloane 1991, 104). Instead of many family hands at work, the cemetery's landscape crew would now be responsible for its maintenance, and a new position would be created to oversee the work. In 1859 the board of directors for Spring Grove Cemetery gave Strauch the position of superintendent of the grounds and landscape gardener (106). With that decision the responsibility for daily operations of the burial ground moved from loosely managed lot holders to a regulated business overseen by a professional cemetery superintendent. In 1887 the American Association of Cemetery Superintendents was formed to

4.9 Aerial photograph of Harleigh Cemetery in Camden, circa 1930. The design concepts of this early lawn park cemetery are apparent in the photograph. The road system has gradual curves that meander through the landscape. The smaller secondary paths found in the rural cemeteries have been dispensed with and the landscape has a more open pastoral setting. Compare this figure to figure 4.3.
(Reproduced with permission from Harleigh Cemetery.)

promote better design and management of cemeteries (110). The new organization would help to professionalize the cemetery.

HARLEIGH CEMETERY, CAMDEN

In New Jersey the lawn park cemetery design would gain favor in the decades following the Civil War. Some cemeteries adopted certain concepts of the lawn park cemetery while dispensing with others. One of the early lawn park cemeteries that closely followed Strauch's design concepts is Harleigh Cemetery in Camden. Incorporated in 1885, the cemetery was laid out in the southeast section of the city and would grow to encompass approximately 150 acres (National Register Nomination, sec. 7, 1). A wide, curved road system was established that meandered throughout the grounds and around artificial lakes. The landscape opened onto pastoral lawns and thoughtful plantings. Compare figure 4.3 to figure 4.9.

In order to minimize clutter, the cemetery board in 1886 prohibited family lot enclosures. In a move that prevented an overabundance of stock pattern book monuments, a problem despised by promoters of the lawn park

4.10 This historic photograph taken around 1928 shows the landscape techniques
of the lawn park cemetery at Harleigh in Camden. Single-family monuments
were encouraged, allowing for an uncluttered pastoral landscape.
(Reproduced with permission from Harleigh Cemetery.)

cemetery, the board also barred duplicate monuments (National Register
Nomination, sec. 8, 1, sec. 7, 1; see also Sloane 1991, 122).

George E. Rhedemeyer was the landscape architect of Harleigh Cemetery and was responsible for expanding the cemetery to its present size
(National Register Nomination, sec. 8, 1). Interestingly, Rhedemeyer had
previously been responsible for laying out the grounds for pubic institutions
in Ohio and at one time was in charge of the grounds at the State Insane
Asylum in Athens, Ohio, just 140 miles east of Strauch's lawn park cemetery
model in Cincinnati. Rhedemeyer was well known in Ohio and was once
praised by Governor Joseph B. Foraker and then Congressman William
McKinley for his landscape work in that state. His obituary published in the
Camden Daily Mirror on October 10, 1917, mentioned that he was "one of the
best known landscape experts in the country," whose advice was sought after
for "planning cemeteries like Harleigh." It would seem likely that, with connections in Ohio, Rhedemeyer would have been familiar with Strauch's work
(National Register Nomination, sec. 7, 1) (fig. 4.10).

Despite the restrictions placed on lot holders, Harleigh Cemetery
quickly grew in popularity throughout the 1890s. Among the notable individuals laid to rest at Harleigh was Walt Whitman in 1892. Whitman had
been given a free plot by the cemetery board, a move that followed a practice

by promoters of the rural cemetery movement to help garner recognition for the cemetery. Whitman apparently chose the spot for his vault and designed the tomb himself (National Register Nomination, sec. 8, 2).

GREENWOOD CEMETERY, TRENTON

While Harleigh Cemetery closely followed the Strauchian design philosophy of the lawn park cemetery movement, others, like the Greenwood Cemetery Association, incorporated on March 12, 1874, did not follow the concept so rigidly. Incorporated by a number of leading Trenton citizens, including W. W. Ward, who served as the first president, and Charles Bechtel as vice president, it was originally formed as a stock company with seven stock-holders, including, among others, Adam Exton, Daniel R. Bower, and Joseph B. Yard. The organization purchased 120 acres of land that originally belonged to the Anderson farm on the outskirts of Trenton (Greenwood Cemetery Association 1964, 2).

Greenwood Cemetery was a nonsectarian burial ground that encouraged both fraternal and religious organizations to buy lots. The articles of incorporation supported this policy by stating that "any association of persons for burial purposes and also any religious society may purchase and hold lots in said cemetery adjacent to each other in which they may bury, agreeable to any rites and ceremonies of their own, subject only to the rules and regulations adopted by the board of directors of said cemetery association" (Trenton Historical Society 1929, 520). Promoting Greenwood Cemetery as a burial place for all citizens and allowing a greater number of residents from Trenton's varied demographics to utilize it would help to secure its prosperity.

Greenwood Cemetery certainly became a community burial ground with a varied socioeconomic cross-section, which consisted of religious groupings—including several Jewish sections—and other groupings as well, including a veterans' plot dedicated in 1900, which today contains veterans from almost every major U.S. conflict, with the exception of the Revolutionary War (Greenwood Cemetery Association 1964, 3).

The cemetery does, however, have a Revolutionary War connection, which increased its marketability during a period of renewed interest in colonial and Revolutionary War history. On January 3, 1777, General George Washington and his troops marched during the night from Trenton to Princeton on Sandtown Road. Later, when the cemetery was formed, part of the original road transected the property. This historical march was officially recognized on the cemetery grounds in 1914 when the New Jersey Society of Sons of the Revolution erected a granite obelisk and bronze plaque.

Greenwood Cemetery incorporated a series of main roads but dispensed with the clutter of secondary paths. One large central boulevard connected the east and west entrances. The boulevard was a wide, spacious tree-lined thoroughfare that was divided by a center median with more trees. This promenade divided the cemetery into two distinct sections and allowed the road system to branch off from it. Trenton's wealthy citizens purchased plots along the central roadway and in the section to the south, which contained curvilinear roads, while middle-class citizens predominated in the northern section of the cemetery, with its more linear road system.

While promoters of the lawn park cemetery encouraged family monuments and frowned upon the busyness of many individual markers, those in charge at Greenwood did not completely abide by this philosophy. Although many individual markers were erected in addition to family monuments, the cemetery maintained its pastoral, open, parklike setting by prohibiting lot enclosures and limiting an overabundance of plantings. Cedar, pine, and holly trees were preferred, as they were more in keeping with "the original appearance of the region," as opposed to exotic foreign specimens (Greenwood Cemetery Association 1964:2).

The monument styles in the cemetery run the gamut. Adolph Strauch disliked the stock designs and promoted classically inspired memorials (Sloane 1991, 104). Greenwood Cemetery's opening coincided with the popularity of granite and a number of fine granite monuments were erected. While most in Greenwood are pattern book quality, several patrons broke the mold and erected unique memorials. Both the Coxson and Exton family monuments are located along the main thoroughfare and feature granite busts of the male lot owners. The Exton monument, carved by J. M. Gessler of West Philadelphia in Pennsylvania, is the earlier of the two and memorializes one of the cemetery's original stockholders, Adam Exton, who died in 1887.

At Greenwood Cemetery the superintendent enforced the regulations that ensured the proper maintenance of the grounds and deterred the mish-mash appearance of the rural cemeteries where individual lot holders maintained their plots without much oversight. In addition to the superintendent, the staff consisted of office workers, presumably marketing the cemetery and recording burials. The administration building was the old Anderson farmhouse and in 1927 more office space was added. Today Greenwood Cemetery is managed by CMS Mid-Atlantic, a cemetery management firm that continues to plan for future growth and carries on the maintenance of the grounds.

Throughout New Jersey, the landscape and management ideology of the lawn park cemetery was being mimicked. In 1893 the *Newark, N.J., Illustrated* (Leary) printed a photograph of the Clawson family plot and monument in Newark's Fairmount Cemetery, set on an open space of green grass with no

4.11 This photograph taken in 1893 shows the Clawson family plot at Fairmount Cemetery
in Newark. The plot stands in contrast to its predecessors in the rural cemeteries,
which were surrounded with cast iron fencing, hedges, or stone enclosures
(*Newark New Jersey Illustrated*, 1893.).
(Reproduced with permission from the Newark Public Library.)

enclosure. The image, titled "View in Fairmount Cemetery," shows an unmarred pastoral scene stretching out behind the marker (fig. 4.11).

The lawn park style caught on and by the late nineteenth century, older rural cemeteries began to rethink operations and adopted some of the new design and management philosophies associated with the lawn park cemeteries. In 1898 Mount Pleasant Cemetery, the quintessential New Jersey rural cemetery, announced in the local newspaper the *Newark Sunday Call* that the cemetery had new management and changes were being made in the appearance of the burial ground. Rusted iron fences from the mid-nineteenth century as well as hedgerows were being removed. Two years later the cemetery board barred family lot enclosures (Senkevitch 1986, sec. 7, 9; *Newark Sunday Call*, April 17, 1898). The popularity of the lawn park cemetery would continue into the early twentieth century, only to be superseded by yet another design movement—the memorial park.

The grounds of garden and lawn park cemeteries were embellished with structures that not only housed support services but also were intended to entice the public to buy into the new concept. It was hoped that these elegant buildings would make the cemetery more attractive to the public, who consequently would invest in lots. The more lots that were purchased, the better the financial future of the cemetery. This next section will focus on cemetery gates, receiving vaults, chapels, and other structures that would dot the cemetery landscape from the mid-nineteenth to the early twentieth century.

Cemetery Gates, Receiving Vaults, and Other Structures

All the buildings and improvements, which will surpass those of any Cemetery in the Country, will be put up by the Proprietors without tax or charge to the lot holders.

~ *Advertisement for the New York Bay Cemetery Company, 1870 Jersey City directory* ~

GATEWAYS INTO THE CEMETERY

The nineteenth century would see a flourishing of highly decorative gateways into the cemetery. Near the entrances structures were built that served as living quarters for the superintendent, office space, chapels, or reception areas for visitors. In the larger cemeteries an impressive complex of buildings, designed in the architectural style of the period, greeted visitors. Besides support services for the cemeteries, the entrances and their associated buildings served as a boundary between the land of the living and that of the dead.

The earliest rural cemeteries constructed entrances in the classical style. A view of the Orange Cemetery published by Barber and Howe in 1844 shows the cemetery's front boundary delineated by a wooden picket fence (187). The main entrance for horse-drawn vehicles consists of two columns supporting an entablature. To the left of the main gate is a smaller, gated pedestrian entrance. The illustration also shows a small structure in the Greek Revival style, perhaps an office or chapel, located on the left corner of the property (see fig. 4.2).

Mount Pleasant Cemetery also built a classically inspired gatehouse during its formative years. In 1844 a committee was formed by Horace Baldwin, Tunis A. Waldron, and Silas H. Kichiel to prepare plans and review costs for the entrance. Builder Ralph Van Houten was contracted to construct the entrance, which he completed in 1846 (Senkevitch 1986, sec. 7, 3). The entrance gate was a wooden structure in the Greek Revival style (fig. 4.12). It consisted of two small two-story buildings, apparently one room in width, whose facade was framed by pilasters. A projecting cornice connecting the two structures continued over the entrance, forming an entablature that was supported by two Ionic columns. The building to the south was utilized as the cemetery office, while the structure to the north was the superintendent's cottage (Senkevitch 1986, sec. 7, 3).

The basic layout of the entrance gate was similar to that of other rural cemetery gates. If the designers were Baldwin and his committee, they did

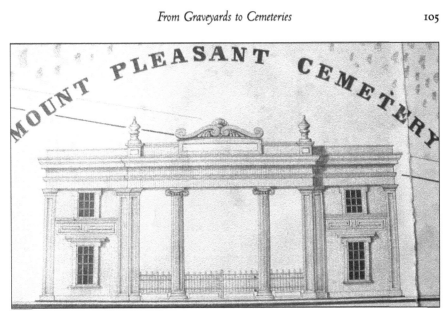

4.12 This illustration appears on an early map of Mount Pleasant Cemetery in Newark and is presumably its first gatehouse. Built in the Greek Revival style, the structure housed an office and superintendent's cottage. The building was replaced with a larger entrance in 1877. (From the collections of The New Jersey Historical Society, Newark.)

have a nearby model at Laurel Hill Cemetery in Philadelphia on which to base their variation. In addition, Kensal Green in London and Low Hill General Cemetery in Liverpool also had classical-style gates similar in form to that of Mount Pleasant (see Curl 2002, 208, 219). Perhaps Mount Pleasant's founders had discovered these examples through widely published period engravings.

The original entrance gate served the cemetery until it was removed in the 1870s; a larger Gothic Revival replacement constructed of brownstone stands today (fig. 4.13). Designed by Thomas Stent, the new structure is similar in style to the brownstone Gothic Revival entrance gate at Green-Wood Cemetery (Senkevitch 1986, sec. 7, 5). It consists of two portals in the form of Gothic arches for the carriage entrance, flanked by two smaller portals through which pedestrians may pass. Rising from the center of the gate is a bell tower that terminates in a cross. On the north side is the superintendent's home and on the south side an office and reception room.

As society began to favor the Gothic Revival style in the mid-nineteenth century, cemeteries built large, ornate Gothic Revival gatehouses. Among the more elaborate was that of the New York Bay Cemetery Company (fig. 4.14). The two-story wooden building featured dormers, spires, and High Gothic wooden detailing. Carriages entered through an arched opening flanked by two wings—presumably an office and a chapel. The 1870 Jersey City directory printed an advertisement for the cemetery which claimed that

4.13 This large brownstone entrance, designed by Thomas Stent, was built in 1877.
Loosely modeled after the entrance at Green-Wood Cemetery in Brooklyn,
it reflects the elaborate Gothic Revival gates that were being constructed
during the third quarter of the nineteenth century.

purchasers of burial lots would be provided with a "lithographic view of the chapel, buildings for superintendents, observatory, [and] gate-way."

In 1867 Cedar Lawn Cemetery in Paterson constructed a rustic Gothic Revival bell tower and on the opposite side a gatehouse in the same style. The two-story structures were covered with red cedar bark. A walkway constructed in a "twig style" connected the two buildings and provided a passageway for carriages to travel beneath (Lanza 1997, 8). By 1872 the cedar bark was stripped off and the buildings were clad in wooden clapboard. The bell tower and reception building were torn down in 1918, when the present granite office building and chapel were constructed. The superintendent's lodge was demolished in 1940 (9).

4.14 A large entrance made a powerful statement about the cemetery. The New York Bay Cemetery constructed this impressive example sometime after the Civil War.
The wooden Gothic Revival building housed an office and chapel. Sadly, it was lost to fire in the early 1970s. (Reproduced with permission from the Jersey City Free Public Library.)

As tastes changed by the late nineteenth century, cemetery structures followed. In the 1880s Queen Anne architecture became favored and Harleigh Cemetery in Camden constructed a cemetery lodge in that style in 1886. In 1902 a gated granite entrance designed by Camden architect Thomas Stephen was built near the lodge (National Register Nomination, sec. 8).

RECEIVING VAULTS AND CHAPELS

Receiving vaults or receiving tombs, as they were also commonly known, were structures designed to temporarily store coffins and were a standard feature of the nineteenth-century cemetery. They were often utilized during the cold winter months when the ground was frozen and it was impossible to dig graves by hand. The vaults, which ranged from simple subterranean structures to ornate, aboveground freestanding buildings, were commonplace in the nineteenth- and early-twentieth-century cemetery. Like gatehouses, several high-style receiving vaults were paired with chapels, creating a convenient segue to a funeral service.

The receiving vault became a standard structure within the nineteenth-century garden cemetery, its expense borne by the cemetery association, which outlined its use in rules and regulations. Some associations, like that of Elmwood Cemetery in North Brunswick, provided use of the vault free of charge so long as the deceased was a lot holder (Kearney Kuhlthau 2005, personal communication). Others, like the New York Bay Cemetery Company, in Jersey City, charged its customers ten dollars for adults and eight dollars for children under ten for a three-month time period (*Rules and Regulations of the New York Bay Cemetery*, 1889).

Receiving vaults were often built away from the prominence of the front gates but rather nestled within the cemetery. The earliest examples were simple subterranean structures built into the side of a hill. If the cemetery landscape was on level earth, the vault was often sunken and the ground mounded over the top. The entrance was decorated in the latest architectural style using brick, sandstone, or granite. Some consisted of simple, restrained features, like the granite facade of the receiving vault at the Jersey City and Harsimus Cemetery. In contrast, the Cedar Lawn Cemetery Company in Paterson built a Gothic Revival brownstone facade for their receiving vault in 1867. The structure, since remodeled, mimicked the receiving vault at Brooklyn's Green Wood Cemetery (Lanza 1997, 18).

In 1857 Evergreen Cemetery in Morristown built its receiving vault from brownstone to include hints of Egyptian Revival designs. As with many other New Jersey examples, carved into the stone above the door are the words "Receiving Vault" and the date of construction. The wording helped to delineate it as a cemetery structure not to be confused with family vaults within the nineteenth-century cemetery.

4.15 The receiving vault at Washington Monumental Cemetery in South River was built in 1906.
It is a simple barrel-vaulted structure with the facade decorated in the latest style
of the period. The interior of the vault is lined with white enameled brick.

Inside, beyond the heavy iron door of the receiving vault, coffins were placed on shelving or stacked. Interior brick was either exposed or skim-coated with cement. Some, like the 1906 receiving vault at Washington Monumental Cemetery in South River, were constructed of white enameled brick, giving the interior an institutional, hygienic quality (fig. 4.15).

Receiving vaults built in rural areas tended to be small and were often subterranean, while larger subterranean vaults and freestanding aboveground structures were most often associated with the urban cemeteries that date into the early twentieth century. In 1918 the rock-faced granite vault of the New York Bay Cemetery in Jersey City had two doors accessing separate crypt locations. It was typical of the larger vaults that were supported by a city population (*Rules and Regulations of the New York Bay Cemetery*, 1918).

Evergreen Cemetery Company in Basking Ridge constructed an over-sized aboveground receiving vault in the early 1900s. The structure, built of finely dressed granite blocks, was T-shaped with an elongated corridor providing access to the vault area. The corridor also served as an interior space for funeral services with natural light coming from side windows punched through the granite walls and open grillwork within the massive bronze doors. A small granite cupola over the vault's roof houses a bell to be tolled during funeral processions.

Both Fairmount Cemetery and Mount Pleasant Cemetery in Newark also built impressive aboveground vaults by the end of the nineteenth century. Each was constructed from brownstone and featured an interior vestibule for services. Also T-shaped, the vestibule accessed the vault area with stone crypts covered with numbered wooden doors, a system permitting the cemetery superintendent to keep accurate records of those entered into the vault.

While most of the larger vaults provided space for services, one would take this concept to another level, quite literally, with a large chapel built over the vault. The Martin Chapel and Receiving Vault at Elmwood Cemetery in North Brunswick marked a high point in vault design when it was originally constructed. The Martin family were wealthy New Brunswickers who lived in one of the grand homes built along Livingston Avenue at the turn of the century (City of New Brunswick 1908, 18). The sons and daughters of Johnson and Emma Ross Martin built the structure to honor their mother and father.

The granite building, completed in 1917, replaced an earlier receiving vault at the same location (map of Elmwood Cemetery, 1887). The marvelous new structure was built into the side of a hill, allowing mourners to enter the chapel from the hilltop. The ground then sharply drops, exposing the lower portion of the building and giving exterior access to the vault. An imposing structure, the Martin Chapel and Receiving Vault, was built with a rock-faced granite exterior and steeply pitched slate roof. Thick, wooden, arched double doors on bronze strap hinges gave access to the chapel area, which consisted of concrete walls and a thirty-foot vaulted ceiling of buff-colored enameled brick and stone ribbing. The reinforced concrete floor was lined with cork, creating a quiet setting. Historically, high-quality stained-glass windows depicting the life of Christ were located in the chapel, with a large window at the front flanked by four smaller windows along the walls.

The structure incorporated new technology, including six electric, Gothic Revival, torch-shaped wall sconces. In addition, an electric heating element was located at each corner of the room to provide warmth during the services. The casket would have been placed at the front of the chapel over an opening that led to the lower level. Two bronze floor lamps flanked the opening and a large stained-glass window, depicting the resurrection of Christ, was set as the backdrop. At the conclusion of the services the casket was lowered onto a carriage in a lower chamber. The carriage would then be wheeled through double doors into the receiving vault, where three rows of iron shelving were located. The casket could be raised to the correct level of shelving with the use of a crank on the side of the carriage. It was then slid into place with the aid of metal rollers. In total, the receiving vault held forty-eight caskets. During its heyday the chapel was decorated with greenery (Kearney Kuhlthau, personal communication), reflecting the natural surroundings. For the mourners it offered a tranquil place of reflection set within Elmwood Cemetery.

Another combination chapel and receiving vault in New Jersey was incorporated into the large stone fortresslike entrance of the Colestown Cemetery. Built in 1858, the vaulted entrance was flanked by a superintendent's lodge and a chapel. Beneath the chapel was a receiving vault.

In addition to wintertime storage, receiving vaults sometimes housed bodies until a burial spot could be secured or a mausoleum constructed. The *Red Bank Register* reported on May 11, 1898, that the body of Charles Macmonagle held a "place in the receiving vault at Greenwood Cemetery. It will be removed to the private cemetery on the Rumson Road as soon as the family vault is completed." The body of New Brunswick resident Emma Ross Martin, who died in 1877, lingered in the receiving vault at Elmwood Cemetery until she was buried over two years later when the family had secured a burial lot (Kearney Kuhlthau, personal communication). Luckily, Emma was not placed in the receiving vault at the New York Bay Cemetery in Jersey City, as prolonged use of more than two years at that location resulted in the body being removed and buried by the cemetery association (*Rules and Regulations of New York Bay Cemetery*, 1889).

Epidemics also impacted on the use of receiving vaults. During the 1918 influenza epidemic the number of deaths quickly outpaced the number of graves that could be dug and bodies soon piled up in receiving vaults. One victim, who had served in the army and lived in New Brunswick, lay unclaimed in a local receiving vault. Over the course of many years the coffin was shuffled back and forth between Elmwood and Evergreen Cemetery until the name wore off the side. In the 1930s, the now unidentified victim was finally buried by a local veterans' organization at Willow Grove Cemetery in New Brunswick (*Home News Tribune*, June 24, 1996).

Receiving vaults provided the basic needs of storage for those who died in the wintertime or who had yet to secure a permanent place of interment. They evolved from simple structures to high-style buildings that reflected the hopes and aspirations of the cemetery associations. When mechanical means of excavating graves became common after the Second World War, some receiving vaults were demolished to allow more room for burials, while surviving structures endured as storage areas, not for bodies perhaps, but for cemetery maintenance equipment.

Other structures graced the grounds of cemeteries as well. In 1870 the New York Bay Cemetery was reputed to have an "observatory" (Jersey City directory, 1870). The cemetery was noted for its views of New York City, the bay, and the ocean (see Sloane 1991, 130). Although the location of this structure is unknown, it may have been an observation deck built on the uppermost portion of the gatehouse.

In 1918 Cedar Lawn Cemetery in Paterson built a rain shelter at its rear entrance. The small stuccoed building, which has since been demolished, offered protection from the elements to the passengers waiting for the Paterson-Hoboken trolley. An electric bell inside the shelter would ring as the trolley approached (Lanza 1997, 68).

Conclusion

The nineteenth century was a period of great change in the way cemeteries were designed and managed. From the earliest hints of burial reform to the large garden cemeteries, and finally to the new designs of the lawn park cemeteries, New Jersey's burial grounds reflect a broader ideology that shaped and guided them. Many of the original design concepts and structures built within them survive today, making New Jersey's examples an important link to society's changing views regarding the treatment of the dead.

« 5 »

Victorian Valhallas

From Markers to Monuments

In presenting my claims for recognition
I hope you will carefully read my petition
I have selected this space to solicit some trade
And tell of some beautiful Monuments I've made.

~ *"The Monument Maker," advertisement for*
Martin A. Adams, 1899–1900 Jersey City directory ~

The nineteenth century saw an unprecedented florescence of gravestone carving. Marble replaced sandstone in new forms: obelisks, statuary, broken columns, and more idiosyncratic memorials were produced in record numbers. In addition to these new forms, the motifs and iconography carved across the surface of the gravemarkers also changed, reflecting different attitudes about religion and the afterlife. The Victorians sentimentalized and in some ways celebrated death like no previous generation. The depiction of their ideas about commemoration was facilitated by new technologies, particularly the increasing use of steam power and pneumatic tools used for carving.

This chapter will examine the evolution of memorials from simple gravestones and headstones to large monuments. Various types of monuments will be defined, including obelisks, broken columns, shafts, canopy graves, and sarcophagi. The variety of carving designs that emerged during this period will also be examined. In addition to the markers and monuments for adults, special memorials for children were crafted, and their characteristics will be discussed. A section of the chapter is devoted to the individuals who created the markers and monuments of the nineteenth century. Their stories will be examined by region.

Markers: Gravestones and Headstones

At the beginning of the nineteenth century, simple tablet markers were the primary form of commemoration. The tablet marker, commonly known as a gravestone, was a single piece of stone erected vertically in the ground. Wealthier individuals might commission a box tomb, a marker that consisted of a large stone slab laid horizontally and supported by stone or masonry sides, or an altar tomb, similar to a box tomb but supported by legs instead of solid sides. At this stage the move to three-dimensional sculpted monuments was limited, however, and even when larger monuments were created, the gravestone was never completely replaced; instead it became the more affordable marker of the time.

By the mid-nineteenth century a different type of gravestone evolved, no longer one piece of stone stuck in the ground but a tablet supported by a base or a series of bases. The tablet was anchored to the base by a key slot or by metal dowels. The term headstone has been used to describe this type of marker. Some modern-day cemetery historians have also called this type of marker a tablet on a base (Strangstad 1988, 39). Such memorials became a standard style for the middle class and would evolve and change in form to reflect the tastes of the time.

Marble became the predominant material during the nineteenth century, a change that reflected a shift in architectural tastes and a desire on the part of society to distance itself from the old burial grounds and the material found within them. In addition, marble was softer and more suited to sculpting. In the sandstone-rich regions of central and northern New Jersey the move to marble was gradual, as sandstone markers continued to be produced well into the nineteenth century. But marble's role in the making of markers was solidifying as notable individuals had their graves marked with the material in newly revived classical forms. Perhaps the most noted early use was in 1837, when carver John Struthers of Philadelphia donated two marble sarcophagi for the reinterment of George and Martha Washington (McDowell and Meyer 1994, 5).

New technology and new transportation routes helped to make the material accessible from the quarries in Pennsylvania and the New England states to New Jersey marble carvers. In addition, steam-powered tools could quickly process the raw material into workable slabs, helping to supply the demand.

MARKERS TO MONUMENTS

The move from markers to large monuments was gradual in the first decades of the nineteenth century. But as time progressed, the cemetery landscape was transformed into a gleaming white, classically inspired sculptural garden.

It was a universal phenomenon, as commentators of the time remarked on the new style and its popularity. English cemetery architect John Loudon looked with favor on monuments because they did not have "the mean appearance of being thrust in like slates, or laid down like pavement" (Curl 2002, 211). In America, writers also remarked on the new styles. With monuments reaching new heights, R. Martin wrote in his 1846 article "Cemeteries and Monuments" that "the tall monument seems intended to strike the eye at a distance, as a memorial seen afar, crowning perhaps a high raised mound" (Martin 1849, 498).

Other monuments became three-dimensional sculpted works of art and, as some modern-day historians, like Elise Madeleine Ciregna, have argued, America's first introduction to the fine arts, with monument commissions helping to sustain a growing class of American sculptors (Ciregna 2004, 101). In 1862 a visitor to the Princeton Cemetery on Witherspoon Street seemed to agree. Observing several newly erected monuments, he stated that "they are all remarkable for the beauty and chaste simplicity of their design." He reviewed the pieces as much more than markers for the dead—rather as works of art, "interesting from their artistic beauty alone" ("The Graveyard at Princeton," 1862, 34).

Monuments were not the same old memorials, but a new form that incorporated classical designs, evoking the architecture of the great civilizations that inspired them, and they were fast gaining popularity with the middle and upper classes. They were created using various sections of stone and by the late nineteenth century were a complex mix of parts. Since it can be a difficult proposition for modern-day cemeterians to describe them, the following description will help to define all the sections.

Starting from the bottom of the monument, the foundation was not meant to be seen but rather to support the weight of the massive aboveground stones. Because of their size, it was important that monuments rest on a sturdy foundation of brick or concrete. Sometimes monument dealers subcontracted the building of the foundation. New Brunswick carver James Sillcocks did so in 1859 when he paid Jonathan Talmadge forty-eight cents to build a foundation for the Bloodgood family monument (Middlesex County unrecorded estate papers, reel 5, file 839).

The next section of the monument was a horizontal stone slab or base resting on the foundation at ground level. Monuments tended to be erected on a series of separate stone bases, often described starting from the bottom as first base, second base, third base, and so forth (Sample 1919, 8). The bases were stepped, leading to a rectangular or square stone, often described as a pedestal, base, or die.

A capstone was placed over the die as a completed feature of the monument, or on more elaborate monuments the capstone acted as a base supporting a statue, tall shaft, column, or obelisk. Shafts and columns were

A   B   C   D   E   F

5.1 Illustration of various marker and monument types. A: Gravestone/tablet,
eighteenth to early nineteenth century. B: Headstone/tablet on a base, mid-nineteenth century.
C: Monument, early nineteenth century. D: Obelisk with mourning pall placed over
the top, mid-nineteenth century. E: Broken column, mid-nineteenth century.
F: Granite monument, late nineteenth century.
(Illustration by Dawn A. Turner.)

squared off at the top to support statuary or a draped urn, while the obelisk
had a pyramid-shaped top. A broken column, a design borrowed from classical times, was another monument style, with the top of the column trun-
cated at an angle (fig. 5.1).

Although there are countless monument styles and variations, the above
represent the basic forms of memorial art in the nineteenth century. With
this basic form the monument dealer has various surfaces on which to
inscribe lettering or create decorations. While inscriptions can be seen on all
parts of the monument, it was the die that served as the surface for inscribing the names of the deceased.

The ability of monument dealers to classify all the parts of a monument
was imperative in order to properly communicate wishes from customer to
carver or from carver to quarry. As an example, a monument dealer needed
to be able to describe the various sections of a stepped base since the first
base could be a dark Quincy granite with a rock-faced finish, while the second base might be polished gray Barre granite with the family surname
inscribed on it. Sometimes carvers added inscriptions at the cemetery and,
because monuments had many sides to them, such as the die with four surfaces on which to carve an inscription, the carver used north, south, west, and

5.2 The marker for four-month-old Juliana Latrobe at St. Andrew's Cemetery in Mount Holly is one of New Jersey's earliest monuments. Dated 1801, the stone features a carved butterfly leaving its chrysalis.

east orientations in communicating to staff and customers where inscriptions or decorations should go (O. J. Hammell Collection, New Jersey Historical Society, folder 61, file 21).

NEW JERSEY MONUMENTS

In New Jersey, the move from markers to monuments has its roots in St. Andrew's Cemetery in Mount Holly. On November 11, 1801, four-month-old Juliana Latrobe, the daughter of noted American architect Benjamin Henry Latrobe, was buried there after her death caused "by the carelessness of a drunken nurse" (Van Horne and Formwalt 1984, 340). To commemorate her short life Latrobe designed a stunning new memorial based on the Classical Revival style, which was gaining popularity at the dawn of the nineteenth century. The simple square stone set on a stepped base resembled a stripped-down version of a Roman altar tomb or small sarcophagus (fig. 5.2). The characteristics of this early memorial would define Latrobe's later works in the Congressional Cemetery in Washington, DC, as well as the monument he designed for Eliza Lewis, the first wife of Louisiana governor William Claiborne, buried in St. Louis Cemetery I in New Orleans (see McDowell and Meyer 1994, 62).

The two-foot, ten-inch-high marble marker for Juliana is adorned with rosettes at the top corners of the die and inscriptions on three of the four sides. One of the inscriptions reads, "To Juliana Latrobe," almost acting as a statement from her parents in dedicating the marker to their lost daughter. On the south side of the memorial is perhaps the most impressive carving. It is a heaven-bound butterfly that has emerged from its chrysalis, a rare and early symbol for this time period, and one that embodies the idea that our earthly form is but a cocoon for the soul, which will emerge and go on to a better life. The Latrobe memorial is New Jersey's earliest monument, a break from traditional gravestones and the beginning of the larger, more multi-dimensional, and classically inspired memorial art that would dominate the landscape of nineteenth-century cemeteries. Curiously foretelling in its design, Juliana's memorial represents the starting point from which markers would be transformed into monuments.

In the second quarter of the nineteenth century, a number of classically inspired monuments were erected in New Jersey cemeteries. The most popular style was a large die with a flat capstone topped with a pyramid-shaped stone or a short shaft rising in height up to eight feet. Examples can be found across the state, notably in the Trenton First Presbyterian Cemetery and the Church on the Green in Hackensack. Early monuments also grace the First Reformed Churchyard of New Brunswick and its neighbor the Christ Church Episcopal Churchyard, containing a marble shaft placed on a square die for Elizabeth Ogden, who died in 1827.

While most rose from a solid square die, other examples of early monuments from the 1830s and 1840s were constructed using sectional pieces, more like a house of cards. The Maryetta Riley monument in the Emanuel Lutheran Cemetery in Friesburg, Salem County, was erected with stone tablatures held in place with corner posts. The weight of a shaft set on a capstone helps hold the marker together. While most monuments were made from marble, several examples in Mercer County were made from a combination of sandstone and marble. The Withington monument in the Kingston Presbyterian Cemetery was erected in 1831 using marble tablets set into a square base. Brown sandstone was used for corner posts as well as for the capstone and shaft. These monuments are a vivid reminder of a time when sandstone was still being employed in the cemetery landscape.

By the 1860s larger and more three-dimensional monuments were transforming the cemetery into an outdoor sculpture museum. Statues and draped monuments, as well as taller shafts and obelisks, competed with one another for prominence in the cemetery. Many urban garden cemeteries, where spacious family plots allowed the construction of a central family monument, contain noteworthy memorials. Notable examples abound in Mount Pleasant Cemetery in Newark as well as in Evergreen Cemetery in Camden, where in 1868 the Richter family erected a monument that looks as

5.3 The Richter monument at Evergreen Cemetery in Camden dates from the mid-nineteenth century and is most likely the work of a Philadelphia marble carver.

if it would be more at home just across the river in the Philadelphia Museum of Art (fig. 5.3). The ten-foot-high monument, most likely crafted by a Philadelphia carver, consists of a large square stone block supported by a base that is elevated on hairy paw feet. The denticulated capstone supports a sculptural piece depicting a cherub in mourning, head resting on one hand while the other hand is placed atop a draped urn.

In addition to Roman and Greek designs, Egyptian Revival elements can also be found in the cemetery and among the most prevalent of these is the obelisk. In New Jersey, the earliest obelisks were often erected on a base that stood flush with the ground. In Barber and Howe's 1844 image of Old St. Mary's Cemetery in Burlington City, one such obelisk can be seen among the ancient stones in the churchyard. Other early examples include the Dows obelisk in Jersey City's Harsimus Cemetery. The towering monument commemorates John C. Dows, who, in the 1850s, while traveling on the clipper

5.4 By the third quarter of the nineteenth century monuments were rising to new heights, often as a complex series of various sections. The Kohbertz family monument at Maple Grove Cemetery in Hackensack exemplifies the late-nineteenth-century eclectic monument.

ship *Sea Serpent*, fell overboard and drowned. At Cedar Lawn Cemetery in Paterson, several early obelisks were erected for the Colt family, and at the Readington Reformed Cemetery in Hunterdon County there is an early example juxtaposed to a later one on a large supporting square block. As the century progressed obelisks were soaring to new heights with the aid of bases and dies to project them further upward. By the late nineteenth century, towering granite obelisks became a prominent part of the cemetery skyline.

By the 1870s and 1880s monuments were reaching astounding heights, often as an eclectic mix of different sections brought together to create ostentatious memorials. R. Martin wrote some thirty years earlier "that all ostentation should be avoided" (Martin 1849, 498). He believed that if this credo was not followed, then "a monument . . . is no longer a memorial of the dead but the folly of the living" (499). The Kohbertz family clearly thought otherwise in 1875 when they erected a family monument in Maple Grove Cemetery in Bergen County. The twenty-five-foot-high monument has a large stone block placed on top of the die (fig. 5.4). The four-sided block has octagonal tablatures, one of which has a carved marble bust of Mr. Kohbertz under glass. A tall shaft then rises from the block and is crowned by a large draped urn. The Kohbertz monument is reflective of many monuments from the late nineteenth century. It was an era when cemeteries contained stones that were a hodgepodge of various architectural designs, characterized by one cemetery historian as "uniquely funerary" (Keister 1997, 89). They are often creative works incorporating elements picked from the pages of a pattern book illustrating Classical, Gothic, Egyptian, and Moorish motifs.

CANOPY GRAVES

Other styles of commemoration were utilized in the nineteenth century with varying degrees of popularity. Among them was the Gothic Revival canopy grave. Dating mainly from the second half of the nineteenth century, the canopy grave features a superstructure supported by columns. It was based on medieval versions that were revived in the early nineteenth century, most notably with the tomb of Heloise and Abelard at Père-Lachaise Cemetery in Paris (McDowell and Meyer 1994, 95).

In New Jersey, one of the better examples of a canopy grave can be found in Holy Name Cemetery in Jersey City (fig. 5.5). Although deteriorated, the canopy grave for Margaret Henwood, who died in 1873, and her husband, Harold, the founder of St. Michael's Orphan Asylum, is representative of the Gothic Revival style, with pinnacles at each corner of the canopy and a cross on a pedestal over the center of the structure. The monument is about twelve feet high and has copper drain pipes to channel the water from the roof onto a surrounding base of black-and-white marble tile.

Not far from Holy Name Cemetery, at St. Peter's Cemetery in Jersey City, is the Mulligan memorial, whose canopy is projected high on the top of the monument. Also found here is another large canopy grave from the 1860s for Father John Kelly.

An early example of a canopy grave can be seen at Old St. Mary's Cemetery in Burlington City. The monument commemorates Edward Grubb, who died in 1867. It is a low structure, about four feet high and five feet long. The overhanging canopy sits on a marble stone block and has marble columns. A stepped granite base supports the entire structure.

SARCOPHAGI

In 1837 Philadelphia carver John Struthers donated two marble sarcophagi for the reinterment of the remains of George and Martha Washington. The event garnered much publicity and was reported in *Harper's New Monthly Magazine* (McDowell and Meyer 1994, 6). A number of early sarcophagi can be

5.5 Revival styles were commonplace during the nineteenth century. The Henwood family monument at Holy Name Cemetery in Jersey City was meant to mimic a medieval canopy grave. The style gained limited popularity in New Jersey during the third and fourth quarters of the nineteenth century.

found in New Jersey. In Perth Amboy at St. Peter's Episcopal Churchyard stands the marble sarcophagus for thirty-nine-year-old Mary Augusta Heyward, who died in 1845. The Daniel Van Syckel sarcophagus rests in the Milford Union Cemetery in Hunterdon County. Dated 1861, it features a funeral pall draped over the top and hanging down the side, partially covering the words "Our Father." The monument stands in contrast to other markers of the same period in the cemetery and may have been made by a Philadelphia marble carver.

Mount Pleasant Cemetery in Newark has a number of mid-nineteenth-century sarcophagi, including the marker for John Taylor and his wife, Charlotte, who died in 1856 and 1864, respectively. Carved from brownstone, it features laurel wreaths and a pair of crossed upside-down torches. In addition to classically inspired designs, Gothic ornamented variations can also be examined in Mount Pleasant. More commonly known as altar tombs, they are similar to sarcophagi but dispensed with the classical lines for Gothic Revival tastes (McDowell and Meyer 1994, 125). Included in this category is the marble Vanderpool monument. Carved by George Brown and Company, the tomb has carved Gothic tracery and quatrefoils.

The sarcophagi found in New Jersey cemeteries do not contain the physical remains of the deceased but rather act as elaborate markers for their graves. Unfortunately, vandals have not realized this and sometimes move the lids to peek inside, hoping to satisfy a morbid curiosity.

BED OR CRADLE GRAVES

Bed or cradle graves make up another type of monument style. More prevalent in southern New Jersey, where Philadelphia marble carvers created some stunning examples, they have the look of a nineteenth-century bed, with headboard, side rails, and footboard. They are often supported on a large marble slab with holes cut through for planting flowers or ivy.

The bed or cradle grave makes its first appearance by the time of the Civil War. It became popular among middle- and upper-class Americans and appears with some regularity in southern New Jersey cemeteries. The popularity of the style wanes by the early 1900s and disappears from the landscape by the 1920s. Notable examples can be seen in cemeteries in Cape May County, St. Andrew's Cemetery in Mount Holly, and Evergreen Cemetery in Camden. Most were produced by Philadelphia marble carvers and tend to be signed by the monument company on the footboard.

DIMENSIONAL URNS

Two varieties of urns can be found in New Jersey. The earliest is a two-dimensional urn carved on a gravestone in the late eighteenth and early nineteenth centuries, which is discussed in chapter 3. The second is a three-dimensional sculpted urn that is sometimes draped with a funeral pall or has an eternal flame rising from its top. Taken from Greek and Roman examples, they were historically utilized for cremated remains, but today are employed as a decorative element crowning the top of a memorial.

One of the earliest and largest examples of a sculpted urn is for Jane Frazee, wife of early American sculptor John Frazee (fig. 5.6). Jane died of cholera in 1832 and was buried at the Old School Baptist Churchyard in South River. While most urns were small in scale, Frazee sculpted a large marble urn as the primary memorial with the epitaph written across the urn's face. In addition, his urn was not short and squat, as others generally are, but tall and slender, giving it a sleek monumental appearance more associated with the grand scale of classical works.

Other later but equally large urns can be found in the state. An oversized example for the Bodine family stands in the Presbyterian Cemetery in Bridgeton, Cumberland County. Sculpted in the mid-nineteenth century, it stands on a square base and measures about four feet in height. The round marble urn has large protruding handles and is draped with a mourning pall.

While most urns were round, the Charles Pitman monument at the Mercer Cemetery has a square urn. Dating from the 1850s, it is similar in

5.6 This important monument for Jane Frazee, the wife of American sculptor John Frazee, is located in the Old School Baptist Churchyard, South River. Frazee carved this impressive urn for his wife after she died from cholera in 1832. The Frazee urn is an early classically inspired monument.

style to the urn used in the cenotaph for George Whitefield in the First Presbyterian Church, Newburyport, Massachusetts, which was designed by William Strickland and crafted by Philadelphia marble carver John Struthers. Another square urn was incorporated into the Bunn monument at the Alexandria Presbyterian Cemetery in Hunterdon County. The monument has a sectional die that is topped with a square urn on which winged cherubs were carved.

Urns were popular motifs and many came in stock styles that could be purchased from monument catalogs. In 1923 the Vermont Marble Company, a business with its roots in the nineteenth century, offered six grades of marble for its plain urns and thirty-nine sizes from which to choose. These ranged from seven inches high and four inches in diameter to thirty inches high and fourteen inches in diameter. Such options gave the customer a total of 234 variations of the urn.

DECORATIVE MOTIFS

As numerous as the various forms of commemoration were, equally endless was the variety of motifs carved upon their surfaces. New Jersey cemeteries offer a wide range of ornamentation (fig. 5.7). Although many of the designs were based on classical motifs, others were not, such as fraternal emblems,

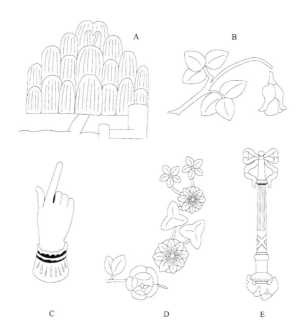

5.7 Illustration of different mid-nineteenth-century tombstone motifs.
A: Weeping willow. B: Broken rosebud. C: Upward-pointed hand.
D: Floral and ivy motifs. E: Downward-pointed torch.
(Illustration by Dawn A. Turner.)

flowers, open Bibles, and sailing ships, to name a few. Architectural elements are frequently found on stones of the nineteenth century and include Greek keys, rosettes, columns, beads, reels, rope molding, and egg and dart motifs. Other common designs of the period include floral decorations, hands, willow trees, urns, and stones with mourning drapery and tassels or funeral palls covering them.

Among the most common designs were floral motifs. They can be found in the shape of a wreath, bouquet, or single flower. Roses and lilies were common on nineteenth-century markers but other flowers were chosen as well. Unusual uses of floral bouquets include those displayed in baskets. The 1871 marker for Annie Claypoole in the Fairview Methodist Cemetery in Cape May Court House is one such example: the basket is tipped over with the flowers spilling out. Other symbolic plant life carved on nineteenth-century memorials included ivy, oak leaves, acorns, and sheaves of wheat.

WEEPING WILLOWS

By the mid-nineteenth century the willow tree, which had previously been carved as spindly and bent over, was erect and covered with foliage, with a vast array of monuments and mourning scenes depicted beneath it. Practi-

5.8 The marker for John Kuhl and Catherine Hoppoch, dated 1830 and 1840, respectively, features a detail of a weeping willow with a male figure in mourning.

cally every nineteenth-century memorial motif can be connected with a willow. All across New Jersey examples of willows with box tombs, altar tombs, monuments, cradle graves, allegorical figures, resting lambs, and angels can be seen.

In the Second Cape May Baptist Churchyard in Palermo the gravestone for Samuel Corson, who died in 1852, and the 1857 marker for his wife, Sarah Ann, feature weeping willows with two different monument types. One has a shaft on a square base with a willow tree while the other has a broken column monument with a willow tree. In addition the carver added a rising (or setting) sun to the scene. James Brower had two weeping willows flanking an altar tomb carved on his stone, while his wife Hannah's stone depicts a box tomb set amid two willow motifs. Both markers are located in the Mercer Cemetery in Trenton, where other weeping willow motifs can be found. In Holy Name Cemetery in Jersey City, the mid-nineteenth century saw willows incorporated into designs reserved for Catholics, including a sleeping lamb, an angel, and a cross.

Allegorical figures can also be found in conjunction with the weeping willow tree. They are often seen in mournful repose, leaning against monuments under the shade of the willow. While most are in classical dress, a few mournful figures wear contemporary, nineteenth-century clothing, and look vaguely similar to characters in Currier & Ives mourning prints. An illegible marble marker in Mount Pleasant Cemetery belongs to this genre, with a mother and child in mourning under the weeping willow. Another unique example was carved by Peter Wakeham of Millstone. It is the gravestone for John Kuhl and Catherine Hoppoch, dated 1830 and 1840, respectively. The top front surface of the stone features a large willow tree with a male figure in a mourning scene (fig. 5.8). The man wears modern clothes with a top hat and is leaning against a monument. By the late 1800s the willow had mostly disappeared from the cemetery landscape.

HANDS

The upward-pointed hand, indicating the way to a better afterlife, had widespread use in New Jersey. The popularity of this motif dates roughly from 1850 to 1870. In addition to pointing hands, several examples of a hand with an open palm displaying a heart can be found in cemeteries in Cape May County. Clasped hands were another motif utilized on New Jersey markers, sometimes carved with amazing detail highlighting the nails and cuff links. Perhaps the most unusual example of a hand motif is the Tindall marker in the Reformed Church Cemetery in Spotswood. The top surface of the stone has a deeply modeled hand holding an hourglass set against a sunset or sunrise.

NAUTICAL THEMES

During the mid-nineteenth century, nautical themes were prevalent in cemeteries along the New Jersey coast. Numerous carved sailing vessels, from sloops to clipper ships, often mark the graves of those whose lives were spent on the sea. Included among such markers is the marble headstone for Captain Jacob Smith, who died in 1861. A schooner under full sail is carved into the top front surface of the stone, located in the Cold Spring Presbyterian Cemetery. In Washington Monumental Cemetery in South River the stone for Enoch Rose, who died in 1862, has a sloop, a single-masted sailing vessel, carved onto it. The sailboat is typical of the vessels that sailed between South River and the markets in New York City, carrying fresh farm produce.

While most nautical depictions show sailing vessels, the Buck family marker in Fairview Methodist Cemetery in Cape May Court House has a side-wheel steamship carved onto the square base. Edmund Buck was only twenty-two when he "accidentally drowned from on board the U.S.S. *Powhatan*" on September 5, 1863 (fig. 5.9). Other nautical-themed markers include several in the Sea Captain's Cemetery in Barnegat, Ocean County. The marble marker for Captain Thomas Woodmansee, dated 1880, has an anchor and capstan carved on the top front surface (Sarapin 1994, 147).

EPITAPH TABLATURES

The section on markers and monuments reserved for the epitaph would also evolve. In the early nineteenth century the epitaph was sometimes surrounded with border designs; however, many inscriptions were carved across the surface of the marker without the use of any framing. By the mid-nineteenth century a raised or sunken tablature was often carved for the deceased's name. Tablatures in the form of a shield were common. They evolved into a variety of shapes meant to give dignity to the inscription.

5.9 Markers in cemeteries along the New Jersey coast often have nautical motifs. The monument for Edmund Buck in the Fairview Methodist Cemetery in Cape May Court House has a carved image of the USS *Powhatan.* On September 5, 1863, Edmund was "accidentally drowned" after falling off the ship.

Scrolls that draped across the surface of the stone and contained the epitaph were also popular.

New Jersey cemeteries are also home to some rare designs. Among them are church landscapes, of which at least three have been documented. They include the Mary Corson marker from 1853 in the Second Cape May Baptist Churchyard in Palermo, which has a carved church with a steeple, graveyard, and hills in the background. Another example of similar style, but unfortunately worn and discolored, is in the Westminster Presbyterian Cemetery in Cranbury. Other unusual designs of the nineteenth century that have been noted in New Jersey cemeteries include a log cabin, sheet music, an axe, a trumpet, and, in Trenton, a carving of machinery in a rolling mill.

Clearly, New Jersey cemeteries offer a variety of markers and monuments and countless decorations, meant to evoke emotion and remembrance of the deceased. But nowhere is this more profound than in the case of markers for children, which this next section will explore.

Markers and Monuments for the Innocent: Memorials for Children

A flower just blooming into life
Enticed an Angel's eye.
Too pure for earth, he said, "Come Home,"
And bade the floweret die.

~ *1882 Monumental Bronze Co.*
catalog, stock epitaph ~

Nineteenth-century memorials for children reflect an expression of great grief translated into stone. They evolve from smaller versions of adult markers in the eighteenth and early nineteenth centuries to sculpted romanticized

works of art in the mid- and late nineteenth century. The designs and
iconography found on children's markers stem from a period when children
represented purity and innocence in an otherwise industrialized and secular-
ized society. They were, as Ellen Marie Snyder described, "innocents in a
worldly world" and the home they had yet to leave was their sanctity (Snyder 1992, 11). Ideas about the importance of family and home were prevalent
during the nineteenth century. John Ruskin wrote that the home "is the place
of peace, the shelter. So far as the . . . hostile society of the outer world is
allowed by either husband or wife to cross the threshold it ceases to become
a home" (13). The innocence of children, their tragic loss to a family, and the
sanctity of home became themes of children's markers.

During the opening decades of the nineteenth century, children's markers were generally miniatures of adult markers. With the coming of age of
the garden cemetery, shifts in attitudes toward death, and the rise of skilled
marble carvers, markers for children evolved into their own genre with child-
oriented motifs, including sleeping lambs, doves, and flower buds. Of the
design elements used extensively in New Jersey cemeteries, the broken rosebud, symbolizing a youth's life that had yet to bloom, with the stem broken,
indicating it never will, was among the most common. For the markers of
infants a closed bud was common, but for young children the bud showed
signs of opening. When three-year-old Wilson M. Stephens "expired" on
February 15, 1860, his parents erected a marker in the Second Cape May Baptist Churchyard in Palermo with such a design. Although usually carved on
the top face of the marker, a broken bud about to bloom was carved near the
base of the Stephens marker. The design was widespread among tombstones
of mid-nineteenth-century New Jersey, so much so that a visitor to the
Princeton Cemetery in 1861 remarked that "numerous 'broken rosebuds'
mark the graves of children, and the device is so often repeated as to become
tiresome" ("The Graveyard at Princeton," 1862, 35).

In no image was the concept of innocence expressed more fully than in
that of a sleeping child (Snyder 1992, 16). The bedrooms of children were
sacred places in Victorian society and a sleeping child was a reflection of
them at their most innocent. In death, children continued to slumber in
another sacred place—the cemetery. Children can be found sleeping on
clouds, roses, plush pillows, and beds, and even inside a clamshell. The tablet
marker of Mellie Hand, who died in 1864, is located in the Fairview
Methodist Cemetery in Cape May Court House. Her parents purchased a
marker with a sleeping child carved on the top face with the wording "Mellie Sleeps" above the scene, further reinforcing that Mellie was not dead but
slumbering in the burial ground. In St. Peter's Cemetery in Jersey City stands
a marker for the Royle children: Sarah, Samuel, and George. Although the
inscription is worn, a date of 1857 can be deciphered for George (fig. 5.10).
The marker features an oversized top on which is sculpted a sleeping child,

5.10 The marker for the Royle children features a sleeping child on a bed of roses. Sculptures of sleeping children are rare; this unusual example is located in St. Peter's Cemetery in Jersey City.

hands clasped on chest, on a bed of carved roses. Other children, like B. Franklin in the Mercer Cemetery in Trenton, were remembered as "Gone So Soon," and represented as slumbering peacefully on a cloud with a dove flying overhead. The marker of Emily [illegible]rth, who died in the 1880s, is a unique example of the sleeping child motif. Borrowing from popular literature of the time, the diminutive marker features a child asleep within a clamshell. Located in Evergreen Cemetery in Camden, the marker was originally a cradle grave, but today the footboard and portions of the side rails are missing.

Full-size sculpted figures of sleeping children erected on square bases were reserved for families of financial means and a number of good examples can be found throughout the state. The marker for Mary Elizabeth Woolverton, who died in 1844, has a three-dimensional child sleeping on a plush pillow in the Alexandria Presbyterian Cemetery. The style was popularized in tombstone pattern books, including Richard Wathan's *Monumental and Headstone Designs*, published in New York in 1875.

Angels carrying children upward to heaven are also evident in the mid-nineteenth century. They come in a variety of styles from uplifting depictions of children riding on the backs of angels toward a better life to images of angels carrying "sleeping" children in their arms. Numerous examples can be found in New Jersey cemeteries, including the Richey children's markers at the Musconetcong Valley Presbyterian Cemetery. Crafted by Philadelphia carver J. Baird, the two cradle graves, each with an angel ascending to heaven, mark the final resting place of the children of Augustus and Anna Richey. The marker for "Our Angel Boy" Walter Mason, who "Died in Boston Harbor" on September 26, 1863, is an interesting variation on both the nautical theme and the heaven-bound angel. Located in Greenwich, Cumberland County, the marker is a cradle grave whose headboard contains a recessed top with a carved scene of an angel carrying a child in her arms and rising from the water and into the clouds of heaven. In the background is a two-masted sailing vessel under full sail.

5.11 The monument for Isabel Bonnell, the daughter of Whitehouse, New Jersey, carver Robert Bonnell, displays a variety of motifs, including angels, baby shoes, three carvings of Isabel, and a rattle.

Sculpted statues of children in life also became popular. Stock sculptures of children helped to keep statuary affordable to the middle class. Some, like the Roshore Withington monument in the Kingston Presbyterian Cemetery, have a stock sculpture of a child holding a basket of flowers. Families who had the means commissioned life-size sculptures depicting the likeness of their children. One of the more notable examples is the monument to Maud Munn in Mount Pleasant Cemetery in Newark. Maud died at the tender age of ten on New Year's Day in 1891. Several days earlier she had finished performing in a Christmas recital when she came down with scarlet fever. Her father commissioned a life-size sculpture of his daughter sitting on a tree stump wearing the dress and slippers that she had worn during her recital.

Other one-of-a-kind markers for children include the memorial for Isabel Bonnell (fig. 5.11). Bonnell was the daughter of Anna and Robert Bonnell, a Whitehouse, New Jersey, marble carver. She was eight years old when she died in 1891. Her father created an extraordinary monument in the form of a cradle grave. The headboard is a four-sided monument topped with a statue of Isabel. Each side and section of the monument is carved with various scenes, including a winged angel holding a banner that reads "Remembered," a dove, a winged angel playing a harp, a cross with an anchor, an image of Isabel holding a lamb, another image of the girl with her arm

5.12 Bertie Harris has perhaps the most impressive child's marker in New Jersey. The basic block of the monument was a stock example produced by the Monumental Bronze Company. However, Bertie's parents had metal replicas of his toys reproduced and placed on the top. The wheelbarrow is filled with toy blocks that have letters and numbers on them.

around a cross and anchor, two hands clasping, another hand holding a rattle, an angel over a sleeping child, and a sleeping child on a Viking ship with an angel overhead. As if this was not enough of a tribute, the footboard is draped with a plush pillow that supports a pair of children's shoes, one upright, the other resting on its side.

Also in the running for New Jersey's most exceptional child's marker is that of Bertie Harris in the Hackensack Church on the Green Cemetery (fig. 5.12). Bertie, who died in 1880, was the only son of Charles and Lizzie Harris. Stricken with grief, his parents erected a stock marker from a monument company catalog but personalized it with replicas of his toys. The marker is made from monumental bronze, an impervious zinc-coated metal marketed as an alternative to erosive marble. It measures five feet, three inches high and stands on a thirty-three-by-forty-five-inch base. The marker was advertised in the 1882 Monumental Bronze Company's "White Bronze Monuments" catalog as design number 207 at a cost of $270 with optional statue of a "kneeling girl" and "kneeling boy" in prayer on top (fig. 5.13). The Harris family decided against the optional statues, instead creating a unique embellishment. Crafted from metal with amazing detail and placed on top of the marker were Bertie's toys, including his riding horse and a small wheelbarrow, which contains children's blocks with numbers and letters clearly visible. To Victorian society, a child playing with his favorite toys was a reflection of a pure and innocent life. Bertie's parents made sure that his toys, an important part of their son's life, were with him in death and further reinforced the sanctity of home through these domestic connections.

5.13 The 1882 Monumental Bronze Company catalog has an illustration of the pattern used for the Bertie Harris monument in Hackensack's First Reformed Dutch Churchyard. Known as design number 207, the marker cost $270 with optional statue of a "kneeling girl" and "kneeling boy" in prayer on top. (Reproduced with permission from Winterthur Library.)

The previous descriptions of markers and monuments are by no means complete. New Jersey cemeteries are a vast outdoor sculpture garden containing stunning memorials with countless design motifs, the product of a period when the monumental arts flourished; the following section will focus on the artists whose skill and vision shaped the cemetery landscape.

New Jersey Monument Makers

Tombs, Tablets, Sarcophagi, Head and Footstones too,
Please give me an order to erect one for you
For I keep them in every conceivable style—
Both ancient and modern, from here to the Nile.

~ *"The Monument Maker,"*
advertisement for Martin A. Adams,
1899–1900 Jersey City directory ~

Stone carvers of the nineteenth century were an integral part of society's fabric, practicing a noble craft that was thousands of years old. They were hoping to create lasting memorial art much as their counterparts did in

5.14 Illustration from Paul Schulze's book *Original Designs in Monumental Art*, 1851. Schulze highlighted a variety of different monument styles. His design book was available to stone carvers, who could replicate the examples in print. This design is similar to that of the Harriet Eldredge marker carved twenty-five years later in Cape May County. (Reproduced with permission from Winterthur Library.)

Egypt, Greece, and Rome. Indeed they saw themselves as purveyors of monumental art. Paul Schulze, the author of the 1851 *Original Designs in Monumental Art*, stated that "no branch of Art is perhaps more intimately connected with the feelings, than the *monumental*." His book, published in Boston, was an important step in recognizing the significance of the monument maker. He hoped that his book would help with "the elevation and promotion of Monumental Art" (fig. 5.14). At least one design from Schulze's book was incorporated into the New Jersey cemetery landscape—the 1875 cradle grave of Harriet T. Eldredge in Cape May County. Even today, New Jersey's cemeteries contain an immeasurable amount of monumental art that impresses and delights contemporary visitors. This chapter will examine, by region, the makers of markers and monuments and their contributions to the cemetery setting.

New Jersey's cemetery landscape was created by a vast array of talent drawn from both local and out-of-state carvers. Skilled full-time carvers worked in urban regions, where a larger population could support the trade, while the more rural sections of the state were home to part-time gravestone carvers with varying degrees of skill. Markers found in rural locations that demonstrate features of high art were usually shipped to the region from nearby centers of carving activity. Southern New Jersey was heavily influenced by carvers from Philadelphia, while the central and northeastern parts of the state were under the sway of carvers working in more heavily populated cities, setting the styles and standards for the region. In 1850 *Kirkbride's New Jersey Business Directory* listed approximately twenty-eight marble workers in the state; by 1860 the number had jumped to fifty-four, as noted in *Boyd's Business Directory*. Certainly not all carvers were recorded in these publications;

in fact the 1866 edition of Talbott and Blood's directory failed to mention the Sillcocks family of New Brunswick, the most prolific carvers of that city. What we do know about those who created the markers and monuments has come from a mixture of historic documents and signed examples of their work in cemeteries across the state. For the period 1800 to 1900 these indicate the presence of at least 225 New Jersey carvers. In addition, out-of-state carvers from Pennsylvania; Washington, DC; New York; Connecticut; Rhode Island; and other states also contributed to the landscape. For historians, New Jersey's cemeteries are an untapped resource, filled with examples from folk to high monumental art, reflecting varying attitudes toward death. It is hoped that the following sections will add to our understanding of those who created the markers and monuments of the nineteenth century and be a foundation for further research.

SOUTHERN NEW JERSEY

Generally speaking, in southern New Jersey, gravestones from between 1800 and 1850 were made in Philadelphia, where a large population and accessibility of material sustained the trade. Later, when New Jersey carvers established a foothold in the region and flooded cemeteries with countless gravestones, the more artistic monuments, markers, and cradle graves would come from highly skilled carvers in Philadelphia. They contributed heavily to southern New Jersey cemeteries, with examples in Cape May, Salem, Cumberland, Gloucester, Burlington, Ocean, and Atlantic Counties. Other Philadelphia memorials made their way to central and northern counties as well, including Mercer, Essex, and Hunterdon. Some carvers created incredible sculpted pieces with undercut lettering and three-dimensional designs. Among the better-known monument dealers whose signed works can be found in New Jersey cemeteries were Steinmetz, J. Baird, Van Cunden and Young, Struthers, and Henry Tarr.

Philadelphian John Struthers was a well-known marble sculptor who worked with architect John Strickland to create a number of notable buildings in that city. After Struthers' death in 1851 his son William continued as a marble carver. His most notable New Jersey commission can be found in Newark at Mount Pleasant Cemetery. Erected in 1854, the large Gothic Revival monument commemorates the founders of the cemetery and ironically was carved from brownstone rather than marble. The base of the monument was signed "Struthers."

Henry Tarr produced a number of markers and monuments in Salem and Cumberland Counties. His most notable achievement, however, is in Hunterdon County in the Alexandria Presbyterian Cemetery. The Woolverton family plot, mainly dating from the 1870s, is a marble lover's delight, with a large central shaft surrounded by smaller cradle graves, headstones, urns with flowers, and a sculpture of a sleeping child for Mary Woolverton, who died in 1844. In addition the entire plot is surrounded by a marble enclosure.

In 1886 Philadelphia monument dealers Van Cunden and Young erected a granite memorial for the Provost family in the Mount Holly Cemetery, not only signing the base with the company's name but also noting that the design was "Copyright[ed] 1886." Other high-style memorials, most likely carved in Philadelphia, have gone unsigned or have had their signatures erode. Such works await future research to help connect the monument to its maker. In addition to Philadelphia carvers, other out-of-state carvers, especially prior to the mid-nineteenth century, supplied markers to southern New Jersey. In the Leesburg United Methodist Churchyard, the Tabernacle United Methodist Churchyard, and the Seventh Day Adventist Churchyard in Cape May County, one can find gravestones from Providence, Rhode Island.

By the mid-nineteenth century a number of southern New Jersey carvers had established themselves and created countless tablet markers and monuments. In more rural locations part-time stone carvers were operating. However, very few signed their work, leaving most of this region's local carvers nameless. In the urban areas, where there was a population to support the marble-carving trade, marble shops were opening by the 1840s. The largest area of activity was in Camden. While there were no stone carvers listed in Camden in the *New Jersey Business Directory* for 1850, by 1860 George Brittain, Christian Kohler, Marc Lang, and George Mott were listed as marble workers. Signed examples by Brittain and Mott show up in Evergreen Cemetery in Camden. J. L. Edwards, who was not listed in either the 1860 or 1866 New Jersey business directory, was clearly operating a marble shop in Camden as early as 1860. Signed examples of his work appear in Cape May County, where he carved an obelisk for Herman Smith in the Seaside Cemetery. His last known signed work is dated 1868 and he does not appear in the Camden city directory in 1877, the first year it lists marble carvers. In fact, of all the marble workers listed in 1860, not one was in business by 1877. Was the competition from Philadelphia too fierce for this first group? By 1890, as the city expanded and the number of cemeteries in operation grew, the number of marble workers had risen to nine, with Michael Riley and Michael Lyons among the more prolific. By 1920 the number of monument firms dropped to five as larger companies bought the smaller businesses and consolidated the trade.

Burlington County had the second largest grouping of carvers in the southern part of the state, primarily located in Mount Holly and Burlington City. Mount Holly sustained several businesses, with J. Reeder and J. Collins among the earliest. Collins was operating a shop in the 1840s. Signed examples of his work can be found in St. Andrew's Cemetery—one such marker for Charles Hughes was signed "J. Collins Stonecutter Mt.

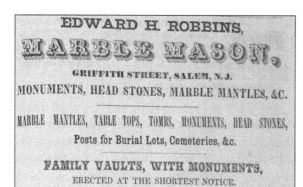

5.15 Like many mid-nineteenth-century marble carvers, Edward H. Robbins of Salem produced a variety of stone products, including marble building elements and tombstones (*Kirkbride's New Jersey Business Directory*, 1850). (Reproduced with permission from the Jersey City Public Library.)

Holly." Reeder, whose known works were all simple marble gravestones, was operating his shop by the late 1840s through the 1850s; then his signed specimens stop appearing in area cemeteries. But by that time Joseph Shaffer and J. Keeler had set up shops in Mount Holly. Shaffer crafted marble tablets primarily, some with weeping willows, including an unusual example carved in 1864 with an American flag above the willow, while Keeler produced both simple tablet markers and numerous monuments. In addition to Mount Holly, Burlington City became a center for marble carvers. The shop of Samuel Sager was located on Union Street in 1860 and in the 1870s C. F. Coleman produced a number of tablet markers on bases that can be found in Monument Cemetery in Beverly and the Odd Fellows Cemetery in Burlington.

Gloucester County had marble workers located in Gloucester City and Swedesboro in 1860. In 1866 M. O'Riley, most likely Michael Riley, who later moved to Camden, was listed as a marble worker in Gloucester City. In Salem County, the city of Salem became a center of carving activity, with C. D. Haines, Edward H. Robbins, and Robert Wildes operating marble shops by the mid-nineteenth century. Haines does not appear in the 1850 *New Jersey Business Directory* but does have at least one signed work, dated 1844, for Ebenezer Peters in St. George's Churchyard in Pennsville. Robbins, on the other hand, advertised in the directory, noting that he sold "Monuments, Head Stones, Marble Mantles." His shop on Griffith Street also supplied "Family Vaults, With Monuments" as well as "Coach Steps, Scrapers, and Spout Stones; Sills and building MARBLE in general" (fig. 5.15).

In Cumberland County, Bridgeton and Millville had areas of carving activity. In Bridgeton George Claypoole operated a marble shop as early as the 1850s. He had competition from J. Gibson, J. Ogden, and Applegate. Both Gibson and Applegate were partners in the 1860s, but by the 1870s Applegate is no longer noted on signed markers with Gibson but instead with Ogden. By the 1880s it seems they went their separate ways as signed stones in both Cumberland and Salem Counties have all three names listed individually. In Millville both T. Cox and W. H. Van Gilder operated marble shops in the 1880s, creating markers that can be found in Leesburg and Port Elizabeth and a cradle grave by Van Gilder at the Head of the River Church in Cape May County.

In that county, Cape May Court House supported a thriving marble-carving industry. Among the carvers there was D. Ballbeck, who in 1849 signed a stone made for Sarah Parson at the Head of the River Church. The simple marble tablet marker has a weeping willow carved on the tympanum. Ballbeck seems to have left the area by 1850, when other carvers like L. Entrikin began to work in the area. Entrikin, whose earliest signed marker is from 1839, was initially from Petersburg; by the 1870s he had moved his operation to Cape May Court House and created numerous monuments, with notable examples in Goshen and the Cold Springs Presbyterian Cemetery. Markers signed "Raymond" also appear in Cape May County. Raymond's marble-carving shops were located in Tuckahoe and Cape May Court House, with the latter location becoming his primary shop by the 1870s. No marble carvers are listed in *Kirkbride's New Jersey Business Directory* as operating in Ocean or Atlantic County in 1850, but clearly carvers whose names have yet to be discovered were creating memorials in these locations.

CENTRAL NEW JERSEY

The counties of central New Jersey—Mercer, Monmouth, Middlesex, Somerset, and Hunterdon—supported a wide variety of carvers who in the early nineteenth century worked primarily in sandstone, but shifted to marble by the mid-nineteenth century. Carving centers developed in Trenton and New Brunswick, where growing cities, newly established rural cemeteries, and access to a thriving customer base helped to sustain the trade. This section will focus on the carvers in central New Jersey and their contributions to the cemetery landscape.

In Mercer County the center of carving activity was in Trenton, where, by 1850, Andrew Allison and Luther Ward had set up competing marble shops (*Kirkbride's New Jersey Business Directory*). Allison was operating in Trenton as early as 1843, when he carved an obelisk for Dr. William Montgomery in the Old Brick Reformed Churchyard in Guilford County, North Carolina (Little 1998, 273). Previously, however, both Ward and Allison had operated in other locations: Ward in New Brunswick during the 1830s and Allison in Easton, Pennsylvania, in the 1820s. By 1855 another competitor in Trenton was the team of Sweet & Crowther, who were listed in the Trenton city directory as "Manufacturer of Monuments, Tombs, Headstones, Posts for Burial Lots." John Sweet formed his own company by 1860 but his name soon disappears from the city directories. One of Luther Ward's workers, John Payran, opened his own shop on State Street in 1875 (Historical Publishing Co. 1883, 169). Payran was a prolific carver and during the 1870s and 1880s he created a number of monuments that can be found throughout cemeteries in Mercer County. Among his competitors was Hugh Swayze, who was born in Morris County in 1849. Swayze may have earlier been operating under the name Weston and Swayze in Lambertville in the late 1860s (Talbott and Blood 1866) and by the early 1870s under his own name in the same location. But during the 1870s Swayze moved to Trenton and opened a shop at 216 East State Street in 1879, where he continued to create markers and monuments (Historical Publishing Co. 1883, 193). John Conroy was another Trenton carver, who started his career in Stockton by 1860 but in 1866 was in Trenton on Greene Street between State and Front (Boyd 1860; Talbott and Blood 1866). After his death, Hugh Conroy took over and operated the business until 1886, when the firm is not listed in the Trenton city directory. Conroy produced a variety of markers and monuments, including a notable family monument with upside-down carved torches in the Hightstown Presbyterian Cemetery.

In 1850 there were three marble workers listed for Monmouth County in *Kirkbride's New Jersey Business Directory*. George Bell and R. R. McChesney were operating independent shops in Middletown Point while Henry Cleaver was working in Red Bank. McChesney was carving gravestones as early as the 1840s. One of his earlier works, an 1842 gravestone for Disborough Appleget, is in the Cranbury Presbyterian Cemetery. The marker has two acanthus panels that flank a willow tree and urn carved into the top face of the stone. Markers carved by McChesney during the 1850s can also be found in the Reformed Church Cemetery in Spotswood, including the 1853 Hannah Jernee tombstone, with a sculpted floral wreath near the top. By 1860 McChesney was in business with F. Lupton; they continued to carve willows as well as floral designs (*Boyd's Business Directory*). By 1866 Lupton appears to be the sole business operator and McChesney disappears from the records. Lupton, who was now operating shops in Middletown Point and Freehold, continued his business into the 1880s, serving a wide geographic area. Signed examples of his work can be found in Middlesex County cemeteries in Old Bridge and Spotswood.

Middlesex County boasted a bustling center of carving activity in New Brunswick. At the close of the eighteenth century the workshop of Aaron Ross was located on Burnet Street. Ross worked in both sandstone and marble, often signing his markers near the base with his initials surrounded by a circular rope border. In 1803 Ross was working in Rahway and advertised in the *New Brunswick Guardian* that "orders for tomb-stones, gravestones, &c left with Joseph Sillcock, in Queen Street, New Brunswick shall be duly executed, and with dispatch on reasonable terms." The "Joseph Sillcock" men-

5.16 Oil portrait of central New Jersey gravestone carver Henry Sillcocks, circa 1820. Sillcocks produced both sandstone and marble gravestones from the early nineteenth century until his death in 1846. (Reproduced with permission from the Cranbury Historical and Preservation Society.)

tioned in Ross's advertisement was part of central New Jersey's most prolific tombstone-carving family. An examination of Middlesex County probate records shows that Joseph was carving stones in the early nineteenth century. Records of payments for tombstones can be documented in 1805 and 1807, and in 1809 he was paid $9.65 for a "headstone and foot stone" for Daniel Freeman (Middlesex County unrecorded estate papers). No known signed examples of Joseph's work have come to light, and he disappears from the probate records around 1810, about the same time that two other Sillcocks family members appear—Henry and Isaac. Henry was the son of Gabriel and his second wife, Sarah Snedeker (Sillcocks family papers, Cranbury Historical and Preservation Society). He was born in North Brunswick in 1793 and operated a monument yard, first in Jamesburg, then in Somerville, and finally New Brunswick (Sillcocks family papers/Hull Family in America, page 345, Cranbury Historical and Preservation Society) (fig. 5.16). Henry, along with Isaac Sillcocks, whose relationship to Henry has yet to be determined, was carving sandstone markers in the 1810s, as evidenced by signed stones in Middlesex and Somerset Counties (see the Elbert Van Coff stone in St. Peter's Episcopal Churchyard in Spotswood by Henry and the Jane Perlee stone in the Hillsborough Reformed Churchyard in Hillsborough by Isaac). Henry was the more prolific of the two carvers, working first in sandstone and then in marble. By the 1820s he was located in New Brunswick, where in 1825 he carved his father's tombstone, noting below the epitaph that the stone was "Erected by his son/Henry Sillcocks/(New Brunswick)" (Sillcocks family papers, Cranbury Historical and Preservation Society). His father was buried in the Cranbury Presbyterian Cemetery, where numerous other Sillcocks-produced markers can be found, some carved with willows and urns. To continue the legacy, Henry's son James Hull Sillcocks, who was born in 1820, took over the business along with his brother Gabriel (born 1822) when their father died in 1846. The New Brunswick city directory for 1855 lists James and Gabriel's marble shop on 51 Neilson Street near the Reformed Church of New Brunswick and the Episcopal Christ Church. Central New Jersey cemeteries are filled with a vast array of markers in different styles signed by James. In contrast, Gabriel did not sign his work and may have produced markers that are signed simply "Sillcocks" or "Sillcocks and Co." as the firm became known by the 1860s. The two brothers used practically every design device in their work, including broken rosebuds for children's markers, floral wreaths, Catholic iconography, upward-pointed hands, and an unusual deeply modeled hand holding an hourglass set against a sunset for Aaron and Ann Tindall in 1869 at the Reformed Church Cemetery in Spotswood. The company's crowning achievement was created near the end of their careers, when they carved the Applegate and Reed family monuments in the Hightstown Presbyterian Cemetery. The plots contain marble headstones and urns as well as two tall, tapered shafts heavily carved with grape leaves.

Around 1876 the Sillcocks company was sold to Edward E. and Charles Kilbourn, who were manufacturing markers and monuments into the late 1880s. James died on October 25, 1880, ending the long legacy of the Sillocks family carvers. He was buried near his father in the Sillcocks family plot in Willow Grove Cemetery in New Brunswick. After decades of carving creative monuments, the family is memorialized with the simplest of gravestones.

New Brunswick was also home to another family of gravestone carvers—brothers Benjamin and James Langstaff. Signed examples of their work appear in the early 1830s and in 1835 Benjamin was paid $22 for a headstone for Peter Runyon (Middlesex County unrecorded estate papers, reel 88, #18222). Their shop was purchased around 1883 by Millstone carver Peter Wakeham, who had moved his operation to New Brunswick about a decade earlier (1883 New Brunswick city directory; Talbott and Blood 1866). The brothers worked primarily in marble but also carved in sandstone. Among their early sandstone examples is the 1845 Henry Blackwell monument in the Lamington Presbyterian Cemetery.

Other New Brunswick carvers of the early nineteenth century include William Brookfield, John Frazee, and Hugh Webster. Brookfield was in business for about a decade, starting in the mid-1820s. He produced several signed tombstones and at least one church wall plaque at the Christ Church Episcopal in New Brunswick. Brookfield is also documented in probate records for Middlesex County. Records exist of payments for stones in 1825 and in 1831, when he was paid $29.47 for a headstone for Elizabeth Runyon (Middlesex County unrecorded estate papers, reel 88, #18177).

Rahway carver John Frazee had a gravestone-carving shop in New Brunswick in 1813, when he joined in partnership with William Dunham (Wasserman 1972, 20). Signed markers by him are rare. Among the few are the Catherine Neilson marble monument at Van Liew Cemetery and the sandstone marker for Johannes Vanliew in the Three Mile Run Burial Ground, signed "Frazee & Co." Webster left an even smaller trace of his work. Two known examples signed by him are the 1817 sandstone marker for Francis Hagaman in the Lamington Presbyterian Cemetery and the 1818 marble gravestone for Alcha Kline in the Readington Reformed Cemetery.

By the time of the Civil War, George Eldridge was operating a marble shop in New Brunswick and by 1886 William Clinton had opened a steam-powered marble and granite works near the entrance of Elmwood Cemetery. The Clinton Monument Company remains in business today, operated in South Brunswick under the direction of Ronald Nelson.

In addition to New Brunswick, carvers were operating in other areas of Middlesex County as well. C. P. Osborn, a possible descendant of Henry Osborn, was carving markers in Woodbridge by 1850, but a decade later was no longer in business (Kirkbride 1850; Boyd 1860). In Perth Amboy William P. Dally was among the early carvers, having opened a shop around 1866.

Bridgewater and Somerville supported the stone-carving trade in Somerset County, where locally quarried sandstone was used extensively in the early nineteenth century. A. Wallace, originally from New Brunswick, was among the early-nineteenth-century carvers in this area. Wallace carved a number of gravestones that can be found in the Bound Brook Presbyterian Cemetery as well as the Stelton Baptist Churchyard in Edison, where he signed a gravestone "A. Wallace Bridgewater." Wallace was one of the earliest to use urn motifs on his gravestones. Urns were sculpted by a number of anonymous carvers in central New Jersey with varying degrees of skill. Wallace's urns display a higher level of craftsmanship, as seen in the Garret Garretson gravestone in the Bound Brook Presbyterian Cemetery. Dated 1810, the marker is decorated with a carved urn and a flame that represents eternal life.

Jacques Vanderbeek opened a marble shop in Somerville in the 1840s, which was in operation into the 1870s, when one can still find signed markers by him in area cemeteries. In Millstone Peter Wakham was also carving marble gravestones in the 1840s. He was listed as a marble worker in the 1866 *New Jersey State Business Directory*, moving his shop shortly afterward to New Brunswick. Wakham did not sign many of his markers, but it is clear that he was working in a large geographic region, as known examples can be found as far south as the Blaw-Nevius Cemetery in Blawenburg.

Isaac Meeker was among the other gravestone carvers working in Somerset County. He was carving gravestones in Summit by 1866, but was apparently operating as early as the 1830s, as evidenced by the Elizabeth Doughty

5.17 The monument to Albert White in Milford's Union Cemetery combines both marble and sandstone elements. The urn and tablatures are marble while the base is sandstone.

marker from 1838 in the Basking Ridge Presbyterian Cemetery and a signed marker from 1833 in Madison's Bottle Hill Cemetery.

In Hunterdon County, Flemington and Lambertville developed as areas of gravestone-carving activity. In addition to the in-county carvers, workers in Easton, Pennsylvania, also supplied markers to cemeteries in Hunterdon County. Lambertville, nestled along the Delaware River, developed as a center of marble carving in the nineteenth century. Among the more prolific and earlier carvers in Lambertville was A. H. Miller, whose signed markers can be found in cemeteries all along the Delaware River. Although Miller is not listed in the 1850, 1860, or 1866 New Jersey business directory, he was certainly in operation during the period between 1847 and 1878, as signed examples clearly show. In addition to Lambertville, Miller apparently was also working in Frenchtown, where in 1869 he carved the David Coughlin marker at the Union Cemetery in Milford. Miller carved a number of marble tablet markers on bases and, in addition, created at least two unique monuments combining both brown sandstone and marble. The 1872 marker for Albert White in the Union Cemetery in Milford has a marble shield mounted on the side of a square brown sandstone base (fig. 5.17). A heavily carved three-foot-tall marble urn rests on the top of the base. The urn is partially draped and a garland of flowers graces the front, then drops along the side. Miller's second example is the Mathews monument from 1871, situated in the Alexandria Presbyterian Cemetery. It has two marble tablatures anchored by iron rods into the brown sandstone base. The draped urn is similar in style to that of the White monument but features a more pronounced carved handle.

Other Lambertville carvers include J. A. Bachman, who was operating a marble shop on Main Street in 1866. Bachman carved a number of marble tablet markers on bases, which can be found in cemeteries throughout Hunterdon as well as parts of Somerset County. By the late 1870s the number of markers with Bachman's signature declined. At about the same time, C. A. Strauss opened his marble shop in Lambertville, creating both marble and granite markers.

Flemington in Hunterdon County also sustained marble carvers, including the team of Pollock and Bullock as well as D. J. Howell. J. Pollock was in partnership with E. R. Bullock, as signed examples from the late 1840s are marked Pollock and Bullock. By the mid-nineteenth century, D. J. Howell was listed as a marble worker in Flemington. Howell created both marble tablet markers on bases as well as monuments. An early example of his monumental work is the 1857 Sheppard family memorial in the Flemington Presbyterian Cemetery. It consists of a square marble base with a large shaft mounted by a draped urn. At each corner of the base are upside-down torches, symbols of an extinguished life. In addition to his shop in Flemington, Howell was also operating a shop in Morristown, Morris County, in 1860 and may have been in business in Clinton, Hunterdon County, in 1866 under the name Howell & Gregory. With two shops in operation, it is possible that Howell was the manager of a growing marble company, buying stock designs from marble quarries and using workers to letter them in his shops. By 1880 Howell seems to have opened another shop or may have moved to Easton in Pennsylvania, as later markers, including the Elizabeth Wilson granite marker in the Union Cemetery in Milford, are signed "D. J. Howell Easton."

In Whitehouse Station, Hunterdon County, Robert Bonnell and Gilbert Melick created numerous marble monuments in the late nineteenth century. Many of their signed examples are crafted from a blue vein of marble and topped with gables. Among their most notable works is the cradle grave Bonnell carved for his daughter Isabel in 1891 and the monument for Melick's wife, Jennie, and daughter Lizzie, who both died in 1881. The marble monument has a carved dove, an angel carrying a child, a winged hourglass, and a broken column. The square die, the portion that contains the family names, has carved columns on the marker's corners, the capitals of which are angels. A three-dimensional sculpted hand holding a bouquet of flowers sits on top of the monument. As if to reserve his place on the monument, Gilbert carved an image of a wooden mallet, a compass, a square, and two chisels—in 1931, under that motif, his name was added.

Hunterdon County also has markers produced in Easton, Pennsylvania. Andrew Allison, who had moved to Trenton by 1843, was operating in Easton as early as 1820. Allison's earliest documented marker, from 1827, was a marble gravestone for Thomas Balby in the Old Greenwich Presbyterian Cemetery. Other marble gravestones signed by Allison dating to the 1830s can be found in the Alexandria Presbyterian Cemetery. A cursory examination of probate records also shows payments to Allison for gravestones. An early documented payment for $23 was made in 1836 by an East Windsor estate for a "tomb stone for the widow" (Middlesex County unrecorded estate papers, box 914647, reel 1).

NORTHERN NEW JERSEY

The largest grouping of carvers resided in northern New Jersey—Essex, Union, Hudson, Passaic, Morris, Bergen, Warren, and Sussex Counties. Those in the urban areas of Newark and Elizabeth supplied a larger geographic region with first sandstone and later marble markers. Less skillfully carved markers produced in rural areas remained within a local region. In addition, some high-style monuments were supplied by out-of-state carvers, mainly from New York.

Essex County holds the distinction as the largest center of tombstone-carving activity in the state during the nineteenth century. In 1850 the number of carvers in that county was more than double that of the next largest (Kirkbride). The center of it all was Newark, where in the nineteenth century, much like the eighteenth century, a prolific group of carvers operated. They worked across a wide geographic area: stones from Newark can be found in cemeteries across the central and northern part of the state as well as other states, including North Carolina.

At the beginning of the nineteenth century, a number of carvers, most of whom have remained anonymous, were carving fully lettered tombstones, void of iconography, from locally quarried sandstone. By the 1820s several nicely carved gravestones signed "Schenck N.Ark" appeared in the area. Of note is the sandstone marker for Josiah Williams in the Orange Presbyterian Churchyard. The stone depicts a deeply modeled image of a willow over a stack of books that sit on a coffin. Little is known about Schenck, who does not appear in Newark's earliest city directory of 1835.

In the second quarter of the nineteenth century, the Grant family, possible descendants of Newark's prolific eighteenth-century carver William Grant, were actively involved in the stone-cutting trade. In 1835 William, Alexander, Wilcox, and Charles are all listed as stonecutters in the Newark city directory. The family operated their business on Quarry Street near High Street, supplying gravestones and building stone. Charles stood out as an active tombstone carver. By 1850 he was operating a carving shop at 107 Market Street and advertised himself as a "Manufacturer of Marble Mantles, Tables, Monuments, Tomb and Grave Stones, of the best Egyptian, Italian, and American Marbles, executed in the best modern Style." He also supplied "stone work for buildings, made to order, of Connecticut or Newark stone." Marble gravestones from the mid-nineteenth century signed by "C. Grant" have been documented in the Newark region (John Zielenski, personal communication). Grant appears to have closed his shop not long after 1860, as he disappears from the Newark city directories and is not listed in Talbott and Blood's 1866 *New Jersey State Business Directory.*

Newark carver Amos Wilcox was making gravestones in the 1830s and by 1840 was located at 140 Market Street, where he then advertised that he was a "Manufacturer of Marble Mantles, Monuments, Grave Stones, and wall plates." In 1860 he opened a studio at 30 Green Street, where two other Wilcoxes joined him: Joseph was listed as a monumental architect and Augustus as a "Sculptor and Carver in all its branches." The company was still in business in 1866, but by 1871 Amos, Augustus, and Joseph are no longer listed in the city directory.

By the 1870s and 1880s a number of large steam-powered marble and granite works were well established in Newark. Among the more notable was the workshop of William Passmore and John L. Meeker, which first opened about 1860. In 1871 they advertised their marble works at 192 Market Street. That same year J. J. Spurr, Gregory and Cox, and George Brown & Company were also operating steam-powered marble and granite works in the area. Brown's works were originally located on Market Street but later relocated to Bellville Avenue, opposite the entrance to Mount Pleasant Cemetery. Brown created a number of notable monuments, taking in a wide patronage. In 1862 and 1863 Brown was commissioned to create the Snowhill monuments at St. Peter's Episcopal Churchyard in Spotswood. The ornate mid-nineteenth-century monuments signed by Brown are a contrast to the locally produced gravestones of the same period. Brown also created the Fireman's Memorial monument in Mount Pleasant Cemetery (fig. 5.18) and in 1911 his son, A. Wallace, designed John Dryden's mausoleum, also at Mount Pleasant (Senkevitch 1986, sec. 7, 24).

However, the czar of nineteenth-century Newark tombstone carving was in fact appropriately named—Czar T. Duncomb. Duncomb was in operation around 1839 with George Timby at 46 Market Street, where they advertised that they were "Manufacturers of Marble Monuments, and Tombs of every description" (1839–1840 Newark city directory). Duncomb signed many examples of his work, from small gravestones to large monuments. In the 1840s and 1850s his dominant style was that of weeping willows draping over

5.18 Fraternal plots were common in nineteenth-century rural cemeteries.
The Fireman's Memorial at Mount Pleasant Cemetery in Newark is one such example,
which is surrounded by former Newark fire hydrants.

urns, which can be found in cemeteries throughout central and northern
New Jersey. In addition to his gravestones, Duncomb created monuments,
including the Smith family monument in the Orange Presbyterian Churchyard. Dated 1846, the marble memorial has a square base adorned with
upside-down torches. Duncomb was operating a marble-carving empire. He
initially operated his shop in Norwalk, Connecticut, where in 1838 he was
acting as a supplier of gravestones to Matthew Lawton, a Wilmington,
North Carolina, cabinetmaker and undertaker (Little 1998, 181). In 1840,
when he came to Newark, he was still shipping gravestones to North Carolina, including four with weeping willows and urns that he carved for the
Foy family graveyard in New Hanover County (182). In 1842, apparently
while still in business in Newark, he was operating a marble-carving shop in
Richmond, Virginia, where he or his assistants sculpted a ledger stone for
William Norwood in the Old Town Cemetery in Hillsborough, North Carolina (276). By the early 1850s Duncomb moved his operation from Newark,
ending almost a decade of work and leaving the New Jersey cemetery landscape with many examples of his craft.

   While Plainfield, Scotch Plains, and Rahway supported carvers in the
tombstone trade, in Union County, the city of Elizabeth had the largest
concentration of activity in the nineteenth century. Among the early carvers
was Noah Norris, who started his career carving sandstone markers at the

close of the eighteenth century. On January 7, 1800, he was paid $10.12 for a headstone for Nathaniel Norris in the Westfield Presbyterian Cemetery (Essex County unrecorded estate papers, reel 2–20, file 189). Carving in both sandstone and marble, Norris used neoclassical designs for his marble markers, carving large urns and willows that appear to be inspired by church wall plaques of the same period. Norris's marble markers can be found in the Basking Ridge Presbyterian Cemetery as well as the Connecticut Farms Cemetery, where he signed several "N. Norris Elizabethtown." He continued to carve markers into the early decades of the nineteenth century. In 1850 John Norris, possibly Noah's son, was carving markers in Elizabeth and by 1869 was joined by other newly opened businesses, including those of George McGhee at 192 Broad and George Stead at 18 Chestnut. All three were still in business in 1873, when three other tombstone carvers opened workshops, bringing the total number to six. Norris was in business in 1880 but just three years later disappeared from city directories, while both Stead and McGhee continued their work into the early 1900s (Elizabeth city directories).

In Plainfield, the Manning shop was in operation for over 135 years, with Lebeus Manning carving marble tombstones dating back to the mid-nineteenth century. In 1869 his business was located on Front Street opposite Laing's Hotel (Elizabeth city directory, Plainfield section, 1869). By the late nineteenth century the business switched from marble to granite, catering to a wide clientele, including Germans who had settled in the Watchung Mountains. Several markers at the Trinity United Church in Warren have German epitaphs. Among them are the granite markers for George and Anna Pabst. The two large headstones are mounted on a single base and the epitaphs are entirely in German. By the 1910s the company was known as L. L. Manning & Son. It ceased operation in the 1990s.

In the mid-nineteenth century Andrew Vanderbeek also operated a marble shop in Plainfield. He is first listed in the 1860 *Boyd's Business Directory*, but was apparently in business earlier as signed stones date back to the 1840s. His relationship with Somerville carver Jacques Vanderbeek has yet to be researched. In the 1870s stones signed simply "Vanderbeek" can be found halfway between Somerville and Plainfield, further compounding the issue of who was carving what.

In Rahway the historic Rahway Cemetery contains a wonderful collection of gravestones made from sandstone as well as later marble markers. Among the carvers with works in the cemetery is Aaron Ross, who in 1803 advertised in the *Guardian or New Brunswick Advertiser* that "in Rahway [he] continues to carry on his business in its different branches." Another local carver was sculptor John Frazee, who was born in the city in 1790. Several signed stones from the 1810s can be found in the cemetery, including the Hannah Terrill marker from 1813 that he signed "Frazee. Engr." [Engraver].

In 1860 marble carver Abraham Abbott was located on Main and Commerce and J. Jardine had his shop on St. Georges above Mechanic Street. Jardine's business had been founded that year and in 1869 was operated by Thomas Jardine (Elizabeth city directory, Rahway section, 1869). The company continued its business into the early 1900s on St. Georges Avenue, near Grand Street, just north of the Merchants and Drovers Tavern; in addition, Jardine had opened a shop across the street from Evergreen Cemetery in Elizabeth.

For Hudson County it was Jersey City and Hoboken that hosted an active tombstone-carving trade. Among the early active carvers in Hoboken was Chris Gregory, whose operation was located at 2 Washington Street in 1866. Jersey City supported a larger number of workers in stone, although most were dealers or stone cutters and may not necessarily have been in the tombstone-carving business but rather the building trade. In 1850 there were at least three carvers in Jersey City, including Alexander Wilson, Wm. & T. Browne, and C. B. Edison. By 1857 Thomas Royle was listed in the Jersey City directory as a stone worker with a full-page advertisement stating that "he is prepared to furnish MARBLE, or any other kind of Stone suitable for building. . . . Monuments and Grave Stones, go out to order, at the shortest notice." Around 1860 James Dickson, James Key, and James Orr were all listed as marble workers in Jersey City. Dickson's became one of the larger monument firms and by the late nineteenth century was a major supplier of large granite monuments for area cemeteries.

By 1890 there were four marble and granite works in Jersey City, including those of Dickson, William Gahagan, and Martin A. Adams (1890 Jersey City directory). Gahagan was born in Pennsylvania and came to Jersey City in 1870, first working for Dickson. In 1882 he opened his own business, which continued into the 1910s (Historical Publishing Co. 1883, 851; Jersey City directories).

Martin Adams was perhaps New Jersey's most colorful monument dealer. Throughout the late 1800s and into the early 1900s, his advertisements proudly proclaimed him "the monument maker" and were sometimes peppered with catchy descriptions and a poem (Jersey City directories) (fig. 5.19).

> In presenting my claims for recognition
> I hope you will carefully read my petition;
> I have selected this space to solicit some trade
> And tell of some beautiful Monuments I've made,
> Tombs, Tablets, Sarcophagi, Head and Footstones too,
> Please give me an order to erect one for you;
> For I keep them in every conceivable style—
> Both ancient and modern, from here to the Nile;
> In Gothic, Corinthian, through renaissance came.
> Mark you the result—my gigantic monumental name;

5.19 Martin Adams was an eccentric monument dealer in Jersey City.
His shop was located across from the entrance to Holy Name Cemetery.
This 1905 advertisement published in the Jersey City directory illustrates Adams' business.
(Reproduced with permission from the Jersey City Public Library.)

> I am famed for my knowledge of art and the trade,
> Though all my vast stock is strictly home-made,
> From the very best quarries all over this land,
> And I am fully prepared to supply the demand.
> In Granite or Marble, for cash, credit, on time,
> I invite all to buy one—they are simply sublime;
> And study this all the way through, in each part,
> Where my business and pleasure commingle with art;
> Quick sale is my motto and at rock bottom price,
> I proclaim that it beats every other device
> In gaining one's friendship, their patronage and trade,
> Now, please excuse me, for I have quite enough said.
>   (1899–1900 Jersey City directory, 68)

Adams was born in Ireland in 1847 and was operating his monument works in Jersey City in the late nineteenth century. His 1898 advertisement explained his location: "If you don't know where 'I'm at,' go stand in front of the Catholic Cemetery gate, on Westside Avenue, near Montgomery Street, Jersey City, face towards the east, as your ancestors are faced" (1898 Jersey City directory, 67). Facing east was an apparent reference to eighteenth-century burials, which were sometimes oriented east so the soul would rise facing the morning sun on Judgment Day. The Catholic cemetery he refers to is Holy Name Cemetery, where signed examples of his granite monuments can be found. Adams was a successful businessman and by 1916 he was reputed to have been a millionaire, with monuments in cemeteries not only in the United States but also in Europe (*Jersey Journal*, January 3, 1916). Also active in charitable organizations, Adams stated that "I hope before the final

5.20 Martin Adams erected his own monument in 1916, more than ten years before his death. Made with columns salvaged from the old Astor House in New York City, it stands sixty-three feet tall in Holy Name Cemetery, Jersey City.

call comes to further help our various local charitable enterprises." In 1916 Adams erected his crowning achievement—his own massive monument in Holy Name Cemetery (fig. 5.20). The extraordinary memorial is almost sixty-three feet tall and was made with salvaged granite columns from the Astor House in New York City. The upper portion of the monument consists of a large granite cross that is perched atop a thirty-foot column (*Jersey Journal*, January 3, 1916). A massive granite base supports the column and four carved Carrara marble statues. Martin Adams died eleven years later on July 20, 1927, by which time his creations, including his own monument, surely solidified his claim to the title "the monument maker."

Paterson was the center of carving activity in Passaic County. In 1829 Benjamin Crane opened a marble works there and between 1838 and 1863 he was in business with Abraham Garrison at 199 Main Street (Lanza 1997, 12; Boyd 1860). Benjamin's son Alfred joined in partnership with his father in 1866 (Historical Publishing Co. 1883, 980) and the firm continued under the name Crane & Son. Markers and monuments produced by the company can be found in a wide geographic region with examples in Bergen, Passaic, and Morris Counties.

Samuel Langstaff was operating a marble shop in Paterson by 1857, when his location is listed in the city directory as 13 Main Street. By 1866 James Langstaff was operating the business at 90 River Street (Talbott and Blood 1866). James was born in Newton in Sussex County and moved to Paterson in 1853 (Historical Publishing Co. 1883, 974). The firm continued to carve markers into the late 1800s, with a notable example, the Zeliff marker, in Pompton Plains, Pequannock Township, in Morris County. The undated marker for Willie, Lizzie, and Mamie Zeliff is a marble tablet stone on a base and has two birds carved on the top face of the stone with one bird drinking from an urn.

Of all Paterson's carvers, the Bamber family was the most prolific, operating their shop over several generations from 1839 to 1951 (Lanza 1997, 12–13). David Bamber started the family business of carving stones in 1839 and almost ten years later moved his marble works to 34 Willis Street (12). His son William entered the stone-carving business in 1867. When David died in 1875, William was faced with the challenge of taking over the business, as well as commemorating his father. For his father's monument he broke away from the traditional tombstone styles and chose instead to carve a life-size marble statue of the man. The full-size figure of the elder Bamber stands proudly atop the monument, looking forward, with the tools of his trade in his hand—the mallet and chisel. His shirt sleeves are rolled up, he wears a brimmed hat, and an apron keeps his double-breasted coat clean. Although the base of the pedestal on which he stands describes him as "at rest," Bamber's eternal pose suggests anything but that. He appears ready at any moment to take a customer's order and carve another tombstone. The impressive monument was included in an advertisement for the Bamber Marble Works in the 1877 *Atlas of Passaic County* (fig. 5.21). The drawing illustrates the company buildings, including the office, with a wide selection of markers in front of the shop. Among them, proudly displayed, is the father's monument. The son can be seen in the drawing, standing in the doorway of the office, gazing at his work. Although the advertisement does not convey William's emotions, one can wonder. He must have been proud of his work, for the statue would have started as an unformed block of marble, with William looking it over and imagining the finished product. As he worked with the mallet and chisel to rough out the figure of his father, did he

5.21 This drawing, published in the 1877 *Atlas of Passaic County*, illustrates the Bamber company
buildings, including the office, with a wide selection of markers in front of the shop.
Among the items displayed is the monument made by William Bamber for his father.
William can be seen in the drawing standing in the doorway of the office, gazing at his work
(*Passaic County Atlas*, 1877).

reminisce about his adolescence, when his father first placed a mallet and
chisel in his hands? As he shaped the features, did he realize that his father's
skills lived on in his hands? One can certainly speculate, but either way the
Bamber monument was unique. In 1883 it was remarked that "this piece of
sculpture has been looked upon and examined by a large number of people,
and pronounced . . . to be of the best and finest workmanship of a native
artist . . . and is a worthy tribute of a dutiful son" (Historical Publishing Co.
1883). Today the Bamber monument can still be seen at Cedar Lawn Cemetery in Paterson. Although the facial features have worn with time, one can
still appreciate William's skill and feel the powerful emotion of a son commemorating his father (fig. 5.22).

   In the northeast corner of the state lies Bergen County, where in 1866 P.
Byrne & Company opened a marble shop in Hackensack. The business,
located on Main Street, carved "Monuments, Tombstones . . . Mural Tablets,
and all other Monumental Work, after new, original, and classic designs."
Byrne continued to carve markers into the 1870s, with signed examples in the
Harrington Park Old Burial Ground and the Woodside Cemetery in
Dumont. The Campbells also operated an early tombstone-carving business.
Signing his work with his initials in both uppercase and lowercase letters, A.
A. Campbell started in the 1830s, carving simple sandstone markers that can
be found in cemeteries throughout Bergen County. Campbell transitioned to
marble by the 1840s and the company continued creating memorials into the
late nineteenth century.

5.22 The monument for marble gravestone carver David Bamber is located at Cedar Lawn Cemetery in Paterson. Carved by his son William in 1875, it shows the elder Bamber with a mallet and chisel.

Among the early-nineteenth-century carvers in Morris County was Leonard Schureman, who had a marble shop in Morristown. Schureman was carving gravestones in the second quarter of the nineteenth century, using weeping willow and urn motifs that can be found on markers in Whippany and at the First Congregational Church in Chester. Schureman formed partnerships with D. J. Howell in the 1850s and Stiles by 1860, but is no longer listed as a marble carver in 1866 (Talbott and Blood). By the time of the Civil War, the firm of Dougherty and Davis had opened a shop in Morristown. They appear to have dissolved their partnership at an early point, but continued to carve markers independently, as signed examples in the Bishop Jane/Evergreen Cemetery in Basking Ridge attest.

During the second quarter of the nineteenth century, Warren County in the northwest part of the state became home to well-carved markers from Easton, Pennsylvania. Both Phillipsburg and Greenwich have numerous signed markers and monuments by Easton carvers. Among them was J. Pollock, whose work can be seen at the Greenwich Presbyterian Cemetery. In 1848 he carved the square-cut gravestone for Susanna Shimer. The marker has an oval tablature with floral designs at each corner. In addition, in the same cemetery, a worn 1850 marble monument with upside-down torches on the base was signed by another Easton carver.

Other sections of Warren County supported local carvers. In 1850 J. W. Wright was listed as a marble dealer in Hackettstown. By the 1860s other carvers were operating there as well. Among them were Cramer and Ward, who signed a gravestone for a member of the Apgar family in 1862. Later, in 1866 Cramer was in business with G. A. Yawger (Talbott and Blood). Yawger was a prolific carver operating in different locales, including Belvidere and Somerville, and in 1881 he was the manager of the Newark Marble Works at 572 Broad Street in Newark (1881–1882 Newark city directory). The Yawger company is still in operation today, across the street from the entrance to Evergreen Cemetery in Morristown, but unfortunately, according to office staff, does not have any records of their early history.

The town of Washington in Warren County also sustained marble carvers, with Jacob Fitts among the earliest. Fitts created five impressive monuments for the Lomerson family plot in the Mansfield Woodhouse Presbyterian Church Cemetery in Washington. Dating to the late 1830s, three of the monuments are square blocks on double bases with a capstone on which is an open Bible. In addition, Fitts carved two identical smaller monuments for children, substituting a sleeping lamb for the Bible. He signed one of the monuments "Jacob Fitts, Marble Works Washington N.J."

By 1860 Josiah E. Lynn had opened a monument shop in Washington and was still in operation by the close of the nineteenth century. Lynn carved a number of marble markers and monuments that can be found in area cemeteries. By the late nineteenth century he had switched to granite and created several large, impressive granite monuments, with notable examples for the Hann and Wycoff families in the Washington Cemetery Association in Washington.

Sussex County in the northwest corner of the state supported an early marble-carving trade in Newton. Daniel Baker was in operation primarily in the 1840s. Several of his stones include an upward-pointing hand, a motif that can be found in the Old Clove Cemetery, Wantage Methodist Cemetery, and Deckertown-Union Cemetery. Baker was no longer working in Newton by the time Charles Crook opened a shop in the late 1850s. In Deckertown, monument dealer A. T. Wolfe produced monuments and headstones from the 1870s into the 1890s. In the more rural parts of Sussex County, away from the primary area of carving activity, professionally crafted markers were shipped into the region, including some signed examples from carvers in Goshen, Port Jervis, and Ridgeberry in New York State, dating back to the 1810s.

The nineteenth century was a period of great evolution in the carving trade. Marble carvers were transformed into monument dealers as markers evolved into monuments. The artisans that created these memorials have long since joined those they commemorated, but leave their legacy behind in countless cemeteries filled with their handiwork. These stones give testament to the work of the Bambers, Sillockses, Wards, Lyons, Mannings, and countless others, including Martin Adams, who invited all to buy one because— "they are simply sublime."

« 6 »

New Technology, New Tools

The Professionalization of the Monument Industry

All the latest improved machinery including pneumatic tools
for carving and lettering.

~ Letterhead, O. J. Hammell Monument Co., c. 1902 ~

The late nineteenth and early twentieth centuries marked a period of great change in the monument industry. Marble, which was the primary material, was being replaced with a more durable stone—granite. The rise in the use of granite in the industry paralleled advances in new technology and tools. New Jersey monument companies found it necessary to update their equipment in order to keep a competitive edge. This chapter will explore the use of granite and the relationship between granite suppliers and New Jersey monument dealers. In addition, the new tools and equipment will be discussed. The chapter will conclude with a cross-section of the markers that make up the granite landscape.

In 1902 Pleasantville monument dealer Oliver J. Hammell was busy filling customer requests for markers. He had placed large orders with a number of stone quarries in Vermont and Massachusetts for both raw granite and finished monuments. The Jones Brothers Quarry in Barre, Vermont, wrote him that year, asking if he was satisfied with the sarcophagus they had shipped (Hammell box 1, folder 1/6). The Guilford & Waltersville Granite Company sent him a postal card informing him that his order number 112, for three pieces of rough granite, was shipped in train car number 4361 on the Baltimore & Ohio Southwestern Railroad (Hammell box 1, folder 1/5). Another letter from the same company mentioned that a second order of stone had to be sent by a drop-end gondola railcar since the company could not get a flat car.

In addition to his monument business, Hammell was the superintendent of the Atlantic City Cemetery. Although this probably benefited his business, which was conveniently located near the front entrance gates to the cemetery, he still had to contend with the daily operations of running a burial ground. In 1902 local funeral director J. P. Crowley wrote him asking to "please bury this still birth child and charge to my account" (Hammel box 1, folder 1/4). In a society where segregation affected both the living and the dead, Crowley added a line mentioning that the child was white.

But 1902 was no ordinary year for Hammell's company. The firm, which had been in business since 1867, was preparing for the twentieth century. In order to stay competitive in the new granite market, it had to invest in new technology and new tools. In August of 1902 Hammell placed an order with the Fairmount Machine Company for, among other things, a line shaft, clutch couplings, pulleys, and a mandrel for a grindstone. The purchase of line shafts and pulleys would enable him to run his equipment with the aid of leather belts connected to a modern gasoline engine. In order to keep his engine in top working order, he purchased from the E. F. Houghton & Co., on Somerset Street in Philadelphia, one barrel of "Cosmolubric No. 20 Engine & Machinery Oil" (Hammell box 1, folder 1/6).

From the H. G. Kotten Company Hammell purchased the latest pneumatic tools. These tools were the most recent development in the industry and made carving into granite easier. The pneumatic tools were linked to rubber hoses that were connected to a compressed air tank. The compressed air drove the pneumatic chisels, similar to the workings of a jack-hammer. The compressed air tank was connected to the line shafts and finally the power source—the gasoline engine. This new equipment enabled the chisels to carve lettering and other designs into the surface of granite. In addition, air compressors also drove sandblasting equipment. After a rubber stencil was placed over the surface of the marker, sand or metal shot was placed under extreme pressure and then blasted at the stone. The sand bounced off the rubber, with the exception of the areas cut out for the decoration or lettering.

In order to properly house his equipment, Hammell constructed new buildings, including a main building that measured 24 feet wide by 157 feet long. His new gasoline engine was housed in an additional room that was twenty-four square feet. In order to facilitate the delivery of granite from out-of-state quarries, a rail line extended from the main line of the West Jersey & Seashore Railroad and entered the main building. Once inside, the stone was lifted by a crane for processing. Hammell spared no expense in outfitting his company's entire operation. Once the new equipment was installed, he turned to the company's office, redecorating it "in the most improved style." With the firm almost refitted, a local newspaper proclaimed that "the Company can pride themselves on having the best equipment and up to date plant when finished that exists in New Jersey." By the fall of 1902 Hammell's new monument company was finished with "all the

6.1 In the late nineteenth century granite quarries in the New England state began to expand as new technology made it easier to quarry and ship the material. Barre, Vermont, was a center of production. Shown here are the quarries located there in 1904.

latest improved machinery" for the twentieth century (Hammell MG 1208 index file).

Rock of Ages: The Granite Revolution

It is difficult to imagine anything more beautiful than the polished surfaces of Rock of Ages Monuments.
> ~ How to Choose a Family Memorial,
> *Rock of Ages Corporation, 1949* ~

Granite was introduced into the cemetery landscape as New England granite quarries were rapidly growing, aided by new ways of quarrying, finishing, and transporting the material. By the second half of the nineteenth century, granite quarries and manufacturing centers could be found throughout the New England states. In Vermont the granite industry was centered in the town of Barre, where quarries had been established and in limited use since the early nineteenth century. It was technology that enabled the granite trade to blossom, as newly developed compressed-air drills and larger derricks were placed in operation at the quarries (fig. 6.1). Some of the new derricks in

6.2 By the early 1900s New Jersey monument shops began to resemble granite stone yards.
The Will Hope & Son Monument Company in Burlington City, shown here around 1925,
displays the latest granite markers. Many of these stones were produced as blanks
by New England quarries.
(Reproduced with permission from Will Hope & Son Monument Co.)

Barre were outfitted with wire cables and gears, and could lift up to eighty
tons of stone (*Granite, Barre, Vermont, USA* 1904). Once taken from the ground,
the granite was sent to finishing sheds, where pneumatic tools and polishing
machines transformed the raw material into cemetery monuments.

Another defining factor in the rise of granite was an improved transportation system. Not only did technology provide the means to produce a
finished product but a rail system provided the means to transport it to the
customer. In Barre train service was first established to the town, then
directly to the quarries. By 1904 this quarry rail line was servicing more than
sixty quarries with thirty miles of track. Trains became the main form of
transportation, with special railcars built to transport large slabs of granite
throughout the United States. New Jersey monument dealers, with rail connections to the New England states, began to resemble granite stone yards
by the early 1900s (fig. 6.2).

By the early 1900s new quarries were discovered in other areas of the
United States as well, adding to the granite craze. In Georgia at the turn of
the twentieth century, deposits were discovered in the northeastern Piedmont region between Savannah and the Broad River. Stretching for twenty-
five miles in length and spanning fifteen miles in width, it was described
by geologists as the Lexington-Oglesby Blue Granite Belt (Granite, www.
georgiaencyclopedia.org). The city of Elberton grew around the industry
and became a production center, shipping monuments to other parts of the
country.

Carving markers by hand with mallet and chisel was now a thing of the
past. The modern way of doing business with mechanized pneumatic tools
and other machinery had arrived. In order not to fall behind, the monument

dealer had to invest in this new equipment. During the third quarter of the nineteenth century, the investment was in steam-powered machinery to cut and polish stones. It was the age of the steam marble and granite works. The Newark city directory of 1871 lists the steam marble works of William Passmore and John L. Meeker at 192 Market Street, and that of 1881 contains an advertisement for George Brown and Company's "Steam Cutting and Polishing Works." Across the state monument dealers were equipping their shops with the latest steam-powered technology.

As the century progressed, gasoline engines replaced steam. Stationary and portable gasoline engines along with air compressors aided monument work. Rubber stencils were placed over the face of the granite marker and the design was sandblasted into the surface of the granite. In 1924 the Alexander McDonald Company in Trenton, located at the gates of River View Cemetery, enlarged their operations to accommodate the latest equipment in the industry. The company had been in business since 1856, when Alexander McDonald came to the United States from Scotland and established a stone-cutting business opposite the gates of Mount Auburn Cemetery in Cambridge, Massachusetts. In 1885 the company branched out and established shops in Paterson, New Jersey, and by 1898 at the gates of Riverview Cemetery in Trenton (*Observer*, April 1930). By 1939 it reported that the greatest changes in the business were the use of sandblasting equipment and portable air compressors in the cemetery (*Trenton Magazine*, July 1939).

The latter had been developed in the late nineteenth century by a number of engine firms. Among them were the Fairbanks and Morse Company, which in 1898, under the direction of James A. Charter and Frank Hobart, had developed a combination gasoline engine and air compressor (Wendel 1993, 115). The following year they took out a patent and by the 1920s the firm was producing both stationary and portable air compressors (118). Other companies supplied the industry as well; an early 1900s trade publication lists thirteen distributors of air compressors and engines (New York Granite Co. 1906, 32). The development of the portable gasoline engine and air compressor made monument inscription more efficient. The equipment was mounted on a truck or wagon and taken directly to the cemetery. Long rubber hoses connected to the compressor were linked with pneumatic tools or sandblasting equipment. Additional names and designs on family monuments could be inscribed in the cemetery.

The use of new tools was one aspect of the professionalization of the modern monument industry. The production of promotional literature and trade magazines by granite quarries and manufacturing companies was another. New Brunswick monument dealer William Clinton received a copy of *Useful Hints for the Monumental Man*. Published in 1906 by the New York Granite Company, the brochure offered advice on how to construct monument foundations and find the right proportions for an obelisk as well as an explanation of the differences between domestic and imported granites. The thirty-two-page brochure also listed numerous suppliers to the industry.

Several trade associations developed in the granite-manufacturing regions to regulate prices and promote the industry. In Vermont in the 1890s the Barre Granite Manufacturers Association, later renamed the Barre Granite Association, was formed. This conglomeration of granite companies looked for ways to consolidate and promote the granite trade. In 1914 the Boutwell, Milne and Varnum Corporation asked a Burlington, Vermont, advertising agency to come up with a slogan to better market the stone. From that came the "Rock of Ages" trademark, a term that had so much success that by 1925 they had renamed their company the Rock of Ages Corporation. By 1930 the company had purchased an additional ten firms and consolidated the way the material was quarried and processed (Clarke 1989, 62). Today the Rock of Ages Corporation continues to be a leader in promoting the Barre granite industry. Monuments produced by the firm have a dime-sized "Rock of Ages" logo near the base of stone.

Granite works in other regions of the United States were following suit. In 1951 the granite companies in Elberton, Georgia, formed the Elberton Granite Association. Markers made by members of the association often bear the signature "EGA."

With a greater dependence on granite quarries, New Jersey monument dealers became middlemen, purchasing stock patterns from granite companies and inscribing them with sandblasted designs and lettering. They provided their customers with catalogs of countless marker types from which to choose a memorial. In 1908 A. L. Hammell visited George Bishop Jr. in Tuckerton with one such pattern book. George's wife, Sarah, had recently died and he was in the process of deciding which marker to purchase. Bishop wrote on April 7 of that year that "we have selected design No. 732 made in Westerly granite at the price of $60.00" (Hammell files).

The type of book George Bishop would have perused contained wonderful large photographs of monuments. Placed lower on the page was a number that corresponded to another book kept by the monument dealers. These estimating or price guide books provided the necessary specifications to order the monument from the granite company (fig. 6.3). If a customer wanted to add on special features, the monument dealer could readily access those designs in the booklets and figure the cost. Some monument dealers created their own stencils, which were carved onto granite blanks. In 1905 the O. J. Hammell Company carefully sketched out a design of a crown and cross from a printed pamphlet provided to them by a customer. In addition, the firm had many Jewish customers who would provide the company with carefully written-out Hebrew lettering. This made it easier for the designer to transcribe the letters into stencils without making a mistake (Hammell file box 61).

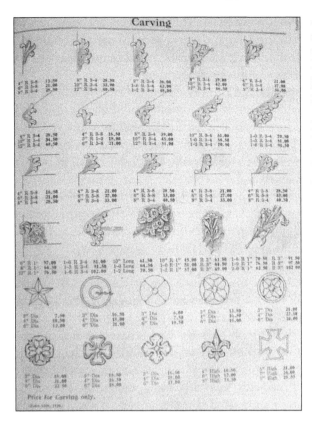

6.3 New Jersey monument dealers acted as middlemen connecting New England–quarried granite stones to a New Jersey customer base. This page from a 1921 estimating book enabled New Jersey monument dealers to calculate the cost of added designs on granite memorials. (Reproduced with permission from the Clinton Monument Company Inc.)

Today the monument industry operates in much the same way. Ronald Nelson of the Clinton Monument Company, an East Brunswick–based business, offers customers three finishes—"polished, frosted, and honed"—for the numerous styles and colors of granite monuments he sells. Speaking in a language that would have been understood a century earlier, he discusses the variation of finishes and how they are achieved. He operates a professional monument company today using the same methods that have been "polished and honed" over the last one hundred years.

New Jersey Granite Monuments

Those very goods I speak of are constantly on exhibition in the shape of beautiful Quincy Granite Monuments, Tablets, Headstones, and Fences, now for sale at ten percent below cost.

~ *Advertisement for monument dealer Martin A. Adams,*
1898–1899 Jersey City directory ~

Initially, the use of granite in New Jersey was limited to support bases for marble monuments. By the mid-nineteenth century granite bases can be

found in central and northern New Jersey, although there are some exceptions in the Newark and Elizabeth region, where brownstone was often utilized. In southern New Jersey early granite bases found limited use, as this
region was dominated by Philadelphia marble cutters.

Both New Jersey companies and out-of-state firms contributed to this
early use of granite. By the 1850s and 1860s a number of skillfully produced
monuments by New York carvers had utilized the material for support. Dudley & See, J. Sharkey, and Jas. Hart Jr., all New York carvers, created marble
monuments on granite bases at the Old Bergenfield South Church in Bergen
County and Cedar Lawn Cemetery in Paterson. Jas. Hart Jr. carved a marble
masterpiece in the Hightstown Cemetery in 1857. The Mary Fielder marker
featured carved upside-down torches, dimensional floral wreaths, and a
draped urn with additional floral decorations. The monument rises eight and
a half feet into the air and is supported by a square granite base.

Alongside out-of-state firms, New Jersey monument dealers also contributed to the granite landscape. In 1853 the Langstaff brothers, Benjamin
and James, carved the Sarah Blackwell marker at the Lamington Presbyterian
Cemetery. The square marble tablet marker has a scroll across the face and a
broken flower bud placed at the top. It sits on a marble base that is then supported by a granite base. The brothers were marble workers who had a shop
at 52 Neilson Street in New Brunswick (1855–1856 city directory). Mid-
nineteenth-century New Brunswick was a bustling center of commerce
whose burgeoning population supported the monuments trade. The city's
accessible rail and river location allowed the shipping of granite from the
quarries to the area. As the century progressed, other New Jersey stone
carvers, including J. A. Bachman and C. A. Strauss, two Lambertville carvers
of the 1870s and 1880s, utilized granite as a base material. The Samuel Brit-
ton marble marker at the Baptist Cemetery in Flemington, carved by Bachman in 1874, is supported by a granite base. At Mount Airy Cemetery in
West Amwell, Strauss erected a marble marker on a granite base for Lavinia
Larison in 1886.

By the time of the Civil War a first generation of granite memorials
appeared in New Jersey. Mainly in the form of obelisks and shafts, these
monuments were produced in the granite-rich regions of the New England
states. Concentrated in the urban Northeast, a number of examples can be
found at Mount Pleasant Cemetery in Newark. Among the earliest is the
1863 granite obelisk for Lewis Lindsly. Nearby the Bolles family monument
from 1865 was crafted by Batterson, Canfield & Company in Hartford, Connecticut. Under the direction of James G. Batterson, the firm was best known
for producing Civil War monuments that dot towns and battlefields across
the Northeast. By the 1870s, with technological advances in working granite,
obelisks and shafts gave way to sculpted granite masterpieces. The Onderdonk monument in Elmwood Cemetery in North Brunswick is one such

6.4 Many early granite memorials in New Jersey were produced by New England quarries. The Onderdonk monument at Elmwood Cemetery in North Brunswick was carved in 1877 by the Smith Granite Company of Westerly, Rhode Island.

example. Eleven and a half feet high, it commemorates members of a prominent New Brunswick family with ancient Dutch roots. Possibly erected after the death of Mary Onderdonk in 1877, the granite monument was crafted by the Smith Granite Company of Westerly, Rhode Island. The memorial features a stepped base with a die topped by a life-sized allegorical mourning figure (fig. 6.4). Carved in granite and draped in a classical flowing robe, she sits among lilies on a rock. Her hands are clasped and her head is cast downward with a sorrowful expression. Other Smith Granite Company monuments in New Jersey include the 1888 Barry sarcophagus in Cedar Lawn Cemetery in Paterson. Decorated with dentil work and rosettes, it was modeled after the Scipio sarcophagus of ancient Rome. Its location among the upper class in Cedar Lawn Cemetery betokened the wealthy status of Henry Adams Barry and his wife, Sarah Jane.

The Milford Granite Company in Milford, New Hampshire, had a hand in the production of the Henry L. Muhs monument, also in Cedar Lawn Cemetery. Henry was a sausage and bologna tycoon who immigrated to the United States from Germany in 1871. The monument was constructed for his son George, who died unexpectedly at the age of twenty-one in 1896. The Muhs monument includes a pedestaled urn covered by a canopy and supported by Corinthian columns. A statue of a neoclassical woman stands atop the canopy. She wears a long, flowing dress and glances downward with a mournful look. Her right hand is slightly extended and holds a flower as if ready to drop it on the grave. The New York City architectural firm of Hoffman & Prochazka designed and copyrighted the monument while New York sculptor Giuseppe Moretti carved the statue (Lanza 1997, 26).

Another outstanding early granite marker is that for Paul Tulane in the Princeton Cemetery. Like many other early New Jersey granite monuments, the Tulane memorial was produced in the New England states, with this example coming from P. Reinhalter & Co. in Quincy, Massachusetts. Paul Tulane was born in Princeton in 1801 and later operated a successful dry goods store in New Orleans. He became a wealthy businessman through such endeavors and made financial contributions to the university that now bears his name. He returned to Princeton, where he died in 1887. His granite monument features a life-sized statue of him perched atop a multi-massed base.

By the early 1900s granite was flowing into a sea of white marble and changing the color of the cemetery to various shades of gray, black, and pink. Although many New England firms contributed to the early emergence of granite, by 1900 other companies were producing monuments as well. The famous New York firm of Presbrey-Leland contributed heavily to the New Jersey cemetery landscape. Their 1952 publication titled *Commemoration: The Book of Presbrey-Leland Memorials* lists for the years 1900 to 1933 an estimated 4,800 New Jersey patrons, including 223 who commissioned mausoleums.

Frenchtown doctor William Finney was a customer of Presbrey-Leland, and commissioned them to construct a mausoleum as well as an impressive granite monument for his son. The Finney monument is located in the Frenchtown Cemetery on a rise overlooking a portion of the burial ground that contains typical granite markers. The monument commemorates William F. Finney, the son of Dr. William and Frances Finney. The inscription on William's monument states that he was born May 24, 1888, and in 1906 enlisted in the U.S. Army. The following year he died in a Jefferson Banks, Missouri, hospital of cerebrospinal meningitis. His monument features a stepped base, central die, capstone, and a large round ball placed on the top. Various shades of granite were utilized throughout the whole monument; gray and a rose granite were chosen for the stepped base, brown for the die, black for the capstone, and gray for the ball. A variety of images including stars, roses, a shield, a cannon, an eagle, and an American flag were carved on the base, die, and capstone, respectively. The die also contained biographical information, including Finney's cause of death. The front face of the monument has a three-foot-high relief carving of William in uniform standing at attention with rifle in hand. Another side of the monument bears an image of the facade of the hospital where he died (fig. 6.5).

As if the monument was not spectacular enough, the family erected a large "pillow"-type headstone at the front of the family plot. Although

6.5 While many granite memorials exhibit stock pattern book qualities, others are one of a kind. The Finney monument in the Frenchtown Cemetery is perhaps the most unusual. Dating from 1907, this masterpiece was made from different-colored granite and embellished with unique motifs, including the facade of the hospital where William Finney died and an image of a soldier in mourning.

carved from one block, the mass of the stone is broken up by tablet-shaped markers separated by sculpted hearts and clasped hands. The tablets bear the names of William and his mother and father. On one side of the stone is an urn with flowers; on the opposite is an image of a soldier, hat off, placing a flag that reads "Comrade" over a grave. There is an obelisk in the background and the branch of an oak tree spreads over the mourning scene.

The Finney monument was clearly not plucked from the pages of a monument catalog but is rather a one-of-a-kind memorial that was designed, crafted, and shipped to a small Delaware River town. It is a testament to the far-reaching impact granite had on the New Jersey cemetery.

By the 1870s New Jersey monument dealers were shifting from marble and offering granite monuments. They ordered stock finished markers or a mixture of raw materials from the granite belts. One such dealer was William Cox, who resided in Cranbury, but was part owner of the Gregory and Cox Marble Works in Newark. The company advertised in 1871 that they had "marble & granite monuments, tombs & headstones of the latest designs constantly on hand." That same year J. J. Spurr's Steam Marble Works in Newark advertised "marble mantels, monuments and headstones" as well as "worker[s] in granite" (Newark city directory). George Brown and Company, also of Newark, set up a monument works on Belleville Avenue opposite

Mount Pleasant Cemetery, where a number of their granite memorials can be found, including a $6,000 commission—the thirty-five-foot-high firemen's monument. Dedicated on June 13, 1888, it is a tribute to those who had served in the Newark Fire Department. From its four-sided pedestal, a tall shaft reaches up toward the sky; on top stands a fireman in full uniform (Senkevitch 1986, sec. 7, 17).

Granite was infiltrating all areas of the state. In 1877 marble carver William Bamber of Paterson was advertising his "Marble and Granite works" at 34 & 36 Willis Street (*Atlas of Passaic County* 1877). In Camden two monument dealers, Michael C. Lyons and Michael Reilly, were producing granite memorials. Lyons was first listed in the Camden city directory in 1877 along with his two sons, Andrew and Simon, and business partner, John Lyons. In 1890 the firm changed names to M. C. Lyons & Sons when John died (Camden city directory, see listing for Rose Lyons). That same year the firm advertised its marble and granite works and by 1900 was located across from Harleigh Cemetery. The company erected several large monuments at Calvary Cemetery in Cherry Hill as well as others in the Camden area. Its most northern documented example was commissioned in 1893 for the Cheeseman family in the Hightstown Cemetery.

Competitor Michael Reilly also appeared in the Camden city directory starting in 1877. His company was located across from the entrance to Evergreen Cemetery on Mount Ephraim Avenue and in 1900 was also advertising granite markers (Camden city directory). Michael died by 1919 and his wife, Margaret, was running the business into the mid-1920s (1919, 1920, 1926). In addition to his local work, Reilly was commissioned in 1893 to make the Alexander Haines monument in St. Andrew's Cemetery in Mount Holly.

In Trenton by the 1880s monument dealer Luther Ward was selling granite memorials. The shift from marble to granite must have been especially difficult for Luther, who had learned to carve marble tombstones from his father, also named Luther. The older Luther was born in New York in 1814 and set up a marble-carving shop in New Brunswick in the 1830s (U.S. Census Bureau 1870). By 1850 he relocated to East State Street in Trenton, where his son eventually took over the business. The younger Luther worked predominately in marble, with numerous signed examples located in cemeteries throughout Mercer, Burlington, and Somerset Counties. Late in his career Ward decided to shift his focus to granite. The company produced typical granite tablet markers with sandblasted filigree (signed examples). In 1887 he was commissioned to carve the simple Ellis marker in Crosswicks Cemetery. Other signed granite examples can be found in nearby cemeteries.

Many simple granite tablet markers were replacing marble by the late nineteenth century. G. A. Yawger, a Somerville monument dealer, produced one of this type in 1884 for John Ten Eick in the Lamington Presbyterian Cemetery. Yawger was also commissioned to erect a granite commemorative marker for the eighteenth-century Reverend Johannes Frelinghuysen in North Brunswick's Elmridge Cemetery in the late nineteenth century.

Thanks to the growing granite trade, by 1915 New Jersey monument dealers had a wide range of textures, styles, and colors to choose from. Their advertisements in the Jersey City directory that year expounded on the skill of their work. Dickson Brothers, prominent Jersey City dealers, informed the public that they were "designers and builders of monuments and vaults," offering "all kinds of granite, slate and marble work." Forty years earlier the word marble would have been the prominent first word in their advertisement, but by 1915 granite had changed the vocabulary of the stonecutter. J. Dickson produced a number of large and complex granite monuments in the Jersey City area, along with a massive forty-foot obelisk in Holy Sepulcher, Totowa. Holy Name Cemetery in Dickson's hometown of Jersey City contains numerous examples of his granite capabilities. Massive multisection monuments as well as granite plot enclosures are evident. Many of the enclosures have floral and sandblasted filigree as added ornamentation. By the 1920s granite had essentially replaced marble as the material of choice, turning New Jersey cemeteries into granite stone yards.

Simplicity and Dignity: The Modern Granite Memorial

Studied restraint and simplicity distinguish the design.
~ Description of George R. Russo's Design No. 114, Second Prize
Association of American Cemetery Superintendents, 1939 ~

While memorial parks restricted marker types, other cemeteries did not, and into the mid-twentieth century a variety of modern granite markers flowed into the cemetery landscape. Most, however, reflected the ideology of the period, when simplicity and dignity were the accepted style. In 1939 August C. Noll, writing in *Contemporaneous Memorial Designs*, stated that "refined simplicity has become the rule rather than the exception in memorial art." Modern markers stood as a "contrast to the heavy treatment which so long characterized [marker styles] in times past" (22).

That same year George R. Russo of Camden, New Jersey, won second prize from the Association of American Cemetery Superintendents for a marker whose style was typical of the period. Russo designed the Rose family memorial, a tall tablet marker, where "studied restraint and simplicity distinguish the design" (Noll 1939, 14). Naturalistic roses were carved at the base of the tablet and the family name appeared near the top. The absence of extraneous ornamentation across the marker's surface helped to ground the monument's simple design. Noll remarked of the memorial that "the elimination of confusing details or spots was characteristic of present-day

memorial design." With the change in the style of markers during the twentieth century, monument dealers looked to reinvent themselves. Some, like
George Russo, considered themselves a new breed of monument designer.
They would change the cemetery landscape visually and apply a new vocabulary to their trade. The monument was to become memorial art and the
dealer—memorial artist.

But memorial art was the exception in the modern cemetery, where rows
of simple rectangular granite tablets dominated the landscape. The tablets
often stand like rows of soldiers in the mid-twentieth-century cemetery, and
have continued as the main form of memorial in modern society. In 1923
Harry Bliss in *Modern Tablets and Sarcophagi* wrote, "Among the unostentatious
memorial forms the tablet has always been held in high esteem. So long and
severe has been its testing and so marked its growth in favor that there is no
possible question as to its place" (73). In 1939 August C. Noll in *Contemporaneous Memorial Designs* noted that "[t]he tablet tops honors as to popularity
among memorial types." Ten years later the Rock of Ages Corporation in
How to Choose a Family Monument showed various placements of tablet markers.
Customers could choose to have a rectangular tablet mounted on a base vertically or horizontally.

Other unique styles of tablet markers evolved in the 1920s, with the
screened or winged memorial as a direct descendant. In 1923 Bliss wrote that
the screen memorial was a modern development of the tablet marker, "one
which has grown in favor during recent years." The memorial consisted of a
central tablet with flanking wings or screens. For those tablet markers that
were mounted vertically, they acted as a buttress, giving a "new effectiveness
in the increased width which they furnish and the sense of support and aid
which they naturally suggest" (98). In addition, the screens provided for a
secluded plot and, as Bliss stated, the "memorial artist . . . mindful of the
need of protection and the wish for privacy . . . has created the screen memorial" (73). In 1939 William E. Brown of Clinton, New Jersey, offered a
screened design reflected in the Van Benschoten family marker. Crafted by
Johnson & Gustafson Company in Barre, Vermont, the horizontal tablet gave
a "sense of protection and privacy" (Noll 1939, 3). Unlike those of most
screened memorials, the wings were designed as one attached piece with a
"conventionalized flower motif" that gave the marker its individuality. Brown
also designed the Burns family marker, whose separate screens were personalized with carved lilies in a recessed panel.

The exedra, a memorial in the shape of a bench, also became popular
during the Classical Revivalism of the early twentieth century. "Its origin as
a memorial may be traced to the funeral banquets of antiquity when the exedra was used as a commodious seat," according to the Presbrey-Leland company (1952, 91). As early as 1919 the "Monument Dealers Manual" (Sample)
offered advice on how to incorporate plantings around an exedra using an

American or Oriental pyramidical, mountain laurel, and azaleas. In 1923 the Vermont Marble Company sold several examples, with the weightiest at 7,500 pounds. No. 1224 from their 1923 monument catalog cost $736 in a light Italian Rutland white marble. During the 1920s and 1930s the exedra gained limited popularity in New Jersey. Often purchased by upper-class families, several examples can be found in cemeteries throughout the state, including a family exedra in the Presbyterian Cemetery in Basking Ridge.

Like markers from the previous century, many monuments were based on classical designs, although often as refined examples of Roman, Greek, and Gothic architectural styles. The sarcophagus, which saw a resurgence in the late nineteenth century, had been transformed by 1940 into stone blocks devoid of any ornamentation. "The sarcophagus is returning into favor. But these memorials today little resemble the ponderous and awkward sarcophagi of yesterday" (Noll 1939, 20). According to the New York monument firm of Presbrey-Leland, which was commissioned to create the Oscar Kohn, Esq., sarcophagus in Orange, New Jersey, "During the last quarter of the nineteenth century it was decidedly the most prevalent of all memorials in our cemeteries—too often ponderous and over-elaborated." The Kohn sarcophagus was an example of the more "simplified in detail" form popular by mid-century. Although modern in appearance, the use of "Egyptian, Greek, Roman, Gothic, [and] Renaissance" styles helped to anchor it in classical design (Presbrey-Leland 1952, 79).

Flower receptacles reappeared in the 1920s and 1930s, though not as elaborate cast iron examples like those found in nineteenth-century cemeteries, but as simple stone receptacles. In 1923 Harry Bliss wrote that "[t]all memorial vases give variety to the cemetery landscape and furnish liberal opportunity for the use of skill in their planting" (148). He went on to further state, "Neither the eye nor the mind ever tires of the thoughtfully filled flower receptacle" (156).

By the mid-twentieth century granite had become the material of choice for the modern memorial. Today it can be found in a vast array of colors and shapes from quarries not just in the United States but in other parts of the world. The long-lasting qualities of granite have guaranteed it a secure place in the cemetery landscape.

« 7 »

New Immigrants, New Traditions

*How am I going to convince an illiterate foreigner, full of sentiment
and emotion, that a thoroughly studied composition of the tablet type
with the décor in the current modern influence is better for the grave of
the child than the carved Lamb for which the soul of him yearns?
Am I supposed to tell him that he is a darn fool and ignorant for
being so sentimental? Am I supposed to give him a high school education
and intensive course in the appreciation of beauty while my
competitor sells him the lamb?*

~ Leland in Matturi, "Window in the Garden" ~

During the nineteenth century New Jersey was transformed by industrialization and immigration. Irish laborers fled the potato famine and came to
work in various industries and along the canals. Italian immigrants left
behind centuries of agricultural poverty for the possibility of a new life in
the New World. European and Russian Jews, aided by benevolent societies
and socially conscious patrons, escaped from pogroms and persecution to
start over in New Jersey. A handful of young Japanese noblemen came to
New Jersey hoping to learn more about the West and jump-start their
nation's move toward modernity. Germany, the site of a failed revolution in
the 1840s, saw an outpouring of migrants, many of whom settled in the German enclaves of Newark, Carlstadt, Egg Harbor City, and Trenton. Other
immigrant groups—Hungarians, Slovaks, Greeks, Danes, and Russians—
added to the mix. Each of these groups brought its own traditions of commemoration to the New World. Today these stones speak volumes about the
traditions of these people and the transformation of their lives.

New Jersey's great ethnic diversity precludes discussing the memorial traditions of all the ethnic groups who have called this state their second home.
This chapter looks briefly at the distinctive gravemarkers produced by immigrants from Africa, Ireland, Germany, Italy, Russia, and Japan. Jewish immigrants' commemorative traditions are also examined.

"Born a Slave, Died Free":
African American Burial Grounds

New Jersey's African American burial grounds are a critically important source of information about the rich history of the state's African American community. Many of them have been lost or forgotten; however, those that remain tell compelling stories.

African Americans have lived in New Jersey since the seventeenth century. Some of the first were slaves, brought from Angola, Madagascar, West Africa, and the West Indies. Lewis Morris of Tinton Falls is reputed to have had nearly seventy enslaved African Americans living and working at his Monmouth County plantation and ironworks (Wacker 1975, 191). An unmarked burial ground associated with these men and women is located near the waterfalls that gave the community its name (Raser 2002, 272). It may be the oldest African American burial place in the state.

Despite the fact that African Americans typically made up roughly 8 percent of New Jersey's population between the years 1726 and 1790 (Wright 1989, 21), the earliest surviving gravemarkers for African Americans date from the early nineteenth century. It seems likely that wooden and other ephemeral memorials may once have marked the graves of other, now forgotten, African pioneers. Moreover, traditional African gravemarking customs, such as grave decoration, have not yet been recorded in New Jersey, but are common in the Southeast and Midwest (Ingersoll 1892; Thompson 1983; Vlach 1978; Bauman 2005).

Despite the northern location, the lot of slaves in New Jersey was a brutal one. In an age of harsh laws, those affecting slaves were exceptionally so. Whipping and branding were common punishments for trivial offenses. Owners contemplating emancipation of their slaves were forced to post sizeable bonds to pay for the long-term maintenance of their freed slaves. Nevertheless, by the early eighteenth century, Quakers, especially in southwestern New Jersey, were advocating abolition. Particularly influential in the fight against slavery was John Woolman (1720–1770) of Mount Holly (Wright 1989, 22).

During the American Revolution, African Americans, hoping for freedom from the tyranny of Great Britain and the no less real tyranny of their masters, fought on both sides. Caesar, a freed slave of Nathaniel Drake from Plainfield, served as a teamster in Captain Davidson's brigade during the American Revolution. Pieces of his broken gravemarker survive in the Scotch Plains Baptist Churchyard.

Ultimately, the Revolution had little effect on the day-to-day lives of most African Americans. The majority remained enslaved on plantations and farms in eastern New Jersey, living under their masters' rule. When death freed them from servitude, they tended to be buried in separate burial

7.1 Jack, a slave of Jonathan Freeman, is buried in Woodbridge's First Presbyterian Burial Ground. His sandstone marker, which was succumbing to the elements, was replaced with this facsimile in red granite.

grounds on these same farms. If they had markers, they must have been made from wood or fieldstone.

In 1793 the New Jersey Society for Promoting the Abolition of Slavery was formed (Price 1980, 54), and in 1804 the state passed a gradual emancipation act. However, it was a half-hearted measure, stating that the children of slaves born after July 4, 1804, were to be freed at the age of twenty-five if male and twenty-one if female. Although the number of enslaved individuals declined, as late as the Civil War a handful of African Americans were still held in bondage in New Jersey.

What may be the oldest surviving gravestone for an African American in New Jersey dates to 1806 and marks the final resting place of "Caesar, an African." Caesar was once the slave of Deacon Nathaniel Drake, a prominent patriot during the Revolution, whose house is now the Drake House Museum in Plainfield. Caesar's marker, now snapped from its base, is located in the nearby Scotch Plains Baptist Churchyard. It was probably carved by Jonathan Hand Osborn and is a typical example of his work, except for its inscription, recounted below. The top of the marker is decorated with the single letter *C*, rather than the monogrammed initials commonly found on memorials from this period (fig. 7.1). Though he was sometimes called Caesar Drake, the last name of his former master did not appear on his gravestone. The sidebars of the marker have a chain-link border. This is likely just a coincidence, but there may be symbolism here as well.

At some point Caesar was freed (Detwiller 1977, 5). However, it is not known when this happened or whether Caesar continued to reside with Drake following his emancipation. The inscription on the marker highlights Caesar's considerable talents. It reads:

> Here rest the remains of
> Caesar, an African,
> Who died February 7th 1806
> Aged 104 years
> He was more than half a century
> A worthy member of the Church in
> This place and closed his life in the confidence of a
>   Christian
> His numerous friends have erected this stone as a tribute
> Of respect to his eminent
> Virtues and piety
>
> [The gravestone is broken at this point.]
>
> When the last trump shall bid the dead Arise
> When flames shall roll away the earth and skies
> While Atheists, Kings, and infidels turn pale . . .
> Caesar will soar from Nature's funeral pile
> To bask forever in his Savior's smile.

This eloquent testament to Caesar is interesting on many levels. For instance, the gravemarker was not erected by family members (in fact, none are mentioned), but rather by "his numerous friends." Such behavior would be more typical of a minister's former congregation. Perhaps Caesar left no family other than the members of his church. In a world where slaves were treated with little respect, this marker notes his eminent virtues and piety. Moreover, Caesar's great age is striking. He had far outlived most of his contemporaries.

Even his name provides insight into the tenor of the times. Certainly, his parents in Africa did not choose to name their son after a long-dead Roman. Caesar, Cato, and other names derived from the classics were often employed by masters for their slaves. Perhaps they saw it as ironic, to name a man deprived of power after powerful figures from ancient history. In Scotch Plains Caesar seems to have lived up to the positive connotations of his name. Other gravestones for African men named Caesar include those of Cesar Van Duyne (1833) in the Bound Brook Cemetery and Caesar Johnson (1826) in Colts Neck (Raser 2002, 50).

Other names from the classics were also used for slaves. A curious document titled the *Bill of Mortality*, which lists all of the burials in Morristown's Baptist and Presbyterian burial grounds between 1768 and 1806 (Cherry 1806), notes four servants named Cato, three Caesars, and a Pompey. Cato the Elder was a Roman statesman, soldier, and author, who while not engaged in affairs of state, farmed. His grandson, Cato the Younger, was a Stoic philosopher of high moral standing, whose fame was increased in the eighteenth century by Addison's play *Cato, a Tragedy*. Julius Caesar and Pompey were contemporaries and political rivals in first-century B.C. Rome. A simple marble tablet survives in the Morristown Presbyterian Burial Ground for Cato the servant of Daniel Phoenix.

A second memorial for a free African American could once be found in Scotch Plains, though today it is missing. It marked the final resting place of David Allen Drake, Caesar's contemporary and perhaps even a relative. His gravestone read, in part, "Born a Slave; Died Free" (Rawson 1974). Both Caesar and David Allen Drake were buried near the edge of the cemetery, likely due to the segregation that affected even the most respected African Americans in life and after death.

In nearby New Providence's First Presbyterian Burial Ground is a simple sandstone headstone for Dinah Cook. Dinah, who died in 1814 at the age of thirty-eight, is described as the "wife of Isaac Cook, a woman of color." Her marker's inscription is also noteworthy. It takes a rather typical epitaph and adds a racial dimension:

> My friends of color that pass by
> And this erection see
> Remember you are born to die
> Prepare to follow me.

Woodbridge's First Presbyterian Burial Ground also contains a single surviving gravemarker for an African American man named Jack. As was often the case, no last name was provided. Jack's gravestone, which was badly eroded, was thoughtfully recarved in red granite several years ago. The result will probably be the longest-lasting memorial for a former slave in New Jersey. His marker simply notes that he was a "colourd [*sic*] man who belonged to Jonathan Freeman, he was a faithful servant. . . ."

Another touchstone to the African American past is the gravemarker of Ambo (1847) in the Rahway Cemetery. Ambo, like Caesar, lived to an exceptional age, one hundred years. Her marker is made from undecorated sandstone. This is curious, as sandstone had fallen out of favor in the region decades earlier. One wonders if the choice of unpopular sandstone in an old-fashioned shape may have meant that the marker was less expensive than would otherwise have been the case.

At the same time the marker is located near other, presumably white members of the Terrill family. A portion of Ambo's epitaph also bears repeating. It reads:

> Born of African parents
> In the family of Abraham Terrill
> She remained a faithful

Servant to him, his children
And grand children until
Her death.

Ambo is described in her epitaph as "born of African parents." Her name is of African derivation. While Jack, who is buried in Woodbridge, has a seemingly commonplace name, it is worth noting that Jack was sometimes an anglicized version of the West African day name Quaco, used for a male born on Wednesday (Genovese 1974, 448). Ambo was apparently born into slavery and later freed, but remained with the Terrill family. Her age is also striking. It seems unlikely that, given the harsh conditions of their bondage, many slaves would live to be one hundred years old. Several alternative explanations present themselves. First, slaveholders may not have known exactly how old particular slaves actually were, simply that they were quite old, making it easier to estimate than to arrive at an exact date. A somewhat more legalistic possibility is that the age one hundred was selected on purpose with the understanding that most contracts do not exceed ninety-nine years, thereby making these individuals free in death, if not in life.

Despite the handful of markers discussed here, and the others that likely survive, these cases were the exceptions, not the rule. Most African Americans in the immediate post–Revolutionary War period did not receive gravemarkers. A review of the minute book of the Samptown Baptist Church (now South Plainfield Baptist Church) revealed that of the six African Americans who were buried in the Samptown Burial Ground between 1796 and 1851, only the last, Rachel Stevens, deceased in 1854, was afforded a tombstone (Drake 1959, 1). While Caesar, Dinah, David, Jack, and Ambo were clearly exceptional individuals, their gravemarkers also show that they were considered important enough to receive permanent commemoration.

African American memorials from the decades before the Civil War are exceedingly rare, despite the fact that more African American burial grounds were being opened. Those African Americans laid to rest in burial grounds associated with churches also become less visible during this period, as the use of "slave names" given by masters (Genovese 1974, 447) declined. Moreover, as freed African Americans chose their own gravemarkers, they were probably less likely to pay extra for inscriptions that noted their former servitude or race.

New Jersey's nineteenth-century African American burial grounds have seen little concerted study. Some rare exceptions include Gethsemane Cemetery in Little Ferry, Bergen County, and the Mount Peace Cemetery in Lawnside, Camden County. These two examples are noteworthy as they highlight the efforts of African Americans to secure decent burial accommodations in the Jim Crow era. Gethesemane's history is particularly enlightening. The land for the cemetery was purchased on November 17, 1860, by three prominent white residents with the goal of serving as a burial ground for the colored population of the village of Hackensack. Burials presumably began shortly thereafter (Geismar 2003, 35). The oldest surviving gravemarker dates from 1878, but burials had been occurring for at least a decade by this point. Gethsemane Cemetery became the focus of a controversy in 1884 with the death of Samuel Bass, sexton of the First Baptist Church in Hackensack. Bass had requested to be buried in the Hackensack Cemetery, an all-white burial ground. Initially it appeared that this might occur, but as his funeral was beginning, permission for the burial was withdrawn (70). Bass was then buried in Gethsemane Cemetery. However, the case did not end there. Governor Leon Abbett protested Bass's treatment and in response the state legislature passed a "Negro Burial Bill" in the 1880s, which made it illegal to deny an individual burial in a public cemetery because of race (72). This was a significant early piece of civil rights legislation in New Jersey.

In 1901 seven African American men incorporated Gethsemane Cemetery, its earlier trustees having died. By the 1920s burials seem to have ceased. Gethsemane is interesting not only for what it reveals about the prejudices of its time, it is also important as the only cemetery in the state where a formal effort has been made to document traditional African American folk markers. Archaeologist Joan Geismar, studying the cemetery, found several pairs of ceramic pipes used to mark graves. Her research revealed several other African American cemeteries with ceramic gravemarkers. This is an intriguing survival of West African burial customs, where pipes are seen as providing a bridge between the spirit world and the natural world (Thompson 1983). Sadly, folk markers like these are in great danger from vandals and even from groundskeepers, who may not recognize their significance.

Mount Peace Cemetery in Lawnside is another good example of a nineteenth-century African American burial ground. Established in 1890, it catered to the needs of African Americans who were still, despite the aforementioned legislation, often discouraged from burying their dead in public cemeteries. Mount Peace Cemetery and Funeral Directing Company was organized as a corporation and sold stock and granted deeds for burial. Among those buried in Mount Peace Cemetery is John Lawson, an African American Civil War Congressional Medal of Honor winner from Philadelphia.

The White Ridge Cemetery in Eatontown, established in 1886, is another large nineteenth-century African American burial ground. According to cemetery historian Edward Raser, "It is believed to be the oldest commercial black cemetery in the state" (Raser 2002, 241). It contains numerous gravemarkers for African American members of the military, who served their country in the Civil War, the Indian Wars, and subsequent conflicts (fig. 7.2). While most of the markers are formally carved from marble and granite, there is also a good selection of folk markers made from concrete. It is a commonplace material in African American burial grounds. Concrete was something of a poor man's marble, which allowed individuals of limited

7.2 Stock certificate for the Mount Peace Cemetery Company, a traditionally African American burial ground in Lawnside, Camden County. (Courtesy of Bryson C. Armistead Sr. and Mount Peace Cemetery Association.)

means to craft attractive, long-lasting memorials. White Ridge, Mount Peace, and Gethsemane are only a few of the many important historic African American burial places surviving in the state. They deserve further study.

Japanese Gravemarkers

Today New Jersey has vibrant South and East Asian communities. One of the first groups of Asian émigrés to make the long trek to New Jersey came from Japan. Prior to Commodore Matthew Perry's 1853 visit, Japan's contact with the outside world was very strictly regulated. Portuguese traders reached Japan in the 1540s. Shortly thereafter, Francis Xavier, later to be sainted, arrived in Kyushu. By the seventeenth century a port had developed at Nagasaki with a small Japanese Christian community. In an effort to control this trade, and to isolate the traders, the Japanese central government constructed an artificial island named Deshima in Nagasaki Bay. It was completed in 1636, but in the year following the Shimbara Rebellion, in which Japanese Christians participated, the central government decided to expel the Portuguese and prohibit Christianity (Heinlein 1990, 2). However, the Dutch, with a small trading community at Hirado, were allowed to remain and transferred to Deshima. Until the arrival of Perry, the Dutch provided Japan's only window and legal means of trade with the outside world. After the arrival of Perry, many young samurai came to America to study. This was part of a policy to solve the crisis precipitated by the foreigners with their clearly superior technology.

Western missionaries also arrived in Japan, including Guido Verbeck, who settled in Nagasaki (Heinlein 1990, 4). Verbeck and other Dutch Reformed missionaries encouraged many of their young Japanese students to

7.3 These marble obelisks with inscriptions in Japanese calligraphy mark the graves of young noblemen who came to America to study in the mid-nineteenth century. Sadly, many succumbed to illness during their American sojourn.

come to America. The first Japanese students to come to New Brunswick arrived in 1866, with the hope of studying military techniques to strengthen Japan's defense. Roughly three hundred students from Japan studied at Rutgers College and Rutgers Preparatory School in the years before 1885 (Burke n.d.). Among them was Kusakabe Taro, the first Japanese student to enter Rutgers College. Sadly, he died of tuberculosis in the spring of 1870 at age twenty-six. He was the first Japanese to be elected to membership in Phi Beta Kappa. His remains were buried in Willow Grove Cemetery in New Brunswick, though his samurai top-knot was returned to Japan (3). Ultimately, nine Japanese students and the daughter of one student succumbed to disease and were buried in Willow Grove Cemetery. Those who survived their studies returned to Japan and rose to ranks of great importance. Kozo Sugiura became the secretary general of the Imperial Navy. Ichizo Hattori became vice president of Tokyo Imperial University and a senator in the Japanese Imperial Parliament. Today the graves of the Japanese students who died in New Brunswick are marked by obelisks in Willow Grove Cemetery carved by local stonecutters, such as James H. Sillcocks (fig. 7.3). While the shafts of the obelisks have their names written in slashing Japanese characters, the bases are inscribed in English. These memorials are somber reminders of the opening of Japan in the mid-nineteenth century.

Another pair of Japanese gravemarkers bears mention. Kashiro and Sydney Kodama are buried behind Christ Church in Shrewsbury. Their ledgers are inscribed with Japanese characters. Kashiro emigrated from Japan to the United States and became a successful merchant. He married a local woman,

Sydney Mowry, and started a family that remains prominent in Shrewsbury to the present day.

Irish Cemeteries

Small numbers of Irish immigrants found their way to New Jersey in the seventeenth century. They continued to arrive in the eighteenth century, and included both Protestants and Catholics. Thomas Warne, whose marker's fragments survive at St. Peter's Church in Freehold, lived, as noted on his gravestone, in the "north of Ireland." It is inscribed on Michael Rynolds's (1763) marker in Ringwood that he was "[b]orn in Ireland, near Mulleganar." However, it was the nineteenth century that saw waves of the thousands of Irish Catholics who would contribute so mightily to the development of the state.

Many of the Irish who arrived in New Jersey during the second quarter of the nineteenth century were employed in the construction of railroads and canals. In the 1830s Irish laborers found work digging the sixty-five-mile-long Delaware and Raritan Canal. Untold numbers died of cholera when it swept through crowded work camps in 1832. Their bodies were buried in unmarked graves along the canal's route, forgotten by society (NJDEP 2003).

In 2003 Robin Boyle, a resident of Lambertville, spearheaded a project to urge the community to do what its predecessors had not done, by recognizing and commemorating the Irish laborers. Today one can find within the picturesque setting of Bull's Island State Park a large granite memorial, with the Delaware River flowing in the background. The granite block, appropriately enough, was taken from one of the canal's locks in New Brunswick and dedicated on St. Patrick's Day in 2003. An inscription on the stone recognizes the contributions of the Irish laborers and permanently commemorates those who perished during the construction of the canal.

Many Irish also came to America following the Great Famine (1845–1851). They settled in little Dublins in Newark, Paterson, Morristown, and Jersey City (Quinn 2004). Catholic churches and Irish Catholic burial grounds soon followed. Some of the finest that survive are in the areas around Newark, Paterson, Trenton, Belleville, Jersey City, and Camden. In their choice of gravemarker forms the Irish differed little from their neighbors. They erected marble and sandstone tablets, obelisks, and the like. Where they differed was in their use of Roman Catholic symbolism on the markers and their pride in homeland. The crucifix was not a widely employed memorial symbol among the primarily Protestant citizens of colonial New Jersey. The typical Irish Catholic marker has a cross at the top, with *IHS*, standing for the first three letters of Jesus' name in Greek (Keister 2004, 147), and the town, parish, or county of origin often listed on the stone.

There are a number of early Irish Catholic burial grounds in New Jersey, including St. Mary's in Gloucester City and St. Peter's Cemetery in Jersey City. The latter is the oldest Catholic cemetery in the Archdiocese of Newark, having been founded in 1849. It is hard to imagine the cemetery's original bucolic surroundings on the outskirts of Jersey City, overlooking the marshes of the Hackensack River; today its setting is markedly different, with Route 1 to the east, the Pulaski Skyway to the south, and industrial buildings and rail lines boxing in the remainder of the grounds.

The earliest burials at St. Peter's Cemetery speak to its Irish roots; family names, such as Doyle, Kelly, Dolan, McNulty, and others are found to have hailed from various counties, including Tyrone, Meath, Carlow, Cavan, Longford, and Cork, and parishes, including Temple Martin, Rowstown, and Castle.

Notably, Father John Kelly of St. Peter's Parish is buried here. Father Kelly was born on March 27, 1802, in Tyrone County, Northern Ireland. He was ordained at Mount St. Mary's College in the early 1830s and became an important figure in the Diocese of Newark, forming three other parishes and founding Holy Name Cemetery in Jersey City. He died on April 29, 1866; a large monument was erected to him near the front gate of the cemetery. The Kelly monument is approximately twenty feet in height and is constructed of granite with arched marble tablatures set into a granite die. A large granite cross tops the monument.

St. Peter's Cemetery is filled with many early Irish markers with Catholic iconography, including about half a dozen crucifixion scenes. Although the earliest gravestones were not signed by the carvers who produced them, later examples, including the Dolan family monument from 1895, were signed by the Irish firm of Kelly & Sons.

Holy Name Cemetery in Jersey City, with markers for hundreds of Murphys and Ryans, is perhaps the quintessential Irish cemetery in New Jersey, though many other ethnic groups are represented as well. From the towns and counties listed on the markers one can derive a good idea of where New Jersey's Irish settlers hailed from. They include Limerick, Cork, Monoghan, Roscommon, Tipperary, and Wexford (fig. 7.4).

Other Irish immigrants followed railroad work and established working-class communities throughout New Jersey. In Hunterdon County a group of Irish Catholics founded St. Ann's Roman Catholic Church. It was built in Hampton Boro in 1867, when Irish Catholics moved to the area to work on the local railroad. The cemetery is located to the rear of the church and bounded by a stone wall. Most markers display Catholic symbolism, many with free-standing crosses placed on top of the gravestones. The markers appear to have been carved by local monument makers who switched draped urns for crosses to better market the memorials to the growing Catholic clientele.

7.4 A typical Irish American gravemarker at Holy Name Cemetery in Jersey City. This marker commemorates Patrick Moran. Note that the town and county of origin are given on the marker.

The Irish continue to be a potent political force in New Jersey today; however, as they have become part of the larger society their distinctive gravemarkers have disappeared from the state's cemeteries. Twentieth-century Irish markers often include Celtic crosses, strong symbols of faith and also Irish nationalism (Jackson and Vergara 1989, 55).

German Cemeteries

During the nineteenth century new waves of German immigrants arrived in New Jersey. Many were Catholic, others were Protestant or Jewish. They came for diverse reasons: lured by economic activities, driven by politics, or drawn by the promise of greater religious freedom. Many settled in cities, Newark and Trenton particularly. Others, often from rural areas, tried their hands at farming. Although German Americans, like Irish immigrants, generally participated in the larger commemorative trends, they did some things differently. Classical figures and mourning angels are common, with gray granite being the most common material employed (Jackson and Vergara 1989, 55). Mausoleums were also constructed. Newark's Mount Pleasant and Fairmount Cemeteries have spectacular mausoleums associated with the beer barons of Newark, such as Gottfried Krueger and Christian Fiegenspan.

In Holy Sepulchre Cemetery, which straddles East Orange and Newark, there is an exceptional collection of German-language markers. Some are marble but many are made from sandstone, a material which had otherwise faded from popularity by the mid-nineteenth century. They are often complex monuments with multiple carved parts. A number of outstanding examples can be found in cemeteries in Trenton and northward. A heavy emphasis is placed on architectural elements, and indeed the markers appear to have been carved by artisans more familiar with the building trade than the cemetery trade. Signed examples are located in Holy Sepulchre Cemetery and St. Mary's Cemetery in Newark.

Many of these markers were crafted by German stonecarvers, though not all memorialize individuals of German descent. The marker "[e]rected by Catharine Flannigan in memory of her beloved husband Peter Flannigan" is located in St. John's Cemetery in Trenton. Peter Flannigan was born in 1821 in Meath, Ireland, and died on March 20, 1877. The brownstone tablet marker commemorating him stands in stark contrast to surrounding white marble memorials both in color and style. The marker features a heavily modeled hood that terminates in rosettes. The oversized hood is supported by the tablet, which has the inscription carved on its face. The inscription is framed by two engaged balusters that each support a bracket. Elements of the monument clearly resemble those of building architecture rather than styles typically found on memorials. Notably, the base of this unusual marker is signed "Hirth."

Henry Hirth was a partner in the stonecutting firm of Hirth, Volpp, & Wiel. In 1875 their shop was located at 122 North Warren Street in Trenton, near St. Mary's Church. George Wiel and Philip Volpp were born in Wurtemburg, Germany, and immigrated to the United States along with many of their compatriots in the mid-nineteenth century. Wiel was the first to arrive in Trenton. In 1859 he was living on Willow Street (Trenton city directory).

A handful of sandstone markers with the same architectural flair can be found in other Trenton cemeteries, including the Mercer Cemetery, where there is a signed Hirth gravestone for Friedrich A. Hirth, who died in 1869. Although Hirth was an accomplished stonecarver, his mark on cemeteries is somewhat limited. He, like other brownstone carvers, probably earned much of his income from late-nineteenth-century building construction, in which the use of brownstone as an architectural element for window and building trim was gaining momentum. His 1875 advertisement seems to lend credence to this notion. It states that the partners were dealers in brownstone and that even though they gave "particular attention" to gravestones, "all kinds of job work [was] attended" (Trenton city directory).

In Newark's Holy Sepulchre and St. Mary's Cemeteries similar architecturally derived sandstone markers for German Americans are common. F. Wipper and J. Loder were two of the artisans who produced them. The

7.5 The Egg Harbor City
Cemetery and Germania
Cemetery, seen here, in
New Jersey's Pine
Barrens, sometimes
display graves covered
with finely crushed
green bottle glass.
The meaning of this
glass is unknown, but
the effect is rather like a
close-cropped sparkly
lawn.

German brownstone carvers were active from the 1850s through the 1880s, and thanks to their choice of material provide some of the most attractive and legible German monuments from the nineteenth century.

German communities such as Carlstadt in Bergen County and Egg Harbor City in Atlantic County also contain fascinating cemeteries with numerous German-language markers. Egg Harbor City was founded by German immigrants in 1855 along the new line of the Camden and Atlantic Railroad. They conceived of the rural town as a way to escape the rampant anti-immigration sentiment then common in American cities. A group of prominent German Americans from Philadelphia purchased 38,000 acres of pinelands. Their goal was to give "Germans in America the chance to build a flourishing agricultural colony, a great commercial and industrial center and to preserve the national qualities of the German element in a homogenous Germanic Population" (Cunz 1956).

From a tour of the Egg Harbor City Cemetery it would appear that the community was, for a while, successful. The cemetery is distinctive. There is very little grass; instead there are square and rectangular plots paved with concrete or crushed green bottle glass (fig. 7.5). In central Europe it is common to have gravel walkways and curbing; perhaps this provided the inspiration for the design of the Egg Harbor City Cemetery. It is arranged with Teutonic precision, and resembles the cemeteries of nineteenth-century German immigrants in Texas (Jordan 1982, 97). The plots have low stone curbs. Others have ceramic curbs in the form of acanthus leaves. These were apparently produced at a local pottery owned and run by German immigrants. The markers vary from small tablets to large obelisks and crosses. Until the twentieth century, most were inscribed in German and often they provide considerable information about where in Germany an individual came from and in some cases their occupation. Eugen von Schwinchamer's marker notes that he was born at Reichstadt in Baiern (Bavaria) and died in Egg Harbor City in 1882. There are several members of the lesser nobility present, counts and countesses. One of the more unusual memorials is a Monumental Bronze obelisk for "Madame Lasthenie Gomez de Wolowski, Prima Dona of the Italian Opera," who died in 1882. However, the forms and decoration of the markers are not particularly divergent from those of other nineteenth-century groups in New Jersey. One especially noteworthy monument commemorates several of the young men from the community who lost their lives during the American Civil War.

Carlstadt in Bergen County was established by German refugees from the 1848 revolution Here too they purchased a tract of land and established a German community, with beer gardens, turnvereins, and singing societies (Gonzalez 2004, 122). The Carlstadt Cemetery also contains large numbers of German-language gravemarkers. However, it lacks the distinctive plots noted in Egg Harbor City.

Other smaller collections of nineteenth-century German-language markers can be found in Trenton and Hamilton Township and in the Coontown Church Cemetery on King George Road in Warren Township, with scattered examples across the state. A fine marble German-language marker commemorates Franz Froehlinger (d. 1857), the purported inventor of salt-water taffy, who is buried near Pleasant Mills, New Jersey.

By the early twentieth century the use of the German language had ceased on most gravestones. Although detailed studies have not been carried out, it seems likely that increasing prejudice against German immigrants during the First World War, which led to the renaming of communities such as German Valley to Long Valley, worked against the maintenance of German culture.

Italian Cemeteries

Italian immigrants began arriving in New Jersey in substantial numbers in the late nineteenth and early twentieth century. They established enclaves in Paterson, Newark, Elizabeth, Trenton, Hammonton, and other cities across the state. Although many of the first immigrants were quite poor, their children and grandchildren often achieved the success they dreamed of. This development of an Italian American middle class resulted in some of the most spectacular gravemarkers ever to be erected in New Jersey's cemeteries.

Italian culture, particularly in southern Italy, focused great effort on funerals. According to folklorist Elizabeth Mathias, "The rural Italian family will deprive itself of its limited comforts and will sacrifice any small reserve it might have accumulated in order to pay for funeral expenses. . . . In fact, behavior surrounding death and burial so permeates daily life in the rural south that the peasants may be described as death oriented" (Mathias

7.6 The Italian American middle class of the early twentieth century invested heavily in elaborate marble sculpture, often representing dead family members. This statue in East Orange's Holy Sepulchre Cemetery commemorates Andrea L. Masi, a musician. Note his trumpet.

1974, 36). She attributes the great attention lavished on the dead to a dread of the return of the soul of the deceased.

Italian American immigrants, often living in isolated enclaves, continued their traditional practices. Funerals provided a means for individuals to show their status within the community (Mathias 1974, 40). As a middle class and indeed upper class or *signori* developed in the Italian American community, they began to purchase elaborate marble gravestones and when possible statuary, which informed all passersby of their success. A family that buried its dead poorly was dishonored.

The result of these practices was a flowering of cemetery art. One of the best places to see this in New Jersey and indeed in the United States is in Holy Sepulchre Cemetery in East Orange. There are dozens of marble statues commemorating members of Newark's Italian American community; soldiers, teachers, musicians, and brides carved out of marble as well as a host of angels pay silent homage to their families' triumphs (fig. 7.6). There are also dozens of enameled portraits on gravemarkers, both simple and elaborate. The faces frozen in time, men in fedoras and women in wedding veils, provide a glimpse of these successful immigrants.

Jewish Cemeteries

Jewish cemeteries outside of New Jersey have seen considerable study by scholars. In Germany, Austria, Poland, and Russia Jewish cemeteries dating back to the Middle Ages survive (Goberman 2000). They are full of carefully carved sandstone gravemarkers bearing elaborate iconography. The quality of the carving equals and probably exceeds the best of North America's colonial carving. Only recently have New Jersey's Jewish cemeteries begun to be studied by researchers (Gradwohl 1998; Gould 2005; Kraus-Friedberg 2003).

New Jersey's Jewish community traces its roots back to the 1690s when Aaron Louzado, a Sephardic merchant, built a lavish home in Bound Brook (Ard 2004, 430). Roberta Halporn, an expert on Jewish cemeteries, notes that American Jews can be divided into three distinct groups and three distinct time periods (1993). The groups are the Sephardim, German Jews, and Russian Jews. The Sephardic Jews, who came originally from the Mediterranean world, were the earliest immigrants, followed by German Jews in the mid- and late nineteenth century, and Russian and Eastern European Jews in the late nineteenth and twentieth centuries.

Aaron Louzado was Sephardic, part of a group of Jews whose ancestors lived in Spain and the Mediterranean world. Expelled from Spain or forced to convert during the Reconquista, many escaped to the Netherlands. Later, some of the Sephardim went to Brazil, where their commercial skills and facility with languages allowed them to thrive. They also immigrated to the Dutch Caribbean colonies, such as Nevis, St. Eustatius, and Curaçao (Halporn 1993, 132). When the Portuguese captured Brazil, the Jews were again expelled. A handful, captured by pirates on their return voyage to Holland, were deposited instead in New York, beginning the Jewish history of that great multiethnic city (133). Although Aaron Louzado moved from New York to Bound Brook in the 1690s, it is not clear where he was buried. The most likely location is New York City's Shearith Israel Congregation Cemetery off Chatham Square. Small numbers of Sephardim settled in the New Brunswick area in the early eighteenth century; however, they seem to have maintained close ties with New York City's Jewish community and were likely buried there.

It was not until the nineteenth century that large numbers of Jewish immigrants began to come to the United States. Most were Ashkenazi Jews from the German-speaking areas of Western Europe. Although many arrived on these shores with few resources other than hope, through hard work many rose to positions of power and influence. They also adopted the styles of the larger American society that surrounded them, in terms of dress, housing, education, and to some extent commemoration (Halporn 1993, 141).

The Eastern European Jews who followed them came from the Russian-dominated countries of Eastern Europe, including Ukraine, Yugoslavia, Bulgaria, Armenia, and Poland (Halporn 1993, 141). They differed from the earlier arrivals in their form of Judaism, often Chasidic, and in their distinctive clothing and dress. Many found work in the garment industry and lived in cramped quarters in the urban ghettoes of the United States. Their cemeteries reflect the sad heritage of the ghetto, where land was precious. Because of this, many Jewish cemeteries have a distinctive appearance, with gravestones crowded in next to each other, and hardly any room to walk. According to Halporn, strict rules had been developed about how to properly bury the dead in such close quarters (147).

New Jersey's Jewish cemeteries reflect the shared heritage of the state's Jewish immigrants, whether they came from Germany, Russia, or Spain. Substantial nineteenth-century Jewish communities were located in Newark, Paterson, and Trenton. The shore towns of Long Branch, Bradley Beach, and Atlantic City hosted Jewish summer tourists and grew to have significant resident populations. During the late nineteenth century another wave of Jewish settlers landed on New Jersey's shore. They came from the Pale of Settlement in Czarist Russia, and had been brought to the United States by generous benefactors, such as the Baron de Hirsh, who hoped to create self-supporting agricultural communities in southern New Jersey. The towns of Norma, Brotmanville, Rosenhayn, and Woodbine were established. The former townspeople and merchants, turned New Jersey farmers, struggled to make a living from farming in the Pine Barrens.

Jewish cemeteries can be found in many parts of New Jersey. Particularly noteworthy nineteenth-century Jewish burial grounds are to be found in Newark, Trenton, and Long Branch. Later burial grounds associated with the agricultural colonies, more recent immigrant communities, and the gradual dispersal of the state's once vibrant Jewish urban enclaves have led to the growth of large, modern Jewish cemeteries in places like Woodbridge and Paramus.

Newark is home to what may be the largest collection of Jewish cemeteries in the state. Alice Perkins Gould, who has written extensively on them, notes five major cemeteries in the South Orange Avenue and Grove Street area near the Garden State Parkway. They include B'nai Abraham Cemetery, Grove Street Cemetery, Talmud Torah Cemetery, and Union Field Cemetery. Other burial grounds are found in the McClellan Street area (Gould 2005, 79). However, most of these cemeteries are divided into smaller sections used by different congregations, as well as benevolent and fraternal organizations. There are roughly 115 such sections (49)

Today, many of these cemeteries are in poor condition. The families that once formed Newark's vibrant Jewish community have moved west to newer suburbs in Livingston and Caldwell. The earliest known Jewish cemetery in Newark was established on Belmont Avenue in the 1850s (Gould 2005, 1). Some Jews were later buried in the new Evergreen Cemetery, in Hillside, a carefully landscaped product of the rural cemetery movement. Others were buried in Newark's Mount Pleasant Cemetery, perhaps New Jersey's finest example of the rural cemetery movement.

As Newark's Jewish population grew, new immigrants from different countries, with slightly different practices of worship, established their own independent cemeteries and purchased sections of already established

7.7 The Workmen's Circle Plot in Newark is typical of nineteenth- and early twentieth-century
Jewish burial grounds. The markers are packed close together, a reminder of the scarcity
of land in the European ghettoes from which many of these settlers hailed.
Also note the fine wrought-iron gate for this plot associated with the Workmen's Circle,
a fraternal support group founded by new immigrants in New York City in 1900.

cemeteries. The result is an amazing collection of gravemarkers and cemetery
gates, particularly in Newark's Grove Street Cemetery. These gates, which
range from simple painted plywood sheets on top of a chain link fence to
elaborate architectural compositions, are true folk art, identifying the sections and providing a glimpse of the diverse Jewish community of twentieth-
century Newark (fig. 7.7).

Jewish gravemarkers are diverse. In Newark's cemeteries gray granite and
white marble are the most common materials. Many of the markers are quite
artistic. The motifs employed differ from those found in Christian cemeteries. Common symbols include the Star of David, the Lion of Judah, menorahs (particularly on women's gravemarkers), and a pitcher for oil, indicating
a Levite, the priest's assistant (Gould 2005, 58). The tree of life and the hands
of blessing, which signify a member of the *kohanim*, or descendant of Israel's
ancient priestly caste, also appear. Inscriptions are in English, Hebrew, German, Yiddish, Hungarian, and Russian. Enameled portraits are also common
(fig. 7.8).

The Jewish cemeteries of New Jersey's Pine Barrens have also begun to
see the scholarly attention that they deserve. These cemeteries are associated
with Russian Jewish agricultural colonists who came from the Pale of Settlement in Russia or from the tenements of New York. These new Jewish
immigrants were at odds with the German Jews who preceded them, and

7.8 Enameled portraits of matriarchs and patriarchs give life to many Jewish gravemarkers from the early twentieth century. These markers are in the Workmen's Circle Plot.

who, having culturally assimilated, had moved into the American middle class. The German Jewish financiers behind this social experiment and the members of the *Am Olam* movement hoped to "normalize" Jewish life through agriculture (Kraus-Friedberg 2003, 3). The reality of the situation was that, rather than working to preserve Jewish life and culture as experienced by the new immigrants, their financial benefactors and some participants in the program were interested in changing them. This posed an interesting challenge for the Jewish settlers, who wished to both become Americans and remain Jews (5). While Jews in Russia had access to local gravestone carvers who knew the deceased and could produce tailor-made headstones, Jews in rural New Jersey had to deal with carvers who often were not Jewish and did not know the deceased. Nevertheless, some traditional Jewish motifs were employed, including candelabras to symbolize the lighting of the Sabbath candles, often on the gravemarkers of women, the tree of life with its branches cut off, the Star of David, and the hand gesture where the middle and ring fingers are separated to create a V shape—a sign associated with Jewish priests or *kohanim*. Although Jews are buried as soon as possible after death, often on the following day, the gravestone was often not erected until a month, or even a year had passed, a custom that continued in New Jersey (7). Finally, pebbles are left on the gravestones to mark the visits of family members and friends. While each new wave of Jewish immigrants adapted to life in the New World, they also selectively retained traditions from their past.

Russian Cemeteries

On Cassville Road in Jackson, New Jersey, tucked in among suburban bi-level and ranch houses, is an underappreciated cultural treasure, the churches and cemeteries associated with Cassville's Russian community. Today the gilt onion domes of two churches, St. Mary's, originally a ceme-tery chapel, and St. Vladimir's, poke through the pines. Surrounding St. Mary's Church is St. Vladimir's Cemetery. Established in 1935, the burial ground is the resting place of thousands of Russian émigrés. It is divided into three major sections, reflective of three major Russian groups found in New Jersey. There is a section containing the graves of Russian immi-grants who came to this county in waves between the late nineteenth cen-tury and the Second World War. Particularly numerous are White Russians, who fled to the United States during and after the Russian Revolution. The most noteworthy of these individuals is General Anton Denikin, whose real life story reads better than most fiction. Although he came from humble origins, during the First World War he rose to the rank of general. He served with distinction, and then, following the Revolution and capture of the Russian royal family, he helped lead the resistance against the com-munists. Despite initial successes Denikin was unable to capture Moscow, and in 1920 he left the Soviet Union, moving first to France, and ultimately in 1946 to the United States, where he died in 1947. He was buried just south of St. Mary's Church. Today his burial site is a place of great inter-est as his reputation has risen with the fall of communism and the beatifi-cation of Czar Nicholas. In 2005 his remains were unearthed, revealing that the general had survived forty-plus years of interment largely unscathed, and he was returned to Russia, where he was reburied at the Donskoy Monastery.

Denikin fought the communist forces with a mixture of peasants, royal-ists, and Cossacks. Also present in St. Vladimir's Cemetery are the graves of numerous Kuban and Don Cossacks. Several of the gravemarkers bear enam-eled portraits of fearsome-looking men, wearing the fur hats and crossed belts of the Cossacks. Most date from the First World War era. At least two individuals who bore the title *ataman*, or leader, are buried in the cemetery (fig. 7.9). One's gravestone is quite simple and shows a photograph of a dis-tinguished-looking man in a business suit. The other bears a large bronze plaque and shows a commanding figure in uniform, complete with mace. Both are buried in front of a small Cossack chapel.

Other individually interesting markers are scattered through this still active cemetery, including memorials for physicians, professors, librarians, and soldiers. One tall obelisk surmounted by a star in front of the church is for local men who died on D-Day. Another marker shows a Russian MiG fighter plane. Many memorials bear icons, particularly of the Virgin Mary.

7.9 Gravestone of a Cossack *ataman* or leader in Cassville's St. Vladimir's Cemetery in Jackson, New Jersey.

Wooden crosses are common. Apparently, some families use them as permanent markers. However, a stockpile of these stacked against a work shed may indicate that they are also used as temporary markers until professionally carved gravestones arrive. Monument shops in Woodbridge and East Brunswick make the markers. Some fine pieces of art are also to be found in the cemetery. These include an abstract figure carved in marble, and a nearly life-sized knight, complete with sword.

Also resting in this cemetery are dozens of Kalmyk Buddhists. The Kalmyks are a unique community. Russian Buddhists who practice Tibetan Buddhism, they hail from the Caspian Sea region of southeastern Russia. Some fled Europe in the 1920s, while others were displaced persons who came to the United States after World War II. Though a small ethnic group, with perhaps three thousand Kalmyks living in New Jersey (Sanderson 2004, 434), their gravemarkers are unique. Most are gray granite memorials, decorated with mandalas—geometric designs symbolizing the universe, an occasional Buddha, and almost always an enameled photographic portrait of the deceased. Some markers show up to half a dozen enameled portraits of family members (fig. 7.10). A recent visit to the cemetery even found one gravestone with a prayer flag flying. The Kalmyk markers are inscribed with a mixture of Mongolian, their native tongue, English, and Russian. They are located in the rear of St. Vladimir's Cemetery.

7.10 Kalmyk Buddhists rest next to Don Cossacks and other Russians in Cassville. This marker commemorates five members of a family. The top of the marker is decorated with a mandala, a traditional Buddhist symbol.

St. Vladimir's Cemetery is a shrine of sorts to individuals of Russian, Cossack, and Kalymk descent. It remains very much an active burial ground today. However, visitors should be aware that because of its privileged status it contains a couple of puzzling markers. At the front of the cemetery, close to St. Mary's Church, there are what appear to be gravemarkers for Igor Sikorsky, Vladimir Ipatieff, and Alexander Gretchaninov. Sikorsky was the inventor of the helicopter while Ipatieff developed high-octane gasoline. Gretchaninov was a composer. Though rumors abound that these three Russian illuminati are buried here, they are not. Rather, the memorials highlight Russian contributions to the modern world for those visiting the church.

Similarly in nearby Pushkin Park there is an outstanding bronze sculpture of Aleksandr Pushkin (1799–1837), the Russian Shakespeare, and commemorative monuments dedicated to the Carpathian Russians who were killed by the Austro-Hungarian forces at Talerhof during World War I. There is also a monument to Jackson's war dead from World War II. Not surprisingly, many, though not all, of the names inscribed on the granite war memorial are Russian.

In Cassville the interesting gravemarkers are not limited to St. Vladimir's Cemetery. There is a smaller burial ground less than a mile down the road next to St. Vladimir's Church. In it are buried not only the remains of several priests and other congregants but also some members of the family that owned this land in the mid-nineteenth century, before the Cossacks had left Russia's steppe for the pine forests of southern New Jersey. Even more intriguing are two marble sarcophagi within the underchurch of St. Vladimir's. They hold the remains of Archbishop Nikon, former White

Army chaplain and archbishop for Washington, DC, and Florida, and Archbishop Vitaly. The latter was largely responsible for the building of the church and during its construction scratched the words "bury me here" on the wall next to where his sarcophagus sits today (Theodora Noordsky 2005, personal communication).

Gravestone Photography

One element common to German, Jewish, and Italian cemeteries, as well as those of many other ethnic groups, is the use of memorial photographs. Photography allowed working-class individuals to commemorate their loved ones in a way that was previously impossible.

Initially, photography, like other forms of portraiture, was limited to those of the middle class or above. New Jersey's earliest surviving example is the Hester Warne marker in the Alexandria Presbyterian Cemetery in Hunterdon County. Hester Warne, who died in 1857, was the wife of John Bellis. He erected a marker that was typical of the upper middle class in the mid-nineteenth century. Its basic form is that of a simple marble tablet marker erected on a double base. Decorative elements include chamfered sides with climbing ivy. Warne opted for other add-ons, including a draped urn on the top with the wording "My Wife" across its surface.

But the most striking embellishment is a surviving photograph of Hester Warne. Set within a porcelain baroque-style frame, it is anchored at the top of the marker just below the urn. A cover, now long gone, once protected the image. The photograph appears to be an ambrotype, an image on glass, which would account for its relatively good state of preservation; other documented examples of early memorial photographs on tin or other ferrous materials have long since disintegrated. Hester appears in a ghostly image on glass; although faded, her facial features and hairstyle are visible (fig. 7.11).

By the 1860s, other examples of photographs can be found on New Jersey markers. Portraits within ceramic frames, or in some cases what is left of them, can be found on gravestones, mainly in Hunterdon County. Other markers in New Jersey contain square niches where photographs were presumably once attached.

The Ann Elizabeth Godfrey marker in Cape May County dates to 1864 and has one such empty square niche in the top face of the stone. A clue to what such niches may have contained can be found in Mount Pleasant Cemetery in Millville. The marker for three-year-old Nellie Barbara, who died in 1873, has a recessed square below the name with a surviving glass cover. Although much faded, traces of an image survive beneath the plate.

By the late nineteenth century, photographs on porcelain became popular. The process had been developed earlier when, by the 1850s, French

7.11 New Jersey's earliest photograph attached to a marker is of Hester Warne. Dating to 1857, the photograph was printed on glass and rests in an elaborate ceramic frame.

photographers Bulot and Cattin had determined how to successfully bond a picture to porcelain, and in 1854 they patented the process (Horne, Montanarelli, and Link 2004, 63).

The process worked like this. First, family members selected an original photograph. Then, the portrait maker took a photograph of the original, thereby producing a negative. Typically the photograph was retouched to remove extraneous objects and isolate the individual. The photograph might then be photographed again and the negative was reproduced on a glass plate. An image on colloidal film was then placed on the ceramic disk and fired, transferring the image to the ceramic body and glazing it (Horne, Montanarelli, and Link 2004, 63).

Italian Americans and other European immigrants were familiar with commemorative photographs from their homelands and continued to incorporate them in memorials in the United States. By 1893 an American company, J. A. Dedouch of Chicago, was producing such photographs on copper plates. The firm remained in business until 2004 (Horne, Montanarelli, and Link 2004, 65).

One of the reasons Italian Americans favored memorial photographs is that they helped sustain family ties with dead relatives. While memories faded, these photographs did not. Moreover, Italian immigrants sometimes kept similar oval photographs of deceased relatives in their homes, photographs that could be reproduced on memorials (Inguanti 2000, 16–17).

Given Jewish proscriptions against the worship of graven images, it may seem curious that memorial photographs are common in early-twentieth-century Jewish cemeteries. However, memorial photographs are also common on Jewish tombstones in the Old World (Levine 1997; Ruby 1995). They are more often found in Conservative and Orthodox cemeteries than in those associated with Reform Judaism (Gradwohl and Rosenberg 1988, 244).

While most images are traditional portraits of individuals, others including family groups, children with toys, soldiers, policemen, and post mortem photographs can also be found. The rise of images on markers coincided with the death of many war veterans. Numerous photographs of Spanish-American War and World War I soldiers in uniform can be found in New Jersey. While most show soldiers, some examples represent the other branches of the military. A few illustrate the horrors of war. In Jamesburg's Fernwood Cemetery there was an image, which has since been stolen, of Willard Snedeker Jr. on crutches, his leg lost in the Meuse-Argonne offensive in 1918.

Post mortem photographs make up another genre; although rare, about half a dozen examples have been documented, mainly dating from the 1910s through the 1930s. The subject is most often a child or adolescent, but a striking post mortem photograph from the 1960s depicting a man in a coffin with his wife standing beside him can be found in a cemetery in Florence.

Today memorial photographs come in all shapes and sizes. They are not limited to the simple ovals and lockets of the past. In the Gypsy section of Rosedale & Rosehill Cemetery in Linden, 8.5-by-11-inch photos may be found. An interesting one is for "Our Playboy" and appears to be the deceased's face superimposed on an issue of *Car and Driver* magazine.

Conclusions

New Jersey's burial grounds were transformed over the course of the nineteenth century. In addition to the development of new types of burial grounds, particularly the rise of the cemetery and the rural cemetery movement, recurring waves of immigration introduced diverse styles of commemoration into the state's burial places. The Africans, Irish, Germans, Italians, Jews, and even the small number of Japanese who came to New Jersey melded Old World traditions with New World technologies and styles to produce unique and lasting memorials, reflecting their heritage and their new circumstances. None of these traditions was or is completely static. All show evidence of change through time, a byproduct of the changing self-definition and worldview of these groups. To date, these markers have seen relatively little study. With more intensive investigation they are likely to yield considerable insights into the lives of the people who became Americans.

« 8 »

Alternative Gravemarking Traditions; or, When a Gravestone Isn't a Gravestone

Ethnic cemeteries abound in folk art. Some is the product of long-held traditions, while other folk monuments were produced because professionally carved markers were too expensive. Other markers, made from metal and other materials, reflect new styles in commemoration that never quite caught on. This chapter, building on the previous discussion of ethnic gravemarkers, looks at folk memorials made from metal, ceramic, concrete, and even glass. Concrete markers were popular with Italians, Poles, and African Americans. Iron crosses graced the graves of German, Italian, and Polish immigrants, while clay workers in Trenton and Perth Amboy, immigrants from England, Denmark, Italy, and Germany, erected ceramic memorials, which are lasting tributes to their skills.

Most of these markers were handmade in relatively small quantities, though some were mass-produced. The reasons they were made vary. Some are found in areas where workable stone is not common and were probably an alternative to expensive professionally carved gravemarkers. Others highlight the skill and craftsmanship of the workers who produced them, or may reflect a fascination with new media that seemed superior to marble, sandstone, and granite. Finally, cost played an important role in the decision to select a gravemarker made from a material other than stone. For a potter of limited means, a ceramic marker must have seemed like an attractive low-cost alternative to a traditional gravestone.

Metal Gravemarkers for Iron Men

At first glance iron seems like a poor material for the manufacture of permanent gravemarkers. It rusts and decays and has a limited lifespan. However, iron gravemarkers have a long history. In Great Britain, cast iron memorials dating from as early as the seventeenth century have been found (Willats 1987). They became much more common in the nineteenth century (Mytum 2004, 61). Most imitate common gravestone forms.

Metal gravemarkers are found in small numbers throughout New Jersey, with noteworthy concentrations in the Pine Barrens, and also in Sussex and Warren Counties. This bipolar distribution reflects the locations of the state's nineteenth-century ironworks. Some of these markers were probably expedient memorials produced because professionally carved gravestones were expensive to purchase and erect. They also speak to the skills of the foundry workers who cast them. Later in the nineteenth century, zinc alloy gravemarkers, marketed under the trade name Monumental Bronze, were sold as an inexpensive long-lasting alternative to traditional gravestones. Most Victorian cemeteries have one or two. Iron crosses, either produced by blacksmiths or cast in foundries, are also found in Roman Catholic cemeteries, particularly those of German and Italian immigrants.

The oldest surviving iron gravemarker made in New Jersey is not located in New Jersey. It is found in the Trinity Cathedral burying ground in Pittsburgh. It is a piece of iron, presumably cast, measuring about four feet high and two feet wide. Its shape is like that of contemporary gravestones, with a rounded top and square shoulders. It is inscribed with *NI* at the top and the year 1747, marking the grave of Nathaniel Irish Sr. According to a modern bronze plaque on the marker, Irish was born in the West Indies about 1680 and died in Hunterdon County, New Jersey, in 1747. He was originally buried in a cemetery near Union Furnace, New Jersey. After the burial ground became defunct, Irish, along with the iron marker, was moved in 1961 to rest next to his son in Pittsburgh (Harris 1987, 9).

The Irish memorial is similar to iron gravemarkers produced in New Jersey's Pine Barrens during the 1820s and 1830s. New Jersey's first ironworks was established at Tinton Falls, in Monmouth County, in the 1670s. However, it was not until the eighteenth century, with increased demand for iron due to the French and Indian Wars (1754–1763), that the ironworks of the Pine Barrens came into full blast. Forges and furnaces were established at Batsto, Weymouth, Martha, Stafford, Speedwell, Cumberland, and Aetna (Boyer 1931). Their products included pig iron, stove castings, tools, firebacks, hollowware, and water pipe (Veit 1993, 40). During both the Revolutionary War and the War of 1812, the ironworks turned out cannonballs and other metal products to aid the patriots' cause (Beck 1961, 31). Most importantly, for our purposes, they also produced gravemarkers.

While the Pine Barrens contain all the resources necessary to produce iron—ore flux to facilitate the melting process and fuel in the form of charcoal—the region is noticeably lacking in workable stone. Most of the area's earliest gravemarkers were imported from Philadelphia or occasionally

8.1 Cast iron gravemarkers at Batsto, dating from the 1820s.

northern New Jersey, New York, and New England. Homemade markers, made from wood, bog iron, and perhaps ballast stone, were also employed. The Atsion Churchyard, as late as the 1990s, had a fine small wooden marker with head-and-shoulder form, presumably made out of a long-lasting wood like cedar. Sadly, it was undated and its inscription was illegible.

At some point in the early nineteenth century an industrious iron worker in the Pine Barrens decided to make a cast iron gravemarker. The inspiration may have come from firebacks being produced at the ironworks. Firebacks, which resemble gravestones, were used to protect the brick walls of a fireplace from the heat of the fire. However, New Jersey's cast iron memorials may also be seen as part of a longer tradition of iron gravemarkers in Great Britain, dating back to the late Middle Ages (Mercer 1914, 15; Mytum 2004, 61; Willats 1987).

In the Pine Barrens, iron gravemarkers were made from roughly 1810 to 1840. Approximately forty are known to survive. They are located in Atlantic, Burlington, Cape May, and Cumberland Counties. Particularly large collections are associated with Batsto's Pleasant Mills Cemetery and the Cumberland Methodist Episcopal Churchyard. At least three ironworks produced them: Batsto, Weymouth, and Cumberland Furnace, also known as Budd's Iron Works (Boyer 1931, 48).

The markers vary from roughly half an inch to over one inch in thickness (Veit 1993, 40). They were made in forms typical of gravestones from the period, including the tripartite or cherub shape, an urn-topped form, a shallow arch, notched shallow arch, and head-and-shoulder form (fig. 8.1). The largest stands 42 inches tall, while the smallest, a head-and-shoulder marker at the Cumberland Methodist Episcopal Churchyard, measures 13.5

inches tall (40). An example on display in the Batsto Village visitors center reveals something not seen on the markers still found in burial grounds. They have feet, an iron flange that extends perpendicularly from the base of the markers, and presumably helped them remain upright in the sandy soil of the Pine Barrens. Many of the iron gravemarkers are paired, with some used as headstones and others as footstones. Most of the markers are undecorated and uninscribed. However, those at Basto/Pleasant Mills have inscriptions in a shallow cursive hand and are nearly illegible. The markers at Weymouth are more legible, presumably because the lettering was cut more deeply into the molds. The largest surviving marker, for Reverend Abijah Davis (1817) in the Mount Pleasant Cemetery in Millville, has a number of small decorative elements.

None of the markers appear to be deteriorating. Instead, they appear to have reached a state of equilibrium with the environment. This may relate to the manufacture of iron using charcoal instead of coal, thereby imparting fewer sulfur impurities to the finished product and lessening the oxidation rate (Rolando 1992).

Today the deep brown cast iron markers stand out in contrast to neighboring white marble stones; however, they may once have been painted. During an archaeological survey of an abandoned Methodist cemetery in Hammonton, R. Alan Mounier (1988, 10) found an iron gravemarker that had been knocked down. Its underside retained bits of white paint, presumably because that surface had been protected from the weather.

Sadly, we have no primary documents that refer to the manufacture of iron gravemarkers in the Pine Barrens. It seems likely that they were made by iron workers for family members and friends (Veit 1993, 42). They may have been unofficial products, like the glass canes, pipes, and other whimsies made by glassmakers at the day's end or during breaks (Pepper 1971). By the mid-nineteenth century New Jersey's bog iron industry was in decline and would come to be replaced by glass manufacturing, paper making, and cranberry farming (Moonsammy, Cohen, and Hufford 1987). The production of iron gravemarkers thus ended as well.

Those found in the Pine Barrens are generally quite simple with minimal decoration. However, there are a handful of iron gravemarkers, some highly ornamented, that date from the mid-nineteenth century. They include fanciful markers that resemble Gothic Revival churches, others shaped like iron shields, and simple bannerlike memorials with spindly legs. Perhaps the most magnificent of these is a Gothic Revival cast iron marker in the Bloomfield Cemetery, an attractive and well-maintained garden cemetery in Essex County. Dating from 1850 and once painted black, it is a well-lettered high-relief casting. With "W. Lane, Paterson" at the base, it marks the final resting place of Amelia M. Lane (fig. 8.2). Very curiously, the late Barbara Rotundo found almost identical markers in the Oakwood Cemetery in

8.2 Amelia M. Lane's cast iron marker (1850) in the Bloomfield Cemetery is a fine piece of Gothic Revival ironwork. It was cast by the Lane Foundry in Paterson.

Montgomery, Alabama, and in Danville, New Hampshire; however, a search of Paterson cemeteries failed to reveal any others. The marker would have been an attractive alternative to typical marble memorials.

There are also a handful of well-made cast iron gravemarkers in New Jersey's Highlands region. They are arch-shaped memorials with very elaborate floral borders. They were produced in the 1860s and 1870s. Some mark the graves of members of the Warner family. Examples may be found in the Stillwater Cemetery and the Bevans Cemetery in Peter's Valley. Like the Pine Barrens markers, they seem to have weathered their century plus of exposure to the elements quite well. Although a few examples of these markers have been found, they too seem to have been a short-lived experiment.

A very unusual and quite elaborate cast iron marker may also be found in Mount Holly. Dated 1871, it is shaped like an urn and has an embossed lamb on one side. Lettered on the front and top, it commemorates seven-year-old Harry Alan Kirkham. The lamb, beautifully cast, was typically a mourning symbol on Victorian children's gravemarkers.

More puzzling are the small bannerlike markers found in Mount Moriah Cemetery, Mount Holly. They are embossed with the name of the deceased on a small rectangular plaque, beneath which hangs a metal banner reading *father* or *mother*, with iron swags in either corner. Marked with the name of a Philadelphia foundry on the reverse, they seem to have been an inexpensive metal alternative to other more traditional memorials, and in this case were employed in an African American burial ground.

One other form of iron gravemarker deserves discussion: the iron cross. These gravemarkers vary tremendously in ornamentation and size. In New

8.3 Iron crosses, made by blacksmiths from bar stock, can be wondrous pieces of art. This fine example marks the grave of Mary Krchnayt (1881–1907). It is located in Holy Sepulchre Cemetery in East Orange. Markers like this were popular with immigrants from Germany, Austria, and Eastern Europe.

Jersey they are most often found in larger late-nineteenth- and early-twentieth-century Roman Catholic cemeteries, particularly those associated with German, Italian, and Polish immigrants. Similar markers are common on the Great Plains, where they have been found from the Canadian prairie provinces south to Texas and from Illinois west to Montana (Kloberdanz 2005, 161). Many are associated with Roman Catholic German-Russian settlers. The markers were made by blacksmith artisans. Interviews with surviving blacksmiths and their children indicate the work was painstaking and time-consuming. It could take from a week to several months of part-time work to complete a marker (Vrooman and Marvin 1982, 51). Each artisan seems to have had his own style. Some drew their designs on paper or the dirt floors of their shops before working the iron, while others worked from their imagination. Originally the markers were painted, often black, silver, or blue (51). They were sold or traded for produce, and were considerably cheaper and more attractive than the locally available gravestones.

Arguably, the finest surviving example in New Jersey is an exceptionally fanciful iron cross located in Holy Sepulchre Cemetery in East Orange. It marks the grave of Mary Krchnayt (1881–1907) and is a tour de force of the blacksmith's art. The memorial has a granite base, an exceptionally elaborate filigree body, complete with an affixed crucifix, and rays shooting out of the top. The entire composition stands about six feet tall. It has a short inscription in German (fig. 8.3).

Also noteworthy is Mary A. Pavone's cross in St. Mary's Cemetery in South Amboy. It too is the work of a master craftsman. The inscription plaque notes that Mary (1885–1911) was the wife of S. J. Lanza, perhaps the artisan responsible for the cross. Handmade iron roses wrap around the marker like a vine and arrows extend outward in all directions from the central plaque.

Simpler crosses are typically the norm. They range from roughly three to five feet tall. Some were made from sections of pipe screwed or welded together. Others were made by blacksmiths out of bar stock, and others still were cast. The latter are sometimes called foundry crosses (Kloberdanz 2005, 174) to distinguish them from the crosses forged by blacksmiths. While highly ornamented cast metal crosses have been found in the Plains states (Horton 1997, 111), they are uncommon in New Jersey. Madison's St. Vincent's Cemetery has a good collection of simple iron crosses made for Italian Americans. They date from the 1910s and 20s. Several have affixed copper letters, such as might have been used as house numbers.

Mercer County is home to some outstanding iron crosses. Many are found in Holy Cross Roman Catholic Cemetery in Hamilton Township. Particularly well represented are foundry crosses, some bearing rectangular plaques with personal information about the deceased. Though never as popular as granite or marble markers, these iron crosses are most common in Italian and Polish burial grounds dating between 1890 and 1930.

In addition to folk markers, there were also mass-produced metal gravemarkers. The most famous of these were manufactured by the Monumental Bronze Company of Bridgeport, Connecticut. There was, however, a New Jersey connection. A resident of Chautauqua County, New York, named M. A. Richardson was unhappy with the condition of gravemarkers in his local burial ground and decided to find a more lasting and attractive material (Rotundo 1989, 264). After considerable experimentation, he decided on cast zinc as the solution to the problem, and with a partner, C. J. Willard, endeavored to manufacture them. Richardson and Willard contracted with W. W. Evans of Paterson, New Jersey, to produce these unusual markers; however, Evans soon gave up and the Bridgeport firm of Wilson, Parsons and Company purchased the rights to manufacture them (265). The company continued to cast their distinctive memorials until 1930.

Monumental Bronze

Although the gravemarkers were sold under the trade name Monumental Bronze, they were not bronze at all, but rather were produced from a zinc alloy. Perhaps Monumental Bronze had a better ring to it in the advertising world. They ranged in size from tiny obelisks and tablets to enormous statues. The material is, as the advertisements state, quite long lasting, and appears unaffected by weathering. It has a bluish gray color that stands out in a cemetery filled with otherwise homogenous white and gray marble markers. Although many Monumental Bronze memorials were manufactured to look like stone, they are easily identified by their appearance, and when lightly struck, they ring hollow.

According to Barbara Rotundo (1989, 267), the markers were cast using plaster molds. Although the molds had many pieces, the hot metal fused together to form a very durable monument, which could be affixed to a stone base. Early markers had a smooth gray surface, while later examples were sandblasted. This innovation gave them a more stonelike appearance. While the markers' bodies were mass-produced, they were individualized through the application of tablets with the names and dates of the deceased, or other pertinent information. One bit of folklore associated with these memorials is that the hollow metal memorials were used to stash booze during Prohibition (284).

At first the company did well and subsidiaries and affiliates were established in Chicago, Detroit, and Philadelphia. Apparently, the markers were sold by salesmen and from catalogs. Presumably, the memorials already erected in cemeteries led to further sales. Prices varied from a low of two dollars to a high of five thousand (Rotundo 1989, 275). Given that most cemeteries contain only a handful of Monumental Bronze markers, it seems that a career in sales for the company was not a surefire way to riches.

In addition to Monumental Bronze memorials shaped like gravestones, statuary was also produced. Civil War soldiers, in both Union and Confederate uniforms, are quite common. There are two particularly noteworthy white bronze markers in New Jersey and hundreds of other good examples. The first is a statue of a Puritan, possibly Robert Treat, the founder of Newark, that stands over the Old Settler's Crypt in Fairmount Cemetery. The statue, which was erected in 1889, rests on a base that provides important information about Newark's settlement, including a map of the first purchase, complete with replicas of the Native leaders' signatures, a depiction of the first landing at Newark in 1666, and a list of the first settlers. The base of the memorial also bears the inscription "Monumental Bronze Co. Bridgeport, Connecticut." Recently restored, the monument will remind visitors to Fairmount of Newark's history well into the future (Veit and Nonestied 2003, 174) (fig. 8.4). The second is Bertie Harris's marker in Hackensack (see fig. 5.12).

Ceramic Gravemarkers

Besides metal, fired clay was also used to produce gravemarkers. In ancient China, a Qin Dynasty emperor was buried with a magnificent army of terracotta warriors, and ancient Romans occasionally used terra-cotta gravemarkers. Much later, in seventeenth-century England, potters occasionally shaped

8.4 This statute of a Puritan over the Old Settlers' Crypt in Newark's Fairmount Cemetery is an excellent example of the sculptural potential of Monumental Bronze.

gravemarkers from clay. Later still, during the eighteenth century, a material that came to be called Coade stone was invented in Great Britain by a Mrs. Eleanor Coade, though similar artificial stones had been produced even earlier. Coade stone was a form of terra cotta that was made in molds. The individual pieces were then attached to each other with a slip of clay. Her factory produced a variety of gravemarkers from large neoclassical designs, such as the Grecian urn on the monument in St. Mary-at-Lambeth commemorating the infamous Captain William Bligh, to small plaques set into marble gravestones (churchmouse.com). Although the popularity of Coade stone faded after the factory temporarily closed in the 1830s, ceramic gravemarkers continued to be made in nineteenth-century Great Britain.

In the southeastern United States, particularly Georgia, Tennessee, and Alabama, researchers have found a variety of ceramic gravemarkers (Oldshue 1987; Smith and Rogers 1979; Zug 1986). Moreover, in parts of Ohio where sewer tile was once manufactured, gravemarkers crafted from this material have been found.

Ceramic gravemarkers were another short-lived commemorative solution to the dearth of workable stone in the Pine Barrens. At the Maurice River Friends Burial Ground in Port Elizabeth, Cumberland County, there are five curious ceramic gravemarkers. Only three of them are inscribed. These include a headstone and a footstone marking the grave of Ann Stanger, who died in 1815, aged twenty years. There is also a marker for a sixteen-year-old girl named Hannah. Unfortunately her last name is partially illegible. It dates from 1817. All of the markers are quite small, under a foot tall, and they are rather thick, about two inches deep. They have the typical cherub shape of

8.5 William Price's brick-red gravemarker in St. Andrew's Cemetery, Mount Holly, is an early and unusual ceramic memorial.

eighteenth- and early-nineteenth-century gravestones in the region. They were made from coarse sandy clay and then glazed. Today they stand as reminders of Port Elizabeth's glassmaking past. One of the steps in the manufacture of glass was melting down cullet—broken pieces of recycled glass in thick clay crucibles. The clay employed to make these simple grave-markers was apparently the same material used to produce crucibles, turned to a more lasting purpose by enterprising potters.

In St. Andrew's Cemetery in Mount Holly there are also a handful of early-nineteenth-century ceramic gravemarkers. Especially noteworthy is a headstone and footstone for William Price, who died in 1804 (fig. 8.5). Though shaped just like contemporary marble markers, they are made from brick-red clay fired to stoneware hardness. The headstone is inscribed in a very fine cursive hand. Curiously, around the edges of the Price headstone are five small holes, perhaps related to the manufacturing process. The question of who made the marker is unresolved. A redware potter is known to have worked in Mount Holly during the nineteenth century, but there is no record of his having produced ceramic gravemarkers (Branin 1988, 101–104). Making the marker even more curious is the fact that members of the Price family, such as Xerxes Price, were noted potters in other parts of the state. For now the ceramic gravemarkers in Mount Holly remain a local mystery.

Other mid-nineteenth-century ceramic gravemarkers probably survive. Father Henry Beck, the famous collector of New Jersey folklore, wrote about visiting a forgotten graveyard at the Union Clay Works in the Pine Barrens, today within the Brendan Byrne State Forest, where he found three fired-clay gravemarkers. According to Beck, one marker bore the inscription, "Put away your dresses—you won't need them any more" (Beck 1961, 147).

New Jersey's finest ceramic gravemarkers date from the 1870s through the 1930s and were made from terra cotta. They are found in a band running across the state from Trenton in the south to Linden in the north, with the vast majority concentrated in Perth Amboy and Woodbridge, two great centers of clay mining and ceramic manufacture. They are also found in small numbers on Staten Island, New York.

Terra cotta was a popular architectural material in turn-of-the-century America, and was used in place of stone. Contemporary commentators billed it as "a piece of granite made in two weeks" (Veit and Nonestied 2003, 174). It was seen as a supermaterial that was inexpensive to manufacture, could imitate stone, easily took a glaze, was fireproof and easy to clean, and could be sculpted and molded. Moreover, it was billed as lasting forever. Introduced into American architecture in the mid-nineteenth century by architect Andrew Jackson Downing, terra cotta was not widely employed until the late nineteenth century, when the building of steel frame skyscrapers provided a ready market for the material. With steel frames, terra-cotta cladding, and elevators, the construction of the skyscraper became possible, and America's skyline was transformed. Perth Amboy and Woodbridge's cemeteries were transfigured as well. Dropped in among the homogenous white and gray markers were over one hundred ceramic memorials, some of which were quite colorful.

Most of the cemeteries containing terra-cotta memorials are associated with various Catholic denominations. Noteworthy clusters can be found in Alpine and St. Mary's Cemeteries in Perth Amboy, Hillside Cemetery in Metuchen, and St. James and Holy Trinity Cemeteries in Woodbridge.

The earliest terra-cotta gravemarker identified in New Jersey so far is dated 1870. However, it displays a faux granite finish that was not invented until decades later; therefore it must be backdated. A second marker, this one for the Sofield family, dated 1873, is also likely backdated as the first factory in Perth Amboy did not open until 1875. The marker is a large, yellow glazed terra-cotta cross with four small marble tablets bearing personal information about the deceased (fig. 8.6). Interestingly, an individual named E.V.R. Sofield was a potter at Alfred Hall's Pottery in South Amboy in 1874 (Branin 1988, 185).

Alfred Hall, who is buried in a terra-cotta-embellished mausoleum in Alpine Cemetery, Perth Amboy, was almost single-handedly responsible for the growth of the terra-cotta industry in the Raritan Valley. A manufacturer

8.6 The Sofield family monument in Perth Amboy's Alpine Cemetery combined a terra-cotta body with marble plaques. (Reproduced with permission from *Ceramics in America.*)

of yellowware and bricks, he made the transition to terra cotta in the 1870s. This proved to be a propitious move as his pottery had been struggling to stay in business.

Terra-cotta gravemarkers come in many forms, including tablets, crosses, pedestals surmounted by urns, obelisks, and statues. Some were simply made while others were lavishly decorated. They range from recycled architectural terra cotta with undertakers' plaques attached to magnificent obelisks and exquisitely modeled ceramic floral arrangements. Crosses were the most popular form for terra-cotta memorials, with just under half of all dated markers cruciform (fig. 8.7). Columns and tablets were seen before 1880; obelisks, sculpture, and full-blown statuary appear by 1902. In size they range from less than six inches tall to seven or eight feet in height. In general they are very colorful; this is true of both the unglazed markers, which are often red or buff, and glazed pieces produced after 1894 (DeKay 1895, 365). In some cases, rather than glazing the entire marker, its lettering or decoration was accented with blue, black, gold, or red glaze.

Many of the markers from the 1870s and 1880s are unique works of art, but by the 1920s what appear to be mass-produced memorials struck from the same molds had become common. Among these latter were tall obelisks occasionally topped with golden crosses, with black accented lettering (fig. 8.8). At first glance they appear to be made from gray granite, but when chipped it can be seen that they are actually ceramic with a granitelike glaze, another example of the versatility of this medium.

8.7 This unlettered tile and terra-cotta gravemarker in Hillside Cemetery, Metuchen, is a colorful piece of ceramic folk art. The border is blue while the plaque and center are white.
(Reproduced with permission from *Ceramics in America.*)

8.8 Terra cotta was a material that could imitate many others. This obelisk in Alpine Cemetery, Perth Amboy, appears to be made from granite but is actually a textured, glazed terra cotta called Granitex. (Reproduced with permission from *Ceramics in America.*)

Also mass-produced were small pillow tablets associated with the Danish Brotherhood and Sisterhood (DBS), a fraternal order founded in 1882 by Danish veterans of the American Civil War (Chittenden 1983). They do not bear the name of the deceased but rather a variety of symbols associated with the DBS. These memorials might be considered supplemental, rather like the cast iron fraternal markers and flag holders sometimes placed by the graves of veterans and members of other groups. However, in some cases individuals, perhaps those who could not afford professionally carved gravestones, received only a DBS marker. At the other end of the socioeconomic spectrum were the terra-cotta-embellished mausoleums of the factory owners, such as those for Karl Mathiasen (d. 1920), the first president of the New Jersey Terra Cotta Company, in Perth Amboy's Alpine Cemetery, and the Hansen family, which was closely associated with the same industry.

It is likely that the manufacturing process was not particularly different from that for architectural terra cotta. After the ceramic markers were sculpted or molded, they were carefully fired at a controlled heat. Some were dipped in or painted with a solution of glaze. Colors were applied at this point. After glazing, the terra cotta was fired in immense kilns, a process that lasted ten days or more. Sometimes pieces shrank during the firing. To reduce distortion in the kilns, large pieces were often composed from several smaller ones (Veit 1997, 163).

The artisans who made these memorials are, today, after the passage of a century, mostly anonymous. In an 1895 newspaper article about Trenton's clay-based industries, a journalist described seeing a "boy carving in the soft brown clay the inscription for a memorial plaque" (DeKay 1895, 657). Nels Alling, a talented Danish sculptor who immigrated to the United States to work in the terra-cotta industry, has been credited with producing many of the markers for St. Mary's and Alpine Cemeteries (McGinnis 1960, 43). Unfortunately, Alling does not seem to have signed his work, making it that much harder to attribute the markers to his workshop.

One of the finest surviving markers is for Bruno Grandelis and dates from 1905. It is located in Metuchen's Hillside Cemetery. Bruno was only four years old when he passed away. The monument shows young Bruno in a sailor suit, being carried heavenward by an angel as roses spill out of his open coffin (fig. 8.9). The back of the marker is inscribed in Italian, *Tuo Padre Fece*, or "Your father made this." Although unsigned, the marker was clearly the work of Geremia Grandelis, Bruno's father, who was born in Campolongo, Italy, trained as a sculptor in Venice, and came to America in 1893. The Grandelises settled in Perth Amboy, and while here, he produced decorations for the Metropolitan Theater in New York, the National Cathedral and Supreme Court in Washington, and the Parliament Building in Ottawa, as well as many private commissions. Grandelis worked in marble, bronze, and terra cotta. He died in 1929 (www.comelicocultura.it).

8.9 Bruno Grandelis's monument in Hillside Cemetery, Metuchen, is one of the finest surviving terra-cotta gravemarkers. It depicts young Bruno (1901–1905) being carried heavenward in the arms of an angel. Bruno's father, Geremia, was a well-known sculptor. (Reproduced with permission from *Ceramics in America*.)

Recently several signed examples of his work were found during the restoration of Shepard Hall at City College of New York (Carl Stein 2004, personal communication).

Other markers were clearly for clayworkers and their family members. A fine example is the Owen Revell memorial in Perth Amboy's Alpine Cemetery. It consists of a rustic cross surrounded by ivy, lilies, and ribbons (fig. 8.10). On an unrolled scroll sculpted from terra cotta is inscribed, "[E]rected by his sorrowing relatives and friends of Lambeth England" (Veit 1997, 181). Lambeth, like Perth Amboy, was a center of ceramic manufacture. There are also terra-cotta markers in Trenton's Riverview Cemetery and in burial grounds in Princeton and Rocky Hill.

The terra-cotta gravemarkers that are found in Woodbridge, Metuchen, Perth Amboy, Linden, Rocky Hill, Princeton, Trenton, and nearby on Staten Island were most popular with new immigrants. Although the majority are inscribed in English, others have been found in Danish, Italian, German, Hungarian, Polish, and various Slavic languages. Perth Amboy was a city of immigrants, many of whom found work in the clay industry, and opted to memorialize their loved ones with ceramic gravemarkers, a choice that may have been influenced by pride in craftsmanship, as well as cost, and perhaps

8.10 Owen Revell's terra-cotta gravemarker in Perth Amboy's Alpine Cemetery is exceptionally detailed. Revell was a native of Lambeth, England, a city known for its potteries.
(Reproduced with permission from *Ceramics in America*.)

ethnic preferences. It seems likely that factories in other states manufactured them as well. Scattered examples have been noted in California and upstate New York. Curiously, terra-cotta markers from the same period can be found in Ireland.

One other factor that may have contributed to the decision to use terra-cotta gravemarkers was a public health catastrophe, the influenza pandemic of 1918–1919. This disease, arriving on the heels of World War I, exacted a terrible toll, killing a disproportionate number of young adults. Three times as many terra-cotta memorials were erected in 1918 as in any other year in the decade (Veit 1997, 196).

These unusual ceramic gravemarkers reached their zenith in the years between 1910 and 1920, then rapidly fell out of use. There had been attempts to formalize the production of terra-cotta gravemarkers. Two letters and accompanying photographs in the archives of the New York Architectural Terra Cotta Company refer to this concept. Both date from 1915. They are all that survive of a correspondence carried on between Henry Hiss, a monument dealer from Woodland, New York, and Walter Geer, representing the terra-cotta firm. Geer proposed the manufacture of monuments that he called *Tanagras*, derived from a term used for ancient ceramic figurines. In one of these letters he wrote: "We believe, therefore, that this would be an ideal

8.11 These numbered terra-cotta tubes were used to mark indigent burials in the Atlantic City Cemetery. Similar markers have been found at potter's fields across the state.

name for our product, both because of its historical connection with the Terra cotta ornaments, and because it is a name which is easy to remember and easy to pronounce, and at the same time does not convey the idea of 'terra cotta'" (Veit 1997). While Geer and Hiss may have been trying to formalize something that the clayworkers in the factories were already doing, it does not appear that they were successful.

However, there was one exception in potter's fields across the state. Ceramic tubes, with numbers stamped on top, were regularly used to mark graves during the late nineteenth and early twentieth centuries. They were also employed to mark out sections of cemeteries. Recent archaeological excavations at the Snake Hill Burial Ground in Secaucus recovered numerous ceramic markers. Unfortunately, they had all been displaced. Those in Elmwood Cemetery in New Brunswick remain in their original locations, and there are dozens stacked and ready for use at the Atlantic City Cemetery (fig. 8.11). Very inexpensive and long-lasting, ceramic markers were a boon to the management of burial grounds for the indigent.

The timing of the markers' demise is puzzling as the factories continued to make terra cotta in sizeable quantities into the 1930s and some factories, such as Federal Seaboard Terra Cotta, survived the Depression and lasted until the 1960s, albeit in much reduced form. A combination of factors led to the declining use of ceramic memorials. Most are found in less prestigious sections of cemeteries. Improving economic conditions, particularly after World War II, may have made them less attractive. Meanwhile, the terra-cotta companies never fully recovered from the one-two punch of the Great Depression and World War II. Moreover, the children of the first-generation immigrants who employed so many of these markers had become part of the larger society by the 1930s and 1940s. Writing in the 1920s, a cemetery superintendent in Bridgeport, Connecticut, had complained of the "weird taste of the foreign element for freakish monuments and such" (Matturri 1993, 30). Perhaps the residents of Middlesex County's clay district saw things the same way. A brick red or cerulean blue gravemarker may have seemed a bit gauche to the younger generation.

Glass Gravemarkers

Another material that was employed for gravemarkers in the late nineteenth and early twentieth century was glass. We have found none that were made entirely of glass, but in Trenton, Lakewood, and undoubtedly other cemeteries, there are a handful of small table-style gravemarkers with large glass insets bearing the name of the deceased. One fine example in Trenton's Riverview Cemetery marks the resting place of Martin J. Van Ness, who died in 1913, and his wife, Mary, who died in 1928 (fig. 8.12). It notes his service in Co. E of the 4th NJ Volunteer Infantry. The insets are thick black glass. It appears that the background behind the names was sandblasted down to reveal the inscription. While glass markers hold up to weather well, they are in great peril from misguided lawnmowers, and several of the examples we saw had been shattered. Furthermore, they were in reality glass plaques affixed to granite markers. Perhaps at some point it became apparent that simply using granite markers would be easier and result in a more long-lasting memorial. Glass gravemarkers were another idea that never really caught on.

8.12 Martin (d. 1913) and Mary Van Ness (d. 1928), who are buried in Trenton's Riverview Cemetery, have an unusual gravemarker, which displays their personal information on a thick black glass plaque.

Concrete Gravemarkers

If terra-cotta was "a piece of granite made in two weeks," concrete was the poor man's marble. Compared to ceramics and metal, concrete makes a relatively late appearance in New Jersey's burial grounds. It was first employed for gravemarkers in the late nineteenth century. Concrete was very inexpensive, easy to work, and relatively long-lasting. It rapidly became the material of choice for those with limited budgets hoping for a permanent memorial. There are probably more twentieth-century folk markers made from concrete than from any other substance. They were most common from the 1880s through the 1930s (Gordon Bond and Stephanie Hoagland, personal communication). However, they are still being manufactured today. Concrete gravemarkers are particularly common in African American, Italian American, and Eastern European burial grounds. They are certainly not unique to New Jersey, nor to this country.

Scholars researching historic cemeteries in other parts of the United States have noted the presence of numerous concrete headstones in African American burial grounds in the South and Midwest (Little 1998, 258; Rogers 2002; Vlach 1978), but there has been little research on these markers in New Jersey. Most were made by anonymous craftsmen. They range from simple slabs, with names scratched in using a nail, stick, screwdriver, or some other pointed implement, to elaborate, highly ornamented, well-made memorials.

The north Jersey city of Linden, best known for its refineries, is also home to a growing necropolis, in the Rosedale & Rosehill Cemetery, which claims to be the largest burial ground in the state. Calvary Cemetery, a predominantly Polish burial ground, established in the early twentieth century, lies nearby. It contains a unique collection of concrete memorials. Many are inscribed in Polish.

Crosses are the most common form. They are quite variable in design, ranging from simple one-piece crosses, presumably constructed around a core of rebar, to extremely elaborate multipiece compositions with tri-lobe crosses, and even concrete coping or posts for grave fences. Some incorporate photographs of the deceased, encased in concrete. These are not always the usual oval memorial photographs bonded to porcelain that are found in Eastern and Southern European burial grounds, but rather standard photographs set in concrete behind small panes of glass. Others have crucifixes and coffin plates—small metal plaques, typically attached to coffins, with vital information about the deceased. A handful of the most elaborate markers have small inset marble plaques with key facts about the deceased as well as ornamental patterns highlighted with white bathroom tile. The effect is quite attractive.

The quality of the concrete employed varies greatly. Some markers are made from a concrete that contains large quantities of gravel and is quite

8.13 The Anna Misak memorial (1928) in Linden's Calvary Cemetery is a good example of a concrete gravemarker. It is ornamented with bathroom tile. The reverse of the marker notes that it was made by Frank Blasko, builder, and provides his phone number.

hard, while others appear to be made with a greater proportion of sand. Many of the markers are painted, and it seems likely that most were once painted white or silver, with their lettering and sometimes their decoration picked out in contrasting colors.

Members of a Polish fraternal order have copper medallions depicting an eagle and the letters *AME RYKI*. Several memorials have a steplike shape. Some markers are also topped by iron crosses. The artisans who crafted these memorials are unknown, with one exception, a fine multipiece concrete cross for Anna Misak, dated 1928, which is inscribed on the reverse, "Frank Blasko, Builder, Curtis St., 815, Linden." Blasko had good reason to be proud of his handiwork (fig. 8.13).

One of the most important surviving colonial burial grounds in the state, with several hundred eighteenth-century sandstone markers, is that of Woodbridge's First Presbyterian Church. Tucked away in the rear corner of the cemetery are a few dozen concrete markers. Dating from the early twentieth century, they mark the resting places of Hungarian immigrants who settled in central New Jersey's Clay District, where they mined clay and made bricks. Their gravemarkers are distinctive. While there are some crosses, many of the markers are tall, narrow, round-topped, and obelisklike, resembling the monoliths erected by the Ethiopian Christians at Axum and showing traces of robin's-egg-blue paint. What, if anything, the form and color of the markers meant is unknown. However, the color blue is associated with heaven in Christian theology.

8.14 Although undated and uninscribed, this is one of the finest surviving concrete gravemarkers in the state. It appears to represent a church and is located in St. Mary's Stony Hill Cemetery, Watchung.

Italian Americans, many of whom were involved in the building trades, often employed concrete gravemarkers. St. Vincent's Cemetery in Madison, New Jersey, home to some fine hand-wrought iron crosses, also holds a number of nicely made concrete crucifixes, with toy glass marbles serving as decoration and to pick out names and dates. They date from the early twentieth century and mark the graves of Italian American immigrants.

A particularly notable concrete gravemarker, presumably for an Italian American, though it is uninscribed, is found in St. Mary's Stony Hill Cemetery, a Roman Catholic burial ground in Watchung. It is shaped like a small church, with a niche, perhaps for a saint's statue, in front. On one side there is a depiction of a communion chalice (fig. 8.14). Mount Calvary Cemetery in Neptune Township also has a good collection of concrete gravemarkers and homemade mausoleums. Several of the markers in this cemetery have coffin plates, small metal plaques inscribed with vital information about the deceased, stuck to their faces. These plates were typically employed to identify coffins, but here were used to add some permanent lettering to folk markers.

African Americans also made widespread use of concrete gravemarkers. Most are quite simple, but there are examples decorated with marbles, colored letters, and other found materials. One of the few studies of the manufacture of concrete memorials was by Barbara Rotundo, who examined the work of Merry E. Veal, a Mississippi gravestone maker. What she recorded about his work is informative and likely relevant to New Jersey. Veal began by making gravemarkers for friends, but soon found that he was "moonlighting on a regular basis." Rotundo interviewed him nearly thirty years after he had begun making markers, and by that point he had produced more than three hundred (1997, 90). The markers are made with wooden forms. Curves are produced using industrial belting. Armatures to strengthen the markers are made from old cemetery display stands, and the letters are inscribed free-hand with a fourteen-penny nail. Veal employs a putty knife to smooth surfaces, and paints the finished markers light gray with acrylic paint. He makes a variety of gravemarker forms, including arches, mushroom-top stones, square markers, and crosses. His earliest markers cost only fifty-seven dollars, with an additional fifteen for installation. Presumably, the now anonymous African American, Italian, Polish, and Hungarian artisans whose work is represented in New Jersey's historic burial grounds followed similar practices.

It deserves mention that, to date, the very elaborate concrete gravemarkers found in the southeastern United States, ornamented with conch shells and other materials (Jordan 1982), have not been recorded in New Jersey. However, with a few noteworthy exceptions, very few detailed studies of African American burial grounds have been undertaken. Here, too, serious researchers could make important contributions to our understanding of local folk art.

Conclusions

Gravestones aren't always stone. Nearly every other long-lasting material known to man has been employed to commemorate the dead. From simple wooden markers to iron crosses, concrete obelisks, ceramic statuary, and glass plates, nearly everything has been tried, with variable results. What these markers have in common is that they are unusual examples of folk art produced for public display by artisans who are now largely anonymous. Some memorials are incredibly well made, such as the terra-cotta gravemarkers of central New Jersey. In many cases they are clearly the work of professional artisans. Similarly, the iron gravemarkers of the Pine Barrens were likely the work of talented foundry workers. Other markers were crudely made. Many were products of poverty, not a poverty of talent, but a lack of stone or, more importantly, a lack of capital that precluded purchasing a permanent stone memorial. Perhaps more so than any other category of gravemarkers, these memorials are endangered. Often they are not recognized as art. In fact, they are seen as unsightly distractions in orderly modern cemeteries. Unthinking cemetery groundskeepers may remove them, as they would wilted flowers. More effort should be made to preserve and record these ephemeral reminders of our past.

« 9 »

Mansions of Immortality

Mausoleums and Columbaria

The waning decades of the nineteenth century would see another evolution in memorial art that continued into the twentieth century—the mausoleum, a structure that represents the apex of splendor and wealth, housing and commemorating the dead to a degree not seen since the ancient pyramids. Elaborate mausoleums for wealthy families were constructed in cemeteries across New Jersey. This chapter will start off by examining the evolution of these "mansions of immortality." While many of the mausoleums were meant to house multiple family members, they were not the best utilization of space, as some consumed large cemetery lots. By the 1910s a new breed of mausoleum emerged—the community mausoleum. This was a massive structure in which thousands could be laid to rest. It was a contrast to the family mausoleum, as it provided a place of entombment for people of all economic backgrounds and not just the wealthy. The next section of this chapter will explore the rise in community mausoleums as cemeteries looked for ways to conserve space within rapidly filling burial grounds. Community mausoleums were often designed with columbaria—niches for cremated remains. This represents the pinnacle of space utilization in the modern cemetery. The chapter will conclude with an examination of the history of cremation and the mansions designed to house cremated remains.

The Evolution of New Jersey Mausoleums

The cemetery changed from a landscape of smaller gravestone markers in the early nineteenth century to large mansions for the dead—mausoleums—by century's end. A mausoleum is a large, stately tomb, or a building housing such a tomb. Classically, it is associated with Mausolus, the Persian king of Caria in what is now Turkey, whose massive mausoleum was built around 350 B.C. and considered one of the seven wonders of the ancient world (Boardman 1995, 28). From a modern perspective, the resurgence of the mausoleum

9.1 This brownstone vault for Sylvester Van Buskirk at Evergreen Cemetery in Hillside was constructed in 1854. By century's end the family vault would be replaced by the family mausoleum.

was rooted in part in the accessibility of an adequate building material, namely granite. This stone provided the structural stability and strength required for above-ground buildings. Previous to the widespread use of granite, brick arched subterranean structures known as vaults had been built. Vaults had been used in New Jersey by families of financial means since the eighteenth century. Relatives of prominent central New Jersey resident Cornelius Low were entombed in the vault of Henry Vroome in the mid-eighteenth century (Schuyler 1885, 431).

By 1854, the year that Sylvester Van Buskirk built his family vault in Hillside's Evergreen Cemetery, vaults could be found in burial grounds throughout New Jersey (fig. 9.1). The facade was often constructed of brownstone and ornamented in the style of the time. The dearly departed were within the embrace of the earth, protected by a gate or stone door, providing the surviving family members with a sense that their loved ones' remains were secured.

The first generation of mausoleums appeared in New Jersey by the second half of the nineteenth century. Often constructed of stucco, brick, or brownstone, they tend to be low structures that hug the ground—half above and half below. But as the century progressed they rose into freestanding structures like the Sayre mausoleum. Built in 1875 in Mount Pleasant Cemetery, Newark, it is constructed from bricks with quoins and other detailing picked out in brownstone. As granite became increasingly available in the late nineteenth century, mausoleums began to dot the cemetery landscape, the dearly departed protected not by the earth but by massive, fortresslike granite walls.

Granite's remarkable hard quality made it more suitable for monument construction than the softer marbles that had been used up until that time.

9.2 Improved transportation made it easier to ship large pieces of granite to New Jersey monument dealers. As this picture illustrates, larger blocks were transported on special railcars (*Granite, Barre, Vermont, USA* 1904).

The Dusenbery mausoleum in the New York Bay Cemetery, Jersey City, is one of the early all-granite mausoleums in New Jersey. Built in 1887, it has simple rusticated granite blocks forming its four walls and larger granite slabs for its roof.

Granite quarries were opening in the New England states, with the heart of the industry in Barre, Vermont. By the early 1900s these operations had expanded, as new technology made it easy to quarry the raw material. Finishing equipment transformed the granite into design elements for cemetery monuments and mausoleums. By 1904 over 250 lathes, column cutters, and polishing machines were in operation in the city of Barre alone and the number of companies went from six to over one hundred (*Granite* 1904, 9).

Another defining factor in the use of granite was an improved transportation system. In some cases factories built special railcars to help transport large slabs of granite throughout the United States (fig. 9.2). New Jersey cemeteries, with close proximity to the New England states, began to resemble granite stone yards.

Societal changes also had an impact on mausoleum construction. The late nineteenth century saw an influx of immigrants, who provided the necessary labor to build mausoleums. In addition, skilled immigrants, such as Italian stonecarvers, were employed by quarries and monument companies to produce decorative elements (Clarke 1989, 29 and 32).

As industrialization continued to grow, so too did the industrial wealth of a rising upper class. Mausoleums became the ultimate expression of the wealth and status that they had attained in life. It's no wonder that mausoleums contain a *Who's Who* of nineteenth- and early-twentieth-century soci-

9.3 The mausoleum for Henry Ranken at Flower Hill Cemetery in Hoboken is typical of the Romanesque-style mausoleums built in the 1890s. It features an oversized draped urn and is constructed of both polished and rock-faced granite.

ety. Nearly all New Jersey mausoleums were constructed of granite, with crypts and interior detailing done in marble. The largest concentration of mausoleums is located in the urban northeast region of the state; however, examples can be found in small towns in every corner of New Jersey where at least one wealthy citizen opted for a mausoleum. The granite-walled Dusenbery mausoleum in the New York Bay Cemetery was quickly joined by others. In 1891 Henry Ranken built his mausoleum in Flower Hill Cemetery, Hoboken, and in 1892 the Muir and Gouland mausoleums were constructed in New York Bay Cemetery (fig. 9.3). Most mausoleums of the 1890s have rusticated granite walls, stepped granite roofs, and an oversized draped urn or marble statuary perched at the peak. They resemble Romanesque architecture, often including arched doorways and columned entrances with both rough-cut stone and polished granite.

Another early New Jersey granite mausoleum is located in Elmwood Cemetery in North Brunswick. It was built for Christopher Meyer, a Bavarian immigrant who died in 1888, having made his fortune in the rubber industry (*New Brunswick Sunday Times*, March 1, 1936). His eclectic granite mausoleum reaches the height of a four-story building. Although the date of its construction is somewhat difficult to ascertain, the structure does represent an early and architecturally impressive example of a granite mausoleum. As with most such structures, interior detailing consists of marble crypts and walls. Stained-glass windows and a mosaic tile floor complete the interior

9.4 Newark beer baron Gottfried Krueger built New Jersey's most elaborate mausoleum at Fairmount Cemetery in Newark. Constructed between 1896 and 1899, this massive granite memorial has a number of funerary motifs, including a winged hourglass and four urns with eternal flames (*Granite, Barre, Vermont, USA 1904*).

ornamentation. The mausoleum was built to house ten members of the Meyer family and includes four additional crypts in the floor. An iron gate and a massive four-inch-thick granite door guard the entrance. The space between the gate and the lock requires a ten-inch brass skeleton key to open the door (Kearney Kuhlthau, personal communications).

Although the 1890s saw additional pattern book mausoleums popping up in cemeteries, more architecturally inspired structures can also be found. One example aspired to be the ultimate expression of wealth in death. Gottfried Krueger was a Newark beer baron whose immense earnings afforded him a large mansion for his earthly life. But Krueger also commissioned a stunning mansion for his eternal slumber. A masterpiece of art and funerary design, Krueger's mausoleum is located in Newark's Fairmount Cemetery (fig. 9.4). Built from Barre granite and designed by Gustavus Staehlin, it was erected between 1896 and 1899. The mausoleum's exterior is ornamented with a number of funerary designs, including eternal flames, laurel wreaths, upside-down torches, and a winged hourglass carved into the tympanum. The interior is equally impressive. A main chamber is bathed in light from oval windows punched into the top wall of the structure as well as skylights in the dome of the roof. The mausoleum was designed with twenty crypts in the main chamber. A sunken floor revealed an additional eight crypts and two marble sarcophagi. An antechamber below the sunken floor housed another eight crypts, bringing the total number of crypts to thirty-eight (fig.

9.5 The interiors of mausoleums were equally impressive. Most contained stained-glass windows and other embellishments that were seen only by family members. This illustration shows the interior of Gottfried Krueger's mausoleum in Newark's Fairmount Cemetery (*American Architect and Building News*, September 23, 1899).

9.5) (*Granite* 1904, 15; *American Architect and Building News*, September 23, 1899).

With a growing market, New Jersey monument companies began to add mausoleums to their repertoire of cemetery work. In 1895 Thomas Jardine & Son advertised in an Elizabeth city directory that they were man- ufacturers, importers, and dealers in monuments, mausoleums, and head- stones. Their location opposite Elizabeth's Evergreen Cemetery and the Jewish cemetery of B'nai Jeshurun, both well-patronized burial grounds, ensured a steady supply of customers who could afford to erect mau- soleums. Many elements of the mausoleum advertised by New Jersey mon- ument dealers were quarried and finished in New England towns. In 1904 roughly two-thirds of the granite quarried in Barre, Vermont, was shipped as a finished product, some to New Jersey monument dealers, who acted as middlemen in obtaining the elements and then constructing them at the cemetery (*Granite* 1904, 7; see also the O. J. Hammell collection, New Jersey Historical Society).

Architecturally, they borrowed heavily from classical designs. Some, like the 1902 Hobart Memorial Mausoleum, with its Doric columns, mimicked Greek temples. Designed by Henry Bacon, who also designed the Lincoln Memorial, it measures thirty feet long by nineteen feet wide by twenty-two feet high, with three large granite slabs forming the roof. The central ridge stone alone weighs forty-three tons (Lanza 1997, 29). Other classically inspired mausoleums include the c. 1910 Dickson mausoleum in Evergreen Cemetery, Morristown, with a copper roof and interior mosaic tile work; the

9.6 Egyptian Revival styles gained popularity for cemetery monuments in the early 1920s after the discovery of King Tutankhamen's tomb. Charles F. Harms built New Jersey's only pyramid-shaped mausoleum after a trip he took to Egypt. The mausoleum, complete with two carved granite sphinxes to guard the entrance, is located at Flower Hill Cemetery in Hoboken.

c. 1908 Young mausoleum in New York Bay Cemetery, Jersey City; and the c. 1898 Butts mausoleum in Flower Hill Cemetery, Hoboken. This last-mentioned granite masterpiece has two statues flanking the entrance. One depicts the angel Gabriel, trumpet in hand, ready to call Theophilus and his family (office staff from Evergreen, New York Bay, and Flower Hill Cemeteries, personal communications).

Besides classically inspired designs, Egyptian Revival styles account for a large category of mausoleums. These often have columned entrances with lotus leaf capitals, a winged orb hovering over the doorway as a cavetto cornice molding completes the Egyptian Revival theme. One such example is the Eisele mausoleum, built in the 1920s in Fairview Cemetery. It is perched near the top of a hill overlooking the Meadowlands. The owner added, as a final touch, two carved granite sphinxes to guard its entrance.

The ultimate expression of the Egyptian Revival, however, is the pyramid mausoleum of Charles Frederick Harms. Located in Flower Hill Cemetery, Hoboken, the Harms mausoleum was built prior to 1923 after Harms's interest in astronomy led him on a trip to Egypt, where he was awed by the massive monuments for the kings of these ancient lands (*Jersey Journal*, January 15, 1968). Harms ruled over his own operations—a lighterage company in Hoboken—and, like the ancient rulers of Egypt, he had enough financial independence to construct his own pyramid, albeit on a much smaller scale (fig. 9.6). The twenty-foot-high mausoleum is built from granite and also has two sphinxes guarding its entrance. The Harms mausoleum is the only example of the pyramid style in New Jersey.

9.7 New Jersey's first electrified family mausoleum is located in Mount Pleasant Cemetery in Newark. Built in the early 1930s, the mausoleum has two alabaster urns with light bulbs inside them.

Throughout the 1910s and into the 1920s, smaller, pattern book–style, mass-produced mausoleums became accessible to the upper middle class (Keister 1997, 5). These mausoleums are found in large numbers throughout New Jersey cemeteries. Often added to the setting of older mausoleums, they were situated in the most prominent parts of the cemetery and became the millionaires' row for the dead.

In the millionaires' row of Mount Pleasant Cemetery in Newark is the Downing mausoleum (fig. 9.7). This relatively diminutive structure from the early 1930s would take funerary technology to a new level as New Jersey's first electrified mausoleum. The interior features two marble sarcophagi flanked by two granite pedestals, each topped with a lighted alabaster urn (field examination 1997). The electricity would also provide other comforts. Parthenia, the widow of Paul Downing, would often come to visit. During the winter months, within the cold, quiet solitude of the mausoleum, she would huddle next to an electric heater for warmth. Mrs. Downing followed her husband in 1961. Before her death she established a trust fund to pay the electricity bills so her eternal light would never be extinguished (Scott Willman, personal communications).

In the same cemetery is the Dryden mausoleum. Built in 1911 for John Dryden, the founder of the Prudential Life Insurance Company, this massive granite mausoleum features a domed roof with a heavy bronze door. The lavish touches did not stop at the door, however; a large marble urn was placed in the center of the floor (field inspection 1997). The mausoleum was designed by A. Wallace Brown and built by George Brown and Company of Newark (*Newark Evening News*, August 18, 1912).

9.8 Recently arrived immigrant groups, many of whom were acquiring newfound wealth, built their own folk art mausoleums. The Alba family mausoleum in Woodbridge, constructed in the 1950s, is one such example.

The many interior features of mausoleums are often seen only by family members with access. Stained-glass windows are a common design element. Usually built into the rear wall, they provide subdued light and feature typical funerary iconography, such as angels, laurel wreaths, upside-down torches, and sunset scenes. On rare occasions memorial portrait windows have been commissioned. Several mausoleums boast stained-glass windows designed by Louis C. Tiffany. Other interior features include mosaic tiles and marble statuary. Combined with the exterior elements, these luxurious appointments allowed Victorian mourners to replicate the social hierarchy of life in death.

Later, in the twentieth century, new immigrants who were experiencing their first taste of financial success began erecting their own mausoleums, just as the dominant culture was beginning to shift to less ostentatious memorials. These folk mausoleums are interesting in their own right, often employing unusual materials, such as cobblestones and handmade fittings. In Our Lady of the Most Holy Rosary Cemetery in Woodbridge, an Italian Catholic burial ground, two homespun mausoleums can be found. The Sinatra mausoleum, constructed of stone with perched statuary at each corner, was constructed in the 1930s. The nearby Alba mausoleum, with its ancient-looking features, was built in the 1950s of stone in a circular design with a domed roof (fig. 9.8). Although both required a certain amount of funds to construct, they speak more to the availability of Italian stonemasons. St. Michael's Parish Cemetery of the Byzantine Hungarian Rite hosts another homemade mausoleum. This small structure has an ornate half-timbered facade with a wooden door and hand-wrought hardware. Its design evokes architecture from the family's Eastern European roots. Other fine vernacular mausoleums can be found in Mount Calvary Cemetery in Neptune Township.

Community Mausoleums

In 1927 a monumental dedication took place in Newark's Fairmount Cemetery. It was the opening of a mausoleum, a "Mansion of Immortality," as it was later termed. Known as the Fairmount Memorial or Fairmount Temple of Rest, this massive three-hundred-foot-long, four-story mausoleum could hold a community of four thousand. The main block of the structure contains the chapel area, a marble staircase, and an elevator large enough to hold a coffin. A heating system provides warmth for mourners in the wintertime. Two large wings flank the central block and provide space for single crypts as well as family rooms (field inspection 1998; Deacy 1930).

The community mausoleum rose from a need to maximize space in older rural garden cemeteries "yet accommodate a large number of interments in a befitting manner" (Deacy 1930, 9). A decade earlier, the personal mausoleums of wealthy individuals like Gottfried Krueger had represented the pinnacle of funerary monuments. The community mausoleum took a step toward democratization by providing a mausoleum for all. One of the earliest is located in Greenwood Cemetery near Trenton. The construction of "The Greenwood Abbey" was authorized by the cemetery association in 1919. Built by the Sanitary Mausoleum Company of Reading, Pennsylvania, the Abbey was a small yet dignified community mausoleum with stained-glass windows and skylights (Greenwood Cemetery Association 1964). Its granite exterior and white marble interior provided an up-to-date alternative to traditional in-ground burials.

Throughout the 1920s and into the early 1930s, larger and larger community mausoleums were being constructed near urban areas in all parts of the state. The Fairview Mausoleum in Cliffside Park was built between 1927 and 1930 at a cost of $2.5 million (Anthony Mauro December 2004, personal communications). The four-story structure stretched for a city block. An Italian Renaissance–style patio gave the mausoleum an elegant and timeless look (fig. 9.9).

Like earlier pattern book mausoleums, the community mausoleums often had similar qualities. The building entrance opens onto a central lobby area, which serves as a gathering place for funeral services. Often it is the most decorative space, with rugs, tapestries, soft lighting, and other features that offer a sense of comfort. Radiating from the central block are wings that provide space for the departed. Single crypts could be purchased as well as gated private rooms. The latter often feature an elaborate entrance, multiple crypts, and stained-glass windows, just as the family mausoleums did.

Today community mausoleums have become an answer to increasingly crowded cemeteries. Not only do they maximize space but they also help to bring some of the cost of the funeral back to the cemetery. Since no monument or vault is needed, the cemetery can charge more money for the crypt

9.9 The Fairview Mausoleum in Cliffside Park was built between 1927 and 1930. This painting from the late 1920s illustrates the original design, which featured an Italian Renaissance–style patio. (Reproduced with permission from the Fairview Mausoleum Co.)

than a traditional in-ground burial; in turn the cemetery receives a larger profit that would otherwise have gone to vault companies or monument dealers. Crypts that are eye-level, near stained-glass windows or statuary can sell for even more (Evergreen Cemetery board of directors, personal communications). Several modern community mausoleums were built in the late twentieth century. One of the largest is located in Holy Cross Cemetery, North Arlington. The cemetery was established in 1915 and by 2004 held over 254,000 burials. Over the last decade alone the cemetery averaged 4,218 burials a year. A community mausoleum was constructed in 1980 and has since been added onto, bringing the number of crypts to 28,000 (Catholic Cemeteries, Archdiocese of Newark, *www.rcan.org*).

Cremation

His ashes should be scattered on the waters of the Hackensack River
because of the many happy fishing trips it had afforded him.
> ~ *"His Ashes on the River,"*
> New York Times, *May 22, 1912*

While community mausoleums maximized space in older nineteenth-century cemeteries, many also provided areas called columbaria—niches for urns containing cremated remains. The columbaria conserved even more space and paralleled a rise in cremation.

Although the oldest known graves in New Jersey are cremations from thousands of years ago (Stanzeski 1996, 44–45), the state's first modern cremation took place on April 2, 1907, at the Rosedale & Rosehill Crematorium in Linden (Alan J. Kroboth, personal communications; see also *A Guide to the Cremation Practice at Rosehill*). The new facility provided customers with not only cremation services but also a columbarium to house the cremated remains and a chapel in which the funeral services could be conducted. The cremation process was carried out on the lower level of the building, which housed the retorts, the chambers that held the remains during cremation. Above the retorts were two floors with rooms that contained niches for urns holding ashes. The exterior of the granite structure was rather boxy and nondescript, yet its austere fortresslike appearance offered a sense of security and permanence to those who chose to utilize its services and house the cremated remains of their loved ones there.

Other crematoriums quickly joined the ranks. Just two weeks after the state's first modern cremation, the New York and New Jersey Cremation Company was incorporated in North Bergen, Bergen County (incorporation papers on file in the crematorium's office). The company had purchased Becker's Castle, a nineteenth-century brownstone mansion on Hudson Boulevard, and converted it into a crematorium and columbarium.

In 1908, bracing for an influx of cremation companies, the New Jersey state legislature adopted regulations for crematories, requiring that they obtain a local municipal health permit and that no ashes be scattered outside the building (MacCrellish and Quigley 1908, 530–531). This reaction was justified as cremations nationwide were on the rise. In 1907 a total of thirty-three crematoriums were operating in the United States. Just six years later in 1913 fifty-two crematoriums had opened, performing ten thousand cremations that year (see Historical Statistics, Cremation History, www.cremationassociation.org).

Cremation was certainly becoming an accepted alternative to traditional burial since its modern introduction in 1876, when Francis Julius LeMoyne, a doctor and staunch abolitionist, constructed America's first crematorium on the outskirts of his hometown, Washington, Pennsylvania. Cremation was slowly gaining acceptance in late-nineteenth-century society as a result of new attitudes toward religion, a less sentimental notion of death, and a greater health consciousness that viewed it as a sanitary method of disposing of the dead. It was argued by those in favor of cremation that the process safely returned the body to its natural decayed state more efficiently and quickly than in-ground burials, which essentially did the same thing but over a longer period of time (Sloane 1991, 144 and 156).

9.10 This photograph, taken about 1907, shows the newly remodeled Becker's Castle in North Bergen as the home of the New York and New Jersey Cremation Company. Remodeled again in the 1930s, the building still stands today as the Garden State Crematory. (Reproduced with permission from the Garden State Crematory.)

With each passing decade both the Rosedale & Rosehill Crematorium and the New York and New Jersey Cremation Company were performing more cremations. The latter was housed in Becker's Castle, an imposing brownstone structure set back from the road on the west side of Hudson Boulevard (fig. 9.10). The building consisted of a projecting three-story front block with a cross-gabled roof flanked by two-story wings and circular towers, which rose above the entire complex. The elaborate exterior was matched by an equally impressive interior with Victorian wood paneling, molding, and a richly decorated staircase that traversed the three floors of the main building.

In 1907 the New York and New Jersey Cremation Company remodeled Becker's Castle, turning it into a mansion for the dead. A two-story wing was added to the south side. The interior of the castle was redone, using a combination of original woodwork and new decorations. Near the entrance by the staircase was a mosaic tile floor with the company logo inside a laurel wreath. A chapel was located nearby and featured paneled walls, a beamed ceiling, Gothic Revival pilasters, and stained-glass windows. The interior space was divided into rooms with thousands of niches in the walls for urns. The rooms on the main floor featured entrances with ornate Gothic Revival woodwork, while the doors to the rooms on the second floor were flanked by pilasters with Corinthian capitals (photographs on file in the crematorium's office).

Located on the lower level of the building were the old retorts, which today have been replaced by three modern ones. When the old retorts were replaced, the crematorium's manager saved the large iron front and rear sections and incorporated them into a basement wall, giving modern historians a rare glimpse of New Jersey's oldest cremation works. The iron front wall of the two retorts stands about nine feet high and is twelve feet long. The framing consists of riveted metal with two large, heavy iron doors that allowed access to the chambers. Below each door are two smaller iron doors, which helped to regulate the draft. In large raised letters across the top front surface of the retorts are the words "New York & New Jersey Cremation Co." The iron rear wall, which today is displayed side by side with the front, housed the burning unit, which at one time was oil-fired. Glass viewing windows allowed the operator to gauge conditions inside the chambers.

The early patrons of the New York and New Jersey Cremation Company were overwhelmingly German, having had experience with the practice in their home country. However, it was not exclusively a German tradition as cremations had taken place in France, Italy, England, Denmark, Sweden, and Switzerland by the turn of the century (Sloane 1991, 152). The crematorium's success with this ethnic group came partly from its location in a heavily populated German neighborhood within a larger German immigrant enclave. In May 1908 three out of the seven cremations performed there were for people who were born in Germany. Between the first and twenty-eighth of the following month, there were thirteen cremations, five of which were for natives of Germany and two for natives of Austria (records on file in the crematorium's office).

The crematorium was taking in customers from a wide geographic area. As the name suggests, the New York and New Jersey Cremation Company had a percentage of clients from New York City. In May 1908 five of the seven cremations were for New York City residents while the following month reflected a mixture of people from New York City, West Hoboken, Hoboken, and the local neighborhood of Union Hill (records on file in the crematorium's office).

Many customers opted to purchase family niches where the cremated remains would be housed. The niches were sold with optional bronze doors with large beveled-glass windows (fig. 9.11). Even though this was an additional embellishment, most families chose this configuration. Many of the niches were also lined along the sides and top with plush fabric in shades of pink, purple, white, and black. Most striking, however, are the ornate urns containing the cremated remains. The earliest examples, dating from 1907 to 1915, are metal urns in classical styles, often with fancy handles and eternal flames, standing about sixteen inches high. They are decorated with floral motifs and name plates. Some of the urns were probably silver-plated, though much of the shine has been lost over time. Others were meant to mimic the age of the ancient pieces they were copying and have patinated surfaces. Several urns from this period were also made from stone. By the 1920s and 30s other styles of urns became common, most with refined lines

9.11 The interior of the building was remodeled with thousands of niches to house cremated remains. The niches are filled with elaborate urns and personal memorabilia. (Reproduced with permission from the Garden State Crematory.)

and styling. Other designs, not in the shape of urns, were also utilized and made to look like miniature caskets or mausoleums.

The niches also lent themselves to displays of personal effects and other unique decorations. They were filled with family photographs, fraternal memorabilia, wax flowers, military medals, coffin plates, and business cards; several even have Christmas decorations. Many of the niches were arranged decades ago and may be viewed today as untouched time capsules in the recessed walls of the columbarium.

Advocates in New Jersey saw cremation as a means to safely and efficiently combat social problems. In 1916 Miss Anita Grish, superintendent of the Poor Fund in Jersey City, was faced with a budget crisis when the cost of burying the city's paupers rose higher than what the city had allocated. In an effort to find a solution, a quote was obtained from a nearby crematorium. The charge of twenty-five dollars was still higher than the twenty-two dollars for interment proposed by local undertaker Joseph McGuire. But Grish thought cremation was the most sanitary and up-to-date method and that competition from other crematoriums could cut that price in half. In meetings with Mayor Mark M. Fagan, Grish also suggested it might be more economical at some point for the city to build a small crematorium of its own (*Jersey Journal*, April 19, 1916).

Although a municipal crematorium would not be realized, during the 1920s and 30s cemetery companies understood the importance of constructing a crematorium to keep up with the interest in cremation. At Trenton's Ewing Cemetery, the association constructed its own crematorium on the cemetery grounds in 1933 (office staff, personal communications). Other cemeteries that did not go so far as to build crematoriums still tried to cash in on the cremation craze by building columbaria to house the ashes. Both the Fairmount Temple of Rest in Newark's Fairmount Cemetery and the Fairview Mausoleum in Cliffside Park were large community mausoleums constructed with columbaria to cater to customers who chose cremation. An outstanding columbarium was built in Paramus's George Washington Memorial Park in the early 1950s. Known as the All Faiths Memorial Tower, the ten-story structure remains New Jersey's most ambitious columbarium.

Cremation gained a stronger foothold in 1964, when the Vatican relaxed its long-standing opposition to the practices with the condition that cremated remains were placed within sanctified grounds—a Catholic cemetery (Catholics and Cremation, www.rcan.org). With the acceptance of cremation by Roman Catholics and its long-approved use by other religious groups, the number of cremations in New Jersey skyrocketed. By the 1990s monument and granite companies responded to this demand by offering cemeteries a variety of retorts and preassembled columbaria. The Granit Bronz Company of Cold Spring, Minnesota, in a color brochure distributed at a 1997 New Jersey cemetery conference, offered from forty to fifty-six niches in a columbarium shipped as a fully assembled unit. The granite-clad columbarium was made with durable polystyrene-lined niches, offering cemeteries greater utilization of space. The brochure further explained that "the commonly held notion that cremation is a cost-driven choice is not true. In fact, the majority of those who choose cremation are educated, middle-to-upper class and looking for desirable options to memorialize cremated remains." Whether or not that depiction of the crematorium customer is true, cremations continue to rise in New Jersey. Close to 20,000 cremations were conducted in 2005 in the state's thirty-one crematoriums. The Rosedale & Rosehill Crematorium was among the busiest, having performed 4,200 cremations that year (Alan J. Kroboth, personal communications).

As populations increase and cemetery space dwindles, the need to maximize space has become ever more apparent. Both cremation and community mausoleums have helped to address these concerns by providing cemeteries with optimized utilization of limited space. This trend has its roots in the early twentieth century and has now become an important part of contemporary practice.

———

Family mausoleums, community mausoleums, and columbaria to house cremated remains have helped to shape the cemetery landscape. They are reminders of differing ideology in the treatment of the dead and in part a need to maximize space. These mansions of immortality continue to be built today, many along side earlier examples, illustrating a trend that has been embraced by modern society.

« 10 »

Modern Marvels

The New Cemetery Aesthetic

Compared to the Victorian cemetery with its high art or the burial grounds of our colonial predecessors and their rustic memorials, the modern cemetery seems like a sterile and uninteresting place. Closer inspection reveals that the late-twentieth-century cemetery and its markers have as much to say about our society as previous generations' burial places did about theirs. In this chapter we examine the rise of the modern cemetery movement, and take a look at the decline and revival of mortuary art thanks to the arrival of new waves of immigrants from Asia, the Middle East, and Eastern Europe, as well as the development of new techniques, technologies, and materials for gravemarkers.

The modern cemetery movement, expressed in the memorial park, has its roots in Glendale, California, with the establishment of Forest Lawn Memorial Park in 1917. Dr. Hubert Eaton, its founder, was convinced that most cemeteries were "unsightly stoneyards." He envisioned "a great park, devoid of misshapen monuments and other customary signs of earthly death, but filled with towering trees, sweeping lawns, splashing fountains, singing birds, beautiful statuary, . . . noble memorial architecture" (Forest Lawn Memorial Park Association 1955, 2). The George Washington Memorial Park in Paramus, established in 1939, provides a glimpse of this new aesthetic as its architects imagined it. The rolling parklike terrain is punctuated only by trees and a large chapel. Like Dr. Eaton's Forest Lawn, this memorial park, in its simplicity and implicit statement that "less is more," is a striking contrast to the cemeteries of an earlier generation (fig. 10.1).

Memorial parks with flush-to-the-ground markers rose in tandem with the development of power mowers and as such they show the clear effect of changing technologies on gravemarker form. Postwar cemeteries and memorial parks contain countless flush bronze memorials, generally bearing only minimal biographical information. The flat uniform tablets of memorial

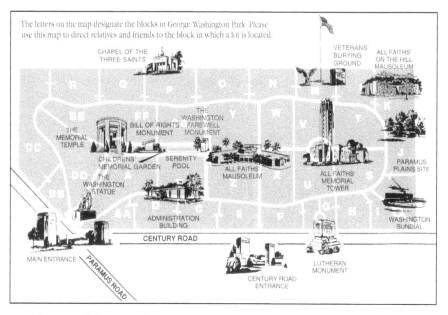

The letters on the map designate the blocks in George Washington Park. Please use this map to direct relatives and friends to the block in which a lot is located.

10.1 This map of George Washington Memorial Park in Paramus reveals a typical design with simple road systems to facilitate the flow of automobile traffic. Gone are the winding roads found in the nineteenth-century cemetery.
(Reproduced with permission from the George Washington Memorial Park, Paramus.)

parks, carefully arrayed in rows, also parallel the rise of the modern suburb. Perpetual-care Levittowns, they speak of the uniform culture of mid-twentieth-century America, where normalcy was highly valued, and any deviation was suspect. They are the product of the company man in the gray flannel suit.

More recently, cemetery art has seen a revival. Monument carvers are employing new technologies, particularly granite etching, which allows anything that can be photographed to be transferred to a gravemarker, from wedding snapshots to pictures of the deceased's restored hot rod car. Color is also being reintroduced to cemeteries, albeit in a limited way, through the use of overpainting on stone. Ethnic cemeteries hold even more breathtaking art. Some especially significant burial places examined in this chapter include St. Andrew's Ukrainian Orthodox Cemetery in South Bound Brook, the Chinese sections of Cloverleaf Memorial Park, Princeton Memorial Park, and Rosedale & Rosehill Cemetery in Linden. The latter also has distinctive Muslim and Gypsy sections. We close with a brief discussion of Laurel Grove Cemetery in Totowa, home to some extraordinary modern gravemarkers, as well as exceptional Muslim and Eastern European memorials, within an already noteworthy garden-park-style cemetery.

The Memorial Park Movement: Ideology and Design

The Burial Estate of Tomorrow
> ~ *Advertising slogan on billboard in 1938 construction*
> *photograph of the George Washington Memorial Park* ~

In 1917 a new cemetery emerged in Glendale, California. Known as a memorial park, it was designed and managed differently from those of the previous century. Pre-need services, perpetual care, and the cemetery beautiful entered the trade vocabulary as ostentatious monuments, at-need burial sales, and difficult-to-maintain grounds of the last century vanished. In New Jersey during the 1930s, this new cemetery and its ideals would emerge with regularity.

In Glendale, California, on New Year's Day in 1917, Hubert Eaton stood on a hill overlooking a small unkempt cemetery that had recently been placed in his care. Wondering what course of action to take, he soon envisioned a radically new cemetery with a management style decidedly different from what had been known before. His thoughts would later be carved in stone and proudly displayed in the cemetery, to become known as the Builder's Creed.

> I believe in a happy eternal life.
>
> I believe those of us who are left behind should be glad in the certain belief that those gone before, who believed in Him, have entered into that happier life. I believe, most of all, in a Christ that smiles and loves you and me.
>
> I therefore know the cemeteries of today are wrong, because they depict an end, not a beginning. They have consequently become unsightly stoneyards full of inartistic symbols and depressing customs; places that do nothing for humanity save a practical act, and that not well.
>
> I therefore prayerfully resolve on this New Year's Day, 1917 that I shall endeavor to build Forest Lawn as different, as unlike other cemeteries as sunshine is unlike darkness, as eternal life is unlike death. I shall try to build at Forest Lawn a great park, devoid of misshapen monuments and other customary signs of earthly death, but filled with towering trees, sweeping lawns, splashing fountains, singing birds, beautiful statuary, cheerful flowers, noble memorial architecture with interiors full of light and color, and redolent of the world's best history and romances.
>
> I believe these things educate and uplift a community.
>
> Forest Lawn shall become a place where lovers new and old shall love to stroll and watch the sunset's glow, planning for the future or reminiscing of the past. A place where artists study and sketch, where school teachers bring happy children to see

the things they read of in books, where little churches invite, triumphant in the knowledge that from their pulpits only words of love can be spoken, where memorialization of loved ones in sculptured marble and pictorial glass shall be encouraged but controlled by acknowledged artists; a place where the sorrowing will be soothed and strengthened because it will be God's garden. A place that shall be protected by an immense endowment care fund, the principal of which can never be expended—only the income therefrom used to care for and perpetuate this Garden of Memory.

This is the builder's dream, this is the builder's creed.

> (Builder's Creed, on display at the entrance
> to the Great Mausoleum, Forest Lawn Memorial Park;
> see also Forest Lawn Memorial Park Association 1955, 2)

Eaton's statement was a clear reaction against "the misshapen stoneyards" of the nineteenth century. During that period cemetery associations began to realize the difficulty of maintaining and managing such elaborate grounds. Other critics commented on the problem in the early 1900s. In search of ways to reform cemeteries, J. J. Gordon in 1915 wrote a piece titled "The Ideal Cemetery—Memorial Park." Gordon, much like Eaton, envisioned a cemetery with natural and artistic features, devoid of monuments (Sloane 1991, 161).

Although the kernel of the new cemetery had been planted a generation before, it was Eaton who would nurture and market it. He made his memorial park a joyful, uplifting place by embellishing the grounds with large fountains and re-creating Renaissance sculpture and statues. Since Eaton viewed the ostentatious markers of the previous century as "inartistic symbols," only flush-with-the-ground bronze tablatures were permitted. Families desiring to further improve the plot could erect statuary approved by the cemetery association (Sloane 1991, 167; Mitford 2000, 103). This helped to control the "noble memorial architecture" by having an acknowledged artist sculpt it. As if influenced by the Hollywood studios, Eaton created his own artificial backdrop, constructing re-creations of churches and chapels, modeling them after existing structures in England and eighteenth-century America. Eaton marketed the cemetery through an aggressive pre-need sales program. He established an ideology of what he called the "memorial impulse," which, as David Sloane writes, "drove people to preserve and to create so that [our] lives would be remembered in the future" (Sloane 1991, 166; Mitford 1963, 101).

With this new ideology and intensive marketing, Forest Lawn's popularity grew in the 1920s and its philosophy was emulated in other areas of the United States. In New Jersey memorial parks appear by the 1930s and by the end of World War II the list included, among others, Lakeview Memorial

Park, Crest Haven Memorial Park, Hollywood Memorial Park, Colonial Memorial Park, Graceland Memorial Park, and George Washington Memorial Park.

HOLLYWOOD MEMORIAL PARK, UNION TOWNSHIP

This memorial park was formed after a dispute between the cemetery association and the township over a tax assessment for improving Stuyvesant Avenue. Dating back to the early 1900s, the cemetery association had owned and operated Hollywood Cemetery on the east side of Stuyvesant Avenue. By 1931 they purchased an additional seventy-four acres across from the cemetery and on the west side of the street. Cemeteries are usually tax exempt but by 1938 the land on the west side had not been used for burial purposes and Union Township did not consider it a cemetery. Viewing the property as taxable, the township imposed an assessment of over twenty thousand dollars when it improved the roadway in front of the cemetery. The levy was upheld during a Union Township Committee meeting on November 7, 1938, where the cemetery's colorful lawyer Otto A. Steifel argued that, since garbage dumps were exempt, they would turn the cemetery into a dump in order to escape taxes. He further implied that it was not the cemetery's fault for its non-use and that "a way out would be to import a gunman from Chicago to shoot up the people of Union and then you would have people dying fast enough to fill it up." The back and forth banter continued until town council member Charles Wagner charged that "the cemetery had defaulted in every one of its obligations and that it was a commercial enterprise . . . it is unfair, and for this association to get out of paying these assessments is the rankest injustice." Steifel then jumped to his feet, protesting, "The statements of counsel are almost libelous. Such Bolshevik statements against the law, coming from this township's counsel are out of order" ("Union Upholds Cemetery Levy," November 8, 1938, Union Public Library). In the end the only way out of the tax problem was to utilize the land as a cemetery. In 1938 Hollywood Memorial Park was established and the development of the grounds as a cemetery began ("Seeks to Modify Cemetery Decree," July 28, 1943, Union Public Library).

Today Hollywood Memorial Park is situated along the west side of Stuyvesant Avenue on a gently rolling landscape, punctuated by two creeks that meander through. At the front entrance is a bowl-shaped Art Deco fountain dating to the burial ground's early years and in keeping with Eaton's vision of "splashing fountains." The cemetery is divided into large sections with statuary and rustic bridges that cross the creeks to provide access to the western portion. A community mausoleum, built in 1953 and since expanded, is located near the southern section of the memorial park. The grounds today are under the care of Cemetery Management Services (CMS), which owns and operates a number of New Jersey cemeteries.

LAKEVIEW MEMORIAL PARK

Along Route 130 in Cinnaminson, Burlington County, is Lakeview Memorial Park. Serving parts of southern New Jersey, it opened in the 1940s and embraces much of Eaton's philosophy. Broad, sweeping vistas of park land, lake, and a picturesque stone arch bridge are some of the design elements of Lakeview Memorial Park. But perhaps the most poignant memorial section in the cemetery is Babyland. A concept direct from Forest Lawn's Lullaby-land and Babyland, this section was designated for children and meant to celebrate, uplift, and be a "tribute to the golden days of childhood . . . an enchanted memorial to the everlasting happiness in a child's heart" (Forest Lawn Memorial Park Association 1955, 17). Admittedly, Lakeview Memorial Park's Babyland is not as elaborate as Eaton's creation, whose inspiration lies in its namesake, a poem by E. A. Brininstool:

> *Babyland*
>
> You strain your ears to catch a note,
> That drifts, in cadence soft and low,
> From out the Heaven Land remote,
> Where all the little children go.
>   (Forest Lawn Memorial Park Association 1955, 17)

OTHER MEMORIAL PARKS

Some memorial parks were the result of failed attempts to establish traditional cemeteries. Crest Haven Memorial Park started out as the West Ridgelawn Cemetery in 1905; by the 1930s it had financial troubles and was taken over by a new group of individuals, who in 1936 decided to create a modern memorial park. In other areas of the state, memorial parks were extensions of existing cemeteries, giving customers both options. Such is the case with the Colonial Memorial Park in Trenton. Dating from the 1930s, it was laid out next to an existing cemetery incorporated in 1899. The two adjacent burial grounds offer contrasting designs within a span of about thirty years (office staff 2005, personal communication)

PERPETUAL CARE

Perpetual care became a hallmark of the memorial parks of the 1930s. Prior to that time, cemetery plots were endowed by individual families, mostly the wealthy, who could afford to do so. What developed was a haphazard system that resulted in well-maintained plots for those with money, while the plots

10.2 Perpetual care became a hallmark of the memorial park. The entire cemetery was managed by a lawn maintenance staff instead of individual families taking care of their plots, as was the practice in the nineteenth century. (Reproduced with permission from the George Washington Memorial Park, Paramus.)

of those without financial means were neglected. Fred Morrow of East Brunswick recalls that, during the 1940s at Chestnut Hill Cemetery, a garden-style cemetery dating back to 1863, families would pay the superintendent to maintain their plots. At times when the grass and weeds grew too high, the Old Bridge Volunteer Fire Department would come to the cemetery to burn it off (Fred Morrow 2005, personal communication).

The memorial parks of the 1930s introduced the concept of perpetual care for their entire membership. No longer was careful upkeep of plots reserved for those who could afford to endow them; as a 1942 advertisement for Hollywood Memorial Park would point out, the modern memorial park provided "perpetual care on every lot" (Union directory, 1942–1943). The New Jersey Cemetery Act of 1971 supported perpetual care by requiring that a percentage of the sale of graves be placed within a perpetual trust fund for the continued maintenance of the entire burial ground (Title 8A).

GEORGE WASHINGTON MEMORIAL PARK, PARAMUS

Promotional photographs of the George Washington Memorial Park from the 1940s showed a landscape of traditional Victorian stone yards in contrast with the modern memorial park. Busy employees were riding around on newly developed mowers while other crews trimmed bushes and trees and planted flowers (fig. 10.2). During the 1950s the landscape crew at the George Washington Memorial Park created some of the largest tulip beds in the state (Frank DeGeeter Jr. 2005, personal communication). The entire site, not just individual lots, was now cared for. Since tombstones were replaced with flush ground tablets, the maintenance became easier and mowers no longer had to navigate through a sea of monuments.

10.3 Pre-need sales were marketed as an alternative to at-need services. As this advertisement from the 1930s illustrates, important decisions were not meant to be made during trying times under harsh conditions. Pre-need sales enabled cemetery patrons to choose wisely. (Reproduced with permission from the George Washington Memorial Park, Paramus.)

The well-manicured lawns, plantings, and statuary of the memorial park were aggressively marketed by the cemetery associations. Historically, cemetery plots were often purchased at the time of death, what became known as at-need sales. By changing to a pre-need system the memorial park could quickly make money with which to invest. Memorial park operators railed against the old way and stressed the importance of pre-need sales. A photograph used in 1940s promotional literature for a New Jersey memorial park showed a grieving couple looking over a snow-covered plot in the dead of winter (fig. 10.3). Death could strike at the most inopportune moments, as the marketers implied, and these difficult choices were not meant to be made during difficult times.

Although many New Jersey memorial parks share Forest Lawn's ideals of perpetual care, pre-need sales, and "sweeping lawns devoid of misshapen monuments," they have hardly become the place for a "school teacher and happy children," as Eaton envisioned. However, the George Washington Memorial Park in Paramus is a good example of Forest Lawn in New Jersey. It opened in 1939 after a group of civic-minded individuals met to discuss the need for a modern memorial park in Bergen County (History and the George Washington Memorial Park 1949, 18). Under the direction of Frank DeGeeter, the association decided upon a ninety-eight-acre tract of land along Paramus Avenue that "was unsurpassed in a glorious natural beauty" (19). The parcel was also chosen for its historical and Revolutionary War connections. The founding members were proud that "the strong tides of history have surged back and forth across the fields and slopes of which George Washington Memorial Park is now a part" (3). The cemetery was to embody a theme of patriotic ideals that was part of the colonial revivalism of the 1930s. The very name of the memorial park evoked the struggles of General George Washington, the Revolutionary War, and the formation of our new country. The history of the cemetery, written in 1949, describes the Revolutionary War as "a time of misery and want, but a time that, in retrospect, also was full of the glory of the new nation's birth" (12). It was in these patriotic feelings in an area rich in Revolutionary War history, within a growing and changing community, that the memorial park anchored its theme and meaning. It advertised itself as the "burial estate of tomorrow" but did so without losing touch with the past. It was an ideology based on Eaton's combination of religious and patriotic values that helped to market the memorial park to a Protestant middle-class society.

The grounds of the George Washington Memorial Park were well laid out with water, drainage, and cemetery structures. The road system was accessed by two gates. The main entrance, on Paramus Avenue, featured a fountain flanked by two octagonal gatehouses designed by noted Philadelphia architect Albert Westover Jr. They were constructed from Indiana limestone in 1940 (George Washington Memorial Park, Art and Monuments n.d., 1). Westover's design was restrained, with simple modern lines and recessed cornices embellished with five-pointed stars. Prominently displayed on both gatehouses were circular tablatures, each with a bust of George Washington. The "splashing fountain," a concept envisioned by Eaton at Forest Lawn, originally consisted of a high, shooting central stream surrounded by lower jets of water, with the added feature of electric lights.

A winding roadway skirted the perimeter of the cemetery while another central road ran straight to the rear of the property. The roads were laid out well to accommodate traffic and dispensed with the wasted space of smaller secondary roads often found in the nineteenth-century cemetery. A colonnaded structure erected in 1939 was positioned at a gentle rise in the land. After the Second World War, sculptor Carl Paul Jennewein was commissioned to create a memorial for the interior space. The work consisted of a bronze drum nine feet in diameter and fifteen feet high, inscribed with the names of fifteen hundred men and women from Bergen County who died in World War II. Dedicated in 1949, the memorial was unveiled by Mrs. Stella Landowski, who had lost three sons in the war (George Washington Memorial Park, Art and Monuments n.d., 2). From the War Memorial the ground rolls out before the visitor, offering a panoramic view of the sweeping lawn and reflecting pool. It is also from this point that the visitor can see the tower of the largest structure erected in the cemetery.

The ten-story, 154-foot-high All Faiths Memorial Tower is the most prominent structure in the George Washington Memorial Park and perhaps the most impressive of any found in other New Jersey memorial parks. Work on the building commenced in 1952 and it took two years just to complete the interior of the first two floors. The structure was built with a chapel on the first floor and a second floor containing niches for cremated remains. An eight-story tower rises up, topped by open fretwork of stone, to which a carillon was later added. The interior of the building is equally impressive, with walls, floors, and moldings of polished marble. The brass railing of a marble staircase holds panels with different zodiac signs. The All Faiths Memorial Tower was an impressive undertaking, designed for use as a chapel and a place for cremated remains. It was also a means to attract the public and bring them into the park. Since 1960 carillon concerts have been given there every Sunday afternoon (Frank DeGeeter Jr. 2005, personal communication). In 1968 a thirty-two-pointed star with over six hundred lights was added to the top of the All Faiths Memorial Tower. When lighted it can be seen from twenty-five miles away (*54th Annual Report and a Guide to George Washington Memorial Park* 1993, 21).

Much like the cemeteries of the nineteenth century, the memorial park included structures and attractions to entice visitors and potential customers. But instead of family memorials, receiving vaults, and the other trappings of death found in graveyards of that period, the memorial park offered a celebration of life by making it a place for the living as well. From 1948 to 1990 the George Washington Memorial Park held outdoor Easter services in the cemetery, with the All Faiths Memorial Tower serving as a backdrop (fig. 10.4). Thousands turned out as a band played music while an opera singer sang hymns that were broadcast on WPAT radio. The services became so popular that several ministers from area churches complained of declining Easter attendance (Frank DeGeeter Jr. 2005, personal communication).

The idea of the cemetery as an attraction for the living was further reinforced in December when a light and music display was exhibited at the front entrance. With the water turned off, cemetery staff erected four thirty-foot-tall papier-mâché angels over the fountain. An enchanted wintertime experience ensued as Christmas music and lights filled the air. People flocked to the cemetery and the display became so popular that it caused traffic jams on Paramus Road; it was eventually discontinued at the request of the local police. But for years prior, visitors had come to the George Washington Memorial Park to celebrate the joys of the season. Much like the festive music that played, their merriment flowed—just beyond the gates—across the perpetual garden of memory.

Today the cemetery continues to cater to the living by carrying on the tradition of erecting "noble memorial art." Under the direction of Frank DeGeeter Jr., new works of art have been added to the grounds. In 1990 a monumental statue of George Washington kneeling in prayer was placed

10.4 The memorial park was meant for the living as well. Special events were held there, including Easter services. This photograph, taken about 1960, shows a large gathering at an Easter service in the George Washington Memorial Park.
(Reproduced with permission from the George Washington Memorial Park, Paramus.)

near the front entrance. Several years later two bronze sculptures of *Joy* and *Love* were erected at opposite ends of the reflecting pool. The four-foot *Love* depicts a young girl standing on a rock with arms raised toward a flock of sea gulls. *Joy* is represented by a young boy playing a panpipe as several butterflies flutter overhead.

The memorial park marketed much more than just a burial place. It was a park setting that was designed to uplift. Although some have strayed from the ideals of the movement's founder, Hubert Eaton, New Jersey memorial parks provide a dignified community cemetery with impressive grounds for their membership. In addition, as a direct result of the memorial park, pre-need sales and perpetual care have become part of the vocabulary of modern society.

The Revival of Cemetery Art

While the carefully scripted memorial park aesthetic shows no sign of abating, some cemeteries remain bastions of individuality, where extraordinary modern gravemarkers continue to be erected. In New Jersey Asian, Eastern

European, Gypsy, Hispanic, and Middle Eastern cemeteries deviate considerably from the norm and provide a rich view of the lives and customs of these immigrant groups. What remains to be seen is how long their distinctive commemorative practices will persist. Are they fated to decline with time and acculturation or will they remain strong into the future?

CHINESE CEMETERIES

As noted in chapter 6, New Jersey is home to some of the oldest Asian markers in the eastern United States, the Japanese graves in Willow Grove Cemetery. These Japanese students were followed in the 1870s by a group of sixty-five Chinese workers who were brought over to work at James B. Hervey's Passaic Steam Laundry in Belleville (Liestman 1994, 20–33; Burnett 1986, 56). Despite protests from nativist groups, the number of Chinese working at the laundry continued to increase. However, under pressure from local labor groups, who felt that the hard-working Chinese posed a threat to their livelihoods, these workers were let go. Some moved to Newark, which was home to a vibrant Chinatown in the years before the Second World War.

After the 1965 abolition of federal quotas on immigration, the number of Chinese immigrants, first from Taiwan and later from mainland China, began to increase. Today there are roughly a hundred thousand Chinese Americans living in New Jersey (Li and Skeete 2004, 148).

Chinese death rituals are quite distinct from those of the larger Euro-American population and have seen considerable anthropological study. Although they vary considerably across China, some common practices include feng shui, which translates as "wind and water" and refers to positioning graves as well as residences in a way that is harmonious with the elements of nature (Rouse 2005, 24–25). Both the location and the shape of the grave were important. An omega-shaped grave with the person's head buried up against the slope of a hill was seen as particularly beneficial (10). Exhumation was also common. According to Wendy Rouse, describing nineteenth-century Chinese funerary rituals in California, "Two to ten years after death, community members, or hired exhumers appointed by the proper district association, excavated the bones from the local cemetery and shipped them back to China. Offerings of food, liquor, and money were offered to the ancestors. These offerings occurred not just at the funeral but at other important holidays, particularly in August during the Hungry Ghost festival, when Daoists believe, the dead returned to earth in search of food and other necessities" (23).

The earliest Chinese burials in New Jersey date back to the late nineteenth century. However, in accordance with a tradition that the deceased must rest near their forefathers, the bodies of Chinese were often shipped back to China for burial. Those interred in cemeteries were exhumed when funds permitted. On June 25,1888, the *New York Times* published the following:

> *To Remove Dead Chinamen's Bones*
>
> Three Chinese merchants, Moy Ah. How, Wong Ye Shin, and Lee Ma Yu, representing the Six Companies of San Francisco, arrived here last Saturday evening, bent on rather a novel mission. The surplus in the treasury of the Six Companies syndicate has grown so large that the managers have voted to reduce it by shipping to China the bones of every dead Chinaman in the United States. The committee is here to visit the different cemeteries in the East and have the Chinese who were buried here because their friends were too poor to ship them to China immediately after death disinterred and forwarded to their native land. The gentlemen are staying at the Chinese Club in Chatham Square and will start their tour of inspection on the first cool day that presents itself. They say that there is no particular superstition connected with the removal of these bodies, but that it is done simply to gratify the natural wish that one has to have his bones rest near those of his forefathers.

Possibly the earliest Chinese burials in New Jersey were located in the pauper section of the New York Bay Cemetery in Jersey City (Halporn n.d., 24). According to *New York's Chinatown*, by Louis J. Beck, Chinese burials took place here in the 1880s and "for economy's sake, bodies were buried as many as possible in a single grave, the coffins resting one on top of the other" (Beck in Halporn n.d., 24). However, no markers remain today.

The earliest extant Chinese gravestones are located in East Ridgelawn Cemetery in Clifton. A marker denotes that the plot was purchased by the Chinese Charitable and Benevolent Association of Newark. Behind it are simple, low granite tablet markers with inscriptions in both Chinese and English, dating back to the 1920s. Among the earliest are those for Ho Chong and Eng Jon, dated 1928. Other than the Chinese inscriptions, there is little to set them apart from the other markers in the cemetery.

The situation in modern Chinese sections of cemeteries is quite different. Particularly noteworthy examples can be found in Cloverleaf Memorial Park in Woodbridge and Princeton Memorial Park in Allentown. Headstones in these cemeteries often have a distinctive form. They may be decorated with images of bamboo shoots, dragons, waves, and flowers. Some designs are painted in red for good luck, while others might be rendered in full polychrome colors (fig. 10.5).

Chinese cemeteries often have informal and sometimes formal furnaces—they can be simple tin cans—in which to burn sacrificial paper ("Hell") money, joss sticks, and other offerings. There may be altars for performing religious rites and there are often large stone gates marking the

10.5 Modern Chinese American gravemarkers in Cloverleaf Memorial Park.

entrance to a particular section of the cemetery. Many of the Chinese graves in New Jersey cemeteries are associated with various fraternal organizations. At Rosedale Cemetery they include the Kai Pun Residents Association, the San Kiang Charitable Association, and the China Buddhist Association.

Food offerings are also common on recent graves and particularly during the Ching Ming festival on April 6. This day is an important time to maintain the graves of one's ancestors. The Chinese believe "all fortune or misfortune stems from the reverence or lack thereof of one's ancestors. These departed ancestors still have similar physical needs (hence, the leaving of food, drink, and gifts) and can assist those still bound to earth" (Keister 2004, 159).

What is perhaps the most spectacular and often photographed modern gravemarker in the state is in Rosedale Cemetery in Linden. It is a life-size Mercedes-Benz commemorating the life of Ray Tse (fig. 10.6). Ray's dream was to have his own Mercedes when he grew up. However, he died while studying in Hong Kong as an exchange student. Rumors that he died in a car accident are false. Ray lost his life to pneumonia. The marker is a Mercedes 240D stretch limousine, created in 1983 by carvers Dante Rossi and Warren Sheldon at Rock of Ages in East Barre, Vermont (Keister 2004, 245). The only things missing are the rear-view mirrors and hood ornament. The cost was $245,000. Ray's brother David commissioned the car. Ray's mausoleum, located immediately to the left of the Mercedes, is equally interesting. It is guarded by two Chinese lions, symbolic protectors of the grave.

ST. ANDREW'S CEMETERY: A BIT OF UKRAINE IN NEW JERSEY

Although a far cry from the Chinese cemeteries and sections in Linden, Woodbridge, and Princeton, St. Andrew's Ukrainian Orthodox Cemetery in

10.6 The Ray Tse marker in Linden's Rosedale Cemetery is a life-size
Mercedes 240D stretch limousine (1983).

South Bound Brook is another stunning modern burial ground. It holds perhaps the greatest collection of outdoor cemetery art in the state.

Dominating the site is St. Andrew's Memorial Church, which points
heavenward like a rocket. On the front lawn of the church is a striking
bronze statue of Saint Ohla, princess of Kiev and grandmother of Prince
Volodymyr the Great, who was responsible for converting the Ukrainian
people to the Orthodox faith.

St. Andrew's is a "national" cemetery, as the prerequisite for burial there
is that the deceased be of Ukrainian birth or lineage (Graves 1993, 39). Most
of the gravemarkers bear inscriptions in Ukrainian, though some also have
English translations. In addition to the usual genealogical information—
name, date, and sometimes place of birth, quite a few of the markers make
mention of the deceased's occupation. There are memorials for generals,
artists, scientists, and philosophers. One noteworthy gravemarker is shaped
like a bridge and commemorates Mykola Szaborski, a "builder of bridges,"
another has a large etched image of Yaraslov Kulynych and his movie camera
and notes that he was a film director. Artistic motifs drawn from Ukrainian
folk art are also employed, including wheat sheaves, *kalyna* or the guilder rose,
which symbolizes sadness, and a form of embroidery called *nyz* (Graves
1993). Other markers show madonnas in folk dress.

Ukraine has had a long and troubled history. Claimed by Poland, Czarist
Russia, and later the Soviet Union, it struggled for freedom for much of the
twentieth century. In 1986 it bore the brunt of the Chernobyl disaster.
Finally in 1991 it became an independent non-nuclear state. Nevertheless,
even today, Russia appears to covet its neighbor's land. Many markers note
military service, particularly during the Ukrainian War of Liberation,

10.7 This life-size bronze Cossack marks the grave of artist Mykola Muchyn, located in St. Andrew's Cemetery, South Bound Brook.

1917–1920. Others bear crests of military units, including the symbol of the Ukrainian scouts, a fleur-de-lis, intertwined with a *tryzub*, or trident.

There is also a good deal of sculpture in the cemetery, including a larger-than-life bronze Cossack emerging from behind a boxwood (fig. 10.7), which marks the grave of artist Mykola Muchyn, who was famous for his sculptures of Cossacks (Graves 1993, 63). There are bronze death masks, modernistic crucifixes, and sculpture of all sorts. Even the wooden gravemarkers in the cemetery are symbolic. Birch branch crosses are common. They were used for soldiers in Ukraine, but appear more widely distributed here.

Folklorist Thomas Graves has called St. Andrew's Ukrainian Cemetery "an entryway into contemporary Ukrainian culture" (1993, 70). It is this and more; it is an outdoor museum, a monument, and a history lesson all in one. Here the visitor gets a glimpse of Ukraine's history, the struggles of its people, and their successes here in the New World.

FORGOTTEN IN LIFE, REMEMBERED IN DEATH:
GYPSY GRAVEMARKERS

Gypsies are one of New Jersey's most poorly documented subcultures. They are an invisible minority, except for a handful who practice as fortune tellers. One might expect a corresponding low profile in death, but such is not the case. Their gravemarkers are elaborate, well made, and often information-packed. They provide a rare glimpse into the lives of this distinctive group of people who are otherwise hidden in plain sight.

Gypsies, or more properly Roma, Rom, and Romani, likely had their origin in India over fifteen hundred years ago. Their language belongs to the Indo-Aryan or Indo-European group, and has until recent years been unwritten (Maas 1975, 49). Wandering musicians, tinkers, fortune tellers, entertainers, traders, and, according to some, tricksters, they had reached Europe by 1000 A.D. (Patrin: Timeline of Romani History). Their name derives from the belief that their ancestors came from Egypt (Erwin 1993, 105). Especially large numbers migrated to Romania, Hungary, Germany, France, Spain, and Great Britain. Their history is one of persecution. Many nations have forbidden their entry, and some of those in which they do live have attempted to tightly control their movements and limit their rights. During the Second World War thousands were exterminated by the Nazis. Today there are perhaps one million in as many as sixty tribes of Gypsies living in the United States (Maas 1975). The exact number in New Jersey is unknown.

Gypsies were certainly present in New Jersey by the mid-nineteenth century. They belong to several different tribes. Some are of Eastern European origin, while others hail from England and Ireland. Their tribes are led by kings or queens.

Gypsies in nineteenth- and early-twentieth-century New Jersey traveled about the countryside in colorful wagons, traded for horses, and told fortunes. Gypsy funerals have attracted media attention for over a century (*New York Times*, August 1, 1881). Ruth Eby, a young girl in the early twentieth century, described a gypsy camp in Edison at a place called the Gypsy Rendezvous by Route 1:

> It was well named because that is the center of where the gypsies met; all the gypsy tribes in the country east of the Mississippi, which took in plenty of gypsies . . . would come every fall to meet. I think there may have been a hundred wagons in that forest. It was a sight I shall never forget, it was so exotic. Each group of people had their own camp fires with big pots cooking food, horses all tethered around, the women in purple and red clothes, draperies and music—very inflammatory music. Sometimes people were dancing and shouting. It was indescribably lovely to see those gypsies. They would come every year and stay for about a month. And then all of a sudden overnight without any noises or goodbyes, like magic they disappeared. . . . But the word would get around fast and every citizen would run and tell his neighbor, "Get your horse in the barn because the gypsies are leaving." Gypsies had a bad name for thievery, you know.   (Eby 1977, tape 2)

Other Gypsy tribes camped in Madison, Morris County, and Newark.

Several New Jersey cemeteries have been popular with Gypsies and remain so. They include Mount Olivet Cemetery in Elizabeth, Evergreen Cemetery in Hillside, Hollywood Cemetery in Union, and Rosedale & Rosehill Cemetery in Linden. Gypsy funeral rites were important opportunities for clans to meet and pay their respects to the honored dead (Erwin 1993, 110). A description of the 1925 funeral of Nicholas John, king of the Romany Gypsies, in Oakland Cemetery, New York, recorded that "[b]eside the grave the coffin was opened and King John's followers stood in line to kiss his bearded face through the opening. Some dropped coins on his chest. A portly woman with black and red dress and bodice poured wine on the face. The coins, reporters were told, will pay the dead gypsy King's fare on Charon's ferry" (*New York Times*, February 8, 1925).

One of the most famous Gypsy burials to occur in New Jersey was that of Naylor Harrison in 1928. Harrison, also a king of the Romany Gypsies, is buried in the Madison Cemetery in Madison, New Jersey. He was born in England, and came to the United States with his parents. After traveling throughout the continent he settled in Morristown, where he lived in a "hut of boards and canvas." Despite these rustic quarters he was an exceptionally successful businessman. For his funeral "[n]o expense will be spared . . . and Harrison will be buried in a silver-lined casket" (*New York Times*, June 3, 1928).

Gypsy funerals continue to be elaborate. In 1974 the funeral of Queen Mary Mitchell in Linden included church services in Paterson, followed by a parade through the cemetery led by a horse-drawn hearse, accompanied by "men and women in bell-bottomed pants and platform shoes as well as some traditional gypsy styles—sashes and long dresses." She was buried next to her son under a "huge burial stone with tall marble columns bearing her picture" (*New York Times*, March 24, 1973).

Two especially good sites for visiting Gypsy graves are Evergreen Cemetery in Hillside and Rosedale & Rosehill Cemetery in Linden—the resting place of Mary Mitchell. Evergreen Cemetery, located near the Waverly Park racetrack, became popular with Gypsies in the early twentieth century. In 1926 John Smith was the first Gypsy buried there. Today it is estimated that three thousand Gypsies have been buried at Evergreen (Turner 1991).

Gypsy gravemarkers show a preference for red and black granite. Some are decorated with paired urns or a colonnade. Many are incredible works of art. At Evergreen Cemetery, some noteworthy examples include the colonnaded marker for Singing Sam Stevens, made from black granite with gilt lettering. The square columns are decorated with musical notes. A granite record, including some of his best-known songs, is displayed between the columns on the left and his electric guitar on the right. There is also a granite etching of Sam strumming the guitar. A cassette tape player on a bench enabled visitors to hear Sam's music (fig. 10.8).

10.8 Singing Sam Stevens was a famous Gypsy musician. He is buried in Hillside's Evergreen Cemetery. Note the guitar and gold record. The marker is decorated for Christmas.

Nearby, George ("Big G") (1992) and "Loveable Rose" Nicholas are commemorated by a similar marker, ornamented with enormous initials of the deceased as well as a carved madonna. Enameled portraits of George and Rose also decorate the front of the gravestone. Another noteworthy memorial marks the future resting places of Estevano (Steve) and Matrona Costello. It reads like a résumé of Roma life. Steve is described as an international legend, a man known all over the world, judge-lawmaker, inventor, singer, composer, musician-entertainer. He and his wife are depicted twice on the marker, first as a young couple in Gypsy garb and then as a mature couple in formal wear.

An equally impressive collection of Gypsy gravemarkers can be found at Rosedale & Rosehill Cemetery in Linden. Among the noteworthy are those of Butch Wando (1992), again of black granite with gilt lettering, complete with a Rolls Royce emblem, and John Lazo (1986), a champion of Romany rights. Although the Gypsies remain hidden, their markers bring an unparalleled vibrancy to New Jersey's cemeteries.

HISPANIC CEMETERIES

New Jersey is also home to sizable contingents of Latin American immigrants. Since their arrival has been relatively recent, their memorial traditions have seen little formal study. However, their gravemarkers also merit mention. Popular motifs include Christ crucified, the head of Christ wearing a crown of thorns, and floral decorations, often quite elaborate. A number of Hispanic gravemarkers can be seen in Perth Amboy's Alpine Cemetery.

MUSLIM CEMETERIES: BORN IN CAIRO,
DIED IN NEW YORK CITY

Muslim cemeteries and sections of burial grounds are among the most recent
additions to New Jersey's funerary landscape. Rosedale & Rosehill Cemetery
in Linden is home to hundreds of both Gypsy and Muslim graves. Laurel
Grove Cemetery in Totowa also has exceptional Muslim sections, as does Jersey State Memorial Park in Millstone. Ethnicity is an important part of a
person's identity during life, and continues to be so in death (Francis, Kellaher, and Neophytou 2005). Many new immigrants plan on returning home
and being buried in their first communities. However, due to circumstances
beyond their control—marriages, sudden deaths, financial setbacks—this is
often not possible.

Today, New Jersey is home to about four hundred thousand Muslims.
Their funerary practices are distinct. Muslims are typically buried as soon as
possible after death. They follow a practice called *janaza*, which requires that
the body be washed, wrapped in a shroud, and buried within twenty-four
hours (Kent 1997, NJ 10). The bodies are washed and prepared for burial by
members of the same sex. Although traditionally Muslims prefer to bury
their dead without coffins, wooden coffins are sometimes used. The
deceased's body should face toward the east and Mecca. Graves are often
raised slightly above ground level. Muslims also prefer to be buried among
other Muslims.

Traditional Muslim funerary practices are completely legal, but
many cemeteries refuse burials without vaults and caskets. Two that permit such burials are Seaside Cemetery in Mays Landing and Makbarat
As-Salaam in Millstone (Kent 1997, NJ 10). A visit to a Muslim section
of a cemetery highlights the diverse origins of New Jersey's recent
arrivals. In Rosedale & Rosehill Cemetery there are markers for immigrants from Kabul, Afghanistan; Cairo, Egypt; and Najaf, Iraq. The
gravemarkers are moderately sized and beautifully decorated. Common
images include the Koran, mosques, palm trees, pyramids, and the cres-
cent moon. Most are professionally carved in granite, but there are some
in slate or marble, their lettering highlighted with paint. Dates are often
given using the Islamic calendar and inscriptions tend to be in both Ara-
bic and English.

At Laurel Grove in Totowa there are numerous gravemarkers for immigrants from the Muslim world, especially Turkey. Many of the graves are
raised in the style prescribed by Islamic teachings, and most are abloom with
flowers. Memorials often show the Hagia Sophia and other emblematic
images of Turkey (fig. 10.9). On occasion one sees a small, wooden anthropomorphic marker, presumably being used until a professionally carved stone
arrives.

10.9 The Hagia Sophia in Istanbul and a Koran are depicted on this gravemarker in Laurel Grove Cemetery, Totowa.

The Exceptional Stone

Ethnic cemeteries are Meccas for lovers of modern gravestone art. However, space permits us only to touch upon a handful of the most exceptional burial grounds. While non-ethnic cemeteries tend to be more restrained in their artwork, granite etching and modern carving techniques are allowing individuals to select highly individualized gravemarkers, often reflecting occupations or hobbies. Totowa's Laurel Grove Cemetery, an enormous, well-maintained modern cemetery, with more than eighty-five thousand interments, has several of the finest of these memorials. Two that are particularly well known were created for Sal Giardino and his daughter Kim. Sal's is a giant black marble light bulb with lettering across it in the style of lightning bolts that reads, "World's Greatest Electrician, Lic. #409" (fig. 10.10). The base of the marker is decorated with an image of Sal and an electrical outlet—carved from stone, of course. Kim Giardino is buried next to her father. Her memorial has a picture of a peace sign superimposed on a map of the world. These two fine markers are the work of Sgobba's Monument Works in Totowa (Moran and Sceurman 1997, 4).

In Rahway's Hazelwood Cemetery another modern marvel can be found. On one side of the gravemarker for Bruce Berman (d. 1998) there is

10.10 Sal Giardino's headstone in Totowa's Laurel Grove Cemetery notes that he was the "world's greatest electrician." His marker, made from black granite, is shaped like a light bulb and is complemented by a small nonfunctioning electrical outlet.

an enameled portrait of the deceased and his family. The inscription describes him as a gentle man, talented teacher, and artist. The obverse of the marker is even more striking. What appears to be Bruce's face is carved in such a way that it appears to be pushing out of the stone toward the viewer. It resembles nothing so much as the cryogenically frozen Han Solo in the movie *The Empire Strikes Back* (fig. 10.11). Below the startling sculpture is Bruce's web address, www.bermananimation.com. Sadly, the link seems to be dead.

There is also humor to be found in New Jersey's modern cemeteries. William Hahn's gravemarker in the Princeton Cemetery is inscribed with the simple epitaph, "I Told You I Was Sick." Another humorous marker commemorates Dorothy "Christiansen" DeCarlo (1936–1992). Located in the Colestown Cemetery in Cherry Hill, it is engraved with a Bingo card. But the William R. Ware marker in the Pleasant Mills Cemetery truly has the last laugh. Its epitaph reads, "Enlightened, Enchanted, Embalmed, Nyuk, Nyuk Nyuk."

Pet Cemeteries

Another relatively recent development is the pet cemetery. No longer is a small patch in the back corner of the yard sufficient for Rover. On the front lawn of Monmouth University's Wilson Hall are gravemarkers for the dogs of Hubert and Masie Parsons, heirs to the Woolworth fortune. Leo the Lion, whose roar graced MGM movies, was buried on the Volney Phifer animal farm in Gillette in 1938 and Elsie the Cow from the Borden Milk Com-

10.11 The Bruce Berman gravemarker in Rahway's Hazelwood Cemetery not only is inscribed with Bruce's Web address, but appears to show a face and hands pushing through the stone.

pany was laid to rest at the Walker-Gordon farm in Plainsboro in 1941 (*New York Times*, April 5, 2006; Sullivan 2006, 40).

Many communities have pet cemeteries. Atlantic City has one that was established in 1918. It is the final resting place of "over 3,000 animals: dogs, cats, horses, monkeys, guinea pigs, mice, canaries, parrots, etc." (Branin 2001, 70). Some of the residents include the Diving Horse from Atlantic City's Steel Pier and Rex the Wonder Dog. Other pet cemeteries can be found in Forked River, Hamilton Township, and Vineland, but the true Valhalla of pet cemeteries is Abbey Glen Pet Memorial Park in Lafayette. It has both a columbarium for cremated pets and a mausoleum for pet remains. There are even vaults for in-ground burial. Essentially all the accoutrements to send one's pet off in style are provided. The landscape is manicured and decorated with tasteful sculptures. It is a full-service modern lawn cemetery designed for pets.

Conclusions

The twentieth century has seen significant changes in the state's cemeteries. The rise of the memorial park introduced a new aesthetic, where the emphasis was not on individual headstones but on fine art and scenic landscapes. Attempts were also made to preserve cemeteries for the long term through the institution of funding for perpetual care. Outstanding examples of the memorial park ethos are George Washington Memorial Park in Paramus, Lakeview Memorial Park in Cinnaminson, and Hollywood Memorial Park in Union.

Despite the memorial park designers' insistence on minimalist monuments, the reality has been somewhat different. New immigrants from Asia, Eastern Europe, the Muslim world, and specific subcultures, like the Gypsies, have continued to erect monuments that reflect their distinctive beliefs and heritages. They add color and interest to the state's modern burial grounds and will likely be studied by historians and anthropologists for years to come.

A worldwide network of stone suppliers and improved carving techniques, such as stone etching, are allowing more and more elaborate images to be placed on long-lasting granite markers. Individualism is also increasingly driving the choice of shape, decoration, and inscriptions for grave-markers: light bulbs, cars, pianos, and even high-top sneakers can now be found in the state's cemeteries. Pets, important members of many modern families, are also receiving gravemarkers in cemeteries little different from those where their masters are buried.

New Jersey's cemeteries are evolving and continue to reflect our society's changing values. Many of the same economic trends that shape other businesses are affecting the cemetery business. The stone supply is now global, carving is done in part with computers, and regional and national cemetery management corporations, such as CMS (Cemetery Management Services), have developed. As they have for centuries, New Jersey's burial grounds and the gravemarkers in them continue to reflect the values, history, and cultures of this intriguing state.

« 11 »

New Jersey's Burial Grounds Past and Present

The city resolves that provisions be made at once for the removal of the bodies buried in the Old Burying Ground to some suitable location.

~ *Newark city directory, 1887* ~

New Jersey's historic burial places are a treasure trove of information for genealogists, historians, art historians, archaeologists, and indeed anyone interested in local history. But what is their future? In 1886, after years of legal wrangling, Newark's historic Old Burying Ground was developed and the bones and headstones removed to Fairmount Cemetery. In the most densely populated state in the nation, where real estate commands a premium, few burial sites are sacrosanct. Within the last decade massive nineteenth- and twentieth-century cemeteries, containing thousands of interments, have been relocated. Rural family plots lie forgotten in thickets and marble and granite monuments in urban cemeteries litter the ground as though some giant had knocked them over. Fewer and fewer individuals go to visit the burial sites of friends and family, preferring to avoid the inevitable as long as possible. The situation seems bleak.

Legal protection for New Jersey's historic burial places is limited. The state Cemetery Board regulates active public burial grounds, but has no oversight of private, religious, or inactive burial grounds—the vast majority of cemeteries in the state. However, local ordinances may provide some measure of protection for historic burial grounds and increasingly friends groups and historical and genealogical societies are taking an active interest in preserving these sites. Several of the state's historic burial grounds, such as Madison's Bottle Hill or Hillside Cemetery, have seen extensive restoration efforts. Skilled conservators can reset almost any monument, and patch and clean markers to a close semblance of their original appearance. Other historic graveyards, such as Woodbridge's First Presbyterian Burial Ground and

Shrewsbury's Christ Episcopal Church, are points of pride for their congregations, who regularly host tours for history-minded individuals.

Popular interest in cemeteries, after decades in abeyance, is returning. There are organizations for individuals interested in historic burial grounds, including the Association for Gravestone Studies. This is not simply a forum for scholarly discussion of gravemarkers, but also serves as a clearing house of information on cemetery restoration and interpretation. Popular magazines like *Weird New Jersey* regularly feature interesting and unusual gravemarkers, and television shows such as *Six Feet Under* draw attention to what the muckraking journalist Jessica Mitford referred to as "the last great necessity" (2000).

Moreover, modern burial grounds are no less intriguing than those employed by past generations. The cemetery of the twenty-first century is likely to be owned by a national or international corporation. It may follow the memorial park aesthetic begun in the early twentieth century, with flush markers and carefully selected artwork and plantings, or it may be full of personalized memorials, taking advantage of the latest techniques in laser etching. The stone used is as likely to have come from South America or India as from Elberton, Georgia, or Barre, Vermont. In this world of the future, digital recordings of the deceased and testimonials that can be downloaded and played are taking the place of traditional headstones. Green burials, which avoid the potential pollution of embalming fluids and costly coffins fit for Egyptian pharaohs, are becoming popular. Here the deceased is returned to the earth in a shroud woven from an organic fiber to decay as naturally as possible. There may be no markers at all in the burial ground, though in some cases the deceased is marked by a computer chip that can be located with a GPS receiver—the ultimate marriage of high tech and low tech in a burial. Cremation is becoming increasingly popular too, and, as cemeteries run out of room below ground, mausoleums grow taller and taller.

Settlers began to bury their dead in New Jersey in the colonial period. Sandstone slabs and headstones marked these early pioneers. Inscribed in English, Dutch, and German, they reflected the varied heritages of these settlers. Although no early Native American gravemarkers remain, ancient burials have been unearthed by archaeologists, and commemorative monuments for a handful of noteworthy individuals have been erected. Wooden markers and fieldstones were also used for many graves. As time went by, these home-made memorials gave way to professionally carved stones, wrought in sandstone, marble, and slate. Some are richly ornamented with skulls and crossbones, cherubim, and willow trees; others are free of any decoration. All reflect the societies and individuals that produced them. By the late eighteenth century, gravestone carving was thriving in northern New Jersey, with skilled artisans in Newark, Elizabeth, Woodbridge, Rahway, and

New Brunswick. Carvers more often signed their markers, hoping to capture some small part of the market, occasionally even noting the price. Some carvers, such as John Frazee, outgrew their mundane commemorative pursuits and became well-known artists. Others, throughout the state, continued to labor at carving gravemarkers, increasingly in marble, in new classically inspired styles.

In the early nineteenth century, undecorated marble markers carved in the Philadelphia style became the national norm. Some of the first markers for free African Americans appeared in this period. They are reminders of the long reach of slavery in colonial New Jersey.

Family plots, church graveyards, and common burial grounds became increasingly crowded, unsightly, and unsanitary, and, by the early nineteenth century, urban reformers were advocating new forms of burial in professionally designed and beautifully landscaped cemeteries, outside of the urban core. Newark, Trenton, Elizabeth, Camden, Paterson, and, by the end of the nineteenth century, most minor urban centers had their garden or rural cemeteries, though increasingly they were subsumed within the growing cities they had once sought to escape.

Waves of new immigrants from Ireland, Germany, Italy, Russia, and other regions of Eastern and Southern Europe brought their own commemorative traditions to New Jersey's burial grounds. Iron crosses, Celtic high crosses, ceramic gravemarkers, and memorial photographs helped these new immigrants remember their dead. Chinese immigrants tried to have their relatives' remains shipped home, but sometimes their sojourns in America became permanent. Immigrants too poor to purchase professionally carved markers, or possessing the skills to make their own memorials, turned to iron, concrete, and clay to fashion monuments to deceased kin and friends.

During the late nineteenth century, class differences, always present in burial grounds, manifested themselves more strongly than ever before. Cemeteries were segregated by class and memorials for the wealthy grew increasingly ostentatious, as seen in the mausoleums of Newark's beer barons and the elaborate monuments erected by industrialists in Paterson, Trenton, and elsewhere. Later community mausoleums provided more democratic resting places for the urban middle class. Cremation, long denounced by the Catholic Church, gained increasing acceptance in the twentieth century and columbaria were constructed to house the remains of these freethinkers.

The rise of new institutions—state hospitals, prisons, asylums, veterans' homes, and orphanages—in the nineteenth century was accompanied by the growth of institutional cemeteries. Inexpensive mass-produced markers made from concrete, metal, or clay, sometimes marked only with serial numbers, perpetuated the institutionalization of some individuals into eternity.

By the late nineteenth century, new technologies and improved transportation networks were making attractive and long-lasting granite memorials available to the masses. Carvers gave up the chisel for pneumatic drills and increasing standardization became the norm in monument design.

Garden cemeteries, which had once seemed a respite from cramped urban graveyards, were increasingly crowded with a jumble of marble and granite markers. In response, memorial parks, an idea first introduced in California, became popular. New Jersey has several spectacular examples, most notably George Washington Memorial Park. Here the individual gravemarker was deemphasized while the overall aesthetic of a parklike landscape unmarred by gravestones became the norm.

Nevertheless, some chose not to follow this new design. New Jersey's modern burial grounds rarely fall neatly into one category. Elaborate painted gravemarkers for Asian and Muslim immigrants may abut flush bronze markers in today's cemeteries. Immigrants from Ukraine and Russia as well as Gypsies send off their deceased comrades in style with elaborate, artistic, and colorful markers. Individual headstones are as likely to display a New York Yankees logo or a favorite hobby as they are to bear a religious inscription.

New Jersey burial grounds have evolved; they remain diverse and yet they share a commonality—they are a reflection of the people. They commemorate on various levels, telling the stories of the individuals who are interred, but also narrating the tales of those who designed and managed the cemeteries and carved the stones.

Unfortunately, so often in researching history the daily tasks of people go unrecorded, and their stories become lost over time. Those who study cemeteries and gravemarkers certainly ache for descriptive references of cemetery operations and detailed accounts of long-gone stonecarvers.

We therefore conclude with a personal account of a modern monument shop. In writing a book about cemeteries and gravemarkers, we could have chosen to end with a description of a cemetery through the eyes of the superintendent; certainly the stories we have heard over the years are fascinating. Instead we leave the reader with a glimpse into the lives of people who create the monuments, which after all are the essence of the cemetery. The following is our way of honoring these craftsmen, and it is our gift to future historians.

———

It was a cold January day when we drove to Will Hope and Son Monument Company in Burlington City. The president of the company, Thomas Hope, had responded to a questionnaire that we had mailed to over one hundred monument dealers in New Jersey. In his response he had informed us that his firm was founded in 1914; he also wrote that he had old photographs and tools that we could see.

Upon our arrival we are met at the door by Thomas, a man in his thirties, who shows us in. The office area is small with desks to the right and a customer reception area to the left. We sit at a table off to the left corner as Thomas, who is dressed in blue jeans, loafers, and pullover sweatshirt, brings over a briefcase filled with historic photographs and yellowed newspaper clippings that chronicle the history of the company. He explains that his great-grandfather Will Hope, a native of England, purchased the company in 1914 from another monument firm in Burlington. With Thomas looking on, we begin to sift through the materials: photographs of long-forgotten groups of men standing in front of newly erected monuments; drawings of tombstones with their costs—one sketch shows a marker for Lucia Prudent from 1918 at a price of $18—and yellowed clippings from newspapers, including an article from 1960 when Joseph Hope, the son of the founder, went to visit the granite shops in Barre, Vermont.

In the background we hear a police scanner and Thomas's ears perk up for a moment as a garbled voice comes over the radio. He explains that besides running the monument business he is also involved with the local rescue squad.

We soon come across a series of photographs taken in the late 1910s. It shows the office furnished with cushioned wicker chairs. Upon closer examination of the photographs we are amazed to find that the walls were once painted with a cemetery landscape scene. We can see in the mural finely painted miniature monuments. Below the scene is a chair rail and a darkly painted wainscoting that is randomly decorated with stencils of tombstone motifs.

For a moment we stop to compare the photograph with the office today. The painted scene has given way to its modern counterpart—an Astroturf wall that is decorated with examples of bronze tablets for memorials parks. Near the table, lining a shelf, are samples of granite from around the world. Seeing our interest in these, Thomas talks about each one in detail, including its origin. Many of the samples come from overseas; others are from the old quarries at Barre. He even shows us examples of modern design etchings, including laser etching on granite.

Thomas then asks if we would like to see the workshop and the old tools. Without hesitation we accept the invitation and are led through the office past a computer that displays an image of a stencil for a customer's order. He takes us through a door and down some steps into another room. We pass a large printer, which is used to generate the stencils for the face of the markers. In the opposite corner is a large blue air compressor, which powers the sandblasting equipment in a nearby room.

Just around the corner we catch our first glimpse of the workshop. It is an open space with a large garage-type door on one wall. The floor is concrete and the ceiling is open, exposing the old rafters and skylights. To our immediate right is a machine that Thomas says was first used about forty years ago and still receives limited use today. It looks likes a large drafting table with a small iron beam suspended over it. A punch comes off the center of the beam down toward the table. Thomas pulls out trays of plastic letters in different sizes and fonts and explains that these letters are placed in the punch and then pressed into the rubber stencil.

Thomas begins to reminisce about stories his father told of when rubber stencils were melted on a coal-burning stove and then poured over the face of the marker. This had to be done very carefully in order to ensure an even spread of rubber over the stone. The melting rubber would leave a pungent smell in the workshop. Although the odor of rubber no longer lingers in the air, there is a certain musty smell, and as we look around we can sense its source, as a century of clutter overwhelms us.

In one corner wooden cubbyholes hold close to a century's worth of tools, including grinding wheels, wooden mallets, and iron chisels. It looks as though they were placed in their respective compartments decades ago and never picked up again. We quickly zone in on a wooden mallet covered in dust and examine its surface worn from years of use. On the floor in what seems like a bottomless crate is every imaginable iron chisel type. As we pull the various chisels out, Thomas briefly explains what each one was used for. Near the crate are several pairs of what look like small yokes. Thomas says these iron tools were once used by the monument company to set stones in the cemetery.

Behind us someone is sandblasting a design onto a marker. The process is loud and for a moment we turn around to see what is going on. Two workers are busy with monuments. One is sandblasting an image of the Virgin Mary onto a stone while the other, Kevin Thiel, wearing a backward baseball cap and earplugs, applies a white adhesive paste to the surface of a marker. He is dressed in blue jeans and a blue thermal shirt, over which is a white Will Hope & Son company T-shirt.

The marker he is working on sits on a push cart that looks as if it has been in use for the past one hundred years (fig. 11.1). It is made from heavy wooden planks darkened with age and is attached to an iron chassis and wheels. Blocks of wood have been set across the planks to raise the stone from the surface of the cart, thus making it easier to load it on and off.

Against one wall of the workshop are two chambers into which stones are placed for sandblasting. The first chamber is constructed of iron; Thomas opens the heavy metal door and we step inside. Heavy black rubber matting hangs from the sides and several work lights are clipped to various sections of the interior. He explains that the markers are wheeled into the room and then sandblasted using either sand or metal shavings, depending on what surface effect they wish to achieve.

The second chamber appears older and is constructed with a wooden front and iron sides. The side has a viewing window and another opening just below it, in which thick rubber mats also hang. The operator, Rick

11.1 A modern gravestone about to be carved. With the aid of this ancient stone cart, the memorial will be pushed into a sandblasting chamber.
(Reproduced with permission from Will Hope & Son Monument Co., Burlington City.)

Sanderson, can place the sandblasting hose through the rubber mats and gauge his work by looking through the window. An ancient-looking cylindrical sandblasting container about four feet high stands near the booth, bearing a polished brass tag that says, "Manufactured by the Peoria Sand Blasting Manufacturing Company of Peoria, Illinois." Rick wears heavy gloves and is busy sandblasting an image onto the surface of the stone. For a moment he lets us gaze in so we can watch him work. By the light of a bulb we watch the sand bounce off the surface, leaving an impression in the stone—and on us. We ask to take his picture as he works. His talent is clear. He is the modern equivalent of Ebenezer Price and Henry Sillcocks. We hope that his work is of as much interest to future researchers as theirs is to us.

Will Hope and Son Monument Company, like others throughout the state, carries on a long tradition of carving stories in stone. It is hard to predict what the future may hold; perhaps stone gravemarkers may be replaced altogether as other movements gain acceptance. Certainly cremation is on the rise; other forms of commemoration are being introduced as well, such as kiosks with videotaped stories and green burials, as discussed earlier. In any case, our visit with Thomas Hope helps connect an image and a story with the people that create the monuments.

Cemeteries tell the stories of people and perhaps that is what drives us to understand them. We can see those stories from many viewpoints, whether they are those of the designers and managers of cemeteries, the stories the monuments tell us about the people they commemorate, or are told from the perspective of people like Thomas Hope, who continue to create stories in stone for the modern cemetery landscape. Cemeteries have many stories to tell; all we need to do is stop and cast an eye upon this history in the landscape, a window to perhaps the greatest narrative of our past.

BURIAL GROUNDS VISITED

The following appendix lists the burial grounds visited during the course of our research. It is by no means a comprehensive list of New Jersey's historic burial places or a complete list of all the cemeteries we visited. In the course of our research we visited more than 950 burial grounds—too many to include in a list. However, it does include many of the state's most important burial grounds in terms of artwork, landscape design, religious history, and association with various ethnic groups.

C = Colonial or eighteenth-century burial ground
V = Victorian or nineteenth-century burial ground or cemetery
M = Modern or twentieth-century burial ground, cemetery, or memorial park
*Burial ground or cemetery of exceptional interest

Location	Type	Location	Type
ATLANTIC COUNTY		Old Meetinghouse Burial Ground, Smithville	V/M
Atlantic City Cemetery, Pleasantville	V/M*	Westcott Free Burying Ground, Mays Landing	V
Baptist Cemetery, Head of the River, Estell Manor	C	Weymouth Cemetery, Weymouth	V
Boling Cemetery, Port Republic	V	**BERGEN COUNTY**	
Clarks Mill Burying Ground, Port Republic	C	First Reformed Dutch Churchyard, Hackensack	C/V*
Egg Harbor City Cemetery, Egg Harbor	V/M*	French Cemetery, River Edge	C*
Emmaus United Methodist Church and Cemetery, Smithville	V/M	Gethsemane African American Cemetery, Little Ferry	V*
Germania Cemetery, Galloway Township	V/M	Moffat Road Lutheran Cemetery, Mahwah	C
Greenwood Cemetery, Pleasantville	V/M	Old Paramus Reformed Church Burial Ground, Ridgewood	C/V/M*
Head of the River Cemetery, Estell Manor	C/V/M	**BURLINGTON COUNTY**	
Holy Sepulcher Cemetery, Hammonton	V/M	Atsion Churchyard (Samuel Richards' Church), Atsion	V
Smith's Meeting House Burial Ground, Port Republic	C	Batsto/Pleasant Mills Cemetery, Pleasant Mills	C/V*

Location	Type	Location	Type
Beverly National Cemetery, Beverly	V/M	Cold Spring Presbyterian Burial Ground, Cold Spring	C/V*
Cavileer-Sooy Burial Ground, Lower Bank	C	Goshen United Methodist Cemetery, Goshen	V
Colestown Cemetery, Colestown	V	Hand-Somers Cemetery, Swaintown	C/V
Crosswicks Friends Burial Ground, Crosswicks	C	Henry Ludlam Family Cemetery, Dennisville	V
Friends Meeting House Burial Grounds, Burlington	C	Seaville Methodist Churchyard, Seaville	V
Green Bank Cemetery	C/V	Second Cape May Baptist Churchyard/Seaview Cemetery, Palermo	C/V/M
Hillside Cemetery, New Gretna	V/M		
Mount Holly Friends, Mount Holly	C*	Trinity Methodist Church Burial Ground, Marmora	C/V/M
Odd Fellows Cemetery, Burlington City	V/M	United Brotherhood Cemetery, Woodbine	M
Old St. Mary's Cemetery, Burlington City	C/V/M*	Wesley Cemetery, Petersburg	V
Old Lower Bank Meeting House, Lower Bank	V	CUMBERLAND COUNTY	
Orthodox Friends Burial Ground, Crosswicks	C	Cumberland Methodist Episcopal Churchyard, Port Elizabeth	V*
Peacock Family Burial Ground, Chairville	V	Deerfield Church Cemetery, Upper Deerfield	C/V*
St. Andrew's Cemetery, Mount Holly	C/V*	Maurice River Friends Burial Ground, Port Elizabeth	V
St. Mary's of the Assumption, Pleasant Mills	V	Mount Pleasant Cemetery, Millville	V/M
Upper Springfield Meeting House, Upper Springfield	V	Old Presbyterian Church Burial Ground, Greenwich	C/V
Weymouth Cemetery, Weymouth	V	ESSEX COUNTY	
CAMDEN COUNTY		Belleville Dutch Reformed Church, Belleville	C
Evergreen Cemetery, Camden	V	Bloomfield Cemetery, Bloomfield	V/M*
Harleigh Cemetery, Camden	V/M*	B'nai Abraham Cemetery, Newark	V/M
Locust Wood Memorial Park	M	Caldwell First Presbyterian Church Cemetery, Caldwell	C*
Mount Peace Cemetery, Lawnside	V/M	Christ Episcopal Churchyard, Belleville	C
Mount Zion Cemetery, Lawnside	V/M	Congregation Adas Israel, East Orange	V
New Camden Cemetery, Camden	V	Congregation Anshe Russia, East Orange	V
Old Camden Cemetery, Camden	V	Ely Family Burial Ground, Livingston	C
St. Mary's, Gloucester City	V	Northfield Baptist Church, Livingston	C
Union Cemetery, Gloucester City	V	Evergreen Cemetery, Hillside	V/M*
CAPE MAY COUNTY		Fairfield Reformed Church, Fairfield	V/M
Baptist Burial Ground, Cape May Courthouse	C/V*	Fairmont Cemetery, Newark	V/M*

Location	Type
Grove Street Cemetery, Newark	V/M
Holy Sepulchre, East Orange/ Newark	V/M*
McClellan Street Cemeteries, Newark	V/M
Mount Pleasant Cemetery, Newark	V*
Old First Presbyterian Church Burial Ground, Newark	C
Remnants in Memorial Garden	
Old First Presbyterian Church Second Burial Ground, Newark	C
Orange Presbyterian, Orange	C*
Rosedale Cemetery, Montclair	V
Talmud Torah Cemetery, Newark	V/M
St. Peter's Church, Belleville	V
Union Field Cemetery, Newark	V/M

GLOUCESTER COUNTY

Location	Type
Green-Fields Cemetery, Woodbury	M
St. Thomas Episcopal Church Cemetery, Glassboro	V
Stanger Episcopal Burial Ground, Glassboro	C
Trinity Church (New Cemetery), Swedesboro	V
Trinity Episcopal Church and Cemetery (Old Swedes), Swedesboro	C*

HUDSON COUNTY

Location	Type
Arlington Cemetery, Arlington	V/M
Flower Hill Cemetery, North Bergen	V/M*
Holy Name, Jersey City	V/M*
Jersey City and Harsimus Cemetery	V/M
New York Bayview Cemetery	V/M*
Old Bergen Church Burial Ground	C/V
St. Peter's Cemetery, Jersey City	V

HUNTERDON COUNTY

Location	Type
Amwell Cemetery	C/V
Bloomsbury Presbyterian Church	V
Bloomsbury United Methodist Church	V
Case Burial Ground, Flemington	C

Location	Type
Evergreen Cemetery, Clinton	M
Fairmont Presbyterian Churchyard	C/V
Fairmont United Methodist Cemetery	V/M
Frenchtown Cemetery, Frenchtown	V/M
Kingwood Presbyterian Church, Oak Summit	V
Larison's Corner Cemetery, East Amwell	C/V
Locktown Old School Baptist Cemetery, Kingwood	C/V
Milford Union Cemetery, Milford	V/M
Mount Hope Cemetery, Lambertville	V*
Oldwick Methodist Episcopal Cemetery	V/M
Oldwick Zion Lutheran Churchyard	C
Prospect Hill Cemetery, Flemington	V/M
Rockefeller Burial Ground, East Amwell	C/V*
Rural Hill Cemetery, Whitehouse	V
Sergeantsville Methodist Episcopal Church Cemetery	V
Stout-Manners Cemetery, Wertsville	C/V*
Whitehouse Churchyard, Old Haypress, Readington	C
Whitehouse Memorial Park D.A.R. Cemetery	V
Zion Lutheran Church Cemetery, Oldwick	C/V

MERCER COUNTY

Location	Type
Colonial Memorial Park, Hamilton Township	M
Congregation Brothers of Israel Cemetery, Hamilton Township	M
Congregation People of Truth Cemetery, Hamilton Township	M
Congregation Workers of Truth Cemetery, Hamilton Township	M
Ewing Presbyterian Church Cemetery	C/V/M*
First Presbyterian Churchyard, Trenton	C/V*

Location	Type	Location	Type
Greenwood Cemetery, Hamilton Township	V/M	St. Vladimir Cemetery, Hamilton Township	M
Holy Cross Cemetery, Hamilton Township	V/M*	Stony Brook Quaker Burial Ground, Princeton	C
Holy Sepulchre Cemetery, Hamilton Township	M	Stout Farm Burial Ground, Hopewell Township	C/V
Holy Trinity Ukrainian Orthodox Cemetery	M	Workmen's Circle, Branch 90 Cemetery, Hamilton Township	M
Old School Hopewell Baptist Churchyard	C/V/M		

MIDDLESEX COUNTY

Location	Type	Location	Type
Lawrenceville Cemetery	C/V/M	Alpine Cemetery, Perth Amboy	V/M*
Lawrenceville Presbyterian Churchyard	C/V	Calvary Cemetery, Woodbridge	V/M
Mercer Cemetery, Trenton	V/M*	Cemetery of the Ukrainian Catholic Church of the Assumption, Woodbridge	V/M
New Jersey State Prison Cemetery, Hamilton Township	M	Christ Church Cemetery, Sayreville	V/M
Our Lady of Lourdes Cemetery, Hamilton Township	V/M	Christ Episcopal Churchyard, New Brunswick	C/V*
Polish National Catholic Church of Our Savior, Hamilton Township	M	Cloverleaf Memorial Park, Woodbridge	M*
Princeton Cemetery, Princeton Borough	C/V/M*	Cranbury Presbyterian Burial Ground, Cranbury	C/V*
Princeton Memorial Park, Washington Township	M*	Elm Ridge Cemetery, North Brunswick	C/V
Riverview Cemetery, Trenton	V/M*	Elmwood Cemetery, North Brunswick	V/M*
St. Basil's Cemetery, Hamilton Township	M	Evergreen, New Brunswick	V/M
St. Hedwig's Cemetery, Hamilton Township	M	First Presbyterian Burial Ground, Woodbridge	C/V/M*
St. John's Cemetery, Hamilton Township	M	First Reformed Churchyard, New Brunswick	C/V*
St. Mary's Roman Catholic Cemetery, Hamilton Township	M	Hillside Cemetery, Metuchen	V/M
St. Michael's Episcopal Churchyard, Trenton	C/V*	Holy Redeemer Cemetery, South Plainfield	M
St. Nicholas Greek Catholic Cemetery, Hamilton Township	M	Holy Trinity Cemetery, Woodbridge	M
St. Paul's Cemetery, Princeton Borough	V/M*	Metuchen First Presbyterian Churchyard (Old Section), Metuchen	C*
Sts. Peter and Paul Cemetery, Hamilton Township	M	Metuchen First Presbyterian Churchyard (New Section), Metuchen	V/M
St. Stanislaus Cemetery, Hamilton Township	M	New Market Baptist, Piscataway	V
St. Stephen's Roman Cemetery, Hamilton Township	M	Old School Baptist Cemetery, South River	V
		Our Lady of Hungary Cemetery, Woodbridge	M

Location	Type
Our Lady of the Most Holy Rosary, Woodbridge	M
Our Lady of Victories Cemetery, Sayreville	V
Piscatawaytown Burial Ground, Edison	C/V*
Samptown/Hillside Cemetery, South Plainfield	C/V/M
Seventh Day Baptist Cemetery, Edison	C/V
St. James, Edison	C/V*
St. James, Woodbridge	V/M*
St. John the Baptist, Woodbridge	M
St. Mary's Cemetery, Perth Amboy	V/M*
St. Mary's Cemetery, South Amboy	V/M
St. Peter's Episcopal Church, Perth Amboy	C*
St. Peter's Episcopal Church, Spotswood	C
St. Stephen's Cemetery, Woodbridge	V/M
Stelton Baptist, Piscataway	C/V
Three Mile Run Burial Ground, New Brunswick	C*
Trinity Episcopal Church, Woodbridge	C*
Van Liew Cemetery	C/V/M
Willow Grove, New Brunswick	C/V
Washington Monumental, South River	V

MONMOUTH COUNTY

Location	Type
Atlantic View Cemetery, Manasquan	V/M
Christ Episcopal Churchyard, Middletown	C/V*
Christ Episcopal Churchyard, Shrewsbury	C/V/M*
Congregation Brothers of Israel Cemetery, Long Branch	M
Crystal Stream Cemetery, Middletown	M
Daniel Hendrickson Family Burial Ground, Middletown	C/V
Drummond Family Burial Ground, Ocean Township	V
Fair View Cemetery, Middletown	V/M*
First Presbyterian Churchyard, Shrewsbury	C/V/M*

Location	Type
Glenwood Cemetery, West Long Branch	V/M*
Green Grove Cemetery, Keyport	V
Greenlawn Cemetery, West Long Branch	V/M*
Hartshorne Family Burial Ground, Middletown	C/V/M
Hamilton Methodist Episcopal Churchyard, Neptune	V/M*
Hebrew Burial Grounds Association Cemetery, West Long Branch	M
Holmdel Cemetery, Holmdel	V/M
Independent Methodist Graveyard, West Long Branch	C/V
Locust Grove Burial Ground, Eatontown	V
Luyster Family Burial Ground, Holmdel	C/V*
Manasquan Friends Burial Ground, Manasquan	C/V
Marlboro State Hospital Cemetery, Marlboro	M*
Michael Field's Grave, Colts Neck	C
Mount Calvary Cemetery, Neptune Township	M
Mount Carmel Cemetery, West Long Branch	V/M
Mount Pleasant Burial Ground, Matawan	C/V*
Mount Prospect Cemetery, Neptune Township	V/M*
Old First Baptist Burial Ground, Middletown	C/V
Old First Methodist Episcopal Churchyard, West Long Branch	C/V/M
Old Brick (Reformed) Churchyard, Marlboro	C/V*
Old Long Branch Burial Ground, West Long Branch	V
Old Roman Catholic Burial Ground, Holmdel	V
Old Rumson Burial Ground, Rumson	C/V*
Old Scots Burial Ground, Marlboro	C/V*

Location	Type	Location	Type
Old Tennent Churchyard, Manalapan	C/V/M*	Meyersville Presbyterian Churchyard , Meyersville	V/M
Pine Brook Cemetery, Tinton Falls	V/M	Montville Reformed Church Cemetery, Montville	C/V/M*
Polhemus Family Burial Ground, Colts Neck	C	Morristown Presbyterian, Morristown	C/V*
Presbyterian Burial Ground, Middletown	C*	Parsippany First Presbyterian Church Cemetery, Parsippany	C/V*
Robbins Burial Ground, Upper Freehold	C/V	Pleasant Hill Cemetery, Chester	C/V/M
Rose Hill Cemetery, Matawan	V/M	Pompton Plains Reformed Churchyard, Pompton Plains	C/V/M
Ruffin Cemetery, Tinton Falls	M	Rockaway Presbyterian Churchyard, Rockaway	C/V/M
St. Peter's Episcopal Churchyard, Freehold Borough	C*	St. Vincent's Cemetery, Madison	V/M
Schenck-Covenhoven Burial Ground, Holmdel	C	Whippany Presbyterian Burial Ground, Hanover	C/V/M*
Shadow Rest Cemetery, Tinton Falls	M		
Shrewsbury Friends Burial Ground	C/V	**OCEAN COUNTY**	
Throckmorton-Lippit-Taylor Burial Ground, Middletown	C/V	Barnegat Friends Meeting House Burial Ground, Barnegat	C/V
Topanemus Burial Ground, Marlboro	C*	Cedar Run Cemetery, Manahawkin	V/M
Wayside Methodist Episcopal Churchyard	M	Good Luck/Potter's Churchyard, Lanoka Harbor	C/V
White Ridge Cemetery, Eatontown	V/M*	Old Manahawkin Cemetery, Manahawkin	C/V
Yellow Meeting House Cemetery, Upper Freehold	C/V*	Riverside Cemetery, Toms River	V/M
		Sea Captain's Cemetery, Barnegat	V
MORRIS COUNTY		Woodlawn Cemetery, Lakewood	V/M
Boonton Presbyterian Cemetery, Boonton	V/M	**PASSAIC COUNTY**	
Chester Congregational Churchyard, Chester	C/V/M*	Cedar Lawn Cemetery, Cedar Lawn	V/M*
First Presbyterian Churchyard, Succasunna	C/V*	Crest Haven Memorial Park	M
German Valley Rural Cemetery, Long Valley	V	East Ridgelawn Cemetery, Clifton	V/M
John Hancock Cemetery, Florham Park	V	Laurel Grove Cemetery and Memorial Park, Totowa	V/M
Hanover Presbyterian Churchyard, East Hanover	C/V/M*	Ringwood Manor Burial Ground, Ringwood	C*
Hillside/Madison/Bottle Hill Presbyterian, Madison	C/V*	**SALEM COUNTY**	
Hilltop Cemetery, Mendham	C/V/M*	Finns Point National Cemetery, Salem	V/M
Long Hill Cemetery, Passaic Township	V	Friesburg Emanuel Lutheran Churchyard, Alloway Township	C/V
Long Valley German Reformed or Old Stone Union Churchyard	C/V*	Friends Burial Ground, Salem	C/V

Location	Type	Location	Type
New Pittsgrove Presbyterian Church, Daretown	V/M	Somerville New Cemetery, Somerville	V/M
Old Daretown Baptist, Daretown	C	Van-Nest-Weston Burying Ground, Hillsborough	C
Old Pittsgrove Presbyterian Church, Daretown	C/V	Vermuele Family Burial Ground, North Plainfield	C/V

SOMERSET COUNTY

SUSSEX COUNTY

Location	Type	Location	Type
Basking Ridge Presbyterian Churchyard, Basking Ridge	C/V*	Bevans Church, Peter's Valley	V
Bound Brook Cemetery, Bound Brook	C/V/M*	Decker Cemetery, Milford	V
		Deckertown-Union Cemetery, Hamburg	V
Bound Brook Presbyterian Cemetery, Bound Brook	C*	Lafayette Cemetery, Lafayette	V
Hillsborough Dutch Reformed Churchyard, Hillsborough	C	Minisink Church Burial Ground, Montague	V/M
		Minisink Burial Ground, Montague	C/V
Kingston Presbyterian Churchyard, Kingston	C/V	Old Dutch Reformed Cemetery, Flatbrookville	C/V
Lamington Cemetery, Bedminster	C/M*	Old Newton Burial Ground, Newton	C/V
Lamington Presbyterian Churchyard, Bedminster	C/V/M*	Old Stillwater Cemetery, Stillwater	C/V/M*
Mount Bethel Baptist Churchyard, Warren	C/V*	St. Joseph Cemetery, Newton	V/M
		Sparta First Presbyterian Church Cemetery, Sparta	C/V*
Neshanic Cemetery Association, Neshanic	C/V/M	Vaughan Cemetery, Sparta	C*
North Branch Reformed Church Cemetery, Branchburg	C/V/M	Walpack Burial Ground, Walpack	V
North Princeton Developmental Center, Upper Cemetery, Montgomery	M*	Wantage Methodist Cemetery, Wantage	V/M
North Princeton Developmental Center, Lower Cemetery, Montgomery	M*	**UNION COUNTY**	
Old Bedminster Churchyard, Bedminster	C/V	Connecticut Farms Cemetery, Union	C/V*
Old Dutch Parsonage Burial Ground, Somerville	C	Elizabeth First Presbyterian Cemetery	C/V*
Old Plainfield Presbyterian Burial Ground, North Plainfield	V	Evergreen Cemetery, Hillside	V/M*
		Fairview, Westfield	V/M
Presbyterian Church Burial Ground, Pluckemin	C	Hazelwood Cemetery, Rahway	V/M
Rocky Hill Cemetery, Rocky Hill	M	Hillside Cemetery, Scotch Plains	V/M
Roman Catholic Cemetery, Rocky Hill	M	Mount Calvary, Linden	M
St. Andrew's Ukrainian Orthodox Cemetery	M*	New Providence First Presbyterian Churchyard	C/V
		New Providence Methodist Churchyard	V
St. Bernard's Cemetery, Bridgewater	M	Plainfield Friends Burial Ground	V/M
Somerville Old Cemetery, Somerville	V	Rahway Cemetery	C/V/M*

Location	Type	Location	Type
Rosedale & Rosehill Cemetery, Linden	V/M*	Hackettstown Presbyterian Cemetery, Hackettstown	C/V
St. Gertrude's Cemetery, Rahway	V/M	Johnsonburg Christian Cemetery, Frelinghuysen	C/V*
St. John's Episcopal Churchyard, Elizabeth	C	Knowlton Presbyterian, Blairstown	C/V*
St. Mary's Cemetery, Plainfield	V/M	Moravian Burial Ground, Hope	C/V*
Scotch Plains Baptist Churchyard	C/V/M	Old Greenwich Presbyterian Cemetery, Stewartsville	C/V
Springfield First Presbyterian, Springfield	C/V*	Ramseyburg Cemetery, Knowlton	V/M
Springfield Old SAR Cemetery	C*	St. James "Straw Church," Lutheran, Greenwich	C/V/M*
Westfield Presbyterian	C/V*	Sts. Philip and James, Greenwich	V/M
Willcox Family Burial Ground, Berkeley Heights	C	Swayze Family Burial Ground, Hope	C/V*
		Union Brick, Blairstown	C/V

WARREN COUNTY

Location	Type	Location	Type
Blair Academy, Blairstown	C/V*	Yellow Frame Presbyterian, Frelinghuysen	C/V*
First Presbyterian Church, Oxford	C		

GRAVESTONE CARVERS ACTIVE IN NEW JERSEY

The following list of over two hundred early New Jersey gravestone carvers covers the eighteenth and nineteenth centuries. It is based on signed markers, probate papers, advertisements in newspapers, and other primary sources. In addition, Kirkbride's 1850 *New Jersey Business Directory*, Boyd's 1860 New Jersey *Business Directory*, and Talbott and Blood's 1866 New Jersey *Business Directory* were utilized. Prior to 1750 New Jersey's gravestone carvers did not regularly sign their work. However, several anonymous artisans have been identified based on the distinctive characteristics of their carving. They are listed below.

ANONYMOUS ARTISANS (LISTED IN CHRONOLOGICAL ORDER)

Philadelphia Column Carver (1700–1710s). This carver worked soapstone. His markers are found in Philadelphia and also in St. Mary's Churchyard, Burlington City. Many of the markers employ bas-relief columns as a decorative motif. The columns show Doric capitals.

Old Elizabethtown Carver I (1720s–1730s). This carver may have worked in Elizabeth. He carved skulls and crossbones on sandstone. His mortality images were some of the most detailed in colonial New Jersey. He is well represented in colonial burial grounds in Elizabeth and Woodbridge.

Old Elizabethtown Carver II (1720s–1730s). This carver also may have worked in Elizabeth. He sculpted masklike mortality images on sandstone. He is represented in Elizabeth's colonial burial grounds.

Rosette Carver (1720s–1730s). This carver is well represented in Middlesex County. He worked a buff-colored, fine-grained sandstone, carving small rosettes and circles in the tympanum of his markers. His work is also common in Edison (Piscatawaytown), Woodbridge, Metuchen, and Monmouth County.

Common Jersey Carver (1720s–1760s). This carver, possibly from Newark or Elizabeth, sculpted both mortality images and cherubs on sandstone. He is well represented in Woodbridge, Orange, Elizabeth, Whippany, Morristown, and other northern New Jersey communities.

Orb Carver (1770s). This carver, possibly from Newark or Orange, produced cherubs on sandstone, with orbs over the cherub's heads. He is well represented in Morris County.

Roman Haircut Carver (1770s). This carver worked in sandstone, producing high-relief cherubs with their hair combed forward. His markers are found in Orange and Succasunna.

KNOWN CARVERS

Abraham Abbott, Rahway. Listed in 1860 and 1866 New Jersey business directories (Boyd; Talbott and Blood).

Jonathan Acken, Elizabeth. 1760–1800, carved cherubs on sandstone. Represented in Bound Brook, Cranbury, and Elizabeth.

Gabriel Allen, Providence, R.I. Slate cherubs found in New Brunswick and dating from the 1760s have been attributed to this carver (Vincent Luti 2005, personal communication).

George Allen Jr., Providence, R.I. A slate cherub for David Cowell (d. 1760) in Trenton's Presbyterian Churchyard is attributed to George Allen Jr. (Vincent Luti 2005, personal communication).

Andrew Allison. May have originally been from Easton, Pennsylvania; by the 1840s he is operating in Trenton. Several monuments signed by him are in Riverview Cemetery, Trenton.

Applegate, Bridgeton. 1894 marble monument for the Davis family in the Deerfield Presbyterian Cemetery.

Applegate & Ogden, Bridgeton. Signed 1873 headstone in the Deerfield Presbyterian Churchyard.

James Ayres, Hightstown. Listed in the 1860 New Jersey *Business Directory* (Boyd) as a marble worker. No known signed examples.

J. A. Bachman, Lambertville. 1866 New Jersey *Business Directory* (Talbott and Blood). Signed marble headstones from the 1870s.

A. T. Baillie, Philadelphia. Marble carver active in the 1870s. Several signed markers can be found in St. Andrew's Cemetery, Mount Holly.

Baird & Lamb, Newark. 1850 *New Jersey Business Directory* (Kirkbride).

Daniel Baker, Newton. 1840s–1850s marble carver known for upward-pointed hands.

D. Ballbeck, Cape May Court House. Signed 1849 marble gravestone with weeping willow at Head of the River Church, Atlantic County.

David Bamber, Paterson. Marble carver active from 1839 to 1875.

William Bamber, Paterson. Son of David Bamber, took over his father's business after his death in 1875. Continued to carve markers into the late nineteenth century. Died in 1899 (Lanza 1997, 12).

Isaac Bamber, Paterson. Brother of William, who continued the family business until his death in 1932 (Lanza 1997, 12).

George W. Bell, Middletown Point. 1850, 1860, 1866 New Jersey business directories (Kirkbride; Boyd; Talbott and Blood). Signed examples can be found in several Old Bridge cemeteries.

G. Bennet, Port Jervis, N.Y. Marble carver; signed examples in Sussex County dating from the 1850s to 1870s.

J. Benz, Blairstown. Last quarter of the nineteenth century.

Bonnell & Melick, Whitehouse. Numerous signed marble monuments; many are a blue or striated blue marble. Active during the second half of the nineteenth century. May have also produced markers that are signed just "White House."

Andrew Bower, Philadelphia. Active in the 1780s and 1790s, Bower carved in marble. A marker for Jacob Miller (d. 1787), inscribed in German, survives in the Emanuel Evangelical Lutheran Church of Friesburg.

George Brittain, Camden. Listed in 1860 New Jersey *Business Directory* (Boyd) under "Marble Workers" on Federal Street, corner of Plum.

William Brookfield, New Brunswick. Carver in the 1820s and 1830s. Signed examples in Metuchen and the Hillsborough Reformed Church Cemetery. One signed wall plaque in Christ Episcopal Church, New Brunswick.

S. Brooks, Providence, R.I. Signed the 1843 marble gravestone for Lucy Ann Riggins in the Leesburg United Methodist Churchyard and the 1864 gravemarker for Margaret Cresse in the Tabernacle United Methodist Churchyard, Cape May County.

George Brown, Newark. Marble and granite monument dealer, mid-nineteenth century to early twentieth century. Responsible for the Fireman's Memorial and Dryden mausoleum in Mount Pleasant Cemetery. Carved several mid-nineteenth-century Gothic Revival monuments, including the Snowhill markers in St. Peter's Episcopal Churchyard, Spotswood.

Thomas Brown, New York. Brown carved cherubs and mortality images. He was active from the 1760s through 1790s, working in sandstone. Examples can be found in New Brunswick and Monmouth County (Welch 1987, 52).

Wm. & T. Browne, Jersey City. 1850 *New Jersey Business Directory* (Kirkbride).

J. H. Brush, Bergen County. Signed sandstone examples from 1802 and 1818 at the Bergenfield Old South Church.

John Buckingham. Listed in the 1866 New Jersey *Business Directory* (Talbott and Blood) as a marble worker from Eatontown. No known signed examples.

Byrne & Co., Hackensack. 1866 New Jersey *Business Directory* (Talbott and Blood), listed on Main Street.

A. A. Campbell, Bergen County. Sandstone carver of the 1830s, by the 1840s also carved in marble. Granite monuments dating from the 1870s signed "Campbell."

H. W. Carey, Frenchtown. 1860 New Jersey *Business Directory* (Boyd).

Wesley Chambers, Andover. 1866 New Jersey *Business Directory* (Talbott and Blood), no known signed examples.

Thomas Clark, Newark. 1860 New Jersey *Business Directory* (Boyd).

William Clark, Newark. 1860 New Jersey *Business Directory* (Boyd).

George W. Claypoole, Bridgeton. 1860 and 1866 New Jersey business directories (Boyd; Talbott and Blood) under "Marble Workers," in 1860 listed on Laurel near Commerce. Marble monument for the Fries family at the Emanuel Lutheran Church of Friesburg, Salem, signed "G.W. Claypoole, Bridgeton, N.J."

J. D. Claypoole, Bridgeton, Millville, and Pennsville. Signed examples from 1842 to 1886.

Henry Cleaver, Red Bank. 1850 *New Jersey Business Directory* (Kirkbride).

Clinton, also "Wm M. Clinton," New Brunswick. Monument firm dating to the fourth quarter of the nineteenth century. Signed markers in New Brunswick–area cemeteries as well as a granite monument from 1898 for the Baird family at the Clover Hill Reformed Church, Somerset County. Still in business on Cranbury Road in South Brunswick.

E. A. Cole, Hudson, N.Y. Signed marble gravestones dated 1837 and 1842 in the Old Clove Cemetery, Sussex County.

C. F. Coleman, Burlington. Three signed examples in Cedar Hill Cemetery. All are multiple tablet markers on one common base and date between 1872 and 1883.

J. Collins, Mount Holly. Signed examples from the 1840s in St. Andrew's Cemetery.

J. Collins, New Brunswick. Stonecarver with two signed examples from the 1880s in St. Mary's Church Cemetery, South Amboy.

E. B. Comes, Newark. 1850 *New Jersey Business Directory* (Kirkbride).

Samuel Conger. Signed marker dated 1819 in the Connecticut Farms Presbyterian Churchyard. Carved monograms on sandstone.

D. O. Connell, New Brunswick. Stonecarver in the 1870s. Signed marble markers in South Amboy and North Brunswick.

Hugh Conroy, Trenton. Signed marble monuments from the 1870s. Shop located at 22 & 24 South Greene Street in the 1883–1884 Trenton business directory.

John W. Conroy, Stockton and Trenton. Signed an 1834 marble gravestone for William Sharp in the Sandy Ridge Churchyard "J.W. Conroy C. Bridge, NJ." Listed as working in Stockton in 1860 and 1866 New Jersey business directories (Boyd; Talbott and Blood). Marble markers dating between 1863 and 1875 are signed "J.W. Conroy, Trenton."

J. Cooper, Munsey, N.Y. Signed marble gravestone from 1819 in the Pascack Dutch Reformed Churchyard, Bergen County.

Benjamin Crane, Paterson. Operated a stone-carving shop in Paterson in 1829. Was in partnership with Abraham Garrison; signed markers from this partnership date from the 1850s and 1860s. Son Alfred B. Crane took over the business after Garrison became ill, continued to carver marble markers into the 1880s (Lanza 1997, 12).

J. W. Crane, Bloomfield. Typographic markers on sandstone, signed examples 1834–1838.

Charles Crook, Newton. Marble carver active from 1859 to 1866.

D Carver. Stones lettered in German were signed by this anonymous carver from the 1780s through the 1790s. They are most common in the Stillwater Cemetery.

William P. Dally, Perth Amboy. Signed headstone for Lawrence Kearny in St. Peter's Episcopal Church Cemetery, Perth Amboy, dated 1866. 1866 New Jersey *Business Directory* (Talbott and Blood).

Elias Darby, Elizabethtown. Late-eighteenth-century carver, known for cherubs on sandstone. His work resembles that of Ebenezer Price.

James Dickson, Jersey City. Monument dealer during the second half of the nineteenth century. 1860 and 1866 New Jersey business directories (Boyd; Talbott and Blood). Signed examples in Holy Name Cemetery, Jersey City.

George W. Dillaway, Jersey City. 1860 New Jersey *Business Directory* (Boyd).

Dougherty and Davis, Morristown. Signed marble markers and monuments from the 1860s. H. H. Davis is listed in the 1866 New Jersey *Business Directory* (Talbott and Blood).

C. S. Down, Hackettstown. Signed marble headstone with weeping willow motif, dated 1829, for Margaret Kinman in the Mount Olive Baptist Cemetery.

Czar T. Duncomb, Newark. Marble carver known for upside-down torches and weeping willow and urn motifs. Active from the late 1830s to the early 1850s. Carved markers and monuments; signed examples in Mount Pleasant Cemetery, Newark.

Duncomb & Timley, Newark. Signed markers from 1838 and an 1848 marble gravestone for Ann Halsted in the Old Newton Cemetery.

J. L. Edwards, Camden. Signed examples from the 1860s in Cape May County.

George Eldridge, New Brunswick. Marble worker and dealer at 51 Neilson Street. Signed examples date mainly from the 1860s and can be found in central New Jersey cemeteries as far south as Hightstown. The earliest, dated 1849, is in the Reformed Church Cemetery, Spotswood. Last listed as a marble dealer in the New Brunswick city directory in 1871.

L. T. Entrikin, Cape May Court House. Originally from Petersburg, c.1839. Numerous signed marble markers and monuments in Cape May County dating from the 1870s and 1880s.

Charles Finney, Swedesboro. 1860 New Jersey *Business Directory* (Boyd).

John Frazee, Rahway and New Brunswick. Notable American sculptor who carved gravestones in Rahway from 1811 to 1814 and New Brunswick from 1814 to 1818.

F. Fritz, Philadelphia. Active in the 1820s, signed markers in Cohansey and Cold Springs. Used the Latin phrase "fecit" after his signature.

Fryer, also signed "S. Fryer," Hightstown. Monument dealer with examples in marble and granite dating from 1877 to 1900. One possible backdated marker signed "Fryer, Hightstown," dated 1842. Majority of signed examples can be found in Hightstown.

Gadmus, Clinton. Monument dealer with signed granite examples including the Elvin family monument in Cedar Lawn Cemetery, Paterson.

J. Gibson, Bridgeton. Signed marble marker and monument, 1872 and 1874, Shiloh Seventh Day Baptist Churchyard and Deerfield Presbyterian Churchyard.

Gibson & Applegate, Bridgeton. 1866 New Jersey *Business Directory* (Talbott and Blood). Signed example from 1864 in the Cohansey Baptist Church.

Grant, Newark. Carved willows on marble.

Alexander Grant, Lambertville. 1860 New Jersey *Business Directory* (Boyd) and signed markers.

Charles Grant, Newark. Signed mid-nineteenth-century markers in the Newark area; also listed in 1850 and 1860 New Jersey business directories (Kirkbride; Boyd).

William Grant, Boston, New York City, and Newark. Grant was originally from Boston but was carving in New York by 1740 and shortly thereafter moved to Newark, New Jersey. He was active between the 1740s and 1790s, carving both mortality images and pearshaped cherubs. The largest number of his markers may be found in the Orange Presbyterian and Woodbridge Presbyterian Churchyards (Zielenski 2004, 1:65).

Chris Gregory, Hoboken. 1866 New Jersey *Business Directory* (Talbott and Blood).

C. D. Haines, Salem. Signed 1844 headstone at the Head of the River Church, Atlantic County.

Harrison & Carroll, Jersey City. 1866 New Jersey *Business Directory* (Talbott and Blood).

Jas. Hart Jr., New York. Mid-nineteenth-century marble carver. Sculpted the Fielder monument in the Hightstown Cemetery.

John Hepburn, Gloucester City. 1860 and 1866 New Jersey business directories (Boyd; Talbott and Blood).

John Hocker, Philadelphia. Early-nineteenth-century marble carver. Sculpted the Elizabeth Estelle gravestone, dated 1821, in the Head of the River Church Cemetery, Atlantic County. Used the Latin phrase "fecit" after his signature.

D. J. Howell, Flemington, Morristown. 1860 New Jersey *Business Directory* (Boyd). Signed examples from 1857 to 1861.

Howell & Gregory, Clinton. 1866 New Jersey *Business Directory* (Talbott and Blood).

F. X. Hurle & L. Kislin, Newark. 1860 New Jersey *Business Directory* (Boyd); L. Kislin is not listed in the 1866 edition (Talbott and Blood).

T. Jardine, Rahway. Monument firm from the mid-nineteenth into the early twentieth century.

David Jeffries, probably Elizabethtown. Signed markers from the 1760s until the late eighteenth century in Elizabeth and Scotch Plains. Carved cherubs on sandstone. Possible Ebenezer Price apprentice.

R. R. Jones, Belvidere. Listed in the 1850 *New Jersey Business Directory* (Kirkbride).

J. Keeler, Mount Holly. Marble carver c. 1850–c. 1890; signed examples in Mount Holly cemeteries.

George Kelly, Camden. Listed in 1866 New Jersey *Business Directory* (Talbott and Blood) under "Marble Workers" on 531 Federal Street.

James Key, Jersey City. 1860 and 1866 New Jersey business directories (Boyd; Talbott and Blood).

E. E. Kilbourn, New Brunswick. Also signed stones "Kilbourn & Co." and "Kilbourn & Co. NB." Edward E. Kilbourn was the successor to the Sillcocks Company in New Brunswick. This firm was in operation throughout the 1870s, with the earliest marker for Charles Cozzens at St. Peter's Church in Spotswood, possibly backdated, from 1867.

E. J. Kisling, Newark. Also spelled Keasling, Keisling, and Kislin. 1866 New Jersey *Business Directory* (Talbott and Blood).

Koellhoffer, Newark. Signed brownstone monument for the Bernauer family in St. Mary's Cemetery, Newark.

Christian Kohler, Camden. 1860 New Jersey *Business Directory* (Boyd) under "Marble Workers" on Federal Street, corner of Front.

J. Krouse, Washington. Listed as a marble worker in the 1866 New Jersey *Business Directory* (Talbott and Blood).

Lamson Shop, Charlestown, Mass. Markers attributed to the Lamson shop are present in Woodbridge and St. John's Churchyard in Elizabeth. They are carved on slate and date from the eighteenth century.

Marc Lang, Camden. Listed in 1860 New Jersey *Business Directory* (Boyd) under "Marble Workers" on Market Street below Front.

Langstaff, New Brunswick. Benjamin and James Langstaff were prolific stonecarvers from New Brunswick. They were active from 1830 to 1876. Numerous signed examples in marble; the earliest in sandstone can be found throughout Middlesex and Somerset Counties. Throughout the 1860s and 70s the business is listed at 50, 52, 75, and 149 Neilson Street.

J. Langstaff, Paterson. 1866 New Jersey *Business Directory* (Talbott and Blood). Markers signed Langstaff date from the 1850s through the 1890s.

Samuel Langstaff, Paterson. 1857 Paterson city directory.

Langstaff & Sullivan, Paterson. 1860 New Jersey *Business Directory* (Boyd).

Lazzari and Barton, Woodlawn, N.Y. Signed marker from 1892, Dutch Reformed Church, Belleville.

T. H. Lee, Bordentown. Marble carver active from the 1860s through the 1880s.

Lomason & Neal, Belvidere. Listed in the 1860 New Jersey *Business Directory* (Boyd).

F. Lupton, Freehold. 1866 New Jersey *Business Directory* (Talbott and Blood). Signed examples from 1869 to 1886.

Josiah E. Lynn, Washington. Listed in 1860 and 1866 New Jersey business directories (Boyd; Talbott and Blood). Signed markers "J. Lynn."

M. C. Lyons and Sons, Camden. Signed 1893 granite monument for the Cheeseman family in the Hightstown Cemetery. Other signed examples in Camden.

J. F. Manning, Washington, D.C. Signed granite monument from 1887 for the West family in Cedar Lawn Cemetery, Paterson.

Lebbeus Manning, Plainfield. Later L. L. Manning & Son, marble and granite monument firm operating from the mid-nineteenth century until the 1990s.

Michael Mayer, Newark. 1860 New Jersey *Business Directory* (Boyd).

R. R. McChesney, Middletown Point. Signed 1840s marble gravestone for Disborough Appleget with willow and urn motif in the Cranbury Presbyterian Cemetery. 1850 *New Jersey Business Directory* (Kirkbride). Active 1840s to the 1860s.

McChesney and Lupton, Middletown Point and Freehold. 1860 New Jersey *Business Directory* (Boyd).

Alexander McDonald, Trenton. Scottish carver who arrived in Cambridge, Massachusetts, in 1856 and opened a shop across the street from Mount Auburn Cemetery. In 1885 he opened a shop in Paterson, and another in Trenton in 1898. The business was sold in 1949 to the Independent Memorial Company.

Charles McDonald, Lambertville. 1860 New Jersey *Business Directory* (Boyd).

Isaac Meeker, Summit. Marble carver active from the 1830s to the 1860s.

S. S. Miles, Goshen, N.Y. Signed an 1815 marble gravestone with two weeping willows and urn motif in Fairview Cemetery, Sussex County.

Miller, Lambertville. Signed examples from 1847 to 1878 in cemeteries along the Delaware River.

George Molley, Camden. Listed in 1866 New Jersey *Business Directory* (Talbott and Blood) under "Marble Workers" on 104 Federal Street.

J. C. Mooney, Connecticut Farms (Union). Signed markers 1813–1819. Well represented in the Connecticut Farms Presbyterian Churchyard. Carved urns and willows on sandstone.

H. Moore, New Brunswick. Marble carver active in third quarter of the nineteenth century. Signed marble gravestone, badly eroded, in St. Mary's Cemetery, South Amboy.

W. A. Moore, New York. Signed 1831 marble gravestone for Bridget Myres in the Wycoff Reformed Churchyard, Bergen County.

George Mott, Camden. Listed in 1860 New Jersey *Business Directory* (Boyd) "Marble Workers" on Federal Street, corner of Front.

B. Mullin, Orange. Active from the 1810s through 1830s. Mullin produced typographic markers on sandstone; can be found in Orange.

J. H. Murphy, Flemington. Signed 1869 obelisk for the Holcombe family in the Sandy Ridge Churchyard.

Neal & Hiles, Belvidere. Listed in 1866 New Jersey *Business Directory* (Talbott and Blood).

E. J. Norris. Signed marker from 1819, Connecticut Farms. He carved neoclassical designs on sandstone.

Noah Norris. Signed markers from 1801 and 1803 in Elizabethtown Presbyterian Churchyard. He carved sandstone and later marble, with examples in the Connecticut Farms Presbyterian Churchyard.

J. Ogden, Bridgeton. Signed marble markers and monuments 1880–1886.

C. P. Osborn. Listed in 1850 and 1866 New Jersey business directories (Kirkbride; Talbott and Blood) as a marble worker and dealer in Woodbridge.

Henry Osborn, Woodbridge. Signed markers 1776–1825. Carved cherubs, floral motifs, birds. Represented in Cranbury, Woodbridge, and Scotch Plains.

Jonathan Hand Osborn, Scotch Plains. Signed markers 1779–1810. Also signed as Hand Osborn. Carved cherubs, monograms, and floral motifs on sandstone. Well represented in Scotch Plains and New Providence.

W. Osborn. Signed markers 1807–1845, Metuchen First Presbyterian Churchyard. Neoclassical designs on sandstone.

Osborn and Son, Scotch Plains. Signed marker 1815. Neoclassical design on sandstone, Basking Ridge.

Passmore & Meeker, Newark. Monument dealer during the second half of the nineteenth century. Signed examples in Mount Pleasant Cemetery, Newark.

Patterson, Vanderveer & Co., Freehold. 1860 New Jersey *Business Directory* (Boyd).

J. D. Payran, Trenton. John Payran learned his skills from Trenton carver Luther Ward. He opened his own business in 1875. It was still in operation in 1900 at 401 East State Street.

J. Pollock & E. R. Bullock, Frenchtown and Flemington. Marble gravestone carvers with signed examples from the 1830s to the 1850s.

Ebenezer Price (1728–1788), Elizabeth. Signed markers from 1744 through 1787 and advertisements. He produced cherubs, tulips, and scallop designs. Well represented in Elizabeth, Westfield, Union, and Basking Ridge. His work can also be found in New York City, on Long Island, and as far south as the Carolinas, Georgia, and the Caribbean.

Prior, Reeder and Sons, Trenton. 1866 New Jersey *Business Directory* (Talbott and Blood).

T. H. Prior & Son, Muirheid, Trenton. Marble and granite workers and dealers, 1898 Trenton city directory.

R&S, Camden. 1867 signed marble marker for the Cattell family at the Baptist Cemetery, Salem.

Rawden & Scott, Bloomfield. 1866 New Jersey *Business Directory* (Talbott and Blood).

John Rawlings, Milford. 1866 New Jersey *Business Directory* (Talbott and Blood).

Raymond, Cape May Court House and Tuckahoe. Marble carver with signed examples from 1869 to 1877.

R. Reilly, Camden. Signed 1893 granite monument for Alexander Haines in St. Andrew's Cemetery, Mount Holly.

Michael O'Riley, Gloucester City and Camden. 1866 New Jersey *Business Directory* (Talbott and Blood). Camden marble carver from the third quarter of the nineteenth century.

J. Reynolds, New York. Marble carver, with signed example dated 1819 at the Old North Reformed Church, Dumont.

J. Ritter, New Haven, Conn. Prolific New Haven stone-carving family from the late eighteenth and early nineteenth centuries. Carved the marble gravestone for Sarah Charles in the Whippany Cemetery.

Edward H. Robbins, Salem. Marble carver from the mid-nineteenth century.

Joseph Roberts, Hudson City. 1860 New Jersey *Business Directory* (Boyd).

Joseph Roeder, Newark. 1860 New Jersey *Business Directory* (Boyd). Several signed brownstone monuments from the 1870s in Holy Sepulchre in East Orange.

Rommel, Mount Holly. Signed marble gravestone from 1870 in St. Andrew's Cemetery.

Aaron Ross. Late-eighteenth-, early-nineteenth-century gravestone carver originally from New Brunswick, later moves his shop to Rahway. Signed markers can be found in Elm Ridge Cemetery, North Brunswick, and the Cranbury Presbyterian Cemetery, Cranbury.

Samuel Sager, Burlington. 1860 New Jersey *Business Directory* (Boyd).

Thomas R. Sager, Mount Holly. 1850 *New Jersey Business Directory* (Kirkbride), under "Marble Yard."

Schenck, Newark. Active in the 1820s, carved neoclassical designs on sandstone.

L. Schlumpberger, Weekawken. 1866 New Jersey *Business Directory* (Talbott and Blood).

Leonard Schureman, Morristown. Mainly carved marble gravestones with weeping willow and urn motifs from the 1820s to the 1860s. 1850 and 1866 New Jersey business directories (Kirkbride; Talbott and Blood). Listed in 1860 New Jersey *Business Directory* (Boyd) as "Schureman & Stiles." Markers from the 1850s also appear with the signature "Schureman & Howell" (D. J. Howell).

Joseph Shaffer, Mount Holly. Signed markers "Shaffer," "Shaffer M. Holly," and "J. Shaffer M-Holly." Listed in New Jersey business directories for 1860 and 1866 (Boyd; Talbott and Blood). Documented signed markers from 1858 to 1881 in Mount Holly and New Gretna.

W. A. Sharp, Belvidere. Listed in 1860 New Jersey *Business Directory* (Boyd).

J. Sharpe, Crosswicks. 1866 New Jersey *Business Directory* (Talbott and Blood).

Joseph Sillcock, New Brunswick. Payment for tombstones in 1805 (John Fisher), 1807 (John Allen), and 1809 (Daniel Freeman), unrecorded estate papers for Middlesex County, New Jersey State Archives. One known signed example.

Gabriel Sillcocks, New Brunswick. Marble carver, born 1822. No known signed examples but may have signed stones with signature "Sillcocks & Co."

Henry Sillcocks. Born 1793, died 1846. Signed markers begin in the 1810s with the signatures "Cut by Henry Sillcocks" and "H. Sillcocks NB." Carved gravestones in both sandstone and marble.

I. G. Sillcocks, New Brunswick, c. 1810s. Most likely Isaac Sillcocks. Carved sandstone gravemarkers including the Jane Perlee stone at the Hillsboro Reformed Church. Signature is in script lettering.

James Hull Sillcocks, New Brunswick. Born 1820, died 1880. Marble carver who was the son of Henry and the brother of Gabriel Sillcocks. Earliest signed markers, apparently backdated, appear in the 1820s. Business was sold around 1876.

Samuel Sillcocks, New Brunswick. Signed marker from 1860, Cranbury First Presbyterian Churchyard.

Smith Granite Co., Westerly, RI. Granite monument firm, carved the Onderdonk family monument in Elmwood Cemetery, North Brunswick.

A. Steinmetz, Philadelphia. Signed markers in Salem City and Shiloh.

De Witt Stevens, Newark. 1860 and 1866 New Jersey business directories (Boyd; Talbott and Blood).

J. Stevens, Newark. Active in the 1840s and 1850s.

John Stevens I (1646/7–1736), Newport, R.I. No signed examples, but slate markers in Rumson, Shrewsbury, and Upper Freehold have been attributed to his shop.

John Stevens II (1702–1778), Newport, R.I. No signed examples, but slate markers in Shrewsbury and Piscatawaytown/St. James Churchyard in Edison have been attributed to his shop.

Philip Stevens, Newport, R.I. No signed examples, but a handful of cherubs on sandstone have been attributed to his shop. These markers date from the 1730s (Luti 2002).

William Stevens, Newport, R.I. No signed examples, but cherubs on slate from the mid-eighteenth century found in Middlesex and Monmouth Counties have been attributed to him. Particularly fine examples are present in the Piscatawaytown/St. James Churchyard in Edison and in Christ Episcopal Churchyard, Shrewsbury.

Abner Stewart, Elizabethtown and Marksboro. Price apprentice, worked in sandstone, carved cherubs and a monogram design. Signed markers in Elizabeth dating from the 1780s and 1790s. Signed markers in Warren and Sussex Counties, particularly common at the Yellow Frame Meeting House, from the 1780s through the first decade of the nineteenth century.

Stewart and Ross, Elizabethtown. Signed marker from 1798. Produced monograms. Example in the Cranbury Presbyterian Churchyard.

David Stewart. Signed markers 1804–1812, New Providence. Produced monograms and urns in sandstone.

J. J. Storms, Paterson. Marble carver during the second half of the nineteenth century.

C. A. Strauss, Lambertville. Marble and granite dealer during the last quarter of the nineteenth century.

H. M. Swayze, Lambertville, Trenton. Originally operated a marble shop in Lambertville, then in 1879 moved his business to Trenton. Signed the 1886 Clara Potts headstone in the Mount Holly Cemetery. Signed obelisk from 1866 for the Willis family in Pennington marked "Weston & Swayze."

John Sweet, Trenton. "Sweet & Crowther" listed in 1854–1855 Trenton city directory. John Sweet listed in 1860 New Jersey *Business Directory* (Boyd).

Henry Tarr, Philadelphia. Prolific marble carver active in the mid-nineteenth century. Signed examples can be found in cemeteries throughout southern New Jersey. Carved many high-style monuments and markers.

John Solomon Teetzel, Hardwick. Signed markers from the 1780s and 1790s. Teetzel carved in both German and English on buff-colored sandstone. His work is well represented in the Stillwater Cemetery, the Yellow Frame Presbyterian Churchyard, and the Knowlton Presbyterian Burial Ground.

Samuel W. Thompson, Red Bank. 1860 New Jersey *Business Directory* (Boyd).

Thompson and Venables, Red Bank. 1866 New Jersey *Business Directory* (Talbott and Blood).

S. Tinsley & Sons, Providence, RI. Signed marble gravestone from 1846 in the Seventh Day Adventist Cemetery, Marmora, Cape May County.

Abner Tucker. Signed markers from 1780s, New Providence. He carved cherubs in sandstone.

J. Tucker, Westfield. Signed markers from 1780s, New Providence. He carved cherubs in sandstone (Welch 1987).

William Valentine, New York. Markers attributed to Valentine include an exceptional cherub for John Bourne (1774) in Middletown.

Van Cunden & Young, Philadelphia. Monument firm from the fourth quarter of the nineteenth century. Signed markers can be found in Burlington County.

Andrew Vanderbeek, Plainfield. Mid-nineteenth-century marble carver.

Jaques Vanderbeek, Somerville. Marble carver active in third quarter of the nineteenth century.

P. Vanderbeek, unknown location. Signed sandstone marker with monogram in the Cranbury Presbyterian Churchyard. The signature is located on the back of the gravestone.

W. H. Van Gilder, Millville. Marble carver active in the 1880s. Carved the Hannah Weeks cradle grave, Head of the River Church, Atlantic County.

Wm. Veghte, New Brunswick. Signed sandstone tablet marker for Henry Freeman in the Old Presbyterian Cemetery. In 1837 was paid $14 to carve a tombstone for Thomas Fourt (unrecorded estate papers, Middlesex County, reel 40).

A. W., New Providence. Carved sandstone gravemarkers, active in the 1810s.

Peter H. Wakeham, originally from Millstone, later moved his shop to New Brunswick. Listed in the New Brunswick city directory in 1873 with a residence at 4 Morris Street.

Earliest signed New Brunswick stone dated 1863 in the Reformed Church Cemetery, Spotswood.

L. Ward. Luther Ward, stonecarver in New Brunswick in the 1830s and 1840s. Moved his shop to East State Street in Trenton by 1850. Son, also named Luther, continues the business as late as the 1880s. Numerous signed stones in Mercer and Middlesex Counties.

Uzal Ward (1726?–1793), Newark. Prolific stonecarver, active from the 1740s through the early 1790s. Ward worked in sandstone, producing mortality images, pear-shaped cherubs, floral motifs, and monograms (Zielenski 2004, 1:31). His fine work inspired numerous imitators.

Hugh Webster, New Brunswick. Two known signed examples from the 1810s.

Wilcox & Crane, New Providence. Carved marble gravestones. Signed examples from the 1820s and 1830s can be found in the Presbyterian Cemetery in Basking Ridge.

Amos Wilcox, Newark. Mid-nineteenth-century marble carver, listed in 1850 and 1866 New Jersey business directories (Kirkbride; Talbott and Blood).

I. Wilcox, New Providence. Signed sandstone gravemarker from 1818 for Sarah Miller in the Westfield Presbyterian Cemetery.

Robert Wildes, Salem. 1860 and 1866 New Jersey business directories (Boyd; Talbott and Blood).

Horton D. Williams, Orange. 1860 New Jersey *Business Directory* (Boyd).

R. T. Wilson, Morristown. 1850 *New Jersey Business Directory* (Kirkbride).

T. T. Wilson & Co, Morristown. Signed sandstone gravemarker for David Condit (1837), Whippany Cemetery.

Ebenezer Winslow. The slate gravemarker for Isaac Winslow (d. 1790), in Middletown's Presbyterian Cemetery, is attributed to his uncle Ebenezer Winslow (Vincent Luti 2005, personal communication).

F. Wipper, Newark. Brownstone monument carver in the 1870s. Signed example for the Robrecht family in St. Mary's Cemetery, Newark.

Augustus N. Wolcott, Trenton. Marble carver from the third quarter of the nineteenth century. Carved the Chapman family gravestones in the Crosswicks Cemetery, Crosswicks.

A. T. Wolfe, Deckertown. Signed examples in Sussex County, 1870–1890s.

J. W. Wright, Hackettstown. Listed in 1850 *New Jersey Business Directory* (Kirkbride).

C. S. Young, Ridgeberry, N.Y. Signed marble gravestones from the 1840s in Sussex County.

John Zuricher, New York. Zuricher was active from the 1740s through the 1780s. He worked primarily in New York City. He produced cherubs in sandstone, and sometimes carved in Dutch. His markers are found in small numbers in northern New Jersey, particularly in Hackensack, Metuchen, Middletown, Montgomery, Scotch Plains, and New Brunswick, and in Cape May County.

(BIBLIOGRAPHY)

ARCHIVAL MATERIAL

Burke, Ardath. N.d. Information, Japanese Buried in Willow Grove Cemetery, New Brunswick, New Jersey. Manuscript on file with Richard Veit.

Burlington County Probate Records. New Jersey State Archives, misc. estate papers, reel 2–186.

Condit, John S. 1847. Inscriptions from Monumental Stones in Newark Cemeteries. Manuscript on file at the New Jersey Historical Society, Newark, as "Monumental Inscriptions Essex County, Vol. 1."

Deats, Hiram E. 1925. Dedicate Marble Shaft to the Indian Chief, Tuccamirgan. Reprinted in the *Hunterdon County Democrat*, October 22, 1925. Manuscript on file at the Hunterdon County Historical Society, Flemington, N.J.

Drake, Oliver D., comp. 1959. The Names of Members Deceased That Belonged to the Church at Samptown. Copied from the Original Minute Book of the Samptown Church. Drake Collection, Special Collections, Alexander Library, Rutgers University, New Brunswick, N.J.

Eby, Ruth. 1977. Interviewed by David Heinlan and transcribed by Janena Benjamin, November 22, tape 2. On file at the Metuchen-Edison Historical Society.

Essex County Probate Records, New Jersey State Archives. Unrecorded estate papers, reel 2–19, folders 1–97.

———. Unrecorded estate papers, reel 2–20, folders 112, 121, 139, 142, 174, 175, 176, 189.

———. Unrecorded estate papers, reel 2–21, folders 217, 236, 244, 265.

———. Unrecorded estate papers, reel 2–23, folders 501, 508, 512, 828, 778.

———. Unrecorded estate papers, reel 2–28, folders 1207, 1271.

George Washington Memorial Park. 1949. History and the George Washington Memorial Park. Ridgewood, N.J.: Kirk B. Shivell, Inc. Unpublished manuscript on file at the office of George Washington Memorial Park.

———. N.d. Art and Monuments at George Washington Memorial Park. Unpublished manuscript on file at the office of George Washington Memorial Park.

George Washington Memorial Park Cemetery Association. 1993. *Art and Nature: 54th Annual Report and a Guide to George Washington Memorial Park*. Paramus. December.

George Washington Memorial Park Cemetery Association. 2003. *64th Annual Report*. December.

George Washington Memorial Park Cemetery Association. 2004. *65th Annual Report*. December.

Greenwood Cemetery Association. . 1964. Greenwood Cemetery Association—Ninety Years Old. Unpublished document on file at Cemetery Management Services office or Greenwood Cemetery office, Trenton. Author's collection.

Heinrich, Adam. 2003. "Remember Me . . ." But "Be Mindful of Death": The Art of Commemoration in Eighteenth-Century Monmouth County, New Jersey. Manuscript on file with Richard Veit.

Library Company of Philadelphia. Wainwright Lithograph Collection. H. S. Tarr's Marble Yard, Philadelphia, ca. 1858. Available at http://www.lcpgraphics.org/wainwright/W166-1.htm.

Middlesex County Probate Records, New Jersey State Archives. Unrecorded estate papers, reel 1, folders 148, 168, 169, 180, 183, 184, 186, 194, 196, 203, 204.

————. Unrecorded estate papers, reel 5, folders 839, 856.

————. Unrecorded estate papers, reel 21, folders 4118, 4121, 4151, 4188.

————. Unrecorded estate papers, reel 39, folders 7554, 7645, 7646, 7655, 7675, 7709.

————. Unrecorded estate papers, reel 40, folder 7685.

————. Unrecorded estate papers, reel 70, folder 14760.

————. Unrecorded estate papers, reel 88, folders 18177, 18183, 18232, 18234, 18235, 18270, 18295.

————. Unrecorded estate papers, reel 89, folders 18222, 18443, 18451, 18476, 18487, 18488, 18495.

————. Unrecorded estate papers, reel 99, folders 20309, 20389, 20398, 20417.

O. J. Hammell Monument Company, Records. New Jersey Historical Society. Hammell—MG 1208 box 61, 1875, 1900–1909, and MG 1208 box 1, 1893–1903 Hammell Correspondence

————. 1902. The New Plant of O. J. Hammell Company Nearly Ready. Unidentified newspaper clipping, MG 1208—Index File.

Harleigh Cemetery. 1995. National Register Nomination. New Jersey Historic Preservation Office, Trenton.

Hollywood Cemetery File. Union Public Library. 1926–1947. Various newspaper clippings.

————. 1938. Union Upholds Cemetery Levy. November 8. Unidentified newspaper clipping.

————. 1943. Seeks to Modify Cemetery Decree. July 28. Unidentified newspaper clipping.

Mount Pleasant Cemetery. N.d. Twelve manuscript maps of Mount Pleasant Cemetery. New Jersey Historical Society. 471 N.D. C.

Ross, Aaron. 1797. Broadside. Rutgers University Libraries, Special Collections and Archives, New Brunswick, N.J.

Salem County Probate Records, New Jersey State Archives. Unrecorded estate papers, reel 13.

Somerset County Probate Records, New Jersey State Archives. Unrecorded estate papers, reel 226, folders 9604, 9566, 9628, 9632.

————. Unrecorded estate papers, reel 360, folders 40, 57, 74, 109, 154.

Stofflet, Mary K. 1964. A Study of the Characteristics of the Gravestones Located in Monmouth County, New Jersey, 1664–1800. Paper written for Art 390, Skidmore College, Saratoga Springs, N.Y.

Trenton Public Library, Reference Collection. Scrapbook of Trenton Industries, Independent Memorials. T670, scr. 6, sec. 1.

————. 1939. *Trenton Magazine*, July. Scrapbook of Trenton Industries, Alexander McDonald Company.

————. 1956. Wagner Memorial. Trenton 32.3, March 1956, 28.

———. 1960. And Who's Trenton's Ambassador to Erie? And Who's Trenton's Biggest Maker of Memorials? It's Himself—Lloyd J. Kelly. Filed under Trenton 36, March 1960, 8–10, 26–29.

Turner, Jean-Rae. 1991. National Register Nomination for Evergreen Cemetery, Hillside, New Jersey. Reference number 91000682. On file at the New Jersey Historic Preservation Office, Trenton.

———. N.d. A Self-Guided Tour of Evergreen Cemetery, Hillside, New Jersey. On file at the Evergreen Cemetery office, Hillside, N.J.

United States Federal Census. 1870. Henry Hirth, Seventh Ward, Trenton, New Jersey, 59.

———.1870. John Payran, First Ward, Trenton, New Jersey, 31.

———. 1870. Luther Ward, First Ward, Trenton, New Jersey, 33.

———. 1870. Luther Ward, Seventh Ward, Trenton, New Jersey, 9.

———. 1870. George Weil, Seventh Ward, Trenton, New Jersey, 71.

PUBLISHED SOURCES

Alden, Timothy. 1814. *A Collection of American Epitaphs and Inscriptions with Occasional Notes.* New York: S. Marks.

American Architect and Building News. 1899. *American Architect and Building News* 65. September 23.

Ard, Patricia M. 2004. Jews. In *Encyclopedia of New Jersey*, edited by Maxine Lurie and Marc Mappen, 430–431. New Brunswick, N.J.: Rutgers University Press.

Atlas of Passaic County, New Jersey. 1877. New York: E. B. Hyde and Company.

Baker, Joanne F., and Anne G. Giesecke. N.d. *Recording Cemetery Data.* Worchester, Mass.: Association for Gravestone Studies.

Barba, Preston A. 1954. *Pennsylvania German Tombstones: A Study in Folk Art.* Allentown, Pa.: Pennsylvania German Folklore Society.

Barber, John Warner, and Henry Howe. 1844. *Historical Collections of the State of New Jersey: Containing a General Collection of the Most Interesting Facts, Traditions, Biographical Sketches, Anecdotes, etc., Relating to Its History and Antiquities, with Geographical Descriptions of Every Township in the State.* Newark: B. Olds.

Baugher, Sherene, and Frederick A. Winter. 1983. Early American Gravestones: Archaeological Perspectives on Three Cemeteries of Old New York. *Archaeology* 36:46–54.

Bauman, Timothy E. 2005. The Cycle of Life, Death, and Rebirth: African American Burial Practices in Metropolitan St. Louis. Paper presented at the thirty-eighth annual conference of the Society for Historical Archaeology in York, England, January.

Beck, Henry Charlton. 1936. *Forgotten Towns of Southern New Jersey.* Reprint, New Brunswick, N.J.: Rutgers University Press, 1961.

Behnke, Fritz. 1997. *Paramus: The Way We Were, 1922–1960.* Shippensburg, Pa.: Companion Press.

Benes, Peter. 1977. *The Masks of Orthodoxy: Folk Gravestone Carvings in Plymouth County Massachusetts 1689–1805.* Amherst: University of Massachusetts Press.

Benjamin, Asher. 1827. *The American Builder's Companion.* 6th ed. Introduction by William Morgan. Reprint, New York: Dover Publications, 1969.

Benson, Esther Fisher. 1980. The History of the John Stevens Shop. *Newport Historical Society Bulletin* 112:90–97.

Bliss, Harry. 1919. *Rock-Faced Monuments*. Buffalo, N.Y.: Press of the Monument and Cemetery Review.

Bliss, Harry A. 1923. *Modern Tablets and Sarcophagi*. Buffalo, N.Y.: Harry A. Bliss, Buffalo.

Boardman, John. 1995. *Greek Sculpture, The Late Classical Period*. London: Thames and Hudson.

Boyd, William H. 1860. *Boyd's Business Directory of the State of New Jersey, Together with a General Directory of the Citizens of Newark*. Philadelphia and Camden: William H. Boyd, Directory Publisher.

Boyer, Charles S. 1931. *Early Forges and Furnaces in New Jersey*. Philadelphia: University of Pennsylvania Press.

Branin, Judy. 2001. The Atlantic City Pet Cemetery: Little Pets Rest in Peace. In *Weird New Jersey* (17): 70.

Branin, M. Lelyn. 1988. *The Early Makers of Handcrafted Earthenware and Stoneware in Central and Southern New Jersey*. Cranbury, N.J.: Associated University Presses.

Burnett, Robert B., ed. 1986. *Pictorial Guide to Victorian New Jersey*. Newark: New Jersey Historical Society.

Camden and Gloucester County directory. 1877–1878.

Camden city directory. 1860–1861, 1863–1864, 1865–1866, 1867–1868, 1869–1870, 1875–1876, 1877–1878, 1879–1880, 1883–1884, 1890–1891, 1900, 1904, 1907, 1910, 1913, 1919, 1920, 1926. Camden, N.J.

Caulfield, Earnest. 1991. Connecticut Gravestone Articles. *Markers: The Annual Journal of the Association for Gravestone Studies* 8:9–337.

Chase, T., and Laurel K. Gabel. 1997. *Gravestone Chronicles*. 2 vols. 2nd ed. Boston: New England Historic Genealogical Society.

Cherry, William. 1806. *Bill of Mortality: Being a Register of All the Deaths Which Have Occurred in the Presbyterian and Baptist Congregations of Morris-Town, New-Jersey, for Thirty-eight Years Past*. Morristown, N.J.: Jacob Mann. Reprint, American Civilization Institute of Morristown, pamphlet no. 1, 1968.

Chittenden, Varick A. 1983. *The Danes of Yates County: The History and Traditional Arts of an Ethnic Community in the Finger Lakes Region of New York State*. Penn Yan, N.Y.: Yates County Arts Council.

Ciregna, Elise Madeleine. 2004. Museum in the Garden: Mount Auburn Cemetery and American Sculpture, 1840–1860. *Markers: The Annual Journal of the Association for Gravestone Studies* 21:100–141.

City of New Brunswick. 1908. *City of New Brunswick*. New Brunswick, N.J.: Times Publishing Company.

Clarke, Rod. 1989. *Carved in Stone, A History of the Barre Granite Industry*. Barre, Vt.: Rock of Ages Corporation.

Clayton, W. Woodford. 1882. *History of Union and Middlesex Counties, New Jersey with Biographical Sketches of Many of Their Pioneers and Prominent Men*. Philadelphia: Everts and Peck.

Combs, Diana Williams. 1986. *Early Gravestone Art in Georgia and South Carolina*. Athens: University of Georgia Press.

Cook, George. 1868. *Geology of New Jersey*. Trenton: New Jersey Geological Survey.

Cook, Richard W. 1971. *The Thomas Osborne Family of East Hampton, Long Island with Some of the Descendants in New Jersey and Connecticut, Part I*. Naples, Fla.: Richard W. Cook.

Crowell, Elizabeth A. 1981. Philadelphia Gravestones, 1760–1820. *Northeast Historical Archaeology* 10:23–39.

———. 1983. Migratory Monuments and Missing Motifs: An Archaeological Analysis of Mortuary Art in Cape May County, New Jersey, 1740–1820. Ph.D. dissertation, University of Pennsylvania.

Crowell, Elizabeth A., and Norman Vardney Mackie III. 1990. The Funerary Monuments and Burial Patterns of Colonial Tidewater Virginia, 1607–1776. *Markers: The Annual Journal of the Association for Gravestone Studies* 8:103–138.

Cunz, Dieter. 1956. Egg Harbor City: New Germany in New Jersey. *Report of the Society for the History of the Germans in Maryland* 29:9–30.

Curl, James Stevens. 2002. *Death and Architecture.* Gloucestershire, UK: Sutton Publishing Limited.

Dally, Joseph W. 1873. *Woodbridge and Vicinity: The Story of a New Jersey Township.* New Brunswick, N.J.: A. E. Gordon.

Deacy, William Henry. 1930. Mansions of Immortality. *Through the Ages* 8 (October 8), no. 6.

Deetz, James. 1977. *In Small Things Forgotten.* New York: Anchor Books.

Deetz, James, and Edwin Dethlefsen. 1966. Some Social Aspects of New England Colonial Mortuary Art. *American Antiquity* 36:30–38.

———. 1967. "Death's Head, Cherub, Urn, and Willow." *Natural History* 76 (3): 29–37.

DeKay, Charles. 1895. What Terra-Cotta May Do? *Harper's Weekly* 39:655.

Dethlefsen, Edwin, and James Deetz. 1966. Deaths Heads, Cherubs, and Willow Trees: Experimental Archaeology in Colonial Cemeteries. *American Antiquity* 31:4, 502–510.

Detwiller, Frederick C. 1977. *War in the Countryside: The Battle and Plunder of the Short Hills, New Jersey, June 1977.* Plainfield, N.J.: Interstate Printing Corporation.

Dickinson, Karl A. 1965. Elijah Hughes Account Book and Diary 1774–1775. *Cape May County Magazine of History and Genealogy* 4 (2): 89–99.

Di Ionno, Mark. 2000. *A Guide to New Jersey's Revolutionary War Trail for Families and History Buffs.* New Brunswick, N.J.: Rutgers University Press.

Dimmick, Lauretta. 1992. Thomas Crawford's Monument for Amos Binney in Mount Auburn Cemetery, "A Work of Rare Merit." *Markers: The Annual Journal of the Association for Gravestone Studies* 9:158–195.

Egan, Colin. 1991. The Hudson Underground. *Hudson County Magazine,* Fall.

Elizabeth city directory. 1873, 1879–1880, 1881–1884, 1888–1889, 1895, 1901, 1905, 1909, 1911, 1915, 1921, 1926, 1930, 1935, 1944, 1955. Elizabeth, N.J.

Elizabeth directory including Plainfield and Rahway. 1869.

Ellis, Franklin. 1885. *History of Monmouth County, New Jersey.* Philadelphia: R. T. Peck and Co.

Elmwood Cemetery. 1887. Map of Elmwood Cemetery, New Brunswick, N.J. George K. Parsell, Architect. Available at cemetery office.

Erwin, Paul F. 1993. Scottish, Irish and Rom Gypsy Funeral Customs and Gravestones in Cincinnati Cemeteries. In *Ethnicity and the American Cemetery,* edited by Richard E. Meyer, 104–131. Bowling Green, Ohio: Bowling Green State University Popular Press.

Farber, Daniel, and Jessie Lie Farber. 1988. Early Pennsylvania Gravemarkers. *Markers: The Annual Journal of the Association for Gravestone Studies* 5:96–121.

Fischer, David Hackett. 1989. *Albion's Seed: Four British Folkways in America.* New York and Oxford: Oxford University Press.

Fithian, Philip Vickers. 1990. *The Beloved Cohansie of Philip Vickers Fithian.* With and Introduction and Explanatory Comments by F. Alan Palmer. Greenwich, N.J.: Cumberland County Historical Society.

Flemming, George D. 2005. *Brotherton: New Jersey's First and Only Indian Reservation and the Communities of Shamong and Tabernacle That Followed*. Medford, N.J.: Plexus.

Forbes, Harriette M. 1927. *Gravestones of Early New England*. Boston: Houghton Mifflin.

Forest Lawn Memorial Park Association. 1955. *Pictorial Forest Lawn*. Glendale, Calif.: Forest Lawn Memorial Park Association Inc.

Francis, Doris, Leonie Kellaher, and Georgina Neophytou. 2005. *The Secret Cemetery*. Oxford and New York: Berg.

Frazee, John. 1835. The Autobiography of Frazee, the Sculptor. *North American Quarterly Magazine* 6:xxxi (2–4).

Geismar, Joan. 2003. *Gethsemane Cemetery in Life and Death*. Hackensack, N.J.: Bergen County Cultural and Heritage Commission.

Genovese, Eugene D. 1974. *Roll, Jordan, Roll: The World the Slaves Made*. New York: Pantheon Books, Random House.

Goberman, David. 2000. *Carved Memories: Heritage in Stone from the Russian Jewish Pale*. New York: Rizzoli.

Gonzalez, Evelyn. 2004. Carlstadt. In *Encyclopedia of New Jersey*, edited by Maxine Lurie and Marc Mappen, 122. New Brunswick, N.J.: Rutgers University Press.

Goodman Jr., George. 1973. Gypsies Go to Linden to Bury Their Queen. *New York Times*, March 24, 37.

Gorham Manufacturing Company. 1918. *Catalogue T: Bronze Tablets, Directory Boards, and Letter/Executed by the Gorham Co., Architectural Bronze, New York*. New York: Gorham Manufacturing Company.

Gottesman, Rita S. 1938. *The Arts and Crafts in New York, 1726–1776. Advertisements and News Items from New York City Newspapers*. New York: New-York Historical Society Collections.

Gould, Alice Perkin. 2005. *The Old Jewish Cemeteries of Newark*. Bergenfield, N.J.: Avotaynu.

Gradwohl, David Mayer. 1998. Bendichta Sea Vuestra Memoria: Sephardic Jewish Cemeteries in the Caribbean and Eastern North America. In *Markers: The Annual Journal of the Association for Gravestone Studies* 15:1–39.

Gradwohl, David Mayer, and Hanna Rosenberg. 1988. That Is the Pillar of Rachel's Grave Unto This Day: An Ethnoarchaeological Comparison of Two Jewish Cemeteries in Lincoln, Nebraska. In *Persistence and Flexibility: An Anthropological Perspective on the American Jewish Experience*, edited by Walter P. Zenner, 223–259. Albany, N.Y.: State University of New York.

Granite, Barre, Vermont, USA. 1904. Promotional booklet from the 1904 Louisiana Purchase Exposition. Montpelier, Vt.: Union Card Company. Author's collection.

Graves, Thomas E. 1998. Pennsylvania German Gravestones: An Introduction. *Markers: The Annual Journal of the Association for Gravestone Studies* 5:60–95.

———. 1993. Keeping Ukraine Alive through Death: Ukrainian-American Gravestones as Cultural Markers. In *Ethnicity and the American Cemetery*, edited by Richard E. Meyer, 36–76. Bowling Green, Ohio: Bowling Green State University Popular Press.

The Graveyard at Princeton. 1862. *Continental Monthly: Devoted to Literature and National Policy* 1 (1): 32–35.

Guardian or New Brunswick Advertiser. 1803. Aaron Ross, Stone Cutter, in Rahway. *Guardian or New Brunswick Advertiser*, June 30. Author's collection.

Hall, Peter Dobkin. 1990. The Thomas Phillips & Son Company Collection: Documenting New Haven Stonecarvers of the Nineteenth and Twentieth Centuries. Available at http://ksghome.harvard.edu/~phall/phillipsessay.pdf.

Halporn, Roberta. 1993. American Jewish Cemeteries: A Mirror of History. In *Ethnicity and the American Cemetery*, edited by Richard E. Meyer, 131–156. Bowling Green, Ohio: Bowling Green State University Popular Press.

————. N.d. *Gods, Ghosts, and Ancestors: The Ching Ming Festival in American*. Brooklyn, N.Y.: Center for Thanatology Research and Education.

Hanks, Carole. 1974. *Early Ontario Gravestones*. Ontario, Canada: McGraw-Hill/Ryerson.

Harleigh Memorial. 1928. *Harleigh Memorial*. Camden, N.J.: Harleigh Memorial Inc.

Harper's New Monthly Magazine. 1876. Newark. *Harper's New Monthly Magazine*, October, 660–678.

Harris, Helen L. 1987. Burials in Trinity Graveyard, Pittsburgh, Pa. Trinity Cathedral, Pittsburgh, Pa.

Heinlein, David A. 1990. The New Brunswick–Japan Connection: A History. *Journal of the Rutgers University Libraries* 52 (2): 1–16.

Heye, George G., and George H. Pepper. 1915. Exploration of a Munsee Cemetery near Montague, New Jersey. *Contributions from the Museum of the American Indian, Heye Foundation*, vol. 2, no. 1.

Historical Publishing Co. 1882–1883. *Industries of New Jersey*. 6 vols. Part 1, *Trenton, Princeton, Hightstown, Pennington, and Hopewell*. Part 6, *Hudson, Passaic and Bergen Counties*. New York, Philadelphia, and Newark: Historical Publishing Co.

Home News Tribune. 1996. A City Neglects Its Honored Dead. *Home News Tribune*, June 24.

Horne, Ronald William, Lisa Montanarelli, and Geoffrey Link. 2004. *Forgotten Faces: A Window into Our Immigrant Past*. San Francisco: Personal Genesis Publishing.

Hornor, William S. 1932. *This Old Monmouth of Ours: History, Tradition, Biography, Genealogy, and Other Anecdotes Related to Monmouth County, New Jersey*. Freehold, N.J.: Moreau Brothers.

Horton, Loren N. 1997. The Remarkable Crosses of Charles Andera. *Markers: The Annual Journal of the Association for Gravestone Studies* 14:110–133.

Hubert, Archer Butler, and William Nathaniel Schwarze, eds. 1999. *David Zeisberger's History of the Northern American Indians* [1910]. Lewisburg, Pa.: Wennawoods Publishing.

Hudson Dispatch. 1955. Burial Fee Row Launched Cemetery in Jersey City. *Hudson Dispatch*, July 28.

Hunt, Dr. Ezra M. 1880. *Metuchen-Edison Historical Society Record of Burials in Piscatawaytown Grave Yards as of October 28, 1880*. Metuchen, N.J.: Metuchen Edison Historical Society.

Inguanti, J. J. 2000. Domesticating the Grave: Italian-American Memorial Practices at New York's Calvary Cemetery. *Markers: The Annual Journal of the Association for Gravestone Studies* 17:8–31.

Ingersoll, Ernest. 1892. Decoration of Negro Graves. *Journal of American Folklore* 5:68–69.

Jackson, Kenneth T., and Camilo José Vergara. 1989. *Silent Cities: The Evolution of the American Cemetery*. New York: Princeton Architectural Press.

Jersey City and Hoboken directory. 1849–1850, 1850–1851, 1855–1856, 1856–1857, 1857–1858, 1861–1862, 1863–1864, 1870–1871, 1875–1876, 1880–1881, 1886–1887, 1890–1891, 1898–1899, 1899–1900, 1900–1901, 1905–1906, 1910–1911, 1915, 1918, 1922. Jersey City, N.J.

Jersey City Gazette. 1835. Ancient Relic. *Jersey City Gazette*, July 11.

Jersey City Gazette. 1835. Violation on the Grave. *Jersey City Gazette*, September 16.

Jersey Journal. 1912. To Extend Jersey City Cemetery, May 23.

————. 1916. Martin A. Adams Builds His Own Monument. *Jersey Journal*, January 3.

————. 1916. Pauper Dead Problem Faces City Officials. *Jersey Journal*, April 19.

————. 1916. New Gate Lodge for Cemetery. *Jersey Journal*, July 18.

————. 1927. Martin Adams, obituary. *Jersey Journal*, July 21.

————. 1968. Funeral Customs Changing. *Jersey Journal*, January 15.

Jones, Mary-Ellen. 1971. *Photographing Tombstones: Equipment and Techniques.* Nashville, Tenn.: Association for State and Local History.

Jordan, Terry G. 1982. *Texas Graveyards: A Cultural Legacy.* Austin: University of Texas Press.

Justice, Joseph. 1831. An Act to Incorporate the Jersey City and Harsimus Cemetery. In *Acts of the Fifty-fifth General Assembly of the State of New Jersey,* 87–89. Trenton: Joseph Justice.

Keels, Thomas H. 2003. *Images of America: Philadelphia Graveyards and Cemeteries.* Charleston, S.C.: Arcadia Publishing Company.

Keister, Douglas. 1997. *Going Out in Style: The Architecture of Eternity.* New York: Facts on File.

————. 2004. *Stories in Stone: A Field Guide to Cemetery Symbolism and Iconography.* Salt Lake City, Utah: Gibbs, Smith Publishers.

Kent, Bill. 1997. Remaining Faithful to Islamic Law in Death as Well as Life. *New York Times,* March 9, NJ sec., 10.

Kirkbride, Stacy B. 1850. *Kirkbride's New Jersey Business Directory.* Trenton, Kirkbride.

Kloberdanz, Timothy J. 2005. "Unser Lieber Gottesacker" (Our Dear God's Acre): An Iron-Cross Cemetery on the Northern Great Plains. *Markers: The Annual Journal of the Association for Gravestone Studies* 22:160–182.

Kraft, Herbert C. 1993. The Minisink Site: A National Historic Landmark. *Bulletin of the Archaeological Society of New Jersey* 48:73–80.

————. 2001. *The Lenape-Delaware Indian Heritage, 10,000 B.C. to A.D. 2000.* Elizabeth, N.J.: Lenape Books.

Kraus-Friedberg, Chana. 2003. Building the Wilderness: Identity and Acculturation in the Alliance Jewish Cemetery. Paper presented at the annual meeting of the Society for Historical Archaeology, Providence, R.I.

Landsman, Ned. 1985. *Scotland and Its First American Colony, 1683–1765.* Princeton, N.J.: Princeton University Press.

Lanza, Howard D. 1997. *Gateway to the Past: A Guide to Cedar Lawn Cemetery, Paterson, New Jersey.* Paterson, N.J.: Acquackanonk History Club.

Lawrence, John, Rob Lore, and Paul Schopp. 2001. Raritan-in-the-Hills (28-So-128): Salvage Archaeology of a Pre-Revolutionary War German Lutheran Cemetery. *Bulletin of the Archaeological Society of New Jersey* 56:11–21.

Leary, Peter J. 1893. *Newark, N.J., Illustrated: A Souvenir of the City and Its Numerous Industries.* Newark: William A. Baker.

Lees, Hilary. 2000. *English Churchyard Memorials.* New York: Tempus.

Leiby, Adrian C. 1964. *The Early Dutch and Swedish Settlers of New Jersey.* Princeton, N.J.: D. Van Nostrand Company.

Lenik, Edward J. 1987. Chief Oratam's Burial Site: The Making of a Legend. *Bulletin of the Archaeological Society of New Jersey* 42:27–31.

————. 1996. The Minisink Site as Sacred Space. *Bulletin of the Archaeological Society of New Jersey* 51:53–64.

Levine, Ellen. 1997. Jewish Customs on Death. In *Death and Bereavement Across Cultures,* edited by Colin Murray Parkes, Pittu Laungani, and Bill Young. New York: Brunner-Routledge.

Levitt, James Haskell. 1973. New Jersey Shipping, 1722–1764: A Statistical Study. Ph.D. dissertation, University of Utah.

Li, Peter, and Yoland Skeete. 2004. Chinese. In *Encyclopedia of New Jersey*, edited by Maxine Lurie and Marc Mappen, 148. New Brunswick, N.J.: Rutgers University Press.

Lichten, Frances. 1946. *Folk Art of Rural Pennsylvania*. London and New York: Charles Scribner's Sons.

Liestman, Daniel. 1994. Chinese Labor at the Passaic Steam Laundry in Belleville. *New Jersey History* 112 (1–2): 20–33.

Little, M. Ruth. 1998. *Sticks and Stones: Three Centuries of North Carolina Gravemarkers*. Chapel Hill: University of North Carolina Press.

Ludwig, Allan. 1966. *Graven Images*. Middletown, Conn.: Wesleyan University Press.

Luti, Vincent. 2002. *Mallet and Chisel: Gravestone Carvers of Newport, Rhode Island, in the 18th Century*. Boston: New England Historic Genealogical Society.

———. 2003. Eighteenth-Century Gravestone Carvers of the Upper Narragansett Basin: Gabriel Allen. *Markers: The Annual Journal of the Association for Gravestone Studies* 20:76–109.

Maas, Peter. 1975. *King of the Gypsies*. New York: Viking Press.

Martin, Alvia. 1979. *At the Headwaters of Cheesequake Creek*. Matawan, N.J.: Madison Township Historical Society.

Martin, R. 1846–1847. The Rural Cemeteries of America Illustrated. Reprinted as Cemeteries and Monuments in *The New Englander*, November 1849, 28:498.

Masters, Edgar Lee. 1924. *Spoon River Anthology*. New York: Macmillan.

Matturri, John. 1993. Windows in the Garden: Italian-American Memorialization and the American Cemetery. In *Ethnicity and the American Cemetery*, edited by Richard E. Meyer, 14–35. Bowling Green, Ohio: Bowling Green State University Popular Press.

Mathias, Elizabeth. 1974. The Italian-American Funeral: Persistence through Change. *Western Folklore* 33 (1): 35–51.

McDonald, Frank E. 1975. Pennsylvania German Tombstone Art of Lebanon County, Pennsylvania. *Pennsylvania Folklife* 25 (1): 2–19.

McDowell, Peggy, and Richard E. Meyer. 1994. *The Revival Styles in American Memorial Art*. Bowling Green, Ohio: Bowling Green State University Popular Press.

McGinnis, William C. 1958–1960. *History of Perth Amboy, New Jersey*. 4 vols. Perth Amboy, N.J.: American Publishing Company.

McGuire, Randall H. 1988. Dialogues with the Dead: Ideology and the Cemetery. In *The Recovery of Meaning: Historical Archaeology in the Eastern United States*, edited by Mark P. Leone and Parker B. Potter Jr. Washington, D.C.: Smithsonian Institution Press.

McKee, Harley J. 1973. *Introduction to Early American Masonry: Stones, Brick, Mortar and Plaster*. New York: National Trust for Historic Preservation and Columbia University.

McLeod, Paul Joseph. 1979. A Study of the Gravestones of Monmouth County, New Jersey 1716–1835: Reflections of a Lifestyle. Williamsburg, Va.: Independent Research Project in Anthropology, College of William and Mary.

Mellett, Dorothy W. 1991. *Gravestone Art in Rockland County, New York*. Tappan, N.Y.: Hudson Valley Press.

Mercer, Henry C. 1914. *The Bible in Iron or the Pictures Stoves and Stove Plates of the Pennsylvania Germans*. Doylestown, Pa.: Bucks County Historical Society.

Messimer, Claire. 2000. *Known by the Work of His Hands*. Kutztown, Pa.: Pennsylvania German Society.

Mitford, Jessica. 1963. *The American Way of Death*. New York: Simon and Schuster.

————. 2000. *The American Way of Death Revisited*. New York: Random House.

Monumental Bronze Co. 1882. *White Bronze Monuments, Statuary, Portrait Medallions, Busts, Statues and Ornamental Art Work for Cemeteries, Public and Private Grounds and Buildings / Manufactured by the Monumental Bronze Co. of Bridgeport, Conn, Bridgeport, Conn*. Bridgeport, Conn.: Monumental Bronze Co.

Moonsammy, Rita, David S. Cohen, and Mary T. Hufford. 1987. Living with the Landscape: Folklife in the Environmental Subregions of the Pinelands. In *Pinelands Folklife*, edited by Rita Zorn Moonsammy, David Steven Cohen, and Lorraine E. Williams, 65–230. New Brunswick, N.J.: Rutgers University Press.

Moran, Mark, and Mark Sceurman. 1997. Some Bright Ideas Carved in Stone: An Interview with Anthony Sgobba and Laurie Giardino. In *Weird New Jersey* (9): 31–32.

Mounier, R. Alan. 1988. A Stage II Archaeological Survey of Rosewood Condominiums, Town of Hammonton, Atlantic County, New Jersey. Report prepared for William Lamanna, Hammonton.

————. 2003. *Looking Beneath the Surface: The Story of Archaeology in New Jersey*. New Brunswick, N.J.: Rutgers University Press.

Mount Pleasant Cemetery. 1844. *Sentinel of Freedom*, June 25.

Mytum, Harold. 2004. *Mortuary Monuments and Burial Grounds of the Historic Period*. New York: Kluwer Academic Publishing.

Newark city directory. 1835–1836, 1839–1840, 1849–1850, 1859–1860, 1871, 1872, 1881, 1887.

Newark Daily Advertiser. 1843. Mount Pleasant Cemetery. *Newark Daily Advertiser*, December 16.

————. 1866. Editorial: Our Cemetery. *Newark Daily Advertiser*, January 30.

Newark Evening News. 1912. Solidity and Simplicity of Design in Dryden Mausoleum. *Newark Evening News*, August 18.

Newark Sunday Call. 1898. New Management at Mt. Pleasant Cemetery and the Changes It Is Making. *Newark Sunday Call*, April 17.

New Brunswick city directory. 1855–1856, 1865–1866, 1866–1867, 1868–1869, 1870–1871, 1872–1873. New Brunswick, N.J.

[New Brunswick] *Sunday Times*. 1936. Early Experiments in Rubber Industry Carried on Here More Than Century Ago. *Sunday Times*, March 1.

New Jersey Department of Environmental Protection (NJDEP). 2003. Honoring the Irish Who Built the D&R Canal (Press Release). Trenton: New Jersey Department of Environmental Protection.

New Jersey Journal. 1788. Advertisement: Three Pounds Reward. *New Jersey Journal*, June 4.

————. 1843. Advertisement: Marble Yard. *New Jersey Journal*, December 4.

New Jersey State Legislature. 1838. An Act to Incorporate the Trenton Cemetery Company. In *Acts of the Sixty-second General Assembly of the State of New Jersey*, 138. Trenton: James Adams.

————. 1908. Act to Regulate Crematory Companies. In *Acts of the One Hundred and Thirty-second State Legislature*, 530–531. Trenton: MacCrellish and Quigley, State Printers.

Newman, John J. 1971. *Cemetery Transcribing: Preparations and Procedures*. Nashville, Tenn.: American Association for State and Local History.

New York Bay Cemetery Company. 1889. *Rules and Regulations of the New York Bay Cemetery*. Jersey City, N.J.: Argus Company.

————. 1918. *Rules and Regulations of the New York Bay Cemetery*. Jersey City, N.J.

New York Gazette; and the Weekly Mercury. 1771. Advertisement for Newark Stone Quarry. *New York Gazette; and the Weekly Mercury*, April 8.

New York Granite Company. 1906. *Useful Hints for the Monumental Man.* N.p.: New York Granite Company.

New York Times. 1881. A Romantic Gypsy Marriage: Sequel to the Death of a King of the Gypsies at Elmwood, N.J. *New York Times,* August 1.

———. 1925. Romany King Buried: Gypsies Follow Tribal Rites—Coins Thrown into Coffin. *New York Times,* February 8.

———. 2006. New Jersey Daily Briefing; Sprucing Up a Lion's Grave. *New York Times,* April 5.

New York Weekly Post Boy. 1745. Advertisement for William Grant and Samuel Hunterdon. *New York Weekly Post Boy,* September 30.

Noll, August C. 1939. *Contemporaneous Memorial Designs.* N.p.

Nonestied, Mark. 1999. *Images of America: East Brunswick.* Charleston, S.C.: Arcadia Publishing Company.

Observer. 1930. A New Technique for an Ancient Art. *Observer,* April. Trenton Public Library, Trentoniana Room.

Oldshue, Jerry C. 1987. Ceramic Gravstones of Northeast Mississippi and Northeast Alabama. *Newsletter of the Association for Gravestone Studies* 11 (2): 17.

Ouzts, Clay. 2004. Granite. In *The New Georgia Encyclopedia.* Available at http://www.georgiaencyclopedia.org.

Paonessa, Laurie J. 1990. The Cemeteries of St. Eustatius, N.A.: Status in a Caribbean Community. Master's thesis, College of William and Mary.

Paterson city directory. 1857. Paterson, N.J.

Pepper, Adeline. 1971. *The Glass Gaffers of New Jersey and Their Creations from 1739 to the Present.* New York: Charles Scribner's Sons.

Podmore, Harry J. 1964. *Trenton Old and New.* Revised by Mary J. Messler. Trenton: Mac-Crellish & Quigley Company.

Presbrey-Leland, Inc. 1952. *Commemoration: The Book of Presbrey-Leland Memorials.* New York: Presbrey-Leland.

Price, Clement Alexander, ed. 1980. *Freedom Not Far Distant: A Documentary History of Afro-Americans in New Jersey.* Newark: New Jersey Historical Society.

Quinan, Jack. 1975. Daniel Raynerd, Stucco Worker. *Old-Time New England, Bulletin of the Society for the Preservation of New England Antiquities* 65 (3–4): 239–240.

Quinn, Dermot. 2004. *The Irish in New Jersey: Four Centuries of American Life.* New Brunswick, N.J.: Rutgers University Press.

Rankin, R. N.d. A Slave of the Wire Brush. *Genealogical Magazine of New Jersey.* Article on file with Richard Veit.

Raser, Edward J. 1994. *New Jersey Graveyard and Gravestone Inscriptions Locator: Morris County.* New Brunswick, N.J.: Genealogical Society of New Jersey.

———. 2000. *Jersey Graveyard and Gravestone Inscriptions Locators: Mercer County.* New Brunswick, N.J.: Genealogical Society of New Jersey.

———. 2002. *New Jersey Graveyard and Gravestone Inscriptions Locators: Monmouth County.* New Brunswick, N.J.: Genealogical Society of New Jersey.

Rawson, Marion Nicholl. 1974. *Under the Blue Hills: Scotch Plains, New Jersey.* Plainfield, N.J.: Interstate Printing Company.

Richards, Brandon. 2007. New Netherland's Gravestone Legacy: An Introduction to Early Burial Markers of the Upper Mid-Atlantic States. *Markers: The Annual Journal of the Association for Gravestone Studies* 24:24–39.

Ritchie, William A. 1949. *The Bell-Philhower Site, Sussex County, N.J.* Prehistoric Research Series, vol. 3, no. 2. Indianapolis: Indiana Historical Society.

Rock of Ages Corporation. C.1949. *How to Choose a Family Monument.* Barre, Vt.: Rock of Ages Corporation.

Rogers, Brett. 2002. Impressions of Black St. Louis: Concrete Markers in St. Louis' Greenwood Cemetery. *Pioneer America Society Transactions* 26:26–37.

Rolando, Victor R. 1992. *200 Years of Soot and Sweat: The History and Archaeology of Vermont's Iron, Charcoal, and Lime Industries.* Dover, Del.: Vermont Archaeological Society.

Rosedale & Rosehill Cemetery Association. 2003. *A Guide to the Cremation Practice at Rosehill.* Linden, N.J.: Rosedale & Rosehill Cemetery Association. Available at http://www.rosedale-rosehill.com/images/rosehill_cremation_brochure.pdf.

Rotundo, Barbara. 1989. Monumental Bronze: A Representative American Company. In *Cemeteries and Gravemarkers: Voices of American Culture,* edited by Richard E. Meyer, 263–292. Logan: Utah State University Press.

———. 1997. A Modern Gravestone Maker: Some Lessons for Gravestone Historians. *Markers: The Annual Journal of the Association for Gravestone Studies* 14:86–110.

Rouse, Wendy L. 2005. "What We Didn't Understand": A History of Chinese Death Ritual in China and California. In *Chinese American Death Rituals,* edited by Sue Fawn Chung and Priscilla Wegars, 19–46. Lanham, Md.: AltaMira Press.

Ruby, Jay. 1995. *Secure the Shadow: Death and Photography in America.* Cambridge, Mass.: MIT Press.

Rutland Florence Marble Company. 1911. *Rutland Florence Marble Company, Fowler, Vermont, Price List.* Rutland, Vt.: Tuttle Company.

Sample, O. H. 1919. Monument Dealers Manual. In *The Monument Man's Encyclopedia: A Handbook of Ready Reference to Useful Information for the Monument Craft.* Chicago: Allied Arts Publishing Co.

Sanderson, Sagan T. 2004. Kalmyks. In *Encyclopedia of New Jersey,* edited by Maxine Lurie and Marc Mappen, 434–435. New Brunswick, N.J.: Rutgers University Press.

Sarapin, Janice Kohl. 1994. *Old Burial Grounds of New Jersey: A Guide.* New Brunswick, N.J.: Rutgers University Press.

Schulze, Paul. 1851. *Original Designs in Monumental Art.* Boston.

Schuyler, George W. 1885. *Colonial New York, Philip Schuyler and His Family, in Two Volumes.* New York: Charles Scribner's Sons.

Senkevitch, Anatole. 1986. Mount Pleasant Cemetery National Register Nomination.

Skinner, Alanson. 1913. Types of Indian Remains Found in New Jersey. In *A Preliminary Report of the Archaeological Survey of New Jersey.* Bulletin 9, compiled by Alanson Skinner and Max Schrabisch, 9–40. Trenton: New Jersey Geological Survey.

Sloane, David Charles. 1991. *The Last Great Necessity: Cemeteries in American History.* Baltimore: Johns Hopkins University Press.

Smith, Samuel D., and Stephen T. Rogers. 1979. *A Survey of Historic Pottery Making in Tennessee.* Nashville: Tennessee Department of Environment and Conservation.

Snyder, Ellen Marie. 1992. Innocents in a Worldly World: Victorian Children's Gravemarkers. In *Cemeteries and Gravemarkers, Voices of American Culture,* edited by Richard E. Meyer, 11–29. Logan: Utah State University Press.

St. George, Robert Blair. 1988. Artifacts of Regional Consciousness in the Connecticut River Valley, 1700–1780. In *Material Life in America, 1600–1860,* edited by Robert Blair St. George, 335–356. Boston: Northeastern University Press.

Stansfield, Charles A. 1998. *A Geography of New Jersey: The City in the Garden.* 2nd ed. New Brunswick, N.J.: Rutgers University Press.

Stanzeski, Andrew J. 1996. Two Decades of Radiocarbon Dating from the New Jersey Shore. *Bulletin of the Archaeological Society of New Jersey* 51:42–45.

Stilgoe, John R. 1982. *Common Landscape of America 1580 to 1845.* New Haven and London: Yale University Press.

Stillwell, John E. 1903. *Historical and Genealogical Miscellany; Data Relating to the Settlement and Settlers of New York and New Jersey.* 4 vols. New York. Reprint, Baltimore, Md.: Genealogical Publishing Co., 1970.

Stone, Gaynell. 1987. Spatial and Material Aspects of Culture: Ethnicity and Ideology in Long Island Gravestones, 1670–1820. Ph.D. dissertation, State University of New York at Stony Brook.

Stose, Anna I. Jonas. 1965. Old Tombstones of the Cape. *The Cape May County Magazine of History and Genealogy* 4 (2): 113–116.

Strangstad, Lynette. 1988. *A Graveyard Preservation Primer.* Nashville, Tenn.: American Association for State and Local History.

Sullivan, Allison. 2006. Elsie the Cow. *American Cemetery*, February.

Talbott and Blood. 1866. *New Jersey State Business Directory for 1866.* New York: Talbott and Blood Publishers.

Tarlow, Sarah. 1999. Wormie Clay and Blessed Sleep: Death and Disgust in Later Historic Britain. *In the Familiar Past? Archaeologies of Britain 1550–1950,* edited by S. Tarlow and S. West, 183–198. London: Routledge.

Thayer, Theodore. 1964. *As We Were: The Story of Old Elizabethtown.* Elizabeth, N.J.: Grassman Publishing Company.

Thompson, Robert Farris. 1983. *Flash of the Spirit: African and Afro-American Art and Philosophy.* New York: Vintage Books.

Tiffany Studios. 1898. *Out-of-Door Memorials: Mausoleums, Tombs, Headstones and All Forms of Mortuary Monuments.* New York: Tiffany Studios.

———. C.1913. *Tiffany Favrile Glass, Tiffany Windows, Tiffany Mosaics, Tiffany Monuments, Tiffany Granite.* New York: Tiffany Studios.

———. C.1918. *Tributes to Honor: Suggested Types of Memorial by the Ecclesiastical Department of Tiffany Studios, New York.* New York: Tiffany Studios.

Trask, Deborah. 1985. Tour of Selected Burial Grounds in Northern New Jersey, June 28, 1885. *Newsletter of the Association for Gravestone Studies* 9 (4).

Trenton city directory. 1854–1855, 1859, 1865, 1867, 1874, 1875, 1876, 1877, 1883–1884, 1884–1885, 1886–1887, 1893, 1900. Trenton, N.J.

Trenton Historical Society. 1929. *A History of Trenton 1679–1929.* 2 vols. Princeton, N.J.: Princeton University Press.

Union, New Jersey, directory. 1942–1943. Newark: Price & Lee Co.

Urquhart, Frank J. 1913. *A History of the City of Newark, New Jersey, Embracing Practically Two and a Half Centuries 1666–1913.* New York: Lewis Historical Publishing Company.

Van Der Donck, Adrian. 1968. *A Description of New Netherland.* Edited by Thomas F. O'Donnell. Syracuse, N.Y.: Syracuse University Press.

Van Horne, James, and Lee W. Formwalt, eds. 1984. *The Correspondence and Miscellaneous Papers of Benjamin Henry Latrobe, Volume 1: 1784–1804.* New Haven and London: Yale University Press.

Veit, Richard F. 1991. Middlesex County New Jersey Gravestones 1687–1799: Shadows of a Changing Culture. MA thesis, College of William and Mary.

———. 1993. Iron Gravemarkers in the Pine Barrens: Unusual Products of a Forgotten Industry. *Bulletin of the Archaeological Society of New Jersey* 48:39–44.

———. 1995. A Piece of Granite That's Made in Two Weeks: Terra-Cotta Gravemakers from New Jersey and New York, 1875–1930. *Markers: The Annual Journal of the Association for Gravestone Studies* 12:1–30.

———. 1997. Skyscrapers and Sepulchers: A Historic Ethnography of New Jersey's Terra Cotta Industry. Ph.D. dissertation, University of Pennsylvania.

———. 2000. John Solomon Teetzel and the Anglo-German Gravestone Carving Tradition of 18th Century Northwestern New Jersey. *Markers: The Annual Journal of the Association for Gravestone Studies* 17:124–162.

Veit, Richard F., and Charles A. Bello. 2002. "Sundry Species of Trading Goods": A Comparative Study of Trade Goods Represented in Colonial Deeds and Archaeological Sites from Monmouth County, New Jersey. *Bulletin of the Archaeological Society of New Jersey* 57:66–72.

Veit, Richard F., and Mark Nonestied. 2003. Taken for Granite: Terracotta Gravemakers from New Jersey and New York. In *Ceramics in America 2003*, edited by Robert Hunter, 172–195. Hanover, N.H.: Chipstone Foundation and University Press of New England.

Vermont Marble Company. C. 1906. *Vermont Marble Company's Designs "H."* New York: Grafton Press

———. 1923. *Price List of Monumental Marble, April 2, 1923.* Proctor, Vt.: Vermont Marble Company.

———. N.d. *Children's Designs and Markers.* Proctor, Vt.: Vermont Marble Company.

Vlach, John Michael. 1978. *The Afro-American Tradition in Decorative Arts.* Cleveland, Ohio: Cleveland Museum of Art.

Vrooman, Nicholas Churchin, and Patrice Avon Marvin, eds. 1982. *Iron Spirits.* Fargo: North Dakota Council on the Arts.

Wacker, Peter O. 1975. *Land and People: A Cultural Geography of Preindustrial New Jersey: Origins and Settlement Patterns.* New Brunswick, N.J. Rutgers University Press.

Walsh, Marianne. N.d. New Jersey Transit Trenton Rail Station Rehabilitation Survey. Trenton: New Jersey Department of Environmental Protection, Historic Preservation Office.

Wasserman, Emily. 1972. *Gravestone Designs: Rubbings and Photographs from Early New York and New Jersey.* New York: Dover.

Wathan, Richard. 1875. *Monumental and Head Stone Design.* New York.

Weever, John. 1631. *Ancient Funeral Monuments.* London.

Welch, Richard F. 1983. *Memento Mori: The Gravestones of Early Long Island, 1680–1810.* Syosset, N.Y.: Friends for Long Island's Heritage.

———. 1987. The New York and New Jersey Gravestone Carving Tradition. *Markers: The Annual Journal of the Association for Gravestone Studies* 4:1–54.

Wendel, Charles H. 1993. *Fairbanks Morse 100 Years of Engine Technology, 1893–1993.* Lancaster, Pa.: Stemgas Publishing Company.

West, Joseph H. 1876. *A History of the Village of Hamilton Square, Mercer County, New Jersey.* Trenton: John L. Murphy State Gazette Printing House.

Wheeler, William Ogden, and Edmund D. Halsey. 1892. *Inscriptions on Tombstones and Monuments in the Burying Grounds of the First Presbyterian Church and St. Johns Church at Elizabeth, New Jersey, 1664–1892.* New Haven, Conn.: Tuttle, Morehouse, and Taylor.

Wickes, Stephen. 1892. *History of the Oranges in Essex County, New Jersey, from 1666 to 1806.* Newark: New England Society of Orange.

Widmer, Kemble. 1964. *The Geology and Geography of New Jersey.* New Jersey Historical Series, vol. 19. Princeton, N.J.: D. Van Nostrand Company.

Wildes, Harry Emerson. 1943. *Twin Rivers: The Raritan and the Passaic.* New York: Rinehart and Company.

Willats, R. M. 1987. Iron Graveslabs: A Sideline of the Early Iron Industry. *Sussex Archaeological Collections* 125:99–113.

Williams, Carl M. 1949. *Silversmiths of New Jersey 1700–1825.* Philadelphia: George S. McManus Company.

Williams, Gray. 2000. By Their Characters You Shall Know Them: Using Styles of Lettering to Identify Gravestone Carvers. *Markers: The Annual Journal of the Association for Gravestone Studies* 17:162–205.

Willshire, Betty, and Doreen Hunter 1979. *Stones: A Guide to Some Remarkable Eighteenth-Century Scottish Gravestones.* New York: Taplinger.

Willison, E. C. 1890. *Marble, Granite and Statuary.* Boston: E. C. Willison.

Wright, Giles. 1989. *Afro-Americans in New Jersey: A Short History.* Trenton: New Jersey Historical Commission, Department of State.

Zielenski, John. 2004. Shaping a Soul of Stone: The Soul Effigy Gravestones of Uzal Ward, William Grant, and the Anonymous Pear Head Cavers of Eighteenth-Century, New Jersey: A Stylistic Study and Comprehensive Survey. MA thesis, Montclair State University.

Zug, Charles C. 1986. *Turners and Burners: The Folk Potters of North Carolina.* Chapel Hill: University of North Carolina Press.

WEB SITES

Association for Gravestone Studies. http://www.gravestonestudies.org.

Barre Granite Association. http://www.barregranite.org.

Catholic Cemeteries, Archdiocese of Newark. http://www.rcan.org.

———. Catholics and Cremation. http://www.rcan.org/cemeteries/cremation.htm.

———. Holy Cross. http://www.njcatholiccemeteries.org/HOLYCROSS.htm.

Cremation Association of North America. History. http://www.cremationassociation.org/html/history.html.

———. Statistics. http://www.cremationassociation.org/html/statistics.html.

Descendants of Hugo Van Vredenburgh. http://familytreemaker.genealogy.com/users/r/e/e/William-H-Reed/ODT1-0001.html.

Old Newark Cemeteries. http://www.virtualnewarknj.com/cemeteries.

Patrin: Timeline of Romani History. http://www.geocities.com/Paris/5121/timeline.htm.

INDEX

Mathias, Elizabeth (folklorist), 184
Mathiasen, Karl, 209
mausoleums, 92, 145, 164, 181, 206, 209, 128–228, 248, 257, 260; folk art, 226, 226; homemade, 216; interiors, 221, 222, 223, 223–226; mass-produced, 225; tympanum, 222. *See also* community mausoleums
Mays Landing: Seaside Cemetery, 254
McChesney, R. R. (carver), 138
McClellan, George Brinton, 94
McDonald, Alexander (stone works), 159
McGhee, George (carver), 147
McLeod, Paul (researcher), 10
medallions, copper, 215
Meeker, Isaac (carver), 141
Meeker, John L. (carver), 145, 159
Melick, Gilbert (carver), 143–144
memento mori tradition, 54
memorabilia, 131, 232
memorial parks, 167, 238–240, 262; ideology, 237–238, 257
memorials, nongrave, 162, 179. *See also* cenotaphs
Mendham: Hilltop Presbyterian Church, 37
menorah, 188, 189
Mercer Cemetery Company, 82
Mercer County, 137–138, 202
Metuchen: Hillside Cemetery, 206, 208, 209, 210
Meyer, Christopher, 221–222
Middlesex County, 44–45, 138–141; Van Liew Cemetery, 141
Middletown, 39: Old Presbyterian Cemetery, 58
Middletown Point, 138
Milford Granite Company, 163
Milford Union Cemetery, 121, 142, 142–143
military service, 249–250. *See also* veterans; war memorials
Miller, A. H. (carver), 142
Millstone, 141; Jersey State Memorial Park, 154
Makbarat As-Salaam, 254
Millville, 137; Mount Pleasant Cemetery, 193, 199
minute book [record book], 175
Misak, Anna, 215, 215
Mitchell, Queen Mary, 252

Mitford, Jessica (writer), 260
molding, 224
Monmouth County, 17, 40, 63, 138
Monmouth County Historical Association, 18
Monmouth University, 256
monograms, 54–55, 56, 63, 70, 74, 172, 172, 253; Christ's, 179
monumental bronze, 131
Monumental Bronze Company, 131, 132, 202, 203
monument dealers, 29, 115, 135, 155, 160, 162, 165, 166, 223, 262
"Monument Dealers Manual," 168
monument industry, 155, 159
monuments, 81, 83, 90–92, 93, 96, 112, 113, 166–167; base, 114, 117, 118, 119; brownstone, 81, 90, 92, 134; capstone, 114, 118; to cemetery founders, 90; for children, 154; cost, 160, 161, 169; design, 117; die, 114, 119; eclectic, 119; foundation, 114, 159–160; granite, 82, 92, 93, 94, 102, 148, 154, 164, 180; marble, 92, 95, 121, 141, 143, 146, 148, 151, 154, 162, 169; monumental bronze, 202–203; Philadelphia-made, 83, 95, 120, 121, 122, 129, 135; Russian, 192; signed, 90, 95, 122, 134, 145; tablatures, 117, 120; three-dimensional, 91–92, 114, 117. *See also* Civil War monuments; family monuments
moon, 65, 254
Mooney, J. C. (carver), 56
Moore, Martha, 31
Moorish design, 95, 96
Moran, Patrick, 181
Moravians, 28, 65
Moretti, Giuseppe (sculptor), 164
Morgan, 37
Morris County, 153
Morrison family monument, 92
Morristown, 45, 53, 143, 153, 154, 173, 179; Evergreen Cemetery, 107, 223; First Presbyterian Church Burial Ground, 26, 33; Morristown Presbyterian Burial Ground, 24, 52, 56, 174
mortality images, 40, 41, 43, 44, 44, 45, 46, 54, 60, 61
mosques, 254
Mott, George (marble worker), 135
Mounier, R. Alan (archaeologist), 199

Richard F. Veit is an associate professor in the Department of History and Anthropology at Monmouth University. A historical archaeologist by training, his research interests include colonial and modern gravemarkers, early American material culture, and vernacular architecture. He is the author of *Digging New Jersey's Past: Historical Archaeology in the Garden State* (Rutgers, 2002).

Mark Nonestied is director of exhibits and programs for East Jersey Old Town Village, a project of the Middlesex County Cultural & Heritage Commission. Mr. Nonestied also served on the Board of Trustees of Evergreen Cemetery, North Brunswick. He regularly lectures on cemetery topics, including receiving vaults, nineteenth century cemeteries, and mausoleums.